LIFE LINES

LIFE LINES

Community, Family, and Assimilation Among Asian Indian Immigrants

Jean Bacon

New York   Oxford
OXFORD UNIVERSITY PRESS
1996

Oxford University Press

Oxford   New York
Athens   Auckland   Bangkok   Bogotá   Bombay
Buenos Aires   Calcutta   Cape Town   Dar es Salaam
Delhi   Florence   Hong Kong   Istanbul   Karachi
Kuala Lumpur   Madras   Madrid   Melbourne
Mexico City   Nairobi   Paris   Singapore
Taipei   Tokyo   Toronto

and associated companies in
Berlin   Ibadan

Library of Congress Cataloging-in-Publication Data
Bacon, Jean Leslie, 1962–
Life lines : community, family, and assimilation
among Asian Indian immigrants / Jean Bacon.
p.   cm.   Includes bibliographical references and index.
ISBN 0–19–509972–9; ISBN 0–19–509973–7 pbk.
1. East Indian Americans—Illinois—Chicago—Cultural assimilation.
2. East Indian Americans—Illinois—Chicago—Ethnic identity.
3. Chicago (Ill.)—Social conditions.   I. Title.
F548.9.E2B33   1996   305.891'411077311—dc20   95–49367

1 3 5 7 9 8 6 4 2

Printed in the United States of America
on acid-free paper

For Daniel

Foreword:
Ethnic Assimilation as Social Differentiation and Americanization as Individuation

> It is not always clear, however, what assimilation means. Historically the word has had two distinct significations. According to earlier usage it meant "to compare" or "to make like." According to later usage it signifies "to take up and incorporate." (Robert E. Park, "Racial Assimilation in Secondary Groups.")

Robert Park was never to be satisfied with either definition. When African Americans turned away from white newspapers and began to read only their own, he thought that was assimilation. When American Jews dropped Russian in favor of Yiddish for their newspapers and then dropped that for colloquial English, he thought both were instances of assimilation. When immigrant groups dropped their old-world provincial loyalties only to become old-world nationalists, he thought that was assimilation. As Ralph Turner observes, Park took the long view on assimilation, and it was a very "untidy" process in his hands (Park, xxxiv).

Since then, there have been heroic efforts to make ethnic assimilation tidy. Stage theories generally allow for piecemeal assimilation but on a fairly strict time schedule (Gordon 1964). Wave-like assimilation allows for deviations and backtracking but not a change in destination (Gans 1979). Multi-pot assimilation is assimilation by selective agglutination but with an unavoidable and apparently irreversible enlargement of boundaries (Glazer and Moynihan 1963).

There are also efforts to tidy things up by tossing out the concept of assimilation altogether. When all that is left is the ethnic identity, it is still too valuable as social capital to be abandoned, we are told (Novak 1972). The down side of this is the claim that ethnic identities are largely contrived and thus the pretext for ulterior ends (Barth 1969). Why the pretext should work with others or self we are not told.

All of these approaches have some scope of application, but when added together, they are even more untidy than Park left things. What Jean Bacon does is to separate the problem of formulating a tidy interpretation of ethnic assimilation from the very messy process of assimilation itself. The result, to my mind, is the most original contribution to assimilation theory since Park left the field to others.

To prepare the reader, however, there are a number of things that must be kept in mind, for, if the general principles are clear, their application in real time will tax most people's memory and mental agility. At least they do mine.

First, all immigrant communities are imaginary communities. This is familiar enough from the work of Benedict Anderson (1991) telling us that all communities too large for mutual face-to-face interaction are imaginary ones. But Bacon means that they are imaginary in the additional sense that they are in a state of becoming rather than being. Immigrants imagine their communities out of their exemplary potentials rather than out of their present limitations. That is the reason these communities can be valorized and become the objects of loyalty, defense, collective ambition, and sacrifice. Looked at in the specious present, they are just another group of immigrants trying to make it.

Second, while these communities are imagined out of exemplary instances that are real enough to be taken as news rather than myth, they are not representative of the community's corporate life, nor is their classic narrative of the "typical immigrant career" especially characteristic of individual experience. People know that the community falls short of some ideal. They often believe that others follow the typical immigrant career but know better about themselves.

Third, there is another imaginary community called "the mainstream." Undoubtedly you have heard of it and, like myself, strategically place yourself relative to it depending upon to whom you are comparing yourself. Immigrants know that there is something different about them, something rather indefinite—Bacon calls it "x-ness"—but something that they must work out in the existential dilemma between the immigrant community and the American mainstream.

Taken together, these imaginary communities stand as contrasting and exemplary prototypes. Each is both compelling and repulsive. The ethnic community is a place of solidarity and mutualism. But it is also overrun with ego-trippers and opportunists. The American mainstream represents freedom and opportunity but is rife with sex, drugs, and violence. Individual families are suspended very unevenly between these antipodes. One reason for the unevenness is that there is a third imaginary community, in this case, "back home in India." In the process of emigration, immigrants position themselves with reference to their country of origin, rejecting it, historicizing it, mindlessly accepting it, compromising with it, and so on. Another reason for unevenness is that immigrant families themselves are quite variable. The "Old Country" may now seem as homogeneous as the American mainstream, but the families and individuals from it are not, and they know it. Initial conditions, then, are quite variable. What makes them comparable is the point at which the contrast between self and "back home" is set, thus determining which trajectory the individual or family will follow.

It is essentially within the context of these three imaginary communities that a multitrajectory pattern of social differentiation originates and proliferates. Each community helps constitute a pattern of differences and similarities between itself and the immigrant's self or family. The similarities may be more obvious to an observer, but the differences are what matter most to the immigrant. It is the differences that are problematic, and thus they are what propel organizations, generations, families, and individuals in different directions.

At the organizational level, these differences are revealed in a pattern of fission, segmentation, and unstable confederations. At the generational level, the main divergence is from a first-generation dilemma over whether serving the community is only self-serving to a second-generation dilemma over whether one can really serve oneself by serving the community. At the familial level, the chief point of divergence is over what to preserve in "the heritage" and when to give in to "the mainstream." At the individual level, the decisive problematic is how children reclaim parental experiences as their own, while also staking out a certain separateness for themselves.

All this may seem rather familiar, hardly involving ethnic assimilation or Americanization at all. All of us face the dilemmas of how to liken ourselves to various imaginary communities, how to balance collective and personal objectives, how or how not to give in to "the mainstream," and how to learn from our parents but still be ourselves. What is most evident is a pattern of social differentiation and another of individuation. Immigrant communities, organizations, families, and individuals become more and more different from their initial condition, sometimes converging, perhaps, but more likely not. All this may sound like little more than living and growing up in America, and, at this level, it is. Individuation and organizational proliferation are probably the most general and distinctive features of America. We are joiners and individualists at the same time.

But at another level, the immigrant brings with him- or herself a distinctive world view. For Indian immigrants, Bacon explains, this world view makes its way into their decisions in a much less self-conscious way than do the imaginary communities and family or personal histories. For the first generation, one's own and others' "inner world" of motivation and being are framed automatically in terms of external social relationships rather than inner selves and always according to apparent rank rather than personal or subjective estimation. Essentially, what American culture takes as evidence for an inner self is here turned around.

This framing occurs so automatically that there is no second-order language with which to reflect upon it or with which to examine it critically. Thus, it feeds into East Indian organizational and family life in a confusion of reversed glosses for the same behavior as seen by different generations or by East Indians and "mainstreamers." This adds to the sense of what Bacon calls "x-ness" in the first generation, but it can also confound relations between generations and between parents and children, who find themselves reversing the meaning for the same words. Here, ethnicity is not simply a Barthian boundary hatched up strategically for political or economic reasons.

So, East Indians in Chicago are becoming progressively different organizationally, generationally, and individually. Does this mean that they are also becoming Americanized? For the time being, yes, but Bacon is quite clear that what she has attempted to provide is the general shape of ethnic careers as they steer between different imaginary communities, define subprototypic careers for themselves, and raise their children to be like themselves and unlike others. They become Americans by becoming different from one another and by translating their Indian x-ness into an American x-ness. The mainstream may become more familiar, but there is still an x-ness that puts one at some comparative distance from it.

It is in this sense that being American is being ethnic. Sometimes, of course, the claim becomes so tenuous that we can only say that we are "American." Accordingly, Waters and Lieberson have declared this the newest and among the least studied of American ethnic groups (1988). But even this is not fatal; look at the astonishing revival in the number of Native Americans in the census (Nagel 1995). These very imaginary ethnic groups may be tenuously connected at best, but they are not "only symbolic."

Ethnicity shares in that innocence that Benedict Anderson assigns to nationality (Anderson 1991, 141–54). Our acts in its name are without obvious choice and, thus, without obvious individual responsibility. As in other ascribed imaginary communities, this is a very powerful and fateful symbol, far more powerful than individual occupational achievement. Ethnicity is a symbol that can release individual restraint or harness individual effort in the pursuit of exemplary group achievement. The East Indian community of Chicago is doing primarily the latter.

Whether or not that continues is, as we increasingly say, "contingent." It depends above all on whether or not the Indian community and the American mainstream remain plausible imaginary communities. For they are not just acts of will assisted by guile. As Benedict Anderson makes clear, the imaginary nation was in a plausible state of becoming rather than just a void filled with popular fantasy. As becomes even clearer in this book, the East Indian Chicago community is filled with tangible and exemplary instances of community, instances that stand out all the more against exemplary instances of egoism. The same is true of the imaginary mainstream.

With the advance of social constructionism into every sociological corner, it has come into use for iconoclasm as well. Since nothing is real and there are only symbols, sociological one-upmanship consists of revealing these symbols as only the latest social guile. The trick to staying ahead in this game, according to Lyotard, is to find truth by revealing the next effort to establish it as untruth (1992). Thus, there is a wide retreat from any positive assertion of social regularities or social values. Even some Marxists have been tamed to the point that they no longer "privilege" social class.

The trouble with this sort of intellectual maneuvering is that symbols are real, very real. The East Indians in Chicago are not delusional, nor are they easily deceived. They see, feel, and experience community, the mainstream, and "back in India" in the most exemplary and positive way. They know the other, less attractive side of all three as well. What they single out to aspire to and seek to incorporate into themselves is still more selective than what they see, feel, and experience. But it is real. Symbols are not to be found only in dictionaries, museums, and discourse. They are out there in front of us, in us, and all about us. I do not want to retrace Pierce's debate with James here, but anytime an experience becomes a sign it becomes a symbol for sociological purposes. Exemplary experience, reduced to prototype and projected elsewhere, is the way that we construct reality, present and future. We do not do it out of thin air. Symbols may be selective, but they are not arbitrary.

In doing this we find that some experiences glossed as prototypes make more plausible, more shareable, and more desirable futures than do others. This is what the Indians are doing in Chicago's East Rogers Park. It is not as if they were picking their values out of a list of abstractions in the Human Area Relations Files. One of the achievements of this book, then, is that it allows the reader to follow these experiences as they occur in a community and its organizations, families, and individuals. The story proceeds along a trail of increasing intimacy and detail that invites us to follow Mead's invitation and "take the role of the other." Thus, it delivers social constructionism back to symbolic interactionism and away from the disembodied discourse of post-modernism.

If the readers take this invitation, I think that they will find that many of the things that attract these Chicago East Indians attract them also. Once action is densely contextualized as it is here, there may be fewer differences among us than we may have thought. It becomes easier then to reflect back on how countless other immigrants, perhaps "our immigrant forebears," struggled through similar patterns of differentiation and individuation for something similar that they also found terribly attractive. The wide range of possibilities, on the one hand, and the continuing effort to make real these imaginary communities, on the other, must be counted as something of a national success.

Can it continue? Bacon would be the first to say, "It depends." At a time of planet downsizing and population expansion, the available social space for differentiation and individuation may be contracting. And the New World is no longer so new. But that is another book. Right now, something like the American Dream is recurring out on Devon Avenue.

GERALD D. SUTTLES

References

Anderson, Benedict. 1991. *Imagined Communities: Reflections on the Origin and Spread of Nationalism.* London: Verso.

Barth, Frederik. 1969. Introduction to *Ethnic Groups and Boundaries.* Boston: Little Brown and Co.

Gans, Herbert. 1979. "Symbolic Ethnicity: The Future of Ethnic Groups and Cultures in America." *Ethnic and Racial Studies* 2:1–20.

Glazer, Nathan, and Daniel Patrick Moynihan. 1963. *Beyond the Melting Pot.* Cambridge: MIT and Harvard University Press.

Gordon, Milton M. 1964. *Assimilation in American Life: The Role of Race, Religion and National Origin.* New York: Oxford University Press.

Lyotard, Jean-François. 1992. *The Postmodern Explained.* Minneapolis, Minn.: University of Minnesota Press.

Nagel, Joane. 1995. "American Indian Ethnic Renewal: Politics and the Resurgence of Identity." *American Sociological Review* 60:947–65.

Novak, Michael. 1972. *The Rise of the Unmeltable Ethnics.* New York: Macmillan.

Park, Robert E. 1967 [1914]. *On Social Control and Collective Behavior.* Chicago: University of Chicago Press.

Waters, Mary, and Stanley Lieberson. 1988. *From Many Strands: Ethnic and Racial Groups in Contemporary America.* New York: Russell Sage.

Preface

America is leaving the twentieth century much the same way it arrived, riding the crest of a wave of immigration. Contemporary migrants will transform the United States in the twenty-first century as surely as the first wave recast the nation in the twentieth. One feature of the new immigration that will affect its impact on American society is the class status of these newest Americans, and the lifestyle that class status entails. Unlike their predecessors, a significant number of new immigrants are educated and middle-class. They quickly find good jobs in the primary labor market and settle throughout the suburban landscape.[1]

This book is about one such immigrant group. It shows how a specific collection of individuals—India-born parents and their children living in the Chicago metropolitan area—bound by neither geographical proximity nor institutional ties nevertheless constitutes a community. In doing so, however, this study highlights two interrelated social processes—assimilation and community formation—that shape the lives of just about anyone, native or foreign-born, who identifies himself or herself as a member of a particular group within America.

We often think of assimilation as the process that transforms somebody alien into someone who is part of the "mainstream." Traditionally, this metamorphosis has been measured by movement, over time, from one kind of job to another (grocer's child to investment banker), from one neighborhood to another (the Lower East Side to Westchester), or from one kind of affiliation to another (deacon of the A.M.E. Zion congregation to president of the Rotary Club).

The foregoing describes one possible outcome of the assimilation process. But the nature of the process itself—what actually happens to each immigrant or child of immigrants who ultimately finds a satisfying place for himself or herself as an American—involves a social-psychological process of situating oneself within society at large; it boils down to a question of identity. In the wake of the civil rights movement and its progeny, this typically means identifying with a particular group or subculture and discovering how that group fits into the "mosaic" or "tapestry" of contemporary American life.

These subcultures include not only ethnic groups but also groups based on a whole range of reputed commonalities—commonalities of age, infirmity, religion, sexual orientation, even political ideology. Members of all these groups face the same definitional tasks. They must work out basic identity issues: Who are we? Who am I? What does it mean to be "Latino," "gay," "elderly," or "deaf"? They must also answer the core question of assimilation: Where do we/I fit into "American society"?

The social processes of community formation and assimilation that sociologists once studied in relation mainly to immigrant groups are affecting the lives of an ever-widening circle of Americans. Under these circumstances, our traditional understanding of the process of assimilation deserves scrutiny. "First-wave" immigrant groups forged an identity conspicuously, within self-contained ethnic neighborhoods, in a hothouse environment of family, church, mutual aid society, and political clubhouse. While much of the "second wave" still live in such geographically bounded neighborhoods and institutional frameworks, many do not. Their group identity is no longer grounded in face-to-face interactions within the neighborhood, workplace, school, or voluntary organization.

American "communities," whether consisting of migrants from the same home country or of any like-minded group of native-born citizens, are increasingly based simply on shared social identities. People never come into direct contact with more than a few others who share their identification, yet they continue to see themselves as part of some large, relatively bounded group.[2] This loss of face-to-face interaction raises some serious questions about the basis for community. How does one's identification with a community develop in the first place? What is the relationship between mere identification and the actual content of the identity that attaches to it? What is the relationship between the public side of the community, represented by community organizations and community media, and the private experience of community that affects one's daily life?

Population shifts and technological advances are working together to make the world smaller and its constituent nations more heterogeneous. But however a country's immigration policies may change in response to these phenomena, the trend in this direction is probably irrevocable. Therefore, the issues faced by Chicago's Asian Indians as they grapple with the business of assimilation are increasingly relevant features of American social life generally.[3]

The case studies of the formal organizations of Chicago's Indian community and of the five immigrant families upon which this study rests were greatly facilitated by the generosity of the individuals involved—not only a generosity of time but, more significantly, a generosity of spirit. Much of what I discussed with people was very personal and sometimes very painful. I thank them all for their openness, honesty, and patience.

My colleagues and mentors Richard Taub, Robert Jackall, and especially Gerry Suttles helped me to hone my arguments and to find my way along the long road from dissertation to book. Donna Chenail, Peggy Bryant, Shirley Bushika, and Rebecca Brassard contributed their editorial skills and good humor. Lingxin Hao, Kevin Brown, Wendy Penner, and Daniel Taub were welcome sounding boards for both ideas and frustrations.

Contents

LIFE LINES

1

Introduction

In the thirty years since Congress lifted the onerous restrictions of the 1924 Immigration Act, immigration has once again altered the face of just about every large metropolitan area in the United States. The swelling population of Asian Indians in Chicago and its suburbs exemplifies a growing trend among current immigrants, particularly the increasingly large percentage from Asia. Many come to America endowed with educations and financial resources that the earlier wave of impoverished European immigrants could only dream about for their descendants. Absorbed into well-paid occupational niches, these post-1965 immigrant professionals have options in terms of living arrangements that were not feasible for the majority of their immigrant predecessors. Dispersed throughout the suburbs with other middle-class people of varying backgrounds and interests, these immigrants from India and their families have one thing in common with many of their native-born neighbors: they are all busy constructing identities to alleviate a sense of isolation and to connect with some type of a "community."

To the casual observer, Chicago does indeed have an old-style Indian neighborhood. Visit Devon Avenue in the East Rogers Park section of the far north side of Chicago, and you will see sari palaces, groceries well stocked with Indian delicacies, and electronics emporia offering the latest videos from Bollywood (as India's Bombay-centered movie industry is known). In fact, marking the Indian community's coming of age as a player in Chicago's turf-bound politics, this conspicuous thoroughfare was renamed Gandhi Marg at a city-sponsored ceremony in 1991.

However, the image of a neighborhood-centered community suggested by the bustling atmosphere of this commercial street does not withstand close scrutiny. Inspect the registration stickers on the cars double-parked on the avenue, and you will discover that their owners live in Schaumberg, Oakbrook, and other Chicago suburbs.[1]

Since Asian Indian immigrants have much less opportunity for social interaction with fellow immigrants than has historically been the case, the social network that has carried the heaviest burden in the process of assimilation has been the family.[2] In lieu of the partnership between family and community that once supported immigrant adjustment, the family unit has now become almost the sole locus for one's experience of "Indianness" in America.[3] It is within the family that Indian immigrants and their children determine who they are and where they belong.

The community institutions that have been formed do not provide opportunities for large-scale social interaction but rather offer this dispersed, putative membership a common language for conceptualizing their community and their status in America. This language filters back to families through long chains of social relationships and the ethnic media. Families use these symbolic resources as a way to position themselves within the Indian community and in relation to an imagined mainstream society.[4] However, positioning oneself does not necessarily entail seeing a resemblance between oneself and the community. In fact, individuals and families, though continuing to identify themselves as Indian, repeatedly stress their *distinction* from "other Indians." This interaction between a unitary definition of the Indian community worked out in public life and diverse Indian identities expressed in private life creates a community well adapted to contemporary conditions. It allows for the diversity that results when social interactions among the community as a whole are rare or impossible but still engineers a common identity that members (and nonmembers) can recognize, if not embrace, and utilize to craft a sense of themselves and their place in American society.

Immigrants, Ethnicity, and Assimilation

Sociological thinking about immigrants and the social processes that govern their experiences began as a reaction to turn-of-the-century political debates about the vices and virtues of immigration policy. The great wave of immigrants from eastern and southern Europe who arrived in the United States in the late nineteenth and early twentieth centuries was widely seen as a potential threat to the American way of life. Nativists argued that these new immigrants, this "human flotsam," would contaminate the noble characteristics of the Anglo-Saxon that underpinned the great achievements and future progress of the American nation.[5] Therefore, if these undesirables could not be excluded altogether, at least they should be forced to shed their ethnic characteristics and become as similar to "true Americans" as possible.

More optimistic commentators, such as philosopher Horace Kallen, argued that the American way of life was in fact suited to "cultural pluralism." If in their private lives people continued to cherish their distinctive ethnic traits, common economic and political life would nevertheless ensure national cohesion.[6] In both scenarios, the focus was on the *outcome* of the adjustment process. At the end of the day, would immigrant ethnic groups eventually become indistinguishable from the "native American" national type?[7] Or would ethnic distinctiveness persist?

The new discipline of American sociology, developing primarily at the University of Chicago, adopted from the political realm a concern with the outcome of the adjustment process but strove to articulate what the outcomes for various ethnic groups were rather than what they should be. Most noted a gradual convergence between the immigrant and the native, particularly across generations.[8]

In pursuit of these descriptions, however, sociologists also began to study the social *process* that led to particular outcomes. This process was usually understood as a sequence of stages or states through which the immigrant group and/or individuals passed. Chicago sociologist Robert Park, for example, hypothesized a race-relations cycle—contact, competition, conflict, accommodation, and assimilation—that governed relations between both immigrants and native-born minorities, principally black Americans, and the nonimmigrant white majority.[9]

After a long period of quiescence, scholarly interest in immigration and ethnicity surged during the 1960s and '70s, spurred by renewed popular interest in issues of race and ethnicity. One strand of this second wave of scholarship shared with earlier work a preoccupation with the outcomes of adjustment. However, instead of stressing the gradual disappearance of distinctive ethnic traits, many researchers, examining the cases of third- and fourth-generation European Americans, stressed the persistence of ethnic identification. The great-grandchildren of immigrants continued to see themselves as Italians, Poles, or Jews, feeling a sense of distance from mainstream America.[10]

Further studies have recognized that the nature of ethnicity among these latter-day "ethnics" differs from that of their immigrant ancestors. Ethnicity no longer informs the patterns of daily life but is instead symbolic—manifest in an occasional ethnic meal, an occasional trip to an ethnic event.[11] Moreover, ethnic identification is not constant; it varies over the life course, across generations, and in different situations. Today, one may be "German-English-Irish" but "Irish" on St. Patrick's Day and simply "American" on the Fourth of July.[12]

Another strand of scholarship examined the post-1965 wave of immigrants, shifting the focus from outcomes to the processes that govern ethnic identification and immigrant adjustment. Not unlike the logic behind Robert Park's race-relations cycle, Milton Gordon's influential treatment of assimilation proposed a decomposition of the process into a series of roughly sequential but often overlapping components.[13] Many others have used this model to measure the relative assimilation of different immigrant groups, different generations, or different individuals.[14]

In addition to documenting the stages in this process, contemporary scholars also explore the process of assimilation by exploring the causal factors that shape the immigrant experience. The emergence of super-ordinate ethnic identities such as Asian American, Native American, and Hispanic or Latino have been traced largely to external, structural factors that delimit the identificational and organizational options of these emergent groups.[15] For example, the manner in which various Spanish-speaking groups have been integrated into the economic, educational, and political systems of the larger society, the persistence of structural or institutional inequality, as well as particular public policies have affected the creation and mobilization of a Latino community in Chicago.[16]

In a similar vein, the divergent ethnic identifications of second-generation individuals (whether one is "Jamaican," "Jamaican American," "African American," or just "American," for example) have been traced to variations in class, family structure, the type of school one attends,[17] and "political relations between sending and receiving countries, . . . the state of the economy [and] the size and structure of preexisting coethnic communities."[18]

Focusing more closely on the adjustment processes that shape individual lives, as opposed to the fate of the ethnic groups or cohorts as a whole, the process that is scrutinized is once again one in which broad structural patterns and social conditions influence a pattern of adaptation. The collective household economy and shifting power relations between parents and children and between men and women evident in the family lives of Vietnamese immigrants, for example, are shaped both by the "conditions of economic scarcity and uncertainty" and the "gender equality of family members" that characterize contemporary U.S. society.[19] The unfolding of ethnic identity across the generations of the Punjabi-Mexican community in California is determined in large part by the "regional economic context and public policies," including "the placement of Punjabis in the hierarchy of groups working in California agriculture, . . . federal and state laws governing immigration, citizenship, and access to resources."[20]

During this century of research, scholars have attended to both the outcomes and the processes of ethnic identification and immigrant adjustment. But as it becomes increasingly clear that the outcomes are tremendously variable, the process of assimilation has become the central focus. Studying this process has meant one of two things: either the decomposition of the process into a series of stages or states, or the explanation of outcomes based on variations in structural and other large-scale social conditions.

The present study shares with this literature a concern with the process of assimilation. However, it departs from this tradition in the aspect of the process it addresses. At a general level, the social process of assimilation is indeed *shaped* by both societywide and contextually specific social conditions. In the final analysis, though, the process of assimilation is *brought about* by concrete interactions among specific individuals. The present study departs from the dominant orientation in the literature on ethnic identity and assimilation by focusing on the specific interactive (i.e., social) and reflective (i.e., psychological) *mechanisms* that allow people to grapple with the core questions of identity and assimilation. This social-psychological approach incorporates both the collective dynamics of community life evidenced in ethnic organization and media and the private dynamics of family life that more directly constitute most people's everyday lives. These dynamics, I will argue, work together in a very specific way to create both meaning for people who live as part of a community and the social structure and social action that community insiders and outsiders observe.[21]

Asian Indians in the United States

Asian Indians are one of the many groups of immigrants from Asia, Latin America, and the Caribbean whose population soared after the reform of American immigration laws in 1965. The 1924 Immigration Act had effectively barred all immigration from Asia. When, in 1946, a restrictive quota was introduced to allow limited immigration, the Asian Indian population numbered a mere 1,500 persons; by 1965, it had grown to 10,000.[22] By 1990, however, there were 450,406 persons born in India living in the United States, and 815,447 persons claiming Asian Indian ancestry.[23] Asian Indians, then, are among the midsize immigrant and ethnic groups in the United States (see table 1).

The social and economic characteristics of Asian Indians, however, place them among the more elite immigrant groups. They are the wealthiest and most highly educated of all recent immigrants. Almost two-thirds of Indian immigrants have completed at least a bachelor's degree. Almost half are employed in managerial or professional occupations, and the per capita income is well over twice that of the general population. Two-thirds of Asian Indian immigrants report that they speak English very well, making them among the most English-proficient immigrants (see tables 2 and 3).

The social and economic resources of Asian Indian immigrants in the United States betray the fact that they are largely voluntary immigrants who have come in search of better opportunities to develop their professional careers. In this, they are similar to many of the other recent immigrant streams that include disproportionate numbers of the highly educated.

Yet Indian immigrants also bring with them a distinctive history and culture that differentiate them from many of their fellow immigrants. India houses fifteen major regional languages, most of which have different alphabets and many of which are mutually unintelligible. Although mostly Hindu, about 10 percent of the population is Muslim, and there are small Sikh, Jain, Christian, Parsi, and Buddhist minorities. Caste was officially outlawed by the 1950 Constitution, but caste considerations continue to

Table 1 1990 Foreign-born and Total Ethnic Population for Groups Originating in Asia, Mexico, the Caribbean, Central America, and South America

	Foreign-born	Total population
Chinese*	921,070	1,645,472
Filipino	912,674	1,406,770
Korean	568,397	798,849
Vietnamese	543,262	614,547
Indian	450,406	815,447
Japanese	290,128	847,562
Laotian	171,577	142,208
Cambodian	118,883	147,411
Thai	106,919	85,132
Iranian	210,941	235,521
Mexican	4,298,014	13,495,938
Cuban	736,971	1,043,932
Dominican	347,858	520,151
Haitian	225,393	289,521
Jamaican	334,140	435,024
Trinidadian	115,710	76,270
Salvadoran	465,433	565,081
Guatemalan	225,739	268,779
Honduran	108,923	131,066
Nicaraguan	168,659	202,658
Panamanian	85,737	92,013
Colombian	286,124	378,726
Ecuadorian	143,314	191,198
Guyanese	120,698	81,665
Peruvian	144,199	175,035

Sources: *1990 Census of the Population, The Foreign-Born Population in the United States,* Table 1. Total populations for Mexicans, Cubans, and all Asians are taken from *1990 Census of the Population, General Population Characteristics, United States,* Table 3. Total populations for Haitians, Jamaicans, Trinidadians, and Guyanese are taken from *1990 Census of the Population, Social and Economic Characteristics, United States,* Table 12. Total population of Dominicans is taken from *1990 Census of the United States, Persons of Hispanic Origin in the United States,* Table 3. Total populations for the remaining groups are taken from *1990 Census of the Population, Social and Economic Characteristics, United States,* Table 4. Note *Chinese foreign-born persons include those born in China, Hong Kong, and Taiwan.

inform social relations, and marriage is still overwhelmingly endogamous. Indian immigrants, then, originate from one of the most culturally heterogeneous of modern nations.

Chicago's Asian Indian population, numbering at least 52,232 in the greater Chicago area, is the third largest concentration of Indians in the United States.[24] On most measures, this immigrant population reflects the diversity of the motherland. One can find almost all major language

Table 2 Selected Social and Economic Characteristics of the Foreign-Born

	Education (persons 25 years and older)		Language (persons older than 4 years)
	Completed bachelor's degree or above (%)	Completed advanced degree (%)	Able to speak English very well (%)
General population	20	7	—
Place of birth			
China	31	16	28
Hong Kong	47	19	54
Taiwan	62	36	42
Philippines	43	8	68
Korea	34	12	38
Vietnam	16	4	34
Japan	35	10	44
India	65	38	73
Laos	5	1	28
Cambodia	6	2	28
Thailand	33	12	43
Iran	51	23	61
Mexico	4	1	29
Cuba	16	7	40
Dominican Republic	7	3	31
Haiti	12	4	45
Jamaica	15	5	98
Trinidad-Tobago	16	5	98
El Salvador	6	2	28
Guatemala	14	5	13
Honduras	8	3	40
Nicaragua	15	6	34
Panama	20	7	65
Colombia	16	6	39
Ecuador	12	4	38
Guyana	16	5	98
Peru	21	8	43
Africa	47	22	77

Sources: 1990 Census of the Population, The Foreign-Born Population in the United States, Table 3; *Education in the United States,* Table 1.

Table 3 Selected Social and Economic Characteristics of the Foreign-Born

	Occupation	Income
	(employed persons 16 years and older) Employed in managerial or professional occupations (%)	*Per capita income ($)*
General population	26	14,420
Place of birth		
China	29	15,532
Hong Kong	41	19,118
Taiwan	47	18,551
Philippines	28	17,740
Korea	26	14,358
Vietnam	17	11,012
Japan	39	18,607
India	48	25,275
Laos	7	6,724
Cambodia	10	7,354
Thailand	24	11,064
Iran	42	21,371
Mexico	6	8,483
Cuba	23	16,482
Dominican Republic	11	9,358
Haiti	14	11,894
Jamaica	22	15,327
Trinidad-Tobago	22	15,469
El Salvador	6	8,405
Guatemala	7	9,003
Honduras	9	8,835
Nicaragua	11	8,548
Panama	26	15,408
Colombia	17	13,733
Ecuador	14	13,354
Guyana	22	14,254
Peru	19	14,028
Africa	37	20,117

Sources: 1990 Census of the Population, The Foreign-Born Population in the United States, Tables 4 and 5; *Social and Economic Characteristics, United States,* Tables 34 and 37.

groups represented among Chicago's linguistically based voluntary associations.[25] Religious diversity is evident in the Hindu, Muslim, Sikh, Christian, Jain, and Parsi communities of worship (see appendix A). Castes are similarly diverse but are usually drawn from the "twice-born" castes, those affiliated with the three upper groups in Hindu India's traditional four-tiered caste system.[26] The truly poor in India have little opportunity for migration. The class backgrounds of migrants range from lower-middle-class to upper-class individuals and families.[27]

In light of both the relatively high class status and the internal diversity of the Indian immigrant population, one might expect that the dynamics of assimilation among Asian Indians are likely to be peculiar to this group. If approached from the more usual perspectives used in the study of assimilation, this may be the case. The pace and outcomes of the process for Indian Americans would no doubt differ significantly from those of immigrant groups with less social capital, whose class status makes them vulnerable to a host of structural constraints that better-educated, wealthier immigrants can bypass. Moreover, the internal heterogeneity and Indian cultural heritage of the community surely shape the process of assimilation, distinguishing this group even from fellow middle-class immigrants.

However, this study is concerned not with the social conditions that shape the process of assimilation but with the interpersonal interactions that provide the mechanism for assimilation and community formation. Interpersonal interaction is a ubiquitous feature of the human condition. All communities (those that rest on nonfamilial social networks as well as those that revolve around families) must, through interpersonal interaction, socialize a new generation of members to become part of the community. There are surely variations in the way in which this socialization is carried out. But such variations is evident even among the families included in the present study. However, in demonstrating the centrality of this common human condition to the process of assimilation, I will argue that much of what is true for Asian Indians is true for other communities as well.

Overview

This research grew out of a curiosity about the way in which social interaction shapes the lives of Indian immigrants and their children. While living with a family in northern India, I became acutely conscious that a heightened awareness of social relationships dominated the daily lives of my hosts. Rules about cooking, eating, worship, and demeanor fluctuated with a kind of other-regard very alien to me. Sometimes I ate in the kitchen with the women; sometimes I was asked to eat in the living room with males and visitors so things would "look good." Sometimes low-caste relations were allowed in the kitchen, sometimes not, depending on who was in the house. Sometimes the daughters struggled to wait on me; sometimes I was asked to work with them for hours to help prepare snack packages for catering jobs. The impressions I was gathering in my time with this family were confirmed over and over again in interactions and conversations with others as well. I began to wonder how the kind of social-psychological gulf I experienced might feel to people from India who chose to settle and raise children in the United States.

When I began this research, then, I imagined that the sum total of interactions in families and organizations and among community leaders would be the core mechanism that shaped the Indian community and its collective fate, as well as the lives of individuals of Indian origin. It was only as I became more deeply involved in the research that I began to realize that "the community" had another significance. On one level, individual and group assimilation *was* governed by this amalgam of interactions. At another level, though, the very idea of "the Indian community" was critically important in shaping the self-understanding of individuals in both public and private arenas. As the study progressed, the role that rhetoric—the concepts of "Indian community," "Indian," "Indian American," and so on—plays in the community became increasingly clear. I found that rhetoric links the experiences of Indian-origin individuals, which for the most part occur in the privacy of their own homes, or among a small circle of Indian friends, with the public life of the community as it is carried on in ethnic organizations, ethnic media, and the political machinations of ethnic elites. A rhetoric that describes the "standard" experience of individual members of the Indian community and the community as a whole is what binds together the networks of social interaction that exist in public and private arenas.

The organization of this book recapitulates the intellectual journey I took in order to come to this understanding of how Indian immigrants and their children lead their lives. It culminates by outlining a model for how we might begin to untangle the relationship between the public and private social interactions and that collective entity we call the Indian community. Untangling this relationship is the key to understanding immigrant assimilation in particular and community formation more generally.

The book is in three parts. Part I (chapters 2 through 5) examines the public organizational life of Chicago's Indian community. Chapter 2 examines in greater detail the concept of an Indian worldview, with its focus on social relationships, as a basis for understanding the public life of the community. Chapter 3 explores the organizational network built by the immigrant generation, and chapter 4 looks at the organizational network of the second generation. Chapter 5 examines the stylized rhetoric of intergenerational conflict and second-generation adjustment as it appears in the ethnic press.

This examination of public life explores the differences that exist between the first and second generations in the way each views its organizations and the way each views its identity. Even though the language the two generations use to discuss themselves is often quite similar, the meanings of particular phrases in each generation's usage are quite distinct. Both generations may talk about the "ego problems" inherent in organizational life, but the meaning and implication of this idea are radically different in the two generational contexts. Superficially, the common rhetoric provides a sense of continuity between the immigrant and second generations, but through social interactions in ethnic organizations, the rhetoric gets filled out, embellished, and particularized so that unique generational identities emerge.

Part II, the heart of the book, turns to the processes of change and adjustment experienced by individual families. Chapters 7 through 11 present portraits of five Indian-American families. Each chapter addresses the history of the family members, the particular concerns that grow out of their experiences of Indian and American cultures, and the dynamic processes that characterize family interaction and conflict resolution. In addition, I have framed each chapter around what, in my view, is the central or overarching character of the family as a whole. These overarching themes form the basis for what I call *family idioms*, the unique perspective and language developed by each family. These family idioms play off both the collective community identity (the identities of the first and second generations discussed in Part I) and the individual, personal identities of family members.

In part III, I bring together the discussions of public and private life and return to the general theoretical issues of assimilation and community. Chapter 12 synthesizes the experiences of the five families and the backdrop of public discussion about what it means to be an Indian youth in America. I suggest a model for understanding the processes of change or adjustment experienced and articulated across generations. I have found for these families, as for organizations, that a standard rhetoric of adjustment plays an important role in family interactions.

Each family develops a complex vernacular for talking about itself, which each member seems to share. Some elements of each family's idiom are quite general and infiltrate talk in many families. These elements are often drawn from the public rhetoric of adjustment—contrasts between Indian and American, between boys and girls, between parents and children. Some are highly idiosyncratic, growing out of the unique histories of a particular set of parents and children. Although each family idiom is ultimately particular, what is common is the process by which families develop a language, an idiom, for positioning themselves in relation to the "standard experience" represented in public conversations, and the way individuals within a family position themselves in relation to other family members.

For example, everyone employs the rhetoric of the "two worlds" that has been used so often to describe immigrant experience. Indians are no exception when they talk about themselves as suspended between the world of "back home" and the world of "America," not completely part of either. In public settings, everyone, including members of the families I studied, can come up with this language. It then appears as if there is a consensus that the problems of the community stem from having one foot back home and one foot here in America. It appears as if everyone feels the same kind of duality. However, in more intimate settings, the way people spontaneously describe their lives has little to do with the idea of two worlds. Rather, people tend to describe themselves *in relation to* this prototype of their "problems." Sometimes they draw parallels between their own experiences and this prototype, but more often they draw contrasts. There is a pervasive tendency for people to see themselves as more integrated, more at home, more satisfied than this prototype of dual lives suggests.

Chapter 13 examines the relationship between families and organizations as the social units that constitute the Indian immigrant community. I suggest that there is a genuine division of labor between families and organizations and that each makes a unique, but still interdependent, contribution to the sustenance of the community.

Ultimately, the way families and organizations fit together for Indian immigrants cannot be generalized to other social groups. Rather, the particular relationship that develops depends on the particular historical experiences of the generations and individual members of the community, the particular set of social and moral values rooted in an Indian cultural background, and the meaning these historical and cultural experiences have for members of families and community organizations. The way the Indian community has resolved the tension between the great diversity inherent in family life and the need or desire for a unified Indian community owes much to a traditionally Indian vision of the nature of social life.

However, as is the case with the construction of family idioms, it is not the content of this particular community's way of resolving the tensions between diversity and unity that is paramount. Rather, it is the interaction between families and community organizations as distinct kinds of social units that sustains the idea of community for Asian Indians and, I will argue, other identity-based communities as well.[28] The interaction between individual experiences in families and organizations and the standardized prototypes of experience grounded in the stylized rhetorics of families, organizations, and the community at large provide a model for the process of assimilation. The outcomes and even the trajectories or paths of the assimilative process vary. I suggest that what is common across communities is the interplay between social interaction and idealized, standard prototypes. This dynamic relationship between social interaction and prototypes, then, is the mechanism through which assimilation takes place and the foundation upon which identity-based communities rest.

Assimilation as a social process surely has a special meaning in the context of immigration. But what immigrant groups do to make sense of their lives, to build communities, to pass along a sense of identity and community to their children is not so very different from what any other community does.

I

PUBLIC LIFE

2

The Question
of Worldview

All people carry with them a worldview, a sense of how the social world is
organized.[1] All people carry with them a sense of what a person is and how
persons are related to one another and to the entire complex of social relations that constitute society. This worldview is the product of a person's
experience in his or her culture of origin. To the extent that people share a
cultural milieu that surrounds and delimits their particular experiences of
language, religion, caste, gender, family, education, work, and politics, they
share the worldview constitutive of their common cultural background.[2]

Certainly, there is great variety in the ways individuals within a common culture think about their social world. I believe, however, that people
who share a cultural background understand the way their culture thinks
about social relationships. Even one who holds views different from most
people, or different from his or her parents, still understands what "most
people" or "parents" are thinking. There is a shared understanding, if not
acceptance, of the dominant worldview.

When immigrants arrive in America, they carry with them a worldview
grounded in their culture of origin. Likewise, people born and raised as
Americans share an understanding of an American worldview. The case of
America is complicated, of course, by the fact that the cultural group is not
composed entirely of people who have been living together in one place
for hundreds or even thousands of years. Yet despite individual, regional,
and social group variation, there is a commonly recognized American
worldview. Bellah et al. put it this way:

[B]eneath sharp disagreements, there is more than a little consensus about the relationship between individual and society, between private and public goods. This is because, in spite of [our] differences, [we] all to some degree share a common moral vocabulary, . . . the "first language" of American individualism in contrast to alternative "second languages" which most of us also have.[3]

To the extent that the immigrant's worldview differs from the worldview dominant in America, a type of adjustment must occur that differs from the more observable adjustments of language, dress, food, demeanor, work roles, or family relations. Immigrants must come to terms with the types of persons they see themselves as and the types of persons they are raising their children to be, while immersed in a society founded upon a worldview that may be radically different from their own. Worldview is an integral component of the adjustment process of individual immigrants, their families, and immigrant communities. One of the concerns of this study has been to understand what happens to the worldview of Indian immigrants when it is carried onto American soil.

Attempts to understand and articulate the Indian worldview by both Indian and non-Indian authors have been couched in terms of fundamental differences between "Indian" and "Western" worldviews.[4] This does not mean, however, that all Indians share one worldview and all Westerners (Europeans, Americans, etc.) another. Rather, this contrast is a heuristic device to highlight the distinct features of an Indian worldview by comparison to a set of assumptions about the social world that is more familiar to American readers.

All societies are collections of empirical agents, the physical persons that are the raw stuff of social life. In the Western tradition, we think of these empirical agents as discrete individuals, separate and autonomous, whose "rights are limited only by the identical rights of other individuals."[5] "[They] owe no man anything and hardly expect anything from anybody. They form the habit of thinking of themselves in isolation and imagine that their whole destiny is in their own hands."[6]

In the Indian worldview, there are no "individuals," as they are conceived of in the Western tradition: "persons—or single actors—are not thought in South Asia to be 'individual,' that is indivisible, bounded units, as they are in much of Western social and psychological theory as well as in common sense. Instead, it appears that persons are generally thought by South Asians to be 'dividual' or divisible."[7] This dividual person is subject to changes in his or her fundamental nature. One's quality as a person is not based upon a natural or God-given humanity that is shared with all people. Rather, each person is born with a distinctly different nature or essence, based on the combined essences of that person's parents and the particular circumstances of his or her birth. People are not fundamentally the same but instead are fundamentally different kinds of human beings. Moreover, one's fundamental nature changes over time depending on what one gives and receives, with whom one exchanges, and the context one is in. To remove a person, an empirical agent, from the web of social relationships, then, is to take away part of his or her identity. As one Indian immigrant suggests, "Americans seem to have to be one thing. I and my Indian friends are able to be many different kinds of persons in different situations."[8]

This basic difference in the nature of the person was ingeniously illustrated in an experiment conducted by Richard Shweder and Edmund Bourne. They asked Indian and American subjects to describe the personality, character, or nature of close acquaintances. Indian respondents described friends with reference to concrete contexts—"comes forward whenever there is an occasion to address a public meeting," "brings cakes to my family on festival days," "is verbally abusive to his father whenever they meet at his home." American respondents characterized friends in terms of context-free attributes that they assume do not vary—"stubborn," "arrogant," "a leader."[9]

The authors argue that the difference in emphasis between context-free and context-dependent descriptions cannot be understood in terms of "underlying deficits in cognitive processing skills, intellectual motivation, available information, or linguistic tools" of Indians.[10] Rather, the difference follows from differing "world premises." Shweder and Bourne assert that a "holistic" worldview, one in which the whole is greater than the sum of the parts, informs the Indian response. From this holistic worldview follows the "sociocentric solution" to "the problem of the relationship of the individual to the group, to society, to the collectivity"[11]—a problem all societies must solve. The sociocentric solution "subordinates individual interest to the good of the collectivity."[12] Social relationships and social groups, not individuals, are the fundamental building blocks of society.

In the Western worldview, in contrast, society is envisioned as a straightforward aggregate of individuals. The whole is the sum of the parts.[13] In the Indian worldview, the whole is more than the sum of the parts.

It follows from these two differing conceptions of the person and of the constitution of society that the relations among persons are different as well. In the Western tradition, all people are theoretically equal because each contains within himself or herself, "in spite of and over and above his particularity, the essence of humanity."[14] In the Indian worldview, people do not share a fundamental quality that renders them all equal at some level. Instead, by virtue of their position in the network of social relations, people are inherently different from one another and thus inherently unequal.[15]

This inequality translates into a view of the social world in which persons and social groups are ranked relative to one another. Americans, too, experience social inequality, but their experience differs from the Indian conception on two counts. First, inequality in the Indian context is based on *fundamental* differences between people. In America, some may be richer than others, but Americans still believe that all are fundamentally equal. Second, in America, rankings of individuals and groups are made with reference to other individuals and groups. Mary the doctor has more social prestige than Joe the bookkeeper. Asian Indians are more advantaged than Dominicans because their per capita income is higher. In the Indian system, in contrast, social groups are related to one another through their "rank in relation to the whole."[16] Brahmins are at the top of the caste hierarchy not only because they are different from the caste below them but also because they share certain qualities with the caste immediately below them that differentiate both castes from the castes of lower rank. Instead of a ladderlike system of inequality, it is a system based on concentric circles. Social groups that encompass others are ranked higher than those they encompass.

The context-dependent view of the person not only implies fundamental inequality. It also implies a potential for great fluidity in the social worth of individuals and groups. McKim Marriott argues that relative status is worked out through interpersonal exchange. One gives out substance code ("codes of conduct . . . substantialized in the flow of things")[17] and receives substance code from others. What one takes in becomes mixed with one's prior substance code to create a new blend. The more subtle and homogeneous one's substance code, the higher one's rank. For example, knowledge is more subtle than money, and money is more subtle than grain.[18] Thus, as one takes what is subtle and gives what is gross, one's own substance code is homogenized and made more subtle; one's rank increases.

The link between rank and an unending stream of the "right" kind of social exchanges and the notion that individuals change in different social contexts suggest that the maintenance of relative rank becomes a constant chore. Inherent in this potential for fluctuations in individual rank is an ambiguity about rank. Rank is not given but needs to be established or proven over and over again. Moreover, since rank is not inviolable but is based on behavior over time, rank becomes more and more inscrutable as interactions between people become increasingly infrequent and their lives more compartmentalized. Since Indian immigrants have fewer opportunities for interaction with other Indians than they had in their homeland, the system of ranking implied by the Indian worldview becomes increasingly difficult to manage. This fluidity and ambiguity, we will see, poses significant challenges for Indian immigrants in their attempt to play out an Indian social game in their new home. The community becomes preoccupied with sorting people out.

For immigrants from India, the significance of the Indian worldview is heightened by its confrontation with the generally Western and specifically American worldviews that underpin institutions and social relationships in America. As noted above, the Western worldview sees society as composed of individuals that are at some fundamental level equal to and like all other individuals. These individuals have a persistent and inviolable character that transcends the particular roles they fulfill or the particular social groups to which they belong. They are in some sense "context-free."

Although American society shares this basic orientation with much of the West, the specifically American worldview also accords an important role to the group in social life. Drawing on a long tradition of research on the American character and social behavior, Bellah et al. argue that a counterpart to American individualism is a fervent commitment to group life. For Americans, however, group life is not an involvement "in social relationships that impose obligations not of their choosing." Rather, group life in America is premised on voluntary associations. "The United States is a nation of joiners."[19]

Allan Silver argues that the American concern with group life is further characterized by America's "congregational" culture: "in the congregational perspective, community is constituted by individualism; the congregation is created by the consent of individuals not merely to join it but to create it continuously by their continuous consent."[20]

The American worldview, then, is not totally characterized by the interactions among equal and autonomous individuals in a context-free environment. Group life is also central to the American character. However, group life in the American context cannot be equated with the role assigned to group life in the Indian scheme. Group life in the Indian worldview is premised upon the idea that social relationships are the primary building blocks of society; American group life is premised upon the idea that individual choice is the foundation of group affiliation.

The particular nature of the contrast between Indian and American worldviews helps us understand the distinctions between the organizational activities of first-generation immigrants and their second-generation children. In the following chapters, I will argue that the organizational life of the first generation owes much to the Indian view of the social world and remains an essentially Indian game. Second-generation voluntary organizations, in contrast, reflect an American sensibility about the nature of group life.

In addition, however, the Indian worldview, in its concern with rank and with hierarchical or encompassing relationships, allows us to understand some of the uniquely Indian aspects of the process of assimilation that affect family life (see chapter 12). Finally, the role the Indian worldview assigns to fluidity and ambiguity in social life enables us to come to terms with the relationship between community and family and appreciates the complex nature of their interdependence (see chapter 13).

3

Organizational Life in the Indian Community

Chicago's Asian Indians, like many other ethnic communities, rely upon ethnic associations to organize the public side of community life. The many events sponsored by the community's vast array of Indian ethnic organizations are either stylized, formal affairs, with introductions, speeches, and votes of thanks, or fun-filled family occasions—picnics, fairs, fashion or cultural shows.[1] Behind the facade of well-ordered speeches and banquets and joyful family outings, one will find organizations animated by questions of collective identity (who are we as "the Indian community"? who do we want to be?) and collective purpose (what is the proper order of public life?).

I use the term *facade* reluctantly; I do not want to imply that the events sponsored by community organizations are other than they appear. Personal experience confirms that they are indeed happy occasions for socializing and networking. What I want to convey instead is that organizations in the Indian community are also collectively engaged in a great deal of worrying and hand wringing about collective identity and purpose.

This other side of organizational life only rarely makes an appearance at public events or in the ethnic media. However, it comes up constantly in more private organizational meetings, in informal conversations, and at those moments when circumstances draw these tensions into the realm of public discussion. Interviewees constantly brought up the "problems" of the Indian community, so that I would get a "true picture" of what was going on. This other side of organizational life is far from secret. It is a preoccupation that structures and motivates the network of ethnic associations at least as much as do more straightforward needs for fellowship or political clout.

The Structure and Growth of the Organizational Network

Between July 1990 and December 1991, at least 107 Indian ethnic organizations were active in the Chicago area (see appendix A). The vast majority of those active in community organizations came to the United States in the 1960s and '70s as students, wives of students, or newly educated professionals beginning their careers.[2] Members of this generation see the pattern of growth of the organizational network in Chicago's Indian community as a reflection of their successive life stages.[3]

Many of the first organizations were Indian student associations. These campus groups provided a social life for the young, usually single, usually male students. Through Indian movies, music, and dance programs, these groups would "create a little piece of India."[4]

The networks Indians created on area campuses found parallels outside the campus context in organizations founded by young professional immigrants and students who had completed their educations at American universities. As with the student organizations, most early organizations in the Indian community were established, in theory if not in fact, around issues of interest to "Indians." The pan-Indian identity of these early organizations went hand in hand with their focus on *adult* social needs and concerns. The founder of one early organization described it as a "coffee club" at which young men would discuss issues of political, social, or psychological importance. Other organizations were concerned about the relationship between India and America, acting as advocates for India in attempts to influence U.S. policy. Some were devoted to assisting development efforts back home.

During this period of early professional development, people started families. Young families formed the core of the cultural and religious organizations founded to help immigrants pass on Indian "heritage" and "values" to their children. With the rise of these cultural and religious organizations, the pan-Indian identity of the very first organizations gave way to organizations more tightly focused on the sectarian interests of their members. Religious organizations were Hindu, Muslim, Sikh, Parsi, and Jain. Cultural organizations were organized around Indian states of origin, language, caste, and class.

Finally, as the immigrants approached middle age and their children approached adulthood, community members began to view themselves as permanent residents rather than sojourners.[5] They began, then, to establish political, professional, and cultural outreach organizations to improve the condition of the Indian community within the larger society. This organizational wave contained a mix of pan-Indian and more parochial organizations.

In all three stages of organizational expansion, there were dual motives at work.[6] On the one hand, people wanted to preserve and pass on
"what is good in Indian culture." In the early pan-Indian organizations,
this took the form of movies, concerts, and discussions of things Indian.
Cultural and religious organizations gave parents an additional forum in
which to create an Indian "atmosphere" for their kids. The later cultural
outreach organizations sought to combat the "snake-charmer image" of
India, to provide "Americans" with accurate facts about India's many achievements, and to share with them India's rich cultural traditions. Even political and professional organizations promoted cultural nostalgia along with
their more instrumental goals. The 1991 convention of the Association of
Physicians from India, for example, included a cricket match, three temple
tours, and a "concert by the king of ghazals." A fund-raiser for mayoral
candidate Richard Daley boasted a larger-than-life cardboard cutout of the
candidate, a campaign tactic imported directly from India.

On the other hand, all three phases of organizational development have
also been motivated by dangers posed by the "mainstream."[7] People who
joined the early pan-Indian organizations felt isolated in the new "strange
world" that surrounded them. In their early years as immigrants, many
Indians felt alienated and excluded from American culture. Some were
shocked by women's immodest attire and behavior in the late '60s. For
many, the American standard of living was new and disconcerting. It was
like being "on a different planet." At times, this sense of alienation came
from an active exclusion by mainstream Americans (being pigeonholed at
work into low-contact technical positions, being insulted and snubbed by
new neighbors), but more often it was the result of unfamiliarity and discomfort with the mainstream and a consequent self-imposed social distance.
The "danger" this represented was the loss of social contact altogether, the
danger of isolation. If they were going to have friends at all, friends needed
to be made in the Indian community. The early pan-Indian student and
community organizations provided just such an opportunity for fellowship.

The dangers of the mainstream were more straightforward for those
who became involved in cultural and religious organizations. Speaking on
behalf of the community, one informant suggested that the impetus for
involvement coincided with daughters reaching the age when they might
begin to date. For many Indian parents, "to go out was unimaginable."
These organizations would provide (and have provided) adolescent boys,
and especially girls, with a safe environment for peer interaction.

Although Indian parents tend to talk almost exclusively about the dangers of sex and drugs when explaining their motivation for getting involved
with cultural and religious organizations, Indian social workers and psy-
chiatrists have suggested to me that deeper issues involving parental control over children's lives and obedience are underlying issues—sex and drugs
are merely buzz words. In the second phase of organizational growth, then,
the dangers from the mainstream have shifted from the first generation's

concern with their *own* fate as social beings to their concern with the fate of their children.

In the third phase of organizational expansion, the danger is not to individuals but to the community at large. Indians must unite to ensure that foreign medical graduates are not discriminated against, that their community receives deserved attention and services from city government, and that the general public esteems rather than disparages India and Indian immigrants.

The relationships between these dual motivations has changed over time. In the early stages in the development of the immigrant organizational network, the desire to "preserve the Indian" and the need to "guard against the mainstream" were more starkly complementary. If one could preserve the Indian, one could simultaneously ward off dangers from mainstream culture. This separatist approach did not require thinking about the relationship between the culture of back home and the new cultural environment in which the immigrants found themselves. In the later types of organizations, however, the immigrant community has begun to address that relationship. What is attractive about Indian culture is not just elements that are lacking or reversed in the mainstream. Sex and drugs are not nightmares just for Indian parents. The Indian community is beginning to realize that they are nightmares for mainstream parents as well.

This merger of motives is also evident in the growing focus on positive aspects of the American mainstream. I have heard over and over again about the "aloofness problem," that Indians are not involved in and do not display a real commitment toward American cultural life. There is a growing feeling that Indians "should put something back into the soil which has been so good to us." In terms of the activities of Indian organizations, this translates into Thanksgiving dinners and clothing drives to benefit the poor and homeless and the establishment of pan-Asian social service organizations that also serve non-Asians in need.

The attraction of the mainstream is also evident in organizational efforts to learn more about mainstream culture and how to compete in that domain. Several organizations offer "how to succeed" seminars that highlight the particular cultural tools that are useful in mainstream social and professional life. Seminars provide instruction about fashion and styles of interaction in business settings, as well as the practical aspects of communicating with American bureaucracies—how to write resumes, prepare taxes, or draft wills.

Finally, the third wave of ethnic organizations also has begun to forge a proactive stance toward something called Indian-American culture. In advising parents about how to talk with their children about dating and marriage, organization seminars and opinion articles in the press are increasingly advising the first generation to loosen up, to try making at least some modifications to the traditional Indian ways of doing things. Indians are being told not only that they should adapt their behavior to mainstream institutions but also that their personal values and expectations for their children can undergo some changes without endangering the vitality of their Indian heritage. To become an Indian American need not be seen as a downward step or cultural adulteration.

This story of organizational development depicts a community maturing and becoming more comfortable with and engaged in its role in American society. In addition to this developmental tale, community members offer one other benign, commonsense response to my queries about how there have come to be so many organizations: the expanding immigrant population. More Indians can support more organizations. Population growth also explains the shift away from the pan-Indian character of the earliest organizations. The pan-Indian character was a necessity rather than a conscious choice. "Back then, there were so few Indians." In the early days, Indian immigrants just didn't have the luxury of associating solely with members of their own religious/linguistic/caste groups. Any Indian would do. When the community became large enough, people reverted to their preferences for associating with those most like themselves. In the third phase of organizational growth, with its mix of pan-Indian and parochial organizations, the community has maintained its preference for differential association but has also recognized that it is sometimes advantageous to present a pan-Indian persona to outsiders.

However, these neat stories are only one strand in the Indian community's talk about itself. The other story, the one people will say is the true story about what is currently at issue in the network of ethnic associations, is not so neat and benign. There is a story of significant strain and tension that runs parallel to the story about the wide variety of ethnic associations that have adapted to the changing needs and expanding population of Chicago's Indian community. This parallel story is the story of division and a desperately longed-for unity within the community.[8]

The major theme that dominates current discussions about the organizational network of the Indian community is its fragmentation and lack of unity.[9] This was the "burning problem" identified by community leaders at the 1990 Asian Leadership Conference sponsored by the governor of Illinois. The "problem," as it was encoded on the flip chart during the meeting, read, "How to unite and integrate Asian Indian Americans."[10]

In the past decade, two organizations have been established to provide "one voice for the community" in Chicago: the Federation of Indian Associations and the Alliance of Midwest Indian Associations. Both organizations actively promote the connection of the Indian community to mainstream political and social life. The Federation focuses primarily on creating a political voice for the community (supporting political candidates and intervening with American bureaucracies such as the police and immigration), while the Alliance is more concerned with forging social connections (sponsoring a Thanksgiving dinner for the homeless; running seminars to educate teachers about Indian culture and the particular needs of Indian children; arranging specialized nursing-home care for immigrants' aging parents).

However, the fact that these two organizations vie for the privilege of being "*the* voice of the community" and the fact that, unlike the earlier pan-Indian organizations (the Association of Indians in America, for example), these two groups have adopted federated rather than pan-Indian organizational identities speak to the fundamental role that division plays in the organizational network.

In the late 1980s and early '90s, this division was acted out annually through two parades on Indian Independence Day, one sponsored by the Federation and one by the Alliance. There was considerable argument and at one point even a lawsuit over the issue of parade permits. But year after year, crowds of a few hundred to a few thousand would turn out to watch the supporters of the two associations, with their differing visions of what the parade should be like, march down the same stretch of Michigan Avenue to celebrate the birth of a united Indian nation.

But it is not just the rivalry between the Federation and the Alliance that is symptomatic of the division Indian immigrants see in their community. Divisions are characteristic of the organizational network overall, structuring the day-to-day activities of ethnic organizations as going concerns. As organizations elect officers and plan events, they are constantly engaged in discussions about division and unity in the community. Ultimately, these discussions are what give meaning to organizational life and thereby integrate organizational life into overarching assimilative searches for answers to the questions "Who are we?" and "Who do we want to be?"

Division and Unity: The Dynamics of Organizational Life

There is a genuine sadness about the fact that the community is not united. Editorials in the ethnic press lament the existence of two Indian Independence Day parades, calling it the "shame of the community." One member of an older pan-Indian organization points out that his organization has only 300 members, while some of the language-based associations are able to draw several times that many.[11] That unity is desirable is virtually uncontested. However, the meaning of unity, and the various schemes proposed to foster it, can be understood only in the context of the community's understanding of the source of its division.

The phrase "all chiefs and no Indians" was used by several people to identify the "problem" at the root of the Indian community's lack of unity. There is a hidden meaning here. Although the increasing number of organizations in the Indian community has in part resulted from the splitting of organizations along "cultural" lines (which in the Indian parlance encompasses a mixture of regional, language, religion, caste, and class differences), community members tend to interpret these splits as the result of "ego problems" (a phrase used by nearly everyone). They see the problem as a lack of "Indians," a lack of foot soldiers, not a lack of *Indians*, a lack of people united on the basis of their common Indian heritage.

The division of organizations through splits has been just as important to the growth of the Indian organizational network as the demographic changes taking place in the community as a whole. The split of organizations has occurred among general, religious, and cultural organizations.[12] Each split follows a similar pattern. There are two groups with differing "cultural" backgrounds in a single organization. These perceived cultural differences are based on language, caste, or "professional" versus "business" class diversity.[13] Sooner or later, an occasion arises in which one group (usually, but not always, the numerically weaker segment) splits away.

The three splits of which I have the most detailed knowledge all occurred on the occasion of organizational elections. In each case, there was disagreement about how the organizational leadership should be constituted. Some would argue that organizational leadership should reflect the diversity of the association's membership. Under this scenario, offices should be parceled out so that each of the major cultural groups in the organizations (no matter how small or how large) should have a leadership position. Some organizations had even worked out rules for ensuring that the presidency of the organization would rotate among constituent groups. On the other side were those who argued for a simple rule by majority. Each person should get a vote, and if one cultural group ended up dominating the organizational leadership, so be it. By rights, the leadership should reflect the numeric strength of the organization's membership factions.

But in discussing the details of these conflicts, all informants (including those who witnessed splits revolving around occasions other than elections) brought up the particular personalities involved as a significant factor in the controversy. The leader of one religious organization that suffered a split based along linguistic lines commented, "So now the five six ringleaders each have their own organization. After they split from us, they couldn't even get along with each other." He went on to point out the particular offenders later in our conversation when we were discussing the various associations in his organizational category.

In one general organization, linguistic and regional divisions emerged after the nominating committee had failed to nominate a particular man who had wanted to become president. After he failed to receive the nomination, this man began to claim it was because he was Gujarati. Gujaratis dominated the membership of this particular association. This was sufficient to foment a "takeover" of the organization by Gujaratis through nominations from the floor at election time, allowed by a loophole in the organization's constitution. Ultimately, he succeeded in becoming president. Members from several other linguistic/regional subgroups resigned in disgust to form their own organization. The "ego" of the would-be president was consistently cited as "the problem."

Others who happened to be Gujarati were equally disgusted with this individual's behavior and also detailed his "ego problem." However, for these Gujaratis, the relevant issue was his professional status as a doctor. For them, the division was along class lines.

Informants discussed all seven organizational splits in terms of both cultural group divisions and the ego problems of particular individuals. However, while cultural differences among subgroups of the organization are used as a backdrop in discussing all of these splits, ultimately the community's understanding of these organizational divisions revolves around ego problems—everyone wants to be a chief. There are cultural *differences*, but there are ego *problems*.

This sense that cultural difference is a legitimate basis for understanding and constituting social life (whereas individual personality and ambition cause "problems" in social life) is also apparent in the various strategies used to build community unity. At the Leadership Conference, the answer offered to the question of "how to unite and integrate Asian Indian Americans" was to get each organization to apprise the others of its activities. One organization official reported that although her group had sent out seventy flyers to other organizations regarding a recent event, they had never received any similar announcements. The consensus was that if more organizations followed this example, the community could begin to build unity. The proper way to unite, under this analysis, is by maintaining the unique cultural identities of the various constituent groups and by coming together as representatives of cultural diversity.

This concern with maintaining cultural difference is also evident in the behavior of language-based associations that have splintered into multiple organizations. Splinter groups occasionally sponsor joint events or consider getting back together. Their efforts at reconciliation, however, are always presented under banners such as "the united Telegu community," suggesting the retention of cultural difference even as they cooperate.

A literally concrete example of this "unity in diversity" approach is the building project at one of the local religious centers. The new construction is intended to build cultural diversity into the very architecture of the facility—different parts of the building complex reflect the different architectural styles of various regions of India. As one official told me, "There should be something for everyone."

The leader of one of the early pan-Indian organizations recognized that its picnics are no longer popular. People now have their own cultural groups' picnics to go to, and so the pan-Indian association has to find another niche (aside from social interaction) to fill. This change he described as "only natural."

Cultural groups, then, are the legitimate building blocks of a united Indian community. As long as everyone acts as part of his or her group and the nominal groups, rather then the individuals they represent, are the social actors in the community, all is well. Only when groups see themselves as composed of discrete individuals (i.e., when a group demands power based on the number of individuals it has as members rather than its unit identity as a group) does social life go awry.

Making Sense of Native Explanations

What should we make of the "ego problems" explanation for organizational division? It seems strange that people ignore the interplay between divergent cultural subgroup interests and the ego problems they cite as sources of disunity in the community. Ultimately, it is not divergent interests that cause organizational splits or prevent cooperation or unity but the ego problems of particular individuals. Strange, too, is the fact that people do not recognize a connection between the lack of unity they find so deplorable and the decline of organizations based on a pan-Indian identity in favor of parochial and federated organizations. The multiplicity of organizations is seen only as the effect of disunity, not its cause. For them, the problem is not a lack of *Indians* but a lack of "Indians."

To explain this, we must look to the cultural contexts that serve as the foundation for the community's public life. These contexts are born of the immigrant generation's experiences as people raised in India. They represent the deeply ingrained shared knowledge that forms an unconscious backdrop for current experience.

The Indian Worldview

One of the central features of the Indian worldview is the emphasis on social relationships over autonomous and separate individuals as the fundamental building block of social life. Individuals have meaning only when they are embedded in the context of social relations. Among the salient social relationships in Indian society are relationships of religion, language, caste, and class. These groupings, then, are the foundation of social interaction.

If social life revolves around the relationships between groups, then the parochialization of the Indian organizational network is quite natural and no cause for concern. The parochial groups are the proper building blocks, regardless of how narrowly they are defined. It only becomes a problem when the order (one may even argue "rank")[14] among the constituent groups is disrupted. When a group splits, the new organizations begin to vie with one another to claim the place of the parent organization in the overall organizational network. Every time there is an upset in the order of social relationships, the social world must somehow be put right again, and ambiguities of order must be sorted out. Until the places of the new organizations are clearly established, tension prevails.

A second feature of the Indian worldview, however, prepares the community to deal with this ambiguity of order: the social world is *inherently* ambiguous and fluid. At an individual level, the ambiguity of one's position in the social order can be sorted out through one's social interactions. Exchanges (of goods, services, speech) among people serve as a constant monitor and marker of one's social status. The system of interaction has the potential to disturb the social order (one's purity can suffer from improper interactions), but it is also the mechanism through which social order is maintained and stabilized.

Ambiguity at the level of organizations can be sorted out in a similar fashion. As I will argue below, the behavior of individual members of organizations, particularly as it reveals the basic moral value of selflessness, is used to adjudicate the relative positions of the different organizations as a whole.

These two components of the Indian worldview, then, allow us to understand why it is neither the parochial character of organizations nor their generation through organizational splits that is singled out as the cause of the lack of unity that plagues the community. These divisions are natural and manageable.

The Context of India

If cultural group divisions are a meaningful and legitimate means for constructing organizational life, then why is unity (albeit federated unity) important? In light of the dangers posed by the mainstream and the activist stance of recently conceived organizations, it may seem that unity is desirable because it confers power on the community. Political organizations in particular have rightly noted that their requests are more readily heeded when one voice represents the whole community. They also recognize the mainstream point of view that immigrants from India are simply "Indians"—not Gujaratis or Tamils, not Hindus or Muslims, not Brahmins or Vaishyas. To the extent that the Indian community can fit into the slot open to them, their contact with mainstream institutions will be eased. But it is not only the community's desire to participate in or extract benefits from the mainstream that is responsible for the consensus on the importance of unity. The history of India itself has suggested to first-generation immigrants that unity is a social good.

The first-generation immigrants are "midnight's children," to use Salman Rushdie's phrase for children born precisely at the moment of independence for the newly united (and partitioned) India on August 14, 1947.[15] The connection between first-generation immigrants and the wider context of the history of independent India was illuminated for me one day during a life history interview with first-generation immigrant Lakshmi Iyengar (see chapter 8). She had begun telling me where she was born and where the people involved in her life—parents, grandparents—were at the time of her birth. After an interruption, she continued, "I was born in 1947, which is the year of independence." I spontaneously said, "One of midnight's children." She picked up on the reference, saying that she had read Rushdie's book and saw a lot of connection to her personal experience. Later in the conversation, Lakshmi referred back to *Midnight's Children*, saying that there was "a sense of being charmed because you were born an independence person. There was a sense of nationalism, greatness of India, and all that kind of stuff."

First-generation immigrants, who constitute the bulk of those active in ethnic associations, grew up in postindependence India, at a time of great national self-awareness. Discussions of the importance of unity and the steep price that had been paid in the bloody riots that accompanied the partition of the British Raj into India and Pakistan were common. Although the unity of India was a powerful and positive concept in the childhood experiences of first-generation Indian immigrants, the meaning of unity was not fixed for all time in the years following independence.

The sense of nationalism that Lakshmi experienced as a child has come under increasing pressure from communal interests in the half century since independence.[16] The religious, regional, and caste divisions that have become increasingly apparent during India's recent history have reinitiated discussions about the terms of a unified India, and in some quarters have called into question the value of unity altogether.

Chicago's immigrant community has been an active participant in recent debates about Indian unity. First and foremost, discussions of India's national unity have been occasions to reaffirm the importance of pan-Indian unity as a social good. Unity is not just desirable for the immigrant organizational network. Unity has strong and deep emotional reverberations that connect first-generation immigrants to their remembered and idealized motherland.

In the fall of 1990, the Babri Masjid/Ram Janmabhoomi controversy provoked intense debate about the future of a united India.[17] The controversy arose out of an attempt to erect a Hindu Rama temple (*mandir*) on the site of a still-standing sixteenth-century mosque (*masjid*) in Ayodhya, the reputed birthplace of Lord Rama. The controversy over this site had been voiced before British magistrates in preindependence India and subsequently put on hold by the courts of independent India, which ordered the closing of the site to all worshippers. In the spring of 1990, a lower court magistrate approved the use of the site by Hindus, while final resolution of the dispute was still pending in the supreme court. This move unleashed a wave of Hindu activism concerning the construction of a new temple on the site, including marches on the site and a planned consecration ceremony. Communal tensions flared throughout India and resulted in riots, mob violence, mass arrests, and loss of life in several cities.[18]

In the ethnic press, in articles supplied by Indian wire services as well as those written by immigrants, the Hindu fundamentalist, pro-*mandir* voice is all but overpowered by the pervasive denunciation of communalism. Among those arguing against the Hindu fundamentalists, there are recurrent references to communalism as a challenge to the great Indian secular democracy. If the current communalism is allowed to spread, it is feared that the country will literally fall apart. The current strife has been called "another Partition of Indian society."[19] In an article reprinted from India's *Sunday Observer*, Atul M. Setalwad reminded his audience that at the preindependence Constituent Assembly, Ram Manohar Lohia argued that "if India was not made a secular state, the only result would be fragmentation, an India divided into a Sikh state, a Jat state, a Brahmin state and so on."[20] The very survival of India, then, depends on the triumph of the spirit of national unity over communalism.

This spirit of national unity is defined by the critics of communalism as the spirit of national oneness that transcends (or at least supplements) loyalties to religion, region, and caste—the spirit of oneness that drove the founding fathers Mahatma Gandhi and Jawaharlal Nehru. At the annual Jawaharlal Nehru Memorial Lecture at Cambridge University in 1990, Indian jurist Nani Palkhivala proclaimed:

> The day will come when the 26 states of India realize that in a profound sense they are culturally akin, ethnically identical, linguistically knit and historically related. We shall then celebrate August 15 not as the day of independence but as the day of interdependence—the dependence of states upon one another, the dependence of our numerous communities upon one another, the dependence of the many castes and clans upon one another—in sure knowledge that we are one nation.[21]

The current problems are said to result from people's failure to internalize this feeling of national "oneness":

> People [feel] loyalties not to the abstract concept of India but to their families, castes, religions, or regions. . . . The Indian independence movement, inspired to a large extent by Western concepts of nationalism, has undoubtedly created the *concept* of an Indian nation, but the very existence of these particular loyalties shows that the concept is still not sufficiently deep-rooted to ensure national unity.[22] (emphasis added)

> The real measure of the political crisis that has taken over the country is that the forces which have served as the cement of nationhood—its corps of professionals and educated middle classes in general—have lost faith in *the idea* that is India.[23] (emphasis added)

> Indian nationhood has yet to be firmed up. The melting pot that is India is still in the process of evolution toward a strong nationhood wherein loyalty to the nation takes precedence over loyalties to one's region, religion, caste and language.[24]

> [T]he time is ripe for every Indian irrespective of where they live, to which religion they belong, or to what position they hold in society to rise as one with the single most concern and goal of saving the Nation by maintaining amity and communal harmony.[25]

In a forum sponsored by the recently formed group TOUCH (The Organization for Universal Communal Harmony), one speaker commented that "the rarest commodity in India today is the Indian. He has been driven out by regionalism, communalism, castes, and creeds. But without the Indian there can be no India."

However, mingled with the nostalgic longing for Indian unity ensured by a sense of national "oneness," a second theme emerges that echoes the Indian community's choice of ego problems over cultural difference as the perceived threat to unity in the immigrant organizational network. In almost every statement vilifying the "menace of communalism" (whether excerpted from the Indian press or produced by the immigrant community in America), speakers note that religious difference itself is not the true root of the controversy over the Babri Masjid/Ram Janmabhoomi site. In his last address to the nation before leaving office, Prime Minister V. P. Singh asked, "Wherein is all this conflict? The conflict is elsewhere and religion is only a pretext." Over and over, the self-serving interests of politicians are blamed for the controversy:

> Responsibility for the communalism sweeping the country falls entirely on the politicians.[26]

> The founding fathers of the republic . . . could never have visualized the kind of self-seeking politicians that may rise one day and tear [the Constitution] apart.[27]

> The leaders are not interested in governing or helping India grow as a modern nation. Their sole preoccupation is their power seat.[28]

This accusation is leveled against politicians on both sides of the communalism issue. At a panel discussion of the *mandir/masjid* issue in Chicago, a prominent psychiatrist suggested that "the Mandal dream of V. P. Singh and the mandir dream of BJP was to secure vote banks. Everyone is for himself."[29]

In addition to the lack of unity and its attribution to the actions of self-serving individuals, the problem of representation by numbers versus representation by group is a third theme shared by the *mandir/masjid* dispute and the Chicago community's discussion of its own organizational network. Those who call for the building of the Ram temple and the establishment of "Hindutva" (the Hindu way of life) argue that India is 85 percent Hindu and thus should be recognized as a Hindu state. There should be no personal law for non-Hindu religious communities and no special treatment of minorities.[30] Opponents argue that "what is nationalism to the BJP is 'communal politics' to those who think that India's secular Constitution gives equal weighage to all religions, irrespective of their numbers."[31] Here battle lines are drawn that mirror the immigrant community's disagreements about the role of numbers in the determination of group leadership. Should the leadership be drawn from the cultural group that is the majority, or should leadership rotate among the group's constituent cultural groupings? This is the very disagreement that has occasioned so many organizational splits.

Finally, shame plays a role in the rhetoric of both controversies. Just as the two Indian Independence Day parades are the "shame" of the immigrant community, "[a]ll those who stand for India's composite culture, rule of law, principles of secularism and decency hang their heads in shame as they watch their country blow up in flames of hatred."[32] Moreover, these "shameful happenings"[33] "damage the country's image before the international community."[34]

The *mandir/masjid* issue, then, has occasioned an outpouring of sentiment regarding the importance of national unity and the feeling of oneness that is supposed to serve as the basis of that unity. The emotive tone of this rhetoric helps us to understand why so much regret and sadness attend the immigrant community's discussion of its lack of unity. In addition, a number of themes in the *mandir/masjid* rhetoric are duplicated in the organizational splits rhetoric: the attribution of disunity to ego problems—specifically, political scheming—rather than cultural differences; the concern over groups gaining strength because of their numbers rather than their voices being equal because of their nominal differences; the understanding of disunity as a "shameful" state of affairs.

Finally, members of the immigrant community sometimes make a direct connection between the disunity problems in India and those in the immigrant organizational network. In an opinion piece entitled "A Story of the Throne" ("Kissa Kursi Ka"), a Muslim immigrant leader criticized all of India's political contenders for their self-interested motives in relation to the *mandir/masjid* and other communal issues. He went on to suggest:

> The multitude of Indian Associations in America are too afflicted with the same leadership virus. . . . Mostly leaders of the Indian Associations are busy getting their pictures taken with U.S. senators and congressmen and getting them published in Indian newspapers. The Indian community in the U.S. which is the most educated ethnic group even by U.S. standards is divided vertically along religious lines. There is no communication between subcommunities and each is espousing its own party line. Whatever happened to bringing these people together and espousing an Indian party line, associating with each other socially and eliminating division?[35]

A similar opinion was voiced by a local newspaper editor who told me that "you can't blame them," meaning the leaders of splinter groups in the organizational network, because "it's in their blood." After all, he told me, if you look at the political parties back home, they have four Congresses. (This was a reference to the way the Congress party has split into factions since independence.) There is a clear parallel between Indian politics and the politics of immigrant organizational life. A desire for unity, ego problems, and the tendency to split seem to be "in the blood."

Epic Contests

An understanding of the Indian worldview can help us make sense of the immigrant community's decision to ignore cultural differences as the driving force behind community disunity. The emotionally charged conflict over national unity in India may suggest why unity is so desirable for the community's organizational network. But when first-generation Indian Americans fault "ego problems" for undesirable divisions in their community, what are they talking about? At first glance, it might appear that they are pointing up the difference between an Indian worldview based on groups as the legitimate component parts of social life and an illegitimate individualistic alternative. When people act for their own benefit rather than keeping the welfare of the group in mind, social life goes awry. However, the answer is not so simple.

First, although *ego problem* and *egoism* are by far the most common terms used to describe the source of the community's divisiveness, there are other undercurrents in people's descriptions that reveal a subtle complexity to the term *ego problem*. Ego problems are not just about differences between group-based and individual-based social organization. Ego problems entail critiques of both the use (and the misuse) of social status and greed. These supplementary themes suggest the need for a more subtle context in which to understand these ego problems.

Moreover, the pervasive complaints about others' ego problems occur amidst an intense display of personal achievement. The self, and the boosterish presentation of self, is much more a part of Indians' discourse about themselves than one would expect in a community so vocal about the evils of egoism. Moreover, it is often the very same individuals who complain most vociferously about others' ego problems who display their own accomplishments most vigorously.

Some of this complexity can be unraveled if we consider ego problems in light of the contests between selfishness and selflessness chronicled in Indian epic texts, and in light of a general ethical scheme in which individual efforts are connected to the good of the social whole.

What Are Ego Problems? The ego problems rampant in the community are, in the most literal sense, ascribed to persons busy "promoting themselves." Promoting oneself often translates into wanting to be president of an organization without first paying the appropriate dues in terms of organizational service. The patterns of organizational division, which revolve around contested elections, illustrate the dubious strategy of splitting from existing organizations so that one can become president. However, charges of promoting oneself are not limited to participants in intraorganization conflicts. One newspaper editor, illustrating the ego problem, told me about a young man who asked the paper for a copy of its mailing list. When the editor asked why the young man wanted it, he replied that he wanted to start an organization. The purpose of the new organization was discussed. The editor suggested that the young man take these ideas to an existing organization. The young man replied, "But I want to start my own organization so I can be president and my friend can be vice president."

In addition to seeking the reward of a position, promoting oneself can also mean putting oneself too often in the limelight. This charge was leveled against media personalities who routinely spotlight themselves and their relatives. Hogging the spotlight also occurs at public organizational functions. "Important members" of the organization crowd up onstage and give lengthy, repetitious, and self-congratulatory speeches.

More subtly, ego problems involve considerations of the relative social status of particular individuals. Being president of an organization is a kind of social capital in the community. It can enhance one's chances of being placed on the consulate's list of "prominent Indians in Illinois," securing an automatic invitation to consular functions. It can get one's name mentioned more often in the local press.

Tensions over the distribution of personal social status become acute when a person tries to trade on the high status garnered in one role or position to claim status in the sphere of ethnic associations. For example, one of the most bitter and public splits in the community involved a conflation of organizational and professional status. One witness complained, "They think that every association should have a doctor for president." Yet in the aftermath of the dispute, the doctors withdrew from organizational participation for a time in order to "dissipate feelings of jealousy" in the community. There was a sense on both sides in this dispute that this sort of compounding of high-status positions was problematic.

The problematic nature of attempts to transfer status from one social sphere to another is further supported, through negative example, by the universal praise for the display of inconsistent statuses. Many people have mentioned with great admiration the doctors, chemists, and engineers who sweep up at the temple, volunteer to serve at the Thanksgiving dinner for the poor, or teach Sunday school. It is not the volunteerism alone that is praiseworthy. People are careful to point out that it is the role reversal that deserves particular remark.

Connected to the whole discussion of ego problems, then, is a concern with the role of social status in the organizational life of the community. The wielding of power in one social sphere based on superior status in another social sphere is frowned upon, and people who are perceived to capitalize on their superior positions are accused of egoism. In contrast, the deliberate display of inconsistent statuses—the doctor-sweeper—is praised.

A critique of greed is a second, though less widespread, undercurrent in the community's discussion of ego problems. "Ego problems" in some conversations referred specifically to the inappropriate use of organizations to promote the personal financial interests of members. I was cautioned that some people "see themselves as community leaders, but they are really just serving their commercial interests."

On a more subtle level, greed came into discussions of organizational division metaphorically. Charges of people trying to "buy each other out" were leveled in relation to more than one organizational dispute. Although the "buying" was done with promises of organizational positions rather than money, the choice of words recalls a general concern with the corrupting power of money.

Greed as a source of disharmony in organizational life is buttressed by a much larger concern with greed as a vice in the community as a whole. Greed was offered as an explanation of why unhappy marriages stay intact,

why business participation in community organizations is less than gener-
ous, why one doctor took a lifetime subscription to a community paper in
the name of his one-year-old son. It is the prevalence of this general critique of greed that has encouraged me to read the fewer incidences of discussions of greed in the context of organizational life as significant.

Complaints about ego problems accompanied by the boosterish presentation of self further complicate any simple explanation of the origin of
ego problems in a clash of worldviews. This style of presentation of self first
came to my attention while interviewing organizational leaders. The very
same people who were complaining about ego problems in other organizations were, in the very same conversations, informing me of their own
accomplishments—not the success of their organizations (which might have
been more appropriate in the context of the interview) but their personal
accomplishments. To me, this display of personal accomplishments seemed
very inconsistent with the general disapproval of self-congratulatory behavior. The intensity of the display could be quite discomfiting. At the con-
clusion of our interviews, people would show me awards for their handi-
crafts or display collections of newspaper clippings about themselves and
their civic service.

It was clear, however, that my informants did not feel at all uncomfortable. In trying to make sense of this experience, I first thought that my
informants might be responding to the context of an interview with an
"outsider." Perhaps they were acting on the belief that this sort of behavior was part of "mainstream culture" and therefore that it was acceptable
to "show off" for me. In my interviews and in community newspaper discussions of mainstream culture, American culture is consistently characterized as individualistic and concerned with individual achievements. While
the rules may be different *within* the Indian community (i.e., highlighting
the individual may be bad), people might just be playing the culturally
appropriate game with me.

Upon further reflection, however, I have come to believe that this is
not the case. It is clear that personal achievement (academic, financial,
reputational, etc.) is highly valued, respected, and publicized within the
community itself. When someone is promoted or receives an award from
a mainstream organization, his or her picture appears in the Indian press.
Children who achieve academic distinction are similarly recognized. Indian
organizations themselves give many awards to recognize service to the
organization or the community, as well as to honor scholastic or professional excellence. Award recipients, distinguished individuals, and Indian
political candidates frequently are honored by banquets.

Reviewing the details of how people related their stories of personal
success to me, I found that it was not the fact of the success that was
important but the *recognition* of that success by others. In a few instances,
people even prefaced their success stories by such phrases as "I don't want
to brag, but . . ." or "I'm not trying to impress you with material figures,
but . . ." The way achievement was reported was less often "I did this" than

"I did this, and here is a newspaper article about it" or "here is the ribbon I won" or "due to my good job, attendance or membership grew." While promoting oneself may be disgraceful, being publicly recognized and rewarded for one's achievements is commendable.

One man explicitly commented on the notion that one's accomplishments are worthless unless they are recognized by others. In recapping the history of the Indian community, he said:

> Then they all moved into the professional stage, where they pursued the American dream. The first thing was to buy a car, but since they were professionals, it had to be an expensive car. You go to an Indian event, and all the cars are Mercedes Benz. The next thing was to buy a house. Now they realized the American dream. What the media told them, what everybody told them, they had.
>
> But there was a problem. How to *show* the house? With the car, you could drive it around and people will see, but a house, you need to invite people. There is a need for recognition.
>
> The next thing is where is the house. Address becomes important. Oakbrook, Burr Ridge are considered good. This is a recent phenomenon, perhaps ten years old.
>
> Then, who do you know? Who comes to your house? Senators, congressmen, aldermen, dignitaries from India. The community is stagnating at this stage. We still don't know where to go from here. There is a lot of picture taking. You give $10,000 to the Republicans and you can have your picture with Bush. But what to do after that is not clear.

Granted, there is a lot more revealed in this passage than the value of recognition of achievement over the mere fact of achievement, but this message at least is clear. Therefore, criticizing self-promotion in one breath and sharing the public commendations of their own successes with me in the next were perfectly consistent.

The skeptic still might point out that even if one's achievements are publicly recognized, and even if that recognition is ultimately more important than the fact of achievement itself, personal achievement ultimately comes about because of some variety of self-promotion or greed. Doesn't the business person end up with a Mercedes, a house in Oakbrook, and political clout because of his or her aggressive approach to promoting the business?

Such skeptics fail to look at achievement in an Indian rather than American context. Those I have spoken to in the Indian community do not see personal achievement as the direct result of personal effort. Rather, personal achievement (much like its recognition) seems to originate somewhere else. One prominent leader described his involvement in the community's organizational life as a result of the fact that he was "blessed with resources" and because of this he was "asked to be involved." In stories of financial, professional, and personal achievements, there is much more discussion of being fortunate or blessed than there is of struggle and hard work. If there is discussion of hard work, it is never that one engages in hard work in order to make more money or to be able to move to Oak-brook. Rather, "hard work" is linked to a concern for "the good of the community." In an Indian construction of achievement, then, there is not the same connection among the fact of achievement, the means of self-promotion, and the motive of materialism that is so integral to the arche-typical American success story.

This digression concerning the style of self-presentation in the Indian community adds another dimension to our effort to understand ego problems as the prime mover of community disunity. As with concerns about the proper use of status and the corrupting nature of monetary greed, how-ever, the boosterish presentation of self and the seemingly uncharacteris-tic concern with individualistic achievement become more sensible when seen in connection to the ethical values that provide a moral backdrop for Indian society as a whole.

Selfishness and Selflessness. Ego problems and all they entail can be understood as part of a larger cultural conversation about selfishness and selflessness rooted in the themes of the Indian epic literature. A passage from the *Mahabharata* in which Lord Krishna tries to persuade Arjuna to proceed into battle against his cousins and teachers sums it up. Krishna argues that Arjuna must detach himself from the fruits of his imminent actions (in this case, the death of his loved ones) and concentrate instead on fulfilling his duty as a *Kshetriya*, a warrior. One's duty in life is deter-mined by God, and doing one's duty is a sacrifice to God and thus a supreme moral good. Krishna tells Arjuna:

> Good men eating the remnants
> of sacrifice are free from any guilt,
> but evil men who cook for themselves
> eat the food of sin.[36]

In reference to greed, Krishna's ethical stance in the *Mahabharata* suggests that those who use their organizational positions for personal financial gain (the "evil men who cook for themselves") are clearly in vio-lation of traditional ideas about ethical conduct. However, those whose community service results in community esteem and perhaps increased patronage of their businesses or professional practices are free from blame since they are merely "eating the remnants of sacrifice" (i.e., benefiting incidentally from the selfless performance of community service).[37]

This passage can also help us understand why the public recognition and celebration of the achievements of separate individuals are compatible with the communitywide condemnation of egoism. The personal success of individuals, be it reputational or financial, when it results from fulfill-ing one's assigned role in life, is in fact evidence that one has been engaged in the selfless act of sacrificing to God. Presumably, if one's actions have not been selfless (i.e., one had not been pursuing one's true duty), God would not have granted the boon of success in that endeavor. If one's success is great enough to merit remark by the community, then that recognition may be used as evidence that this success is "free from any guilt," proof that one has been engaged in performing one's true duty.

Community newspapers routinely run profiles of community members. Individuals chosen as the subjects of these portraits have almost always received some public recognition from peers in their field (or, in the case of students, scholastic awards) *before* they are recognized in the immigrant press. I would argue that it is the public recognition of success that protects one's individual achievements from charges of egoistic motivation. In a sense, such recognition is proof that one is fulfilling a calling. Public recognition, then, differentiates deserved success from successes gained through self-promotion.

Finally, the evil of linked statuses is part of the larger contest between selfishness and selflessness. The link is provided by viewing status as a kind of community property. In his analysis of Hindu ethics in the *Gita*, Balbir Singh argues that the ultimate good lies in the cohesion and harmony of the social whole, and that an individual actor's performance of his or her duty is just a means to that end:

> [T]he Gita purports not to be the ethics of the mere individual but that of the social whole of which he is an inalienable constituent. If the good lies in promoting the cohesion of the social whole, all its members can truly share its goodness by discharging the various obligations that accrue to them as a result of their identification with it. The good of the social whole is the good of its constituents as well, and this can be attained only through the greater and greater degrees of their identification with its solidarity and progress.[38]

Statuses achieved through individual accomplishments, then, do not entitle one to power or influence. Rather, the community as a whole is served by the accomplishments of individuals. Since status is ultimately community rather than individual property, it is improper for one to claim one's own status as a source of individual power or prestige.

If individual achievements are community property, then it is easy to see why there is so much criticism of the selfish act of claiming one's status, and the power it confers, for one's own use. But, as with questions of monetary greed, motivation is key. The inscrutable nature of motivation sets the stage for the ongoing debates within the community about who is selfless and who is selfish. Yet the presentation of self through the vehicle of community recognition (i.e., presenting oneself by displaying one's awards) provides a mechanism by which the selfless and the selfish can be sorted out. The selfless are those with awards to show, the selfish are those without. One's moral status is "proved" in some sense.

The community's discussion of "ego problems," then, is more than just a straightforward critique of an imagined American individualistic worldview. It is a reflection of the contest between selfishness and selflessness in the epics, carried out within the community as a whole rather than within each person alone. It is this desire to distinguish the selfish and the selfless in the community that has, at least in part, fueled this enterprise of public recognition.

Power struggles for community leadership are not unique to either immigrant Indians or immigrants in general. But the moralistic character of the community's discussion of organizational life and leadership does resonate strongly with the specifically Indian concern with sorting out the selfless and the selfish. Power struggles within this community have meaning because there is a consensus that in the end it is the selfless who will and should prevail, and that selflessness, working for the good of the community, is the moral quality that is most important to the character of the community as a whole.

Collective Identity, Collective Purpose, and Cultural Shows

The preoccupation and attention to division within the community, and the ego problems that cause it, are part of a quest by the Indian community to construct a collective identity it can feel good about. A major component of this identity is moral correctness, particularly selflessness. This identity is enacted both by the community's attempt to sort out and organize its ethnic associations and through the particular activities ethnic associations sponsor.

I argued that splits in organizations are problematic in part because they create disorder among the ethnic associations. Every time there is an organizational split, the Indian Consulate and a host of other ethnic organizations must decide how to cope with the new organizations. Stories about the reason for the split, and who has the ego problem, circulate freely. Everyone else is forced to make the moral judgments about selfishness and selflessness that can restore order to the network of ethnic associations. This sorting strengthens and refines the community's collective identity. The proper order in the organizational network, which I earlier called the collective purpose, is vitally tied to the community's collective identity.

Collective identity is also enacted through the events that are sponsored by ethnic associations. The informative speakers, honorary banquets, family picnics, and cultural shows all provide occasions for demonstrations of selflessness (working for the good of the community) and public recognition of that selflessness (public thanks are made all around). It is not just in the backstage agonizing or management of organizational splits that support the development of collective identity. The regular public activities of ethnic organizations are bound up in this process as well.

The story the Indian community tells about the expansion of the network of ethnic associations, about organizational developments responding to a growing community with changing needs and an increasing commitment to life in the United States, is reminiscent of classic models of assimilation. Over time, immigrant generations put down institutional and cultural roots and adapt to life in America, trying to make the most of it.

But the dynamics of organizational life and the stories the community constructs around those dynamics reveal the *process* of assimilation at work in real time. The act of constructing a collective identity allows the identity-based community of Indian immigrants to exist. The assimilation of ethnic groups in American society is accomplished in part through the act of becoming a community.

I have paid careful attention in this chapter to the language the immigrant generation uses to talk about organizational life. The language is important because it encodes the meaning people assign to behavior. It helps us understand the insider's view. However, language is also an important social tool. The language of organizational life—division, unity, ego problems—has become a stylized rhetoric, a rhetoric that is called up automatically anytime someone mentions the organizational network or its equivalent, the community. Moreover, this rhetoric provides a link between first- and second-generation organizations. While the sensibilities of organizational life for the first generation remain rooted in Indian heritage and the sensibilities for the second generation are very much American, the rhetoric regarding problems in the community is an undisputed legacy that the first generation has passed on to the second. The process of assimilation also is constituted in part by those mechanisms through which a sense of collective identity and community survives from generation to generation.

4

Organizations
of the Second Generation

The second generation, the children of the immigrants of the 1960s and
'70s, are now coming of age. They have reached a point in late adolescence
and early adulthood when they are poised to make a contribution to the
future of "the Indian community." They have not, however, chosen to filter seamlessly into the organizations set up by their parents. Nor have they
opted to forgo associational ties based on their ethnic heritage altogether.
Instead, they are constructing an organizational network of their own.

The first generation used ethnic associations to construct the collective identity that is the foundation for the Indian community. For these
pioneers, adjusting to life in America, at a collective level, has meant answering questions about identity with resources drawn from the Indian cultural milieu. The motives behind organizational development (a desire to
conserve and protect a cultural heritage) and the way social interactions in
the organizational context are understood (as contests between the selfish
and the selfless that reinforce a particular vision of the communal good)
are both informed by the first generation's Indian background. Assimilation has not been about adopting American ways but rather about constructing a community, with the guidance of symbolic resources drawn from
their past, affording Indian immigrants a place among the various "communities" that constitute American public life.

The organizational life of the second generation also figures into the
process of assimilation. For the second generation, however, organizational
life is governed by resources drawn from both the cultural milieu of America

and the Indian world as represented by their parents. Moreover, the connection between the social interactions embedded in organizational life and the symbolic meaning of the community differs between the two generations. In the first-generation organizational network, action and idea were tightly linked through a stylized rhetoric that gave meaning to organizational activities. Machinations regarding "division," "unity," and "ego problems" affected both day-to-day operations and the community's image of itself. This neat package provided the first generation with a sense of identity as "the Indian community." In the second generation, the processes of assimilation and identity construction work differently. For a variety of reasons, the organizations of the second generation are not bound together in a common dialogue linking action and idea. Thus, collective identity does not emerge from organizational life in quite the same way as it does for the first generation.

Three Types of Organizations

The budding network of second-generation ethnic associations is much more limited in scope than the vast organizational network built by first-generation Indian immigrants. This difference is in part a result of the particular life stage of the bulk of second-generation individuals. While a small segment of the second generation is in the late twenties, the majority is still in college or professional school. Consequently, most second-generation organizations have developed within the larger institutional framework of campus life. Memberships and activities are usually limited to those attending particular institutions, curtailing the second generation's potential to develop a diversified network of organizations. The population of each campus can support only one or two Indian organizations, and communication among campuses is fairly limited. The most common type of second-generation ethnic association, then, is the campus-based Indian organization. Most of the colleges and universities in the greater Chicago area have some sort of Indian student organization.[1] Most are secular, but a few are religious.[2]

In addition to campus-based organizations, there is also a small population of youth branches of first-generation organizations. However, few organizations have successfully maintained a youth branch with an independent identity (i.e., separate officers, autonomy as far as planning activities, etc.).[3] The most visibly active of these has been the youth organization at the Hindu Temple of Greater Chicago. During the study period, this youth organization, now called In the Wings, came into formal being. By the end of the study, other temples and associations were beginning to advertise youth organizations and activities that mimicked the program activities of In the Wings.

At about the same time that this project began, a new type of second-generation organization aimed at postcollege people was starting up. The Network of Young Indian-American Professionals (NETIP) was the first and only free-standing second-generation organization. I was not able to examine this organization as closely as I wished. I will discuss what I do know, and the limits of my access to and knowledge of this organization, below.

It became clear very early in the study that the second-generation organizations, unlike the first, did not have a sense of themselves as a network. There were no federated organizations (parallel to the first-generation Federation of India Associations or Alliance of Midwest India Associations). There were no jointly sponsored events. There was no talk about the "problems" of the second-generation "community." Rather, what was important was the internal dynamic of each individual organization. So, rather than spend time getting to know all the different organizations, I chose to focus on in-depth studies of a selected few: the Indian Students Association at a large public university; the South Asia Club at a private university; Om, a Hindu religious group at another private college; and In the Wings, the youth branch at the Hindu Temple of Greater Chicago.[4] Close attention to the internal dynamics of these organizations revealed that although they do not participate in a collective enterprise devoted to the construction of a "second-generation community," each organization was governed by some similar principles that lend them a kind of common identity as the second generation. These principles as well as the diverse internal dynamics of each organization may be illustrated by three case studies.[5]

Indian Students Association

As of 1991, the Indian Students Association (ISA) at the public university was only three years old. According to the ISA's leadership, five or six years before the new ISA took shape, there had been another Indian student organization. Although none of the contemporary leaders or members to whom I spoke had any detailed knowledge of why the old ISA disbanded, the common wisdom was that it became "too involved in Indian politics" and that there was something about "a speaker who was talking about communism" that caused it to dissolve.

The revived ISA was the brainchild of graduate students from India. The goal was to stay away from politics and have a "more culturally oriented" organization. The Indian graduate students ran the organization for the first year, but in subsequent years, the leadership has been drawn exclusively from the America-raised second-generation undergraduates. The current leaders attribute this change to the graduate students being "busy with their own lives" and realizing that the undergraduates were willing and able to keep the new ISA afloat.

Currently, the ISA has about 100 to 150 members, most of whom are undergraduates. More than half the membership is of Gujarati origin. Officers of the organization were not sure if this reflects the proportion of Gujaratis at the university as a whole. (In the Chicago area, Gujaratis are the largest ethnic subgroup among Indian immigrants.) The gender composition of the membership and the officers is mixed, unlike first-generation organizations where most organizational officials are men.

The organization sponsors what members termed "cultural" and "social" events throughout the school year. On the cultural side, they hold celebrations of Indian and Hindu holidays, such as Diwali and Gandhi Day, and a cultural show in the spring that draws an audience of a thousand people. The cultural show is an opportunity for students to show off their talents. There are skits, dances, music, and a fashion show. Social events include volleyball tournaments, dances, and parties.

In planning and staging events, leaders report three major concerns. First, when parents are involved, particularly for the annual cultural show, they have to take care to moderate their incorporation of American culture into the program. For example, the year before this study began, the fashion segment of the annual show was organized by someone who "was trying to express himself." He featured "Western" fashions, miniskirts, and the like. This offended some parents who under the best of circumstances are unsettled by their daughters "parading around onstage" even in Indian clothes.

Second, the ISA's cultural events tend to emphasize Gujarati culture. The leaders say they do not intentionally focus on Gujarati dances or foods; it is just "what they know." Although they are sensitive about this bias (they brought up the subject with me), they are not sure what they can do about it. It is a concern, but not as much of a problem as the potential conflicts with parents over less than decorous displays of "American culture." Among non-Gujarati association members, I did not detect any resentment of the Gujarati domination of the organization. There is some feeling that the Gujarati students tend to be insular, having mostly Gujarati friends, but there is definitely none of the vehement resentment of ethnic domination that has occasioned the splits of first-generation organizations.

Finally, there is some concern that the association should not sponsor "too many parties." The Indian graduate students are a little like the organization's conscience in this regard, reminding the undergraduates that their first responsibility should be toward Indian culture. For example, at the Diwali party (which is ostensibly a cultural event but in fact becomes more of a social activity), the undergraduates provided a tape recorder to play music. Members brought their own tapes to play, which turned out to be American rock music. Graduate students complained because they felt the entertainment was inappropriate. In retrospect, the undergraduate organizers thought so, too. There is a sense that the cultural and social functions of the organization should be balanced. Although the latter are much more popular and well attended by students, the cultural aspects of the organization's purpose should never be totally ignored.

In addition to concerns that arise regarding the organization's activities, there is also a self-consciousness among the leaders about the problems the organization faces in governing itself. In full-scale organization meetings, this does not seem too big of an issue. The meetings are very informal. There is no adherence to parliamentary procedures. The leaders moderate discussion of upcoming events and ask for participation. There is a tendency to assume that everyone knows the North Indian lingo that peppers people's speech. This sometimes makes it difficult for new members or South Indians, but given the overall homogeneity of the organization, it does not seem to disrupt the meetings.

Problems of governance do arise regarding the election of organizational officers and the distribution of work among board members. In previous years, I was told that after elections, disgruntled losing candidates would sometimes organize events parallel to those organized by the duly elected leaders—same event, same time, different location. In the year during which I followed the organization, there was a more serious problem at election time. Some students running for office requested that there be an additional voting time because the scheduled voting time conflicted with some exams. This request was granted by the outgoing officers. However, at the early voting session, there was a heavy turnout of "new members" who paid the three-dollar membership fee and cast a vote. The candidates who had requested this early election time benefited from the turnout and won the election. There was even a rumor that one of the victorious candidates' supporters had been standing by the voting table, handing out the three-dollar fee to passersby. A considerable scandal resulted, and the election was redone. However, the outcome was the same.

Governance problems also arise in relation to the distribution of work. In my first interview with leaders, one person reported that there were "ego problems" in the organization. Reluctant to give an example, the speaker just commented that one has to "handle everyone." I told other informants that I had been told about ego problems and asked what they thought was meant by that. Some suggested that it had to do with the dirty dealings that had attended the election. Others linked ego problems to the distribution of work among board members. One member suggested that a third of the officers are really "out for the benefit of the club." Another third are moderately involved. A final third, however, are only on the board for the "name," so that they can put it on their résumés. After a successful event, board members will be congratulated, will "get recognized a lot" by other members and parents. The third of board members who are on the board just for the name will get the praise without having contributed to the event's success.

These election controversies and ego problems recall similar issues in the first-generation organizations. There, election controversies occasioned organizational splits based on language or caste divisions. For the ISA, disappointed candidates have held parallel events. First-generation organizations are plagued by all chiefs and no Indians; people want the recognition of leadership positions without first paying their dues of hard work on the organization's behalf. The ISA harbors similar complaints. Although the issues and rhetoric are similar, they in fact hold very different meanings for the two generations of organization participants.

In the ISA, I heard none of the overtones of calamity that characterized first-generation responses. First-generation informants viewed ego
problems and the electoral ambitions of individuals as direct threats to the
integrity of the organizational network. If people were acting for their own
interest and not as part of their subgroup, the stability of the organization
was threatened. In the second generation, ego problems and electoral
ambitions were seen as a much more routine affair. Particular people and
the situations they created may have caused problems, but there was never
any discussion of these problems as serious challenges to group life. Problematic individuals and situations just needed to be "handled." There was
never any concern that these problems would lead to organizational splits.
For the second generation, "ego problem" provided a generic description
for the vagaries of managing organizations rather than an accusatory
label for particular individuals who could throw organizational life into total
disarray.

A final concern of the organization regarded not its internal workings
but its relationship with other student organizations. In an early conversation, I brought up the subject of all the divisions among the first-generation
organizations and asked if my informants saw any of those tensions in the
second generation. They answered that for them the internal divisions
among Indians do not matter too much. They all "speak English together."
However, the main division they see on campus is between Indians and
Pakistanis—"it's a Hindu-Muslim thing."

The week of my first interview was a joint Indian-Pakistani Awareness
Week, so I pursued the topic of Indian-Pakistani tensions.[6] ISA leaders
report that relations between themselves and the leadership of the Pakistani Students Association are quite cordial and cooperative. However, the
members maintain strict divisions. Pakistani students sit in one room of the
main cafeteria, Indian students in the other. A jointly sponsored volleyball
game degenerated into accusations of unfairness and name-calling when
Pakistani and Indian teams faced each other in the final match.

As with first-generation organizations, there are some schemes and talk
about softening the divisions between the two organizations. One route
suggested by some ISA leaders is to sponsor joint events, particularly the
annual cultural show. The Pakistani students have their own show, with
many of the same acts, at the same time of year as the ISA show. In the
year of this study, one of the ISA copresidents wanted to combine the two
shows but found no support for her position from other board members.
At an Awareness Week panel discussion on the problems of the second
generation, one ISA member offered the closing thought that the ISA and
the PSA should cooperate more. The Pakistani moderator of the panel
enthusiastically agreed. Yet there has been no strong effort to bring the two
organizations closer together. (In fact, after the first joint volleyball game,
which ended unpleasantly, the second tournament was sponsored by the
ISA alone.)

Again, this concern with division and rivalry between the ISA and the

PSA is reminiscent of the first-generation concerns about division and unity in the Indian community. However, in the first generation, the concern is about divisions *within* the Indian community. For the second generation, "these differences [in language and caste] are not manifested in us." The second generation is reaching well beyond the usual community boundaries in its concern with relations between Indian and Pakistani students. Moreover, the first generation is much more preoccupied with problems of division and unity than is the second. Nearly everyone in the first-generation organizational network talks about the need for greater unity. In the second generation, it is a minority of students that are concerned with these issues as they apply to the ISA-PSA division.[7]

The final point that should be noted about the ISA is its connection to the Chicago Indian community at large. One of the faculty advisers of the organization is active in the Association of Indians in America and the Federation of Indian Associations. Through these connections, students participated one year in the FIA-sponsored parade. (Although asked, they did not participate in the rival parade because they didn't want to get caught up in the first-generation organizational battles.) Skits for the annual cultural show have also appeared in the comparable cultural shows of first-generation organizations. However, there is no sustained organizational interest in developing these connections. The students selectively contribute to first-generation organizations when asked but do not seek out opportunities for contact.

My general impression of the students involved in the ISA is that they participate in order to meet people and to have fun. Even among officers or at organizational meetings, there is little of the seriousness of purpose that characterizes first-generation organizational leaders and events. While ISA officers and members do work very hard to make the association events successful, the spirit is to make them useful and enjoyable for members rather than to view events as somehow embodying second-generation Indian American identity. There is little of the self-sacrificing "good of the community" rhetoric I heard from the first-generation organizations.

Despite this difference in tone, many of the same problems of first-generation organizations are repeated in the ISA. Ego problems as well as division and unity are frequent themes. However, for the ISA, these issues have different associations and meanings. They are not seen as very serious and tend to be reduced to the level of individual behavior ("handle" those with ego problems, and cooperate with the PSA leadership) rather than expanded into problems that undermine the fabric of the organization.

In the Wings

At the beginning of this study, the only first-generation organization that supported a youth branch with an independent spirit, and even a slightly adversarial relationship with its parent organization, was the Hindu Temple of Greater Chicago.[8] Even at its inception, the HTGC youth project had an independent flair. As opposed to other youth branches that began at the urging of the first generation, the HTGC youth project grew out of the frustration of the second generation with the parent organization's lack of responsiveness to youth needs. The first-generation leaders had been mulling over the problem of how to get young people involved in temple activities. There was a feeling that the college graduates had already been lost and that action needed to be taken if the temple expected the active participation of the younger generation as it moved into adulthood.

At a fund-raising event for the most recent of the temple's ambitious building projects, the standard round of self-congratulatory speeches was under way. One leader suggested that the current construction project, which included a marriage hall, would ensure that young people would remain supporters of the temple, since they would now have a place to get married. A young man, who was asked to speak impromptu as a representative of "the youth," stood up to challenge this analysis.

Although, as he told me, he was expected to continue the self-congratulatory tone of the speeches, declaring the new project a boon to all, he chose instead to speak out on the "real" problem confronting the temple in its attempt to keep hold of the second generation. No one is going to come to get married, he argued, if they do not understand the culture, the religion. Rather than a new marriage hall, what is needed is intensive education for young people. To be kept in the fold of Hinduism, members of the second generation must understand the rituals they are asked to perform.

Audience response was enthusiastic, and the temple president immediately put this young man in charge of the upcoming youth program for the temple anniversary. This spontaneous appointment glossed over the prior committee-level machinations that attempted to fill this youth leadership post with other more politically connected young people.

The youth program that grew out of this initiative combined formal presentations of various aspects of the religion with opportunities for the youth, in small discussion settings, to share their experiences and concerns as second-generation Indian Americans. For the discussion sessions, participants were divided by age group, and group sessions were led by local college students as counselors. The first Youth Day was well attended and well received. Encouraged by this success, the college-age counselors organized additional youth programs in the year that followed. At first, there was some resistance, or at least lack of interest, among the temple leadership. The youth group had difficulty getting financial and advertising support from the temple. However, by the following summer, the informally organized youth project had become a new organizational entity called In the Wings.

After the first Youth Day, I had the opportunity to attend the daylong youth workshops, "Youth Talk" and "Youth Speak." I sat in with the college-age discussion groups. While the counselors usually provided some discussion topics,[9] the actual discussions tended to be freewheeling and often incorporated subjects that were of particular concern or interest to participants.

Two recurrent themes emerged in discussions of a variety of specific topics. First, the notion that both religion in general and specific moral and behavioral decisions are "a personal thing" was repeatedly offered up as a way to come to terms with the role of religion in group members' lives.[10] I first encountered this notion of religion as "a personal thing" during a discussion of temple attendance. The group members had been asked to consider how often they go to the temple and how they feel about going. There followed a discussion about whether it is better to go to temple alone to pray or to go for the big functions. The consensus was that it depends on whether the temple's function is religious or social. Parents, they agreed, go on the festival days because going to the temple is part of their cultural background and revives for them memories of the social atmosphere of India. The second generation, however, does not share these reminiscences and furthermore is not familiar enough with religious practice to have a sense of the meaning of these events. This dual alienation made many in the group uncomfortable with temple attendance altogether. Those who reported positive feelings traced them to a feeling of inner fulfillment—as one woman put it, "a peaceful feeling" derived from experiences of quiet introspection rather than festive celebration.

The idea that religion at its most meaningful is and ought to be a private affair was further reinforced in the reaction of a small group of three to the "assignment" to interpret a series of quotations from the *Gita*, a portion of the *Mahabharata* often called the Hindu Bible. When the larger group of twenty divided into small groups of three or four, the group I was with sat silently reading the two-line quotes for a few moments. After some vague mumbling directed at the air rather than toward one another, I asked why they weren't discussing the quotations. This aroused one of the group to say that the meaning had always seemed pretty obvious to him and there-fore the quotes really didn't need "interpreting." "Besides," he added, "it's a personal thing." Immediately, the other two members of the group joined in and began a discussion of things they had never understood about the *Gita*. They were much more engaged and active in discussing the aspects of the text they had rejected ("caste duty is totally nonfunctional") than the positive feeling about the parts of the texts they found personally meaningful.

In addition to viewing religion and religious feeling in general as per-sonal rather than something shared, the college-age groups at the two workshops repeatedly used "personal" criteria to adjudicate hypothetical questions about morally right behavior. Responses such as "Each person has to draw the line," "Duty is relative, defined by each person," and "Ultimately, you have to make yourself happy" were used over and over.

The second major theme of these discussions—a critique of material-ism in the Indian community—highlighted the groups' concern with "per-sonal" standards of right and wrong. As many in the Indian community have pointed out to me, there is a good deal of conspicuous consumption going on. In chapter 3, I related a tale about the search for social status that involved a transition from car to house, to neighborhood, to pictures with President Bush as markers of social status. Participants in the youth workshops repeatedly raised consumption as a morally troublesome issue. One asked why it is that people feel they can buy a BMW. How can we distinguish between what is needed and what is "attachment to the fruits of labor"? Another participant suggested that there is nothing wrong with being wealthy, but attachment is the problem. For example, would you care if you lost your BMW? Further complexities were introduced by the *Gita*'s admonition against "cravings." Someone suggested that there is a problem when a person has money and says, "I don't crave this house, but I'm going to get it anyway." What's the difference, he asked, between getting and craving?

The groups also viewed human capital choices as similarly troublesome. There was a recurrent complaint that Indian parents push their children into the fields of medicine and engineering. Some felt that it was for wealth and financial security that these pressures were imposed. A medical student commented that he constantly hears other Indian medical students talking about what they are going to acquire when they get out of school. Another commented that as far as education is concerned, parents just see the title. When she switched her major from engineering to psychology, her parents were not enthusiastic. However, when they discovered that she was going to be a "doctor," it was fine. These young people rejected the notion that "society's standards" should shape individual choices. Rather, the individual should satisfy his or her own conscience.

In both their tendency to see religion as something individual and personal and their concern about materialism, members of this group positioned themselves in opposition to their parents, who, they believe, experience life with a much greater concern about the "social." In the discussion about going to temple, the young people criticized the social aspects of temple-going that they saw as part of their parents' motivation.[11] They criticized first-generation materialism on the basis of parental concern with what others will think of them and their family.

The slightly adversarial relationship with the first generation that this group established in its origin and continued throughout its discussions was concretized when the youth project became a formal part of the organizational apparatus of the temple. When temple leadership underwent its regular rotation, the incoming president asked the young man who had spoken up at the trustees meeting and who had coordinated the youth workshops to become the chairman of the temple's Youth Committee. This was the first position of formal organizational power granted to a member of the second generation. Previously, the chairperson of the Youth Committee had been a member of the first generation.

The name "In the Wings" was chosen by the new Youth Committee chairman to provide an identity to the group. He felt that the HTGC youth group needed to be distinguished from all the other youth groups associated with other organizations.[12] Although it has never been articulated, I think there is a second rationale for the name change as well.

Standard temple rhetoric claims that the temple is "dedicated to the youth." On several occasions, I have heard members of the second generation express skepticism about this claim. A young man once asked me if I knew why the temple was built in the 1980s. When I said I didn't, he responded that the first generation talks about it being dedicated to the youth, but it was really a tax shelter. Others have reported that they have heard first-generation temple officials suggest that since their own children are not interested in the temple, the current leadership can look for support in the coming years to the newly arriving immigrants. I think "In the Wings" is a message, perhaps a warning, directed at a first-generation audience. In addition to providing identity to the second-generation group, the name says to the first generation of temple leadership that their own children *are* in fact waiting in the wings to take over. Although the practice of Hinduism may change under this new generation, the inevitability of that transition must be recognized.

In fact, In the Wings has sometimes been explicit in its challenge to first-generation conceptions of Hindu practice. At Youth Day, parents were invited to take temple tours with their children during which the symbolism and character of each deity were explained. The message for parents was that the second generation cannot treat religious expression solely as practice. The second generation is not willing to perform rituals the meaning and symbolism of which remain a mystery. Although many young people concede that their parents do know more about the rituals, they are generally accurate in their accusation that the first generation lacks specific knowledge of the meaning behind its religious practices. Even first-generation individuals have complained to me that their kids always want to know why every little thing is done, when they themselves don't know why. They have just been raised "to do it that way."

In short, then, the formalization of the HTGC youth project, the creation of In the Wings, harbors a message about the second-generation view of religion. Religion is ultimately something that requires expression and understanding in the individual mind. It is not something that can be meaningful if done by rote. By presenting this view to their parents' generation and declaring themselves to be in the wings, the second generation expresses its discomfort with the organizational philosophy of the first generation. For the next generation, community life is not built around organized groups (in this case, organized religion). Rather, organized groups are there to serve and enhance the lives of individuals in the community.

This view of the role of religious organizations harks back to the attitude of ISA members toward their organization. Both leaders and members wanted the organization to fulfill the needs of members. They were not terribly cognizant of or concerned with the organization as an end in itself. Second-generation organizations, both religious and secular, are not outward-looking. They do not see themselves as representatives of their "community" to others in the Indian immigrant subculture or to the mainstream. Rather, members of this generation seem much more concerned with enhancing their own lives through their organizations. This is the major difference between first- and second-generation organizations.

Perhaps, though, this inward-directedness and personalized focus of second-generation organizations, despite the variety of organizations in which it occurs, is simply a function of the youth of their participants. American teenagers (a group of which these second-generation Indian Americans are a part) are self-centered. It may be that as they age, the group aspects of organizational life will become more important. It may be that they will eventually, as the current temple leadership hopes, take over the mantles of power in the first-generation organization network, ensuring that the network will survive largely unchanged.

Yet if one looks a little beyond the college-age group to the oldest members of the second generation, the group orientation of organizational life is still absent. Further, given what has developed so far among the postcollegiate second generation, there is strong evidence that once the excuse of proximity to other Indian Americans in the context of college life has receded, the individualized attitude toward organizational life will tend to disperse rather than unite the second generation.

Network of Young Indian-American Professionals

The Network of Young Indian-American Professionals (NETIP) is the only totally independent, noncollegiate second-generation organization. It was formed with the goal of promoting networking and social service activities among postcollegiate Indian Americans. In its press release, the group said it hoped to become "a social, cultural, and political force" and to "promote unity and harmony among their peers as one group of Indians."[13] Its organizational birth was the joint effort of a second-generation woman recently graduated from an area college and a prominent first-generation doctor. The young woman is credited with "having the idea," but the first organizational meeting took place in the home of the doctor.

A couple of months before I formally began my field work, NETIP had been receiving attention in the immigrant press. The first big event, a party at a nightclub, had been well advertised, and articles introduced the organization in both local newspapers. However, shortly after my first interview with a member and the flurry of press coverage, the organization seemed to disappear from public sight. Repeated phone calls to board members over several months went unreturned.

By chance, I happened to interview, for other purposes, people who had been involved with the organization, some in official capacities. Through these sources, I learned that the organization was still in existence, holding monthly brunches at a downtown Indian restaurant (not a restaurant on Devon Avenue, the heart of the first generation's idea of

"Indian Chicago"). NETIP had also sponsored some other large gatherings (a picnic, a cruise on Lake Michigan) that had not, to my knowledge, been advertised in the local press.

The people I spoke to had several difficulties with the organization. Although they thought the concept of the organization was a good idea, all felt the organization was not living up to its stated goals. Instead of "networking," I heard descriptions of organizational meetings as "a big marriage affair," "a meat market." There was a feeling that the core group of officers was "a bunch of doctors' kids" who did not really have any interest in developing extended social and professional networks in the second-generation community. They were said to have "personal agendas." There was a complaint that people were using the organization membership list to sell insurance. Leaders told one woman who argued for lower event costs (so that events would be accessible to more people) that high costs would ensure that the organization would remain "elite and exclusive." Others outside the inner circle have reported the same difficulty with unreturned phone calls that I had experienced.

Despite what appeared to be a promising beginning, I have been unable to examine this organization in depth. I cannot say whether it represents an aberration resting on the shoulders of a small, select group of individuals or the first in a trend among second-generation organizations.

However, it is notable that despite NETIP's self-described goal of becoming a representative of "unique members of the Indian community,"[14] both within the Indian community and in the mainstream, the group has seemingly chosen to focus on the immediate personal needs of the majority of its members—to find a mate or make a living.[15] In this way, it shares the orientation of other second-generation organizations toward organizational life, that the purpose should be to benefit members rather than represent "the community."

Organizations and Assimilation Revisited

The second generation's organizational life owes at least as much to its members' experiences of American culture as it does to their Indian heritage. On the one hand, the *issues* that arise for members of the second generation in the context of their ethnic organizations are issues that arise out of their Indian heritage. The ISA worries about ego problems yet is proud of its organizational unity. In the Wings tries to educate both themselves and their parents' generation about changes in the practice of Hinduism required to respond to the needs of the second generation. NETIP eases the transition of the second generation to the adult roles associated with work and marriage, but with an Indian twist. On the other hand, the solutions developed have a distinctly American overtone. Again and again, second-generation organizations deal with salient issues by personalizing and individualizing solutions. Although the ethnic organization can provide a forum for the exchange of ideas and an opportunity to participate in common enjoyable experiences, ultimately the way each person resolves heritage issues and the way organizational leaders work through their management problems are the result of individual conscience decisions.

The American solutions stem from the American consciousness that has developed in this generation. Just as the first generation was molded by the Indian cultural milieu, the second generation, collectively, has been molded by its particular historical conditions. Individuals within the second generation surely vary in the extent to which each has internalized American and Indian sensibilities. This range of variation will be amply illustrated in the family studies of part II. Yet overall, in the discussions and choices that are part of organizational life, the individualism of the American ethos is paramount.

In contrast to the American solutions that result from the second generation's exposure to an encompassing American milieu, the Indian issues that so often motivate these organizations develop through more discrete and identifiable channels. The second generation, as illustrated by the ISA, has adopted some of the language of the first generation. "Ego problems," "division," and "unity" all make appearances in second-generation talk.[16] This legacy of rhetoric has supplied the second generation with a vocabulary to discuss certain aspects of public life. On the one hand, this vocabulary provides a concrete link to the first generation. On the other hand, however, the words the second generation has inherited are part of a model of parental behavior that the second generation uses as a point of contrast. Members of the second generation often define issues for themselves by contrast with what they see their parents doing. Whether the matter is division in the first-generation organizational network, parents' lack of knowledge about the symbolic meaning of Hindu rituals, or parents' excessive concerns with what others will think, second-generation organizations see themselves as different from their parents in significant ways.

The confluence of a basic orientation toward social life nurtured by their American surroundings, the legacy of words left to them by their parents, and the parental example that stands as a point of comparison provide the tools that membrs of the second generation use to manage public life. The way these tools work together to make possible essentially American interpretations of heritage-related problems is one significant piece of the real-time process of assimilation manifested in the second generation.

These tools are fundamentally similar to the tools that first-generation organizations use in their collective process of assimilation. Both generations utilize worldview and more concrete and discrete historical realities (the example of nationalism in India or the example of Indian behavior provided by parents) as symbolic resources to understand the issues that arise in organizational life. However, when we look at the way worldview and historical realities interact, the picture is quite different for the two generations. For the first generation, ideational issues (which are informed by worldview and more specific cultural values derived from a shared national background) are closely tied to the practical realities of organizational life (organizational splits, as well as the routine speeches and picnics). The infusion of these everyday interactions with symbolic meaning and the representation of that meaning in a standardized rhetoric are what constitutes a community identity for the first generation.

For the second generation, there is no such tight link between organizational activities and the ideational or symbolic realm. Individual organizations, of course, may be more or less involved in finding symbolic significance in their everyday activities. In the Wings, for example, in its name and through its activities, demonstrates its unique identity in contrast to that of its parent organization. However, the leaders and members of these organizations were not *conscious* of the connections between daily activities and this larger identity issue. Members of the second generation do not construe their organizational behavior as contributing to a grand conversation about "who they are." NETIP, in its press releases, paid lip service to the idea that it was the representative of the second generation, but no feature of organizational life seems to support this symbolic self-consciousness. Second-generation organizations, as a group, did not utilize the interplay of social interactions and ideas to work out a community identity, and consequently did not develop a rhetoric of their own (analogous to first-generation rhetoric) to underscore that link.

It is not accurate, however, to suggest that the second generation, in its public life, is not engaged in the construction of a collective identity as part of its process of assimilation. It has happened, as a consequence of the fact that interorganizational affairs are not paramount in this generation, that its collective identity has not been worked out in organizational rhetoric. Instead, collective identity for the second generation has been worked out in another arena, complementing the assimilative processes at work in its ethnic associations. The *idea* of "the second generation" is developed through "problems talk"—not the problems of organizations but the problems of "the second generation." This problems talk was a common occurrence at all the public forums on the second generation that I attended. In the next chapter I examine the contribution of problems talk to the construction of a collective second-generation identity.

5

Problems Talk:
The Rhetoric
of Adjustment
in the Immigrant Press

In public forums and panel discussions, in the youth columns of the immigrant press, there is a standard way of discussing the adjustment problems faced by "the youth" in the Indian community. Unlike the organizational problems of the first generation or the adjustment problems of immigrants,[1] which only make occasional appearances in public forums or print media, the problems of the second generation are very public and are discussed incessantly.

This "problems talk" has become the identifying rhetoric of "the second generation." Although the problems themselves do not constitute a generational identity in the sense that they answer questions about "who we are as a community," the fact that discussions of the second generation are routinely discussions of its adjustment problems does provide the basis for a kind of generational identity—one grounded in a purportedly common experience. The collective identity of the second generation is built around rhetorically shared tribulations. I say "rhetorically shared" because, as we will see in part II, this *generation's* "problems" are rather poorly represented in the actual experiences of *individuals*. Nonetheless, problems talk is a critical component of a second-generation collective identity, complementing the common individualistic approach to organizational issues that unifies the second generation at another level.[2]

Two Worlds

The adjustment problems of the second generation are summed up in the "two worlds" metaphor. The second generation must live in two worlds—an Indian world at home and an American world in the neighborhood, at school, and on the job. Although this image permeates discussions of adjustment problems, there is an ongoing debate over whether there are indeed two worlds. An illustrative exchange appeared in *Spotlight* in the summer and fall of 1990. As part of the "Growing Up in America" series, one student wrote, "America does have a lot of advantages but also creates some problems for kids stuck between two worlds, like myself." She went on to describe the problem she had explaining what she had for dinner to her friends at school (*dal* and *roti* became Indian soup and bread). She described feeling left out of the social advantages of churchgoing. She was disturbed by the inability of teachers and students to pronounce her name the first time. When studying India, "it felt weird to be the only one who had visited India because they expected me to know everything about it."[3] This is a very typical litany of complaints.

A few months later, a fourteen-year-old responded to the series of articles she had read about the various problems of Indian youth "stuck between two worlds":

> These past few months I have come across a great deal of articles written about the numerous problems Indian teenagers growing up in the U.S. have to cope with and I have a few comments on them. Now, I am not your average teenage Indian trapped in two worlds, *and* I'm not perturbed with people mispronouncing my name, *and* I'm also not having trouble with not dating. We are all teen-agers of the Indian heritage growing up in the U.S. and we, very plainly, just have to deal with it. I want people to know that not *everyone* is having trouble with this, and I am one of those people. I, actually, find it much more exciting coming from India because our lifestyle is so much more fun and different compared to everyone else's. Most of my friends think it is really interesting that I am from a different country and like to hear the language and about the different cultures that we celebrate, so I never feel embarrassed to tell them why I am vegetarian and why my mother wears that little red dot on her forehead.[4] (emphasis in original)

The difference in interpretation between these two young people stems in part from a deep ambivalence within the Indian community concerning the status of Indians in America. Are Indians "better" or "worse" than the mainstream? The young person who *does* envision herself "stuck between two worlds," I think, may feel this ambivalence, while the young person who is *not* embarrassed by references to her Indian heritage does not.

The debate about two worlds that pits Indian against American values and practices often places Indian values and practices on top, as clearly superior to the American alternatives. The standard advice elders give youth and youth give to each other counsels the second generation to take "the best of both worlds." Retain one's heritage, and take what is good from American society (educational opportunity), steering clear of the bad influences (drugs, alcohol, premarital sex, bad language, torn blue jeans).

The fear that "American culture [will] ruin our kids"[5] is best illustrated in debates about dating. Dating, a positive part of American teenage life supported and encouraged by parents, is often indistinguishable from rampant promiscuity in the Indian press. A swami at an area Hindu religious organization instructs the community by answering the question "Why should we denounce dating?" Citing "a medical journal" report that 85 percent of American teenagers suffer from sexually transmitted diseases, the swami suggests, "The problem of dating among teenagers is a hazard to their own health." Further, there is the issue of "purity of race." If even animals are bred to develop "pure" breeds, "is it not essential for human beings to have a pure genetic pool wherein the unwanted genes are awarded in the progeny?" Third, there is the issue of family ties. Dating is something that takes place between a boy and a girl. But according to Indian philosophy, "marriages are never limited between a boy and a girl, but a girl is married to the family." Finally, "In the West the so-called licentiousness under the disguise of freedom for sex has led to a society wherein the only relation between a man and woman is that of sexual attraction. Can't we look toward an opposite sex with holier relationships like sisters, brothers, uncles, aunts? Can't we think that human beings are more than breeding animals?"[6]

This example is perhaps the most exaggerated version of the "American immorality" story I have heard or read, but nonetheless it strikes a chord that runs deep within the Indian community. One author, who "humbly request[s] [Hindu youth] to wake up and save your heritage before it is too late," explicitly places Hindu and American morality in a superior/ inferior relation, declaring, "time and deep studies will convince you of the superior doctrines of your heritage."[7] The author goes on to note that even some Americans are recognizing the superiority of Hindu culture, turning to vegetarianism and being married by Hindu priests. Another article suggests "that all of us have adjusted our personalities so drastically to fare in this fast-paced, egotistical, masochistically working society that we have forgotten that we possess a unique, special, and much more profound social identity that we are liable to lose if we do not start to appreciate it very soon."[8]

However, the two worlds story does not consistently place Indian culture in a positive light vis-à-vis American values and practices. Suggesting that Indian may be inferior to American, the two worlds metaphor sometimes contrasts "Indian" and "modern" rather than "Indian" and "American":

> Being modernized is ok, but don't overdo it. Indians try to be "Americanized" and as a result they outdo the Americans. You should be happy with what you are. . . . You should keep your Indianness, but it is ok to be modernized to an extent. You should be yourself and use wise judgment.[9]

Indians want to dress like Americans, listen to [American] music, and this
also affects their study habits. If you become modernized, that's ok, but we
[Indian teenagers] have a good quality of studying hard, and I see that quality is deteriorating in some teens.[10]

One parent suggests: "Someday, we have to accept the future generation's
'modern' ideas (at which we'll probably be scandalized to our hair roots)
when ours become outdated and old fashioned."[11] While none of these
writers extols the virtues of "modern" over "Indian" (and even view *modern*
with skepticism), the word *modern* does have a generally positive conno-
tation in the Indian-American English-language press. Particularly on the
business and technology pages, and even in the fashion news, modernity
is clearly positive. It is not simply that modern technology is valued while
modern morality and social practices are not. The mere use of the word
modern as the antithesis of *Indian* in this context is enough to sow the
seeds of doubt about the superiority of the Indian half of the two worlds.

But there is further and more persuasive evidence of a haunting fear
of inferiority in the Indian community. In response to the article cited above
that claimed that being stuck between two worlds was *not* a problem for
that writer, a letter to the editor by another teen appeared:

[T]hose of the people who believe that we should become like the Cauca-
sian race just because we live in their country are spineless derelicts. People
who think of themselves as totally accepted by Americans are sadly wrong.
They are not at all happy with the fact that foreigners (mainly Indians) come
to this country and make it big and exercise their culture in public. So some
of you who sit there and think that you've become one of them may not know
what one of them says when you are not around. And no matter who you
are, you can't change your skin's color to match theirs completely or your
parents' values to match your pseudo-American lifestyle. . . . On the subject
of interracial marriages, if you don't understand why your parents are against
it, you are just basically very ignorant. . . . [W]hat is this garbage that "as long
as we believe in our culture and who we are" it's okay? . . . Now with interracial marriage they'll [i.e., the second generation] lose their morals and culture all to an inferiority complex. Once you start to value someone else's
culture, you might as well become one of them. But the question is "Will
they ever accept you as one of them?"[12]

This angry response suggests that the earlier writer's comfort with being
a person of Indian origin in America is self-delusion. Yet this writer's attitude toward the position of Indians in America seems two-sided. On the
one hand, he claims that Americans are jealous of the success of Indian
immigrants. On the other, however, Indians seem shut out of full acceptance because they cannot change their skin color or their parents' values.
Intermarriage puts the Indian partner in an inferior position. Ultimately,
the question is "Will America accept us?" rather than "Do we really want
to blend in?"

This writer's decision to raise the issue of skin color further supports
the notion that the superior/inferior relationship between the two worlds

is problematic. Within the Indian community, there is a long tradition of color prejudice. Being "fair" is a quality, along with being an M.D. or a green card holder, that is used to market one's relatives in the marital ads in Indian-American newspapers. Several people have used skin tone to explain to me Indian attitudes toward white as opposed to black Americans. As one writes, "True, we are hypocrites to point fingers at U.S. racism against Indians, when we haven't thought enough about our color prejudice and our caste prejudice. Many Indians are blatantly disdainful toward African Americans."[13] Thus, for the angry writer to claim that skin color sets Indians apart from "Americans" evokes, albeit indirectly, this notion of lighter being better.

I do not mean to suggest that references to two worlds are motivated by a sense of racial inferiority. The conflict between Indian and American in many discussions is a straightforward debate about how the community can preserve its cultural heritage in the second generation, which through sheer force of history is necessarily growing up American. What I do mean to point out is that a regular feature of print treatments of the two worlds issue is the sense that these two worlds are asymmetrical. One world, and it is not clear which, is superior to the other.

The Issues

Numerous particular adjustment issues are discussed in the Indian immigrant press. However, three stand out as clearly dominant: education, dating, and intergenerational communication. The "education problem" concerns parental pressure on Indian children to do exceptionally well in school and to choose certain preferred professions. The "dating problem" concerns whether or not children should date and also whether they should choose their own spouses. Discussions of the "communication problem" call for more "open" communication between the two generations. These three issues, like the two worlds metaphor, are unified by an underlying concern with the relations between superiors and inferiors. In these specific cases, the concern is less over the relative status of Indian and American than the role of status demarcations in social life.

Education

A typical complaint of a second-generation high school student regarding education runs, "As Indian teenagers living in America, importance has been put on academic performance . . . and that's good motivation for us. But sometimes the pressure gets to be too much. An A+ seems to be the only acceptable outcome of a semester or a year's worth of work."[14] The three themes contained in this passage inform the bulk of the education-related discussions: education as a worthwhile or valued pursuit, the pressure exerted by parents and the community to do well, and the notion that *the best* is the only worthy outcome.

It is clear that education was and is a top priority for Indian immigrants. Many of the 1965–1975 generation of immigrants came to the United States to pursue graduate education. In one reminiscence, a first-generation immigrant recalls, "My first priority was to get a good education, and therefore as soon as I arrived in Notre Dame, I went to meet the Chairman of the Department."[15] The second generation, too, accepts education as a positive attribute: "[W]e [Indian teenagers] have a good quality of studying hard."[16] But what makes education valuable? What sort of education do people seek?

Debates about education pit "education as academics" against a broader view of education that encourages the development of a well-rounded person. The "education as academics" position, billed as the traditional Indian view, leads directly to careers as doctors or engineers. Advocates of the broader interpretation are outsiders to the tradition—members of the second generation or first-generation critics. The teen quoted above cautions that the "good quality of studying hard" "does not mean that teenagers should seclude themselves from American society, and it is good and healthy for Indian teenagers to take part in extracurricular activities, sports, etc."[17] Another adds, "In my school it doesn't seem that the average Indian teen is involved in extracurricular clubs, sports, but are more concentrated in their studies and secluded. I feel they should take more of a part to make them a more rounded person."[18]

Although many first-generation immigrants espouse the broader view of education, the notion that Indians construe education narrowly does persist quite strongly: "As Vipin Malhan says, 'My parents were pretty strict about school and stuff because we're Indian and Indians are supposed to get awesome grades.'"[19]

Why should this narrow view continue to be touted as the Indian view? One partial explanation comes from the historical experience of first-generation immigrants. Their educational experiences in India reflected a hierarchy of educational options that was linked solely to examination scores. Based on high school examination scores, one either went into the preferred college educational programs of medicine and engineering or, as one person put it, "on to other things." To the extent that the narrow Indian view of education refers to this historical background of first-generation immigrants, one can understand the continued equation of the Indian (read "traditional") view with "education as academics."

However, the community is keenly aware of what it takes to succeed in America and knows that good grades alone will not secure success in higher education. For example, the selection criteria for *India Tribune*'s Nehru Youth Award incorporates the typical nonacademic attributes (nonacademic interests or talents and community service) that are necessary for admission to top-tier colleges.[20]

The persistence of the rhetoric of a narrowly defined education (despite the realities of an increasing number of activities being incorporated into this narrow definition) can be understood in terms of the superiority/

inferiority anxiety discussed above. When definitions of what is good and worthwhile remain clear and narrow, it is much easier to sort out the superior from the inferior in some absolute and definitive way.

Even in print, there is evidence that the narrow version of education is bound up with questions of superior/inferior status. A writer asks, "What can we do to help ourselves as parents and youths?" and answers, "We need to maintain honest dialogue about what is really important: the happiness and mature development of children or the fleeting reputation of the family, as reflected in wanting all children to become successful doctors, engineers, etc."[21] In claiming that the "reputation of the family" depends on the children becoming "successful doctors, engineers, etc.," the connection between education and status is carefully framed to draw on the narrow definition of education: children should be doctors or engineers (as opposed to simply being successful in their chosen careers) to bolster the reputation of the family.

A further effort to rein in the criteria for judging superiority/inferiority stems from the third of the education themes noted above: the notion that *the best* is the only worthy outcome. In response to the student who complains that A+ seems to be the only acceptable outcome, the editor of that article adds a story of his own:

> Once I was visiting my friend. The two of us along with his father were watching a movie when comes his sister, 8, with a big smile on her face and two sheets of paper in her hand. She screams, "Daddy look I got a 97 on my exam." The dad looked over the exam and said, "If you hadn't made this stupid mistake, you would have gotten a 100." The little girl's excitement vanished.[22]

The connection between being *the best* and superiority is on the one hand purely logical: if you are *the best*, you must be superior to all others. The criteria are clear and well defined. On the other hand, however, there is a more spiritual sense of superiority that is also connected to being *the best*. In a particularly poignant passage from the biography of the 1991 Nehru Youth Award winner, the imagery is telling: "Ramesha Jagsi has the rare distinction of perfect score (1600) in the Scholastic Aptitude Test. Less than 1 percent of 1.3 million students nationwide achieve such a feat. Her friends said, 'Wow, Ramesha, can we touch you?'"[23] Although this may not seem a very unusual reaction from an American perspective (we often joke about touching someone who has done something special), touching has a special significance in Indian culture. We may joke about luck rubbing off, but in a Hindu scheme, touch is about relationships between superiors and inferiors, particularly the touching of feet. While this writer refers to a "feat" rather than to literal "feet," the homonyms do conjure up a peculiarly Indian meaning for the last sentence.

I suggest, then, that the persistence of the narrow definition of education as the official Indian view and the assertion that for Indians only *the best* is acceptable are both evidence of a persistent concern with being able to sort out the superior and the inferior. The nuances of the two worlds metaphor were suggestive of an ambivalence about the superior/inferior relationship between Indian and American. The problem of education adds a different twist to the superiority/inferiority theme. In this context, we see a concern over finding criteria that can resolve the ambiguities of superior/inferior ranking.

Dating

The second common adjustment issue is dating. As with education, however, the core reference unfolds to encompass a range of meanings and related issues. In much first-generation rhetoric, dating equals promiscuous premarital sex. In his article entitled "Why We Should Denounce Dating," a swami denounces premarital sex. Similarly, one father quoted in an article on "How to Combat Dating Virus" just states, "Children are supposed to achieve something before they start engaging in sexual activity." Another father adds, "I do not agree with the concept of having sex before marriage in guise of dates."[24]

Yet there is some ambivalence evident in first-generation responses to dating. A mother of two young sons asks rhetorically whether it is "right for my son or daughter to date" and responds:

> Maybe it would not be too great a problem if he/she went out in a group; but alone? I am not so sure. What do I do when he/she feels terrible, different and alone on Monday mornings when friends discuss what happened on their dates over the weekend and my child has only been to one of those typical Indian get-togethers? I sense his/her heartache, but I am not sure what the answer is.[25]

Although this writer does not explicitly define dating, she does imply that she recognizes it as an important social activity for teens. Why exactly she feels uncomfortable with the concept is not made clear.

It is mostly up to members of the second generation to catalogue the sources of their parents' anxiety at the prospect of their children going on dates. In addition to the "sex factor," other reasons members of the second generation give for their parents' concern are worries about the effect of dating on the all-important studies,[26] a general notion of conflict with the parents' traditions, and parental concern over whom the child will date (i.e., the possibility of dating a non-Indian).

The definition of dating from the second-generation perspective differs markedly from the overwhelming equation of dating and sex in first-generation rhetoric. For one fifteen-year-old boy, dating is "a process of getting acquainted with another person."[27] While this young man goes on to deny that dating always has to be a matter of "boyfriend and girlfriend," others in the second generation clearly make a connection between dating and marriage, specifically the choice of a spouse. One young woman, after suggesting that parents are opposed to dating because of whom the child might date, goes on to say, "I think [parents] should realize that no matter who we date or who we choose to marry, we will always be the same person that we always were."[28] Another boy comments, "I think kids should be allowed to date because I wouldn't want to marry a lady that I would hate for the rest of my life."[29]

As with the first generation, however, not all in the second generation view dating similarly. One college-age Muslim boy asserts, "I do not need dates to make friends. And why female friends? Being a Muslim, I am completely against dating." The connection between dating and sex is articulated by his friend, who adds, "Divorce rates are higher among sweaty palms than those who wait for a real date until they reach to the appropriate age."[30]

While there are multiple opinions about the dating issue within each generation, the dominant conceptualization of dating in the press rhetoric of the first generation equates dating with premarital sex. For the second generation, dating is seen as a way to get to know people and, perhaps more importantly, a way to meet potential spouses.

Discussions of dating, particularly for the second generation, turn invariably to the question of marriage. There are two issues of concern under the general rubric of marriage. One is the choice between arranged marriage and marriage to a partner of one's own choice.[31] The other is the issue of interracial marriage. Discussions of both these issues have two significant features in common.

First, neither choice of marriage partner nor interracial marriage was mentioned at all by first-generation writers. Yet it was clear from my other field research that this issue is indeed one about which parents have concerns. There are several possible explanations for this seeming anomaly. It may be just a fluke that during the months of my monitoring these issues were not broached by first-generation writers in the Indian immigrant press. Or this lack of attention may stem from the particular life stage of the children. While a few in the second generation have married, the first big cohort of second-generation youth are only now finishing their education. The issue of marriage still lies ahead for their parents. Thus, while parents may be thinking "in theory" about their children's marriages, the absence of imminent decisions may contribute to the scarcity of public dialogues. Finally, and I think most likely, it may be that the issues related to marriage are just unspeakable for many parents. Clearly, there are some in the first generation for whom the marriage question is simply not a concern. They fully expect their children to choose their own spouses and are not particularly concerned about the prospect of intermarriage (see, for example, the portraits of the Iyengars in chapter 8 and the Shenoys in chapter 10). However, for many others, the prospect of a child marrying someone outside the preferred boundaries of caste, religion, status, and race is so threatening as to be unimaginable. Perhaps parents realize that in many instances, they are powerless to control this aspect of their children's lives (unlike dating, when children are still under significant parental control). With silence, perhaps, they try to avoid confronting these realities.

In addition to first-generation silence, the other major marriage issue is the connection the second generation makes between marriage questions and ethics. In discussing both arranged or choice marriage and interracial marriage, second-generation writers justify their positions based on an appeal to an underlying set of values, values that are stereotypically American.

Arguing against arranged marriages, one college student writes, "When parents choose a husband for their girl, they pick him out not for who he is but for what he is. There is something unethical about choosing someone solely because he is a doctor, a computer engineer, or a scientist."[32]

Another writer cites the pro-interracial marriage attitudes he finds among his peers and asks rhetorically, "Why is this?"

> Are we corrupt? Or do we look at the situation from a new, different perspective? . . .
> Obviously, there must be some reason for this path of thinking. We aren't just crazy. It's that we have been exposed to new ideas. . . .
> [A] general, overall advantage for our community and society is that perhaps if people begin to overlook each other's skin color, there just might be hope that we will overcome this titanic problem which exists in our society and is scored with the notorious name—RACISM.[33]

The ethical positions that these two writers describe are clearly contrasted to the ethical concerns of their parents and are rooted in their generation's exposure to "new"—a code word for "American"—ideas. The underlying theme connecting these ethical positions has to do with the relative importance of the "content of our character" on the one hand and the superficial features of social status or race on the other. There seems to be a clear declaration that it is the content of character that is ultimately important.

In addition to rejecting social status as a marker of ultimate human worth, second-generation writers also claim that individual autonomy, so highly valued in American society, should allow them to make marriage and dating decisions on their own. As one young man states emphatically, "Dating should be a personal decision."[34] In regard to interracial relationships, a high-schooler comments, "The person involved in an interracial situation should do what they want, but also respect their parents' views but talk to them."[35] The issue for the second generation is who has the moral right to make decisions regarding dating and marriage.

As with the two worlds metaphor and the specific issue of education, much of the rhetoric surrounding dating and marriage can be linked to a concern with superiority/inferiority. In the context of dating and marriage, the superior/inferior issue manifests itself as a disagreement between the two generations over the role of superior/inferior relations in social life. The treatment of the dating and marriage issues by the first generation provides some evidence that the first generation continues to be deeply concerned about superior/inferior status. The equation of dating and sex and the general silence on the issues of choice and interracial marriage are both telling. It is clear that for members of the first generation the choice of a spouse is not a matter of personal preference and affinity. While there is no direct discussion of the proper avenue for the decision about life partners, it is clear that they do not discuss it in terms of a decision two people alone can make. Dating is not for meeting people, and "choice" marriages are not even worthy of comment. Perhaps first-generation silence results from persistent commitment to the view that marriage is a matter between families (preferably between families of similar caste and class status) and a matter about which parents have considerable input if not complete control.[36]

The first generation's treatment of the relations between parents and children in the context of dating and life-partner decisions provides more direct evidence about the proper structure of intimate social relationships. From the parental perspective, the relationship between parents and children is clearly one of superiors and inferiors. Even the most liberal of first-generation writers who question what the right path is concerning the issues of dating and marriage see all rights resting with the parents. It is solely the parents' choice whether to "give in" or "hold off." There is not even a recognition that parents may simply be unable to exercise this level of control over their children.

The second generation, in contrast, rejects the idea that social life is structured by relations between superiors and inferiors. In their rejection of the notion that "exterior" statuses such as occupation or race are important in issues of dating and marriage in favor of a focus on people's "interior" qualities and in their assertions of the independent rights of children, the second generation exemplifies its rejection of distinctions of superior/inferior in favor of interpersonal equality and personal autonomy.

We must be careful, however, not to extend this rejection of the superior/inferior paradigm in the context of dating and marriage to the second-generation outlook in general. As we saw in the discussion of the two worlds metaphor, some members of the second generation represented in the press do think in terms of superior/inferior, at least in comparing Indian and American culture. I think the general praise for equality and the condemnation of distinctions of superiority and inferiority grow out of the particular issue of dating and marriage. When we move beyond the realm of family and intimate personal relationships, the second-generation rhetoric is much more likely to incorporate concerns with superiority/inferiority. I will return to this point and explore the possible explanations for this phenomenon after an examination of the third specific adjustment issue.

Communication

Unlike the issues of education and dating, there seems to be consensus between the two generations about the "communication problem." For both generations, the central issue is the lack of "open" communication. Time and time again, writers of both generations appeal for "openness." There are two essential features of this openness. First, openness means dialogue as opposed to monologue. One Ph.D. advises parents that "in order to build [a meaningful] relationship we need to listen to our kids more than lecturing them."[37] A second-generation writer suggests that "instead of yelling we should try to explain why we want to go out to the movies with our friends. . . . [T]he road to understanding each other is a two way street and we as well as our parents have to travel half the way to meet the other."[38] For both these writers, a lack of openness is a lack of listening to the other side's point of view.

The second element of openness concerns the place of the child in the parent-child relationship. Press accounts by writers of both generations suggest that children do in fact have certain rights of autonomy and that parents should respect these. One mother comments, "Placing restrictions can only breed resentment, while an open, heart-to-heart chat ensures not only total understanding on both sides, but also sufficient liberty of thought, speech, and action for the offspring."[39] The Ph.D. advisor quoted earlier adds, "[A]s parents it is important for us to . . . try our best to guide our children early in their formative years of character development with a spirit of love and respect for their individuality."[40]

The second generation reiterates its members' rights to some autonomy (which also appeared in relation to the dating and marriage issue) in the context of discussing communication problems: "[O]ur parents have to listen to us and allow us the room we need to grow."[41]

One curious feature of the discussion of communication problems is the plea on the part of second-generation writers to understand one's parents: "Instead of yelling maybe we should . . . try to understand that our parents came from a different environment and weren't raised with all these problems."[42] "Our parents also have a difficult job in raising us between these two worlds. They tend to give us our freedom, but also expect us to honor their background and give them respect. They have to determine what is right considering the values they were taught, and also considering that we were born and raised in America, the country of freedom."[43]

Intergenerational agreement about the communication problem centers on values and attitudes that are antithetical to the traditional Indian view of parent-child relations. Both generations are calling for openness, dialogue, respect for children's individuality and autonomy, and respect for parents' difficult task in raising children in an unfamiliar environment. Parents are admonished to abandon the "tendency to be an authoritarian disciplinarian [rooted in] Indian culture."[44]

In discussions of the communication problem, concerns over superior/inferior status and relationships are absent. One explanation for this absence is that the very idea of communication between parent and child as a desired goal implies a solution that requires a departure from the superior/inferior elements of parent-child relations. Open communication goes hand in hand with a certain degree of equality and mutual respect. Without redefining the communication problem (say, that the problem is that kids are not listening to their parents), the current formulation precludes positive assessments of superior/inferior parent-child relations. Thus, in calls for parental recognition of children's individuality and a certain amount of autonomy, there is an explicit rejection of superior/inferior distinctions in this realm of social life.

I do not think this argument can be sustained. Rather, there is simply a lack of explicit concern with superior/inferior relations in this arena because first-generation calls for open communication are clearly couched in a larger framework that *assumes* a hierarchical relationship between parents and children. The Ph.D. adviser quoted above discusses respect for children's individuality in the context of the parents' guiding role. The other mother who talks about liberty for offspring does so amidst a discussion of parents determining exactly how much liberty children should be allowed. It is simply that open communication is assumed to take place in the context of already established hierarchical relations between parents and children, a relationship in which parents encompass and protect children.

The Implications of Adjustment Rhetoric

The two worlds metaphor, as well as the specific issues of education, dating, and communication, illustrate the variety of ways in which the Indian worldview has permeated discussions about the problems of the youth. There is clearly not a simple unified idea of how hierarchy or concerns about relative status are or should be part of second-generation consciousness or behavior. Although there is a fairly persistent concern with issues of status or relative rank across generations and across the issues of dating, marriage, and education, there is by no means a clear correlation between the idealized Indian worldview described in chapter 2 and what we observe in the print discussion of second-generation adjustment issues. Hierarchy is sometimes a classic encompassing hierarchy, as in the communication issue where openness, a potential challenge to the superiority of parents, is in fact circumscribed by the traditional encompassing role of parents. Sometimes hierarchy is a straightforward linear ranking devoid of notions of encompassing relationships, as in the case of the two worlds metaphor, where the task is to figure out whether Indian or American is better. Moreover, hierarchy is sometimes a concern over sorting out relative rankings, as in education; sometimes a disagreement about the validity of status considerations altogether, as in first- and second-generation disagreements over the role of social status in dating and marriage. While the Indian worldview, with its attendant judgments of higher and lower, clearly informs the way the Indian community expresses its concerns about the fate of the second generation, its effects are by no means uniform.

This variable role played by the Indian worldview in the construction of second-generation "problems talk" makes an interesting counterpoint to the very American approach to social life characteristic of the second generation's management of its organizational network. In concrete interactions, the American sensibilities of this generation are paramount. In the rarefied realm of rhetoric, however, American and Indian sensibilities are more mixed. Attention to the superior/inferior paradigm is coupled with talk about individual autonomy and equality or mutuality in social relationships (even between such obviously unequal partners as parents and children).

The greater role of an Indian worldview in problems rhetoric is in part a result of the fact that the second generation does not produce this rhetoric on its own. First-generation writers play an active role in contributing to this public discussion of the second generation's situation. Indian sensibilities, then, can more easily creep in than they can in the organizational context where the second generation is effectively cut off from its elders, functioning fairly exclusively in its own Indian-American milieu.

Additionally, the very fact that what appears in the press is removed from the realities of day-to-day interactions makes possible a more synthetic mixture of Indian and American sensibilities. The print media is beholden to a plurality of voices and perspectives which meet on an equal footing.[45] In daily life, in contrast, there is no such level playing field, and what emerges from observations of interactions is the winnowing of multiple opinions and a dominant voice.

Yet despite the variable combinations of Indian and American sensibilities evident in print problems talk, this problems talk does provide the second generation a kind of symbolic generational identity. For the first generation, *organizational* life resulted in a collective identity because the concrete interactions within and among organizations were understood to have great symbolic import. The symbolic meanings of actions and activities were captured with stylized rhetoric that reinforced and standardized the symbolism of organizational life. For the second generation, the problems of organizational life were resolved through individualistic solutions—everyone should decide for himself or herself—and none of the issues of organizational life was symbolically important (save, perhaps, for the notion that the second generation is distinctly different from the first). The problems rhetoric of the press, however, does constitute a clear generational identity stored in a standardized rhetoric. Members of the second generation must live between two worlds (even though the extent to which this is problematic for particular individuals may vary). They are under pressure from their Indian parents to do well in school and become doctors or engineers. They quarrel with their parents over the issue of dating. They long for open communication between the generations.

These defining characteristics of second-generation Indian-American experience were repeated in every community discussion of "the youth" that I attended. Moreover, as will be evident in the family portraits of part

II, second-generation individuals use this rhetoric as a marker of the "standard" second-generation experience to which they compare their own experiences.

Although both the immigrant and the second generations come to their generational identities differently, their generational identities together become the anchors for the process of assimilation and the construction of community. At the collective level, the stylized rhetoric of standard generational experiences becomes a kind of beacon to draw people together. In the public sphere, people are happy enough to agree that the rhetoric does in fact capture the essence of their generation, even if their own individual experience deviates from the standard. These generational identities, then, provide the basis for maintaining the idea of a community. At the individual level, however (as we will see in part II), they allow people to differentiate themselves from typical Indians. Yet as long as individuals recognize the standard experience of typical Indians as a point of comparison, the distance they can drift from these prototypes is limited. It makes no sense to compare yourself to a standard with which you have nothing in common. Because individual difference is in effect bounded, the community can continue to exist.

II

FAMILY PORTRAITS

6

Family Life

The public life of the Indian community plays only a small part in the everyday lives of Indian immigrants and their children. People get up, go to work or school, and return at night to share a common space and perhaps a common meal with virtually the only other Indian people with whom they interact on a daily basis. On weekends, they may expand their contacts to include extended family, or Indian friends, but the most fundamental and consistent context in which people experience their common Indianness is that of the family.

This section of the book presents portraits of five Indian-origin families. The focus is not on the material aspects of family life but on the emotional and symbolic character of each family. The portraits are based on a series of interviews in which I asked people to tell me their life story, beginning with when and where they were born and what they remember about growing up. These loosely structured interviews allowed people to speak about their past and, particularly, their current lives in ways that addressed the connection between what has occurred, and the interpretations or meaning they assign to those experiences. Although some people spontaneously introduced their feelings and interpretations of events into our conversations, others began to share these aspects only after I remarked on a facial expression or gesture that indicated shock, puzzlement, distaste, or pleasure. Each of the twenty-one people I interviewed, however, revealed something of the symbolic and emotional side of family life. (Appendix B describes the methodological issues involved in creating these family portraits.)

Each family had a set of core concerns. Some core issues were repeated from family to family. Many families discussed arguments between parents and children over curfews, friends, dating, and personal styles of dress and adornment, a range of issues familiar to most parents and teenagers. In addition, there were issues related to Indianness. What does it mean to be Indian? What aspects of Indian culture should be passed along to children? What do Indian-origin teens and young adults wish that their parents were able to teach them? A similar set of issues confronts many immigrant families. Finally, each family had a set of very particular concerns rooted in the personal histories of parents and the personalities and social environments of children. One family was preoccupied with spiritual and material growth as human beings; another was concerned with maintaining a sense of closeness among family members; yet another was focused on working through day-to-day controversies by intensive discussion and fair-minded, though sometimes painful, compromise.

The particularity of each family was also evident in the language members shared for discussing themselves and the issues that shape family life. Family members shared certain turns of phrase, certain key concepts and contrasts that both connected them to each other and distinguished them from other families. The combination of family-specific concerns and family-specific ways of conceptualizing and discussing family life produce unique *family idioms*. Each family portrait illustrates the overarching family idiom as it relates the events that are of significance to family members, individually and collectively.

In order to appreciate what is common in the assimilation process played out in the family setting, we must first appreciate the uniqueness of individual and familial experience. Theories of assimilation generally abandon a concern with individual difference in favor of highlighting the commonalities of the adjustment process. While it may well be true, for example, that immigrants share a kind of "wavy-line" pattern of assimilation punctuated along the way by easily recognized signposts,[1] it is my argument here that the *catalysts* for that process of assimilation are the specific and infinitely varied interactions among individuals. In light of this, we need to develop an alternative, new type of theory to articulate the relationship between the peculiarities of individual experience and assimilation as a social process.

The key to identifying patterns in the experiences of and interactions among individuals is to pay serious attention to their complexity. In working with the five families profiled here, I saw that interactions and their meanings are indeed incredibly varied. When viewed together, a pattern of interaction and experience does emerge from the family portraits, but the pattern is not fully represented in any one family. Nor does the pattern emerge in a linear form if one reads each family portrait in turn. Instead, each family portrait, rich in its own unique details, provides a sampling of the different elements that constitute the model of the assimilation process laid out in chapter 12.

This model identifies a set of overlapping dynamics that give shape and form to the process of assimilation as it occurs within each family. These dynamics, however, do not determine the trajectory of assimilation. We cannot predict how any family will come through the process of negotiating intergenerational change and adjustment. We cannot predict which families will remain healthy and happy and which will be torn apart. Nor can we predict a degree of assimilation reached in the second generation. We cannot predict who will be more "Indian" and who more "American." Understanding these dynamics, though, does give us a way to conceptualize the process of assimilation that both appreciates the variability of individual experience and renders these experiences in some way comparable or common.

The Dynamics of Assimilation

The first dynamic illustrated in the family portraits is one that ensures a kind of intergenerational continuity. The process of assimilation is not only concerned with intergenerational discontinuities. Rather, it encompasses a modulation of continuities and differences between generations.

In these five families, the issues that arise (controversies over dating or hairstyles or spending time with peers, controversies about the proper ways to treat one's elders, etc.) and the way these issues are talked about or conceptualized originate in the experiences of parents. We might expect that family controversies usually arise from the fact that immigrant parents and their children have been raised in vastly different social environments. In reality, much of what comes up between parents and children is related to issues that arose in parents' own lives. This intergenerational dynamic is responsible for a great deal of continuity between parents and children— not only in terms of *what* is of concern but also in terms of *how* those concerns are articulated. In listening to children and parents talk, it is easy to identify which children belong to which parents. These continuities represent one layer of the process of assimilation, a layer shared by all families—immigrant and nonimmigrant—as part of the process of intergenerational socialization.

A second dynamic governing the process of assimilation concerns the way people define themselves in contrast to others. Just as second-generation voluntary organizations held up immigrant-generation organizations as models of Indianness from which they differentiated themselves, individuals within families refer to various models or prototypes as a way to create distinct identities. One class of models represents a generalized, prototypical Indian experience. Throughout the family portraits, people refer to what happens "back in India" or to what "Indians" are like. These models are used as standards to which people compare their own and their family's behavior. Sometimes people see similarities between themselves and these models, but more often they see differences. There is a persistent tendency for people to see themselves as atypical Indians.

Another class of models that people mobilize in their attempts to carve out identities includes those provided by other family members. In addition to comparing their experiences to those of "Indians," individuals compare themselves to parents, spouses, and siblings. Here, too, the emphasis is on *differentiating* oneself from family members.

Assimilation, as a day-to-day social process, is about creating an identity for oneself that locates one in the social world. The others in that social world, whether they are close and specific (as are parents and siblings) or more distant and less specific (as are "other Indians"), are all part of the background or setting against which one's own identity stands in relief. These characters represent a wide range of Indiannesses to serve as foils for the creation of one's own sense of Indianness.

This dynamic of comparison, central to the creation of a personal Indian identity, is accompanied by certain recurrent themes peculiar to the process of intergenerational change in the Indian-American context. In these portraits, readers will note a recurrent sense of status anxiety in the second generation. At a low but persistent level, young people worry that they are not "good enough" in some way. They worry that they will not match the success of their parents, that they will experience personal failures, or that their activities and life choices may not be sufficiently prestigious or respectable.

A second striking theme is the strong bond that exists between the generations. There is a sense of closeness and involvement that binds even adult children's lives with their parents'. This bond, however, is not an explicitly emotional one, based on the sharing of feelings and thoughts. Rather, it is a kind of practical, physical engagement that creates in children a strong sense of obligation to parents, and in parents a strong sense of protection toward children. In chapter 12, I will argue that these two themes are particularly Indian at some level.

The third dynamic driving the process of intergenerational change in these families stems from their sense of difference from something they refer to as "the mainstream." Above and beyond peculiarly Indian features of the adjustment process, Asian Indians exhibit certain responses that stem from their minority status. As immigrants and their children discuss "the mainstream," the social process they illustrate is one that affects all who see themselves as minorities. The way in which children come to terms with this aspect of their experience is conditioned by their parents' attitudes toward their own minority status, by the environment prevailing in the community in which the children are raised, and by the particular personality of each child.

To understand assimilation as a social process, one must appreciate the layered dynamics that constitute the process. In these families' stories, my commentary will alert the reader to those passages that illustrate these dynamics of assimilation. As I have suggested, however, one cannot see these processes neatly packaged in any single family portrait or laid out sequentially across the portraits. Rather, what one sees are glimpses of these dynamics as the family idioms unfold.

Five Families

The five families profiled below do not know one another and do not have common sets of friends. They represent a variety of class, religious, and caste backgrounds. Each came to participate in this study by a different path. No family I asked to participate refused. They represent, then, a serendipitous, if not strictly random, sample of families currently living in Chicago and its suburbs.[7]

The Nagar Family

Vaidehi—mother, early forties.
Anar—elder daughter, age twenty.
Mausami—second daughter, age twelve.

The Nagars are a Brahman family, originally from Gujarat, in northwestern India. They emigrated to the United States when Anar was a toddler. One distinguishing feature of the Nagar family is the tragedy that struck the family when the father, Raghav, died suddenly in 1984. Many of Vaidehi's concerns revolve around the difficulties, in particular the loneliness, of raising the children on her own. The Nagars are marked as well by the extraordinary thoughtfulness of the elder daughter, Anar, who is able to articulate the psychological tensions she has experienced as a consequence of her feeling at once Indian and American. Also of note is the dramatic difference between the two daughters in the way in which each has responded to her Indianness. The task for Anar has been arduous, while Mausami seems a dynamo of practical, no-nonsense acceptance of "who she is" as a consequence of her birth to Indian parents. These differences in the two sisters point to the effects of the minority dynamic. While both sisters have been subject to the same parental influences, their peer environments have been quite different, as are their personalities. These differences have contributed to their different responses to their status as minority members (over and above their differing views of their Indianness).

The Iyengar Family

Lakshmi—mother, mid-forties.
Shivan—father, mid-forties.
Michael—elder son, age twenty.
Bob—second son, age fifteen.

Like the Nagars, the Iyengars are a Brahman family. Both parents are ethnically Tamil (from a region in southeastern India), but both were raised in large metropolitan centers in North India. The Iyengars are marked by their cosmopolitan, humanist orientation, which has deeply affected the way they have dealt with being Indian in the United States. Lakshmi and Shivan see themselves as Indian in a historical rather than an essential sense. They are historical Indians since they were born and raised in India. They question and resist the notion, however, that their core values or their core selves, their very essences, are somehow Indian. Being a good person transcends cultural boundaries and is not connected to being a good Indian. Their sons are clearly the product of their parents' views of their own Indianness. Just as Lakshmi and Shivan are historically Indian, Michael and Bob are historically American, stressing that their household has more in common with the household next door than with the households of "typical" Indian immigrants. However, the Iyengars do maintain the sense of connection between parents and children that is deeply Indian, although it is manifested in less obviously Indian ways than it is in other families.

The Kumar Family

Ravi—father, mid-forties.
Ratna—mother, mid-forties.
Minakshi—elder daughter, age twenty-one.
Anu—second daughter, age twenty.
Raj—son, age nineteen.

The Kumars' is a Christian household. The circumstances of their immigration from Andhra Pradesh in southern India set the Kumars apart from others in this study. Their immigration was preceded by that of Ravi Kumar's widowed mother, who urged her sons and their families to follow her to the United States. The Kumars, then, came to this country "for good" rather than with the intention of returning to India in a few years' time. This feature of their experience led the Kumar parents to open discussions of the cultural compromises they anticipated they would and would not make in raising their kids in America. The open and often difficult dialogues Ravi and Ratna had before their immigration have carried over to the similarly explicit and conscious conversations they have with their children. This family is characterized by an intensity of communication unparalleled in other families profiled here. The assimilative experiences of the Kumar children have also been shaped by the family's Christianity which acts as a third identity that complicates the relationship between Indian and American and results in a persistent sense of cultural drift among the Kumar children.

The Shenoy Family

Shenoy—father, late fifties.
Durga—mother, mid-fifties.

Psalm—elder daughter, age twenty-eight.
Padma—second daughter, age twenty-six.
Sanjay—son, age twenty-one.

The Shenoys' is the only inter-caste marriage among the five parental couples. Shenoy's natal family was a Brahman family from a small linguistic group in southwestern India. Durga's was a non-Brahman but still caste Hindu family from the Punjab; however, they spent many years of Durga's youth living in East Africa. The Shenoys met and married while both were graduate students in the United States.

The Shenoys, like the Kumars, have a strong third identity that has shaped the assimilative experience of the children. For the Shenoys, however, this third identity is idiosyncratic, centering on a combination of class and a well-articulated philosophy of life which stresses personal growth and development as well as responsibility to fellow human beings. In both the Kumar and Shenoy families, the third identities muddle the sharp contrast between Indian and American that figures into other families' lives. The children in these two families are led to experience their cultural fates as diffusions of culture rather than transformations. They don't see themselves as negotiating the relationships between Indian and American so much as they see themselves as "losing" altogether a sense of cultural belonging. Of the families profiled here, the Shenoys are most similar to the Iyengars in general demeanor and lifestyle. There is very little that is Indian about their daily lives. However, unlike the Iyengar parents, who were troubled intellectually by what was and wasn't Indian about their lives, Shenoy and Durga never spontaneously discussed the concerns of their current lives as in any way Indian. Their children's connections to their own Indian background is consequently very surreal. There is a lack of concreteness in their musings about India and Indians.

The Shankar Family

Shankar—father, early fifties.
Parvathi—mother, mid-forties.
Ganesh—son, age twenty-six.
Veena—daughter, age twenty-two.

The Shankars, a Vaishya caste family from Karnataka, emigrated to the United States in search of economic opportunity and settled rather quickly and easily into a comfortable life. Although each of the other families profiled here has a strong and rather particular sense of the drama of family life, the Shankars were much less forthcoming about the day-to-day rough-and-tumble of their relationships. What I took away from my interviews with the Shankars was an appreciation of the sense of distance between parents and children that troubles both generations. Both parents and children long for closer relationships with each other. The fulfillment of these longings, however, is problematic because of the very different ideas the

two generations have about what constitutes close parent-child relationships. For the Shankar parents, closeness is rooted in being physically
together. They remember the satisfaction they felt living in big families in
India, where simple everyday chores led to meaningful interactions. Veena
and Ganesh, however, want "spending time with parents" to include a psychological kind of closeness, based on understanding and empathizing with
each other's feelings and points of view. In the portrait of the Shankars,
the peculiarly Indian nature of parent-child relations is most fully exposed.

7

The Nagars:
Duty and Heart

Vaidehi Nagar and her two daughters live in a well-kept middle-class neighborhood in a suburb of Chicago. My introduction to this family was through the elder daughter, Anar, a twenty-year-old student I met at a youth workshop at one of the area Hindu temples. My original interest in Anar was as an informant for my study of the second-generation organizations. During the course of our first interview, however, we talked about Anar's own background, her feelings and experiences growing up. Anar was the first second-generation Indian I had spoken to who articulated her experiences in terms of feeling like two distinct people for a large part of her life.

When she discussed this duality, she alternated between describing herself as "living in two worlds" and "feeling like two different people." To me, however, these two terms were not interchangeable. To live in two worlds, behaving differently in different situations, does not necessarily mean one needs to be two people psychologically. I pressed Anar about what made her feel like two different people.

She said that her house had a different "feeling" from the houses of her "white" friends. Her friends' families seemed very unconnected. Their moms didn't seem to care what the kids did. Everyone appeared to go his or her own way. In Anar's family, there was a whole contingent of relatives concerned whenever anyone did anything. Yet, at the same time, she felt that there was a distance between people in her family. She would never talk to her mom like a "friend" in the same way as her friends talked to their moms. Sex and dating were taboo subjects. She remembered being in a car once with a friend and her mother. They passed a cute guy, and her friend's mother honked. Her own mother, Anar said, would never do that.

Anar also talked about home life being "Indian clothes and Indian food." If people ever criticized American culture, Anar just agreed with them (whether she actually felt as they did or not). Meanwhile, at school, she was curling her hair, wearing makeup, organizing socials, and joining clubs. This still left me without a sense of who the "two different people" were. I asked Anar to describe them.

She told me that the person at home has respect for older people. If someone asks you to do something, you just do it—no questions. You also have a different feeling for people younger than you. You watch out for them. There was a time when sitting at the dinner table was confusing. You're supposed to give the food to the older people first, but you're also feeling responsible for the younger ones. Whom to offer it to? At home, you're playing the role. Being good in your parents' eyes.

The person at school is independent, assertive. If you want something, you work for it. The emphasis is not on giving. Happiness comes out of getting. Whenever formal giving is part of school life—volunteering at hospitals, participating in charity fund-raisers—it is done with a sense of what one can get out of it. You participate in a walk-athon because you want the exercise. You volunteer so you can put it on your résumé.

Still, examples Anar gave of her experiences and perceptions, which grew out of her position as a person of Indian origin growing up in "white" America, were not unique. These were feelings and experiences I had heard before, and, to one degree or another, I was to hear them repeated by nearly everyone with whom I ultimately spoke. What was intriguing to me was the particularly psychological interpretation Anar gave to her experiences. What was it that made her feel like two different people as opposed to one person acting differently in different situations?

Intrigued by her story, I asked Anar and her family to participate in my study. The following excerpts from my conversations with the Nagars begin with Vaidehi's childhood memories, marriage, and immigration to the United States. Later come the girls' lives and the concerns and inter-actions that have dominated the family's recent past.

In this family's story, talk about relationships deserves special atten-tion. Vaidehi often explains her behavior in terms of model social relation-ships. Husbands and wives, children and parents should be attuned to the nature of their relationships and behave accordingly. Vaidehi says she began looking for work to be helpful to her husband. She tried to behave with her in-laws as if they were her own parents. She feels bad when her daugh-ters constantly ask why they should do something Vaidehi has requested. This, she feels, indicates a lack of trust, a key component of children's proper attitude toward parents. In the same vein, Anar equivocates about whether behavior results from the roles entailed by certain relationships—

the roles of daughter, mother, sister—or just from the "kind of person" one is. Although her conclusions differ from her mother's, Anar's *attention* to social roles is a legacy of the example provided by Vaidehi. This family, then, illustrates one component of the intergenerational process of assimilation: Parents can have a strong influence on the way their children "think"—not in terms of shaping their children's opinions (although this undoubtedly happens as well) but in terms of shaping the way children interpret their experiences.

Although Anar owes much to her mother, she also feels compelled to interpret her experiences through a different lens from the one her mom provides. In emphasizing the "kind of person" one is, independent of the social roles one fulfills, Anar combines a sensitivity to the content of one's character with a concern for the character of social roles. This interplay between the two sets of motives or explanations for behavior is the key to Anar's construction of her identity. She is both like her mother and different. The play of similarities and contrasts is a second feature of the social process of assimilation, evident as one constructs one's identity *in relation to* the people who surround one.

Just as Anar carves out an identity for herself by positioning herself in contrast to her mother, the family as a whole, through its particular idiom, both partakes of the standard community rhetoric of "adjustment problems" and develops some unique models that define this family as a special case vis-à-vis the standard Indian experience. Both individuals within the family and the family as a whole stake out an identity in relation to others who populate the social environment.

The first floor, the public space, in the Nagars' house is an L-shaped area consisting of living room, dining area, kitchen, and family room. The interior arrangement of space reflects the family members' struggle to come to terms with being Indian, being American, and living in America. The front door opens directly onto the living room, which is furnished tastefully with a sofa, a love seat, and an overstuffed chair. There are framed pictures of Vaidehi and her late husband, Raghav, on the end tables. Alongside Raghav's picture is a small picture of the two girls which they gave to him one Father's Day. On some occasions when I visited, Raghav's picture was draped with flowers.[1]

The dining area is set up in the back half of the living-room space. This combined living and dining space is separated by a wall and an open doorway from the kitchen. In the living and dining area, there is not much to remind one that the occupants of this house are of Indian origin, only a small model of the Taj Mahal on top of the china cabinet. The first time I visited, there was a Christmas tree in the living room decorated with garland, ornaments, and star.

In the kitchen and family room area, however, the Indian presence in the household is very apparent. In the kitchen itself, there is a small countertop temple. A large *tulsi* plant—a plant that is considered holy and adorns most yards in the family's native Gujarat—grows vigorously in the corner. The family occasionally nibbles on the minty leaves to preserve their good health. The family room furniture is all of a wooden Indian-style set, brightly painted with geometric designs. A picture of Krishna playing the flute accompanied by dancing *gopis* hangs above the stereo.[2]

According to the younger daughter, Mausami, friends and relatives usually are entertained in the family room. The living room is used only for formal guests. The first time I went to the house to interview Vaidehi, Anar was away at college. Mausami answered the door and invited me to sit in the living room. Her mother was upstairs resting. In a few minutes, Vaidehi came down the stairs. Her entrance was very impressive. She wore a plain, full, peach-colored cotton sari. Her hair was drawn back in a traditional bun, and she wore a small *bindi* on her forehead.[3] She moved slowly and elegantly. She is a soft-spoken woman, very calm. She began her story in gentle and deliberate English.

> I was born in India. My father was a civil engineer. He started with entry-level position, then he went up to chief engineer for Gujarat state. He was working hard, and people respected him. My mother was a housewife.
>
> As a matter of fact, one funny incident I remember my father told me. Once a year, we had a religious ceremony for Lord Shiva to celebrate the day Lord Shiva and Parvathi got married. So all little kids ride on horses and buggies. People dress up all pretty. My father had a cart with two pedals, and he was riding it. All the ladies were walking behind him. And my mother was five years younger than him, so her mother was carrying her. Then someone told my mother (my grandmother and my father's mother also, they were walking together), since she was carrying my mother, she saw that there was room for one person in my father's cart. So they put my mother in it. She was riding for a while with my father.
>
> My father was older, and he could understand what people are talking about. When he came home, he was sleeping in his mother's lap, and mother and father were talking. After a while, they thought my father was already asleep, so they were thinking, "How did it look when both of them were riding together? How about if it happens that when they grow up, we can ask if they can get married?"
>
> Finally, after so many years, it did happen. So it was kind of surprising that how can this work out? Of course, it was not because of that incident it happened. It's just what happened. My mother's parents asked his parents if they were interested. Then they just match horoscopes, and if they match well, they go ahead and arrange the marriage.
>
> Growing up, I remember I was a little crying baby. If anybody would tease me, I would take it very serious. I was very sensitive. So I remember that. Very sensitive.

When I was in school, I was interested in dancing. From fifth grade, I just started *bharata natyam* classes.[4] My father and mother were both coming to watch my dances in school whenever there was a performance. My principal knew my father very well. So he was often inviting him, you know, when I was dancing. I felt very good. And my mother was also interested in me wearing different saris of hers. My sisters were dressing me up. Doing my hair.

I passed high school and then went for college. I graduated in psychology, and then I started my master of arts in psychology, but I didn't complete it. Just did six months. I got engaged when I was seventeen. Seventeen.

It was beautiful. We got engaged in '66. My husband and his family were living in a different town. From some relative, my parents knew about him. He was doing bachelor's of engineering. They knew that he was a good student. He was very good student. And there were only two kids in his family. He was a very good student. And he was handsome. So they thought this will be a good match.

But before they would decide for engagement, they wanted us to see each other, too. They didn't tell me that this is the reason why we are going to their house. We just went somewhere, and on our way back, they said, "Let's stop by. They live right here." So we stopped by their house. He was there, too. He knew at that time, but I didn't. And I didn't even think that it could be this reason. Because I had two older sisters and one older brother, and none of them were engaged at that time. We went to his house, and we just had general talk at that time. Then, after I came to my house, my mother asked me the next morning, "How did you like him? If you are interested in him, we can . . ." Same way, the horoscope. "If you are interested, we can do that. Otherwise, we won't even talk about it." I didn't say yes or no, but I think it was like if you didn't say anything, but by your behavior, by your reaction, you would find out whether it is yes or no. So then they did ask for his horoscope. Luckily, they matched.

After that, also we met. We did go out for a few times. Then Mother asked me, and his parents also asked him, if we are ready to get engaged or would we like to go for that. We got engaged in '66. I was seventeen. Six months later, he came here, in United States, to study.

See, even in India, I haven't heard of anybody doing that. I mean, nobody talks about that kind of thing. But we had a very romantic time in our engagement. He was writing me a letter every single day. I was answering, but I wasn't as regular as he was. Two or three times a week, I was writing him. And my mother and father, my whole family was happy with how I was going with my engagement.

Then he came back in October '69, after he got his M.S. in industrial engineering. In '70, February, we got married.

After our marriage, I was pregnant almost right away, and I had

Anar within ten months. In India, also there is a custom that when first baby is going to be born, you go home to your family. So when I was about seven months pregnant, we came to my parents' house. After Anar was born, I stayed until Anar was five months old.

But when Anar was two months old, my husband came back here for further study and better job. Because in India, he didn't feel it was that advanced. So he thought, "At this time, good to go back." After marriage, I could go with him, too. So we decided to live here for a few years. Then, later on, we would come back to India.

But first ten months [i.e., after Anar was born] were very hard. I mean, first time, when we were engaged, he was also here, but at that time I was studying. So mentally we were prepared for that. Even though we are apart, we don't like to live without each other, we don't get to see each other, but we knew that we cannot live together. But after marriage, when I had to live there, it was hard. And Anar was also little, and so I had to raise . . . I was living a few days at my parents' house, few days at his parents' house. Both parents would like to enjoy the grandchild.

But after ten months, I came here. I was more than happy to come here, 'cause he was here. And in the beginning, it was just totally new. Every day, when I was walking on this ground, I was feeling like I'm somewhere. Like a different planet. I didn't know anything about outside the apartment. Even in that apartment, I didn't know much about how things run. But one thing I had in my mind, that this is where I wanted to come, because that's where my husband is and I wanted to come to him. So now we're going to make it go as good as we want to. But in the beginning, it's all like that, you have to learn to get adjusted. And I was a student of psychology. I had prepared my mind.

So did you have much contact with other Indians, or with other people?

In the beginning, not that much contact. We did have a neighbor who was an Indian. They had also a boy, little boy, as old as Anar. They also came, I mean she, his wife also came from India just about the same time when I did. So both of us were new. But when we came here, we came in December, so it was very cold. We were not going out that much. But in summertime, we were going toward the lake, take kids to play in the playground. There was a school nearby, so they can play in the summertime. Every afternoon, almost every afternoon, we were getting together.

And then, some of my husband's friends, we were meeting and eating, on the weekends. We were going to their house. We were inviting them over.

Did you have much contact with Americans at that time?

Not that much. We knew couple of families, American families. They were working at my husband's work in the factory. They were older ladies. My husband was taking the time study, and they were best workers, so he knew them more than other employees. They liked him very much.

After I came, they invited us to their house. One lady said, "I had a son." She was working in army when she was young. She was an officer. And she had a son. He would have been Raghav's age if he was alive. So that's how she . . . just think that this is my son. The other woman also, she liked him. She did have kids, and they were living with her, too, but they were not so close to her. Attached so much. Raghav's behavior was very gentle with all the employees. She would say that "I wish my kids were like him." So both of them had that kind of feeling.

Did you have any particular impressions in general of American culture at that time?

I didn't have any. I liked to know more American people, because whenever I came in contact with them, they were very nice. Maybe my major problem was communication. I was not communicating as much as I wish I was. I wasn't very fluent. And also I was very shy and reserved. I wasn't very outspoken. Just wouldn't go out and make friends.

Anar was in day care when she was two. So I was by myself. I was not feeling very good. Of course, my main idea to let her go to day-care center was she would learn this English language. Plus, she could be with other children so she can be in this society. And, of course, she would know to share, whole thing, with others. Because otherwise, she was very possessive.

And if she would go to school, I could work. That way, I can be helpful to my husband. Financially, we would have more. In the beginning, Anar was going to school part-time. After a while, she got more adjusted, and she started going full-time. After she started that, I started looking for work.*

In the beginning, I found first job in the factory. And I was happy that I got the job. But the work wasn't very . . . I wasn't very happy

---

* In Vaidehi's portrayal of her life to this point, we see over and over that she describes it with reference to a series of social relationships. Her description of her parents is dominated by the story of how their casual childhood contact becomes a marriage. Vaidehi as a young girl sees her father's, mother's, and sisters' interest in her dancing as a memorable aspect of that experience, rather than just the fact of her dancing or her own personal enjoyment of the physical experience. Her courtship, her marriage, and the birth of her daughter create yet another layer in the webs of relationships that surround her. Raghav's relations with co-workers are akin to those of family.

When she begins to discuss her life in America, one senses a feeling of discomfort and isolation. Social relationships figure much less prominently in her description of her experiences. In the following description of her efforts to find a job, Vaidehi for the first time seems on her own. However, while the experience itself no longer involves contributions of significant others in her life, Vaidehi interprets the entire work episode as a service to her family.

with working environment. And I should have expected—because in a factory. I just worked there for three days. I couldn't take it. Two days I worked, and I told my husband, "I don't like this." He said, "Don't worry about it. You don't have to work."

When I came from India, I never thought of working. But after I came here, I saw a lot of ladies working, and my idea was that I always wanted to be helpful to my family. So I thought if I can use my knowledge, it would be good if I can. And if I didn't like that work, he said, "You can look for other job."

I think third day I looked for a job, and I found a job, it was surgical needles. Over there, I worked for about eight months. It was nice. You could learn something how to sharpen needles and how to take care of them. This kind of delicate job. But I still felt I should be able to do better than this. I was not able to use my education, and what I wanted to do was to work with other people. One day, one of those ladies that was working with Raghav, she had a sister working at a bank—sister-in-law was working at a bank. So she said, "I'll talk to my sister-in-law, she can find a job for you there. A graduate in psychology should be able to do something." And then she did, and she referred to me to the bank. And I went and got a job there. It was entry-level position, but that's how I started. In six months, I got promotion. And then, in two years, I got another job there, too. With the bank, I was very happy.

In '76, we had to go to India.* We decided to go there for good. It was like parents were not very happy. They were getting older, his parents. And he was the only son, and he felt that he owes his responsibility to his parents in their old age. But in eight months, we decided to come back. It was very frustrating. First four months, he didn't find a job there. Then he found a job, and it was very hard to go from the town where we were living to another town. It was rush rush rush all the time. He was coming home about seven-thirty. After change clothes and take bath and get ready, we'd eat dinner. But then half an hour, just sitting there, he would fall asleep. It was very tiring, and even then he was not very much satisfied with his work. He didn't feel he would do as well as he would do here in those years. So he still thought that, you know, he was still young, and if we did love to live in India, but at the same time, if he was interested in his personal advancement, too, that didn't have a chance in India. In '77, we came here.

What about his parents?

His parents, well, they were not very happy that we had to come back here, but they could see him frustrated all the time. They realized that

---

* While this change of topic may seem rather abrupt, it occurred as it is recorded here. With no intervention from me, Vaidehi switched suddenly from her story about her work life to the episode of the family's return to India. This dramatic return, once again, to discuss the way various social relationships govern the flow of life provided further evidence that this was indeed the idiom of expression most comfortable for Vaidehi.

he was working for the family, not only for himself. But still they did see him getting frustrated so much about not getting good job and like so much hardship going back and forth to work. And they were getting old, but they were not in bad shape. Physically, they were still able to work. They were not totally dependent. Even though they were not happy to be apart from us, but still they agreed okay. And we came here.

After coming here the second time, we were doing very good. Within a year, we had a baby.

Anar has some vague memories of her brief residence in India. She remembers feeling distant from her own parents. For the first time, she didn't sleep with them. In India, she slept in one room with her grandparents and aunt. Her parents slept in another room. She remembers spending a lot more time with her grandparents than with her parents. Her mother was always in the kitchen. Her grandfather would pick her up from school, and she would have to do her homework as he sat and watched.

She remembers going with her mother to visit her mother's parents in Ahmedabad, the state capital. That was a real treat, both because she got to spend time with her mother and because her mother's parents gave her special treatment. Life with her father's parents was very routine—get up, go to school, do homework, go to bed.

Upon the family's return to America, Anar remembers being happy to be back, happy to sit on a toilet, happy to be able to go to the refrigerator to get a glass of soda when she felt like it. She remembers her sister being born and feeling happy that there would be someone else around. She says she also got fat because she and her mom were home eating all the time.

The next major change for the Nagars came in 1983, when Raghav's parents moved from India to the United States to live with their son and his family. Raghav's parents lived with the Nagars from 1983 to 1988 (Raghav died in 1984). The presence of their grandparents exposed the two girls to dimensions of family life that were new and sometimes distressing.

Anar, age thirteen when her grandparents arrived, remembers the changes in family life before her father's death:

> Especially with my grandparents, and in the way my parents dealt with them. Things that I never thought they'd do, once my grandparents were here, they'd start doing. Like before my grandparents arrived, I don't think we'd ever say a prayer before dinner. But once they were here, we'd start doing all these prayers, going to the temple a lot more often. It just seemed like it was a lot more Indian after . . . not that it wasn't before, but it was even more once they were here.
>
> Another thing that I remember is they'd always get me to learn how to be a good, you know, a good girl. Whatever that was. Like it was really important that I made tea for them. But my parents were never really like that. My mom was not like that.

She didn't care whether you made tea for her?

No.

But when your grandparents were here, she made tea for them?

Yeah. She made tea for them, and like I'd come home from school, and this was a big thing. I was supposed to make tea for them.

Do you remember feeling anything about that? You seemed to think it was sort of strange, you had this look on your face.

I was annoyed. I might be covering up with feelings I have about that now, but, just like, "Why do I have to do all this?" It wouldn't make any sense to me. Especially like when they were, I don't think this ever really happened, except for my uncle, but like, the women and the men and their roles, and how like my uncle would never have to do anything. And I was always expected, and if I didn't, I was scolded or whatever.

That never happened before my grandparents came. But I can't imagine a situation where it could have happened, because it was just me. I was pretty much the only child when my sister was born. I guess when things like that happened, my mom would take care of it. So I would always assume it was just her, and that's why she's doing it. If there were people who had to be served, or like the men would be outside and the women would be in the kitchen, and I always thought that was just the way it was in her situation.

Her grandparents' presence also contributed to Anar's "two worlds" moving farther apart. Anar said that throughout her childhood, she felt it was a strain to have her friends visit. There were certain subjects she felt she and her friends couldn't discuss in front of her parents (boys, for example), and she felt uncomfortable about having to explain to her friends why this was the case. Her grandparents' presence exacerbated Anar's embarrassment about having her friends over. Her friends were "too curious" about her grandparents, who always dressed traditionally, her grandfather in a dhoti and her grandmother in a sari.[5] I asked if her mother's sari also made her uncomfortable. No, she said, that was somehow different. Her grandparents were just too much of a spectacle: "They made a scene wherever they went."

Mausami's memories of her grandparents focus more on the period after her father's death. Since her grandparents' departure in 1988 and her sister's departure for college in 1989, Mausami has managed much of her own time before and after school. She says she occasionally gets lonely, but overall she seems comfortable with and appreciative of the responsibility and independence. This contrasts to the period before 1988, when her grandparents were still living with Vaidehi and the girls.

They were always sleeping. If I was watching TV and I'd put it up a bit . . . my grandmother, she's like, "I can hear that. I can hear that."

I have to be really especially quiet. I can't go upstairs and jump around if I wanted to, you know, they're always sleeping.

And I couldn't talk on the phone when they were around. Now, when I'm home alone, if I need to call somebody, if I need to do my homework, I can do it. I don't have to worry about, "Oh, my grandparents are here."

When they were around, we were constantly doing whatever they wanted to do. We ate at like nine o'clock. And now we eat at five-thirty. So it's really different. If my mom comes home late, then we can eat at six o'clock. But not nine at night.

They were just always annoyed with me. And I didn't know what I did. I was in the fourth grade! I mean, how can they expect me to be perfect? And they had these high expectations of me. "Be like your father. Be like your father." You know, "Your dad wouldn't do this." Everything's not the same here as it was when he was growing up.

Both daughters see their grandparents' presence affecting the behavioral patterns of the family in general and their own behavior in particular. Vaidehi sees these behavioral changes as well but goes further to suggest that Raghav's parents' influence on the family was shaped by their changed view of their relationships with Vaidehi and the girls after Raghav's death.

I was happy to have them here, because originally in my mind, I thought, "Whatever is my husband's is mine. They are my parents." And I wanted to make them very happy living here with us. With my husband, I think we enjoyed being all together.

In June '84, my husband passed away. So it was not that long time that we had to be together. As far as I'm concerned, I was doing as good [after Raghav's death] as I was doing before. But I think in their mind, the way to take it was changed, because he wasn't there. They feel that now the relation is not the same anymore. Like they are living with me rather than they are living with their son. And that's why it didn't work out that well. I'm very unhappy about it, but I think that's how it is going to be now.

How do you think that having their grandparents here affected your daughters?

I think they didn't like that that much. Mainly after my husband passed away, it really made very bad effect on them. Whenever they [her in-laws] were going away, like to my sister-in-law's house, they would go there for a weekend. As soon as they would leave, the kids would jump up and down. It looked like free birds. I was happy to see them being happy, but then at the same time feeling sad that this is not how that relationship with grandparents and kids . . .

They were very conservative. I could remember so many times that after my husband died . . . in India, there's a custom that for a year, especially husband's wife cannot even go out of the house, for one year.

Stop celebrating everything. I could understand that celebration just comes out of your heart . . . but then it was like forced upon you—that doesn't have good effect on people's minds. As time was going by, I was trying to lighten up the situation. It was not that I was happy, but in their mind within the first year you cannot do anything. You cannot go out. You cannot invite people. Even if someone comes, you are supposed to cry.

After a while, I was taking kids to McDonald's. Before we used to go every Friday to McDonald's. I would ask them, "Would you like to come?" Then they would talk so much, like you are not . . . and that's the way they would talk—so bad. I would let them talk. I have been student of psychology, so I knew—just let them talk. I wouldn't even go away from that. Mostly, they were doing like that at dinnertime. I would just sit there and let them talk. They would talk so much. Not very happy talk between parents and daughter-in-law.

Now the first Christmas came, six months later. Mausami was just six years old. She would feel that if Santa doesn't come, or doesn't leave a gift, that means that I'm not a good kid. So I didn't want her to feel that way. So I thought, happiness was not there in my heart, but I still wanted to keep the feelings in her heart alive that she was a good girl. So I said, "Mausami, this year we will not decorate our house, but if you be a good girl, I'm sure Santa will come and leave you something." So I bought her a gift. I bought Anar a gift also. And then for my father and mother-in-law, also I wrapped a gift.

Now, I could see that they didn't like that. But then, in the morning, I told them that we're going to open the gifts. I asked them that, "You have to come and sit and open the gifts." I mean, by their reaction, I could see that they didn't like it, but they sat down and they opened. What they found they really loved it, because both of them had picture frames with my husband's picture in it. So I think they liked the gift. They had no reason to say that, "Why did you give us such a gift? This was not day to give and take gifts from each other." For kids, I gave something kids would like; for them, I didn't give something they would normally enjoy. I just gave them the ideal gift. At that time, they needed that. So I think that was all right for that time.

But then, next day, we had to go for India. I stayed there for couple of months, with my parents. I had long talks with my parents, and it was nice.

I was talking about how my in-laws were treating me. I told him that I realized that it is true that they have lost their son, but it is not right to behave with me as if I am criminal. They behaved with me like that. Like I killed their son. And couple of times, I think they were talking behind my back. I didn't know, but Mausami listened. They probably were thinking that Mausami is too little to understand. But I think she did. Whenever I was going to work, and I was telling that this is where I am going, I'll be back by this time. That day, they said,

"I wonder why this early she is going out? Probably she is going to see someone." It was seven in the morning. Usually, I was starting at eight. That day, I had to work extra, so I went early. So Mausami says, "Mommy, Baja and Baji were saying that you probably went to see someone." That hurt me.

When your daughters would get upset during this period, what kind of advice did you give them in terms of what they should do?

I was glad that they were not talking back. They were feeling very bad about it, but they were not talking back to them. That was good about them. And I was also saying to them, "Let them talk. Let them take their anger out. I know how much we are hurt. So we don't have to show them by measurement that this is how much we miss him, how much we are hurt. But let them talk." And that could be with anybody. Anybody in the world can think of you some way, but if you know in your heart that this is right, what can you do about it? If you are wrong, at that time you may want to correct it. And if you are right, no matter how much everybody's going to say, you are going to remain right. I was telling them just to keep calm. And whenever they are not here, and if they are enjoying, just enjoy. But they are our parents, so we cannot just tell them, "Go out. We don't want to have you anymore." Because that is like if Raghav was with us, how would he feel if we asked them to move? They were his parents. And I mean, as a soul, he is still with us. So, like anybody, if they're your parents, you don't want to leave them. As I told you before that I was trying to live with them just like their daughter. And I was trying to treat them as if they're my parents. We cannot just tell them, "Don't live here" or "don't say that." They are raised a certain way, so we cannot teach them. We have to let them do whatever they do, unless it is too much harmful to us. We will live the way we are doing. Still, of course, if they were living happily with us, it would have been more fun.

These last comments suggest how a sensitivity to the proper behavior associated with particular social roles was transferred from Vaidehi to her children. The difficulties the family faced after Raghav's death presented an occasion for the discussion of familial roles, an occasion for Vaidehi to instruct her daughters. In the girls' recollections of events, they tend to focus on the inconveniences their grandparents' presence entailed. Anar remembers the embarrassment she felt at her grandparents' dress and appearance. Mausami remembers having to be quiet and having to eat dinner at an uncomfortably late hour for a small child. However, the girls do share with their mother an analysis of their "grandparent problems" in terms of familial roles and dynamics—what their grandparents were expecting of them, in terms of behavior and demeanor, and how they felt about fulfilling those expectations. It was this particular gloss in both mother's and children's construction of their experiences with grandparents that first alerted me to the importance of social roles for the Nagar family. It was only in retrospect than I began to see this idiom in Vaidehi's interpretation of events in general.

My sense that interpersonal dynamics are a central concern for the Nagar family was strengthened by my conversations with Anar concerning some of the more concrete behavioral issues that arose during her early adolescence. In addition to negotiating what one is and is not allowed to do, which seems to be an adolescent issue in all families, Anar's description of the process of negotiating behavioral limits with her parents is unusually sensitive to the management of interactive dynamics. How should you speak to someone? What can you speak about? What styles of communication are appropriate?

Anar knew her parents disapproved of her curling her hair, wearing makeup, and going to school dances. I asked her how she came to know that these things were taboo.

> I guess . . . two things. It was implicit sometimes. Just the way they talked about what they felt was beautiful, or attractive. Like with my hair. They thought the most beautiful hair was just long and straight, and parted in the middle, you know. I couldn't do that. I didn't like it. But that was still the most beautiful thing to them. Every time I would talk about getting my hair cut or pointing out a hairstyle that I liked, they'd be like, "That's not pretty!" And things like, "We're the ones that have to look at you. It doesn't matter what you think is attractive, we're the ones who have to look at you." I constantly got the message that what I'm seeing as attractive or fashionable is not what they think is okay.
>
> And it wasn't just my mother and father. It was aunts and uncles, too. Just things like, "Oh, it used to be so nice when it was just long and straight, when you were three years old. Ever since you started cutting it, it just doesn't look as nice." It was pretty traumatizing sometimes.
>
> And then, like explicit things. They would take my curling iron away. Or they wouldn't let me buy hair spray. So I'd end up taking my makeup to school or curling my hair at someone else's house. Just so I wouldn't have to cause tension in the house and still get away with what I wanted.

What do you remember about the issue of going to dances and parties?

Well, I could never talk about that. Sometimes when I did mention it, it was always really looked down upon. Or they would talk about other teenagers. Like they were spoiled or something. I remember once, we were at someone's house, and the daughter walked in with her friend. She was probably like sixteen or something, and she said, "Okay, Mom, John's picking me up at so-and-so, such-and-such time." And she went upstairs to take a shower or something. And the whole way back, that's all they talked about. How can she go out with an American boy? And she was going to dances, how that was so bad and how she was so corrupt, and how could her parents let her get away with this?

In terms of more general values you were discussing last time, like respect for elders, the importance of family, how was it that those values were taught to you?

I'd say it was really subtle. I can remember things like going to India and always having to, like, you know, bow down to people, and I never quite understood that. But it was something you just do. So I started doing that all the time. It wasn't only respect for elders all the time, but even respect for people who were younger than you. So all the time, I learned that you're supposed to sacrifice yourself. You know, so if you have something to eat, you should always offer it to people that are younger than you first. But if you're supposed to serve, you should always serve your elders first. Things like that. So, I guess in the way I was supposed to act, I kind of figured it out.

Just as she struggled to find a way to please both her parents and herself with her actions concerning the typical teenage issues of hair, makeup, and boys, Anar has struggled to find a way of managing interpersonal relations that is comfortable for her.

I think I get away with things that I would never get away with when my grandparents were here. Like if I was sitting in the family room, and I'm like, "Mom, can you bring me a glass of water?" That would never happen, you know, I would never even think of asking her to bring me anything. Because she's older, and she shouldn't do that. She's not playing the role of a mother and I'm the daughter who's supposed to kind of take care of, or, you know, do all the chores while the mother sits and rests.

She should say, "No, you should get it yourself." But she's just a considerate person. That's her personality, and she'll want to help out anybody she can.

You see that as being a departure from the Indian style?

Yeah. Just like when my sister asks me to get something for her, I feel really strange about that. I'm like, "You can't ask me to get you something. You're younger than me." What the heck am I doing?! 'Cause I feel comfortable for my mom to bring me things, but I don't feel comfortable bringing things to my sister. But I'll do it anyway, just 'cause, 'cause this whole guilt thing . . . but yeah, there's something that's telling me that that's the way it's supposed to be.

How do you feel when you get together with the male relatives?

Yeah, really yuck. I don't like it at all. My uncle sitting out here and being like, "Bring me this." Or after dinner, just getting up and leaving—I hate that. There's something about Indian men that really repulses me [laughing]. I definitely feel that.

Like I was in India, and I have another cousin who's four years younger than me. I was in the kitchen, by the sink or something, and he was by the refrigerator, and my aunt—his mother—told me to get some water for my uncle. And so I told my cousin, 'cause he was right there by the refrigerator, "You give it to your dad," or whatever. And she looks at me. "No, I told you." I'm like, "He's standing right there." And she said, "No, I asked you to do it." I'm like, "What difference does it make who does it?" She's like, "You're the girl." She explicitly said that. And it was just like, "Oh! I'm not doing it. If he wants water, he can do it himself! I'm not going to do that." And then she just got mad at me. I don't remember if I got it or not, but I remember telling my mom, and how my aunt was so awful, and how she wouldn't tell her own son but she'd tell me. And he was standing closer to the refrigerator.

Did your mother ever try to explain why that is, or explain where they're coming from?

She doesn't agree with it.

Oh, she doesn't?

No.

But you said when the male relatives are here, she'll play that role.

But I don't know if she does that because she's just a nice person, or she feels like they're a guest in her house, or I don't even know exactly why. But I know she doesn't agree with that. 'Cause she said, you know, "That's not right. She shouldn't be doing that." But she said, "Just don't get too upset about it, because that's the way some people think. You're only here for a short time." So I feel like she supports that that's not right. But she doesn't support me yelling at my aunt, who's older than me [laughing].

Later, I asked Vaidehi about the incident with the glass of water. Her answer reveals her own negotiation between what she feels in her heart is right and the demands of social interaction that for her, at least on some occasions, legitimately separate one's feelings from one's actions.

I didn't like the way she behaved. I said, "Anar, she was wrong. But I wouldn't make her my enemy from this moment. Let her behave the way she is behaving. We know that that is not right. I'm not going to do that to anybody. Whether you are my own kids or any other two kids, I'm not going to behave as if male is dominant and female inferior. I don't believe in that. So I'm not going to behave that way. But if some people are behaving, I'm not going to fight with each individual that what you are doing is wrong." If at that time I was present,

I may have commented to my cousin that it is not something right you are doing, but in general, I don't want to fight with individuals because everybody has different ideas. And let them behave the way they do. Of course, it would make you feel bad. Especially these kids, it made them feel very bad. I probably, if I was there at that time, I don't think she would have even done that.

In India, people have been raised that way, that men are the dominant, and all the ladies are supposed to work. So after men eat, they just leave their dishes and go out, and ladies finish the cleaning up. My brother-in-law just walks out, and my sister-in-law, she wouldn't mind, either. I think maybe she minds, but in front of everyone, she doesn't want to talk to her husband nasty way like, "Why are you doing like that?" She probably would tell him at her house. But I don't think that at her house she might be doing that, either, or else he wouldn't . . .

So do you ever say anything? When that happens?

No. 'Cause they don't come every day. And I don't like to make fight about that. But at that time, I don't ask kids to do that. "Anar, now would you take everything away? He is done now. Would you do it?" I just would do whatever I can do myself. And if anybody sees me working would want to help, they help. They're not living here forever, right? If one or two hours, if they are coming, and they behave certain way, just let it go, 'cause you cannot change each person's life. Just enjoy their company. Whatever they have good, enjoy.

We are beginning to see, in both Anar's and Vaidehi's recollections, a refinement of the issue of social roles. It is not just that social relationships blanket one's interpretation of events, as was the case in Vaidehi's stories about her background and childhood. It is not just that one needs to be aware of and conform to the proper behavior associated with different social roles, as in the Nagars' attempts to be a good daughter-in-law and good grandchildren. A sensitivity to social relationships and social roles also introduces a tension between duty and heart, between the behavior associated with particular social roles and the behavior stemming from universalistic moral precepts that transcend particular social roles. Vaidehi resolves this dilemma by arguing that her heart remains her heart, regardless of what behaviors particular social roles might require her to perform. One may do one's duty but remain faithful in one's heart.

The persistent focus on social relationships and roles and the duty/heart issue constitute the core of the Nagars' peculiar idiom. This idiom influences not only family members' understanding of relationships with people outside the nuclear group but also their take on internal family relationships. What follows concerns the relationships between the girls and their mother and the differences family members perceive between the two girls. In addition to continuing the focus on social roles and appropriate behav-

ior, this section introduces a prominent feature of the adjustment process in general: the construction of identities through differentiation.

In the passage below, Anar begins to describe herself and her beliefs using her mom as a point of contrast. In her younger years, Anar's strategy
to avoid conflict with her parents was simply not to communicate with
them. Nowadays, she is trying, quite consciously, to transform her relationship with her mother by openly communicating about her differences
of opinion. That does not mean, however, that the relationships between
mother and daughter is becoming more oppositional. In fact, the next
passages illustrate that the relationship is perhaps less oppositional than
it was in earlier years, when Anar separated herself from her parents. Instead, the newer relationship is based on a mutuality of exchange, which,
although it brings differences into sharper relief, also facilitates a stronger connection. As Anar articulates her own identity in relation to her
mother, the relationship itself becomes a focal point, drawing mother and
daughter more firmly into an interdependent system of familial identities.

> I think I just decided that somewhere down the line, maybe it was
> when I was leaving for college, she needs to know. Because, I mean,
> how much am I going to hide it? I'll give you like a really recent ex-
> ample. My friend Dave wanted to come down and spend three days
> here. She's like, "Uh, no." I'm like, "Why not?" You know, she's like,
> "Well, you two would be here alone when Mausami and I aren't
> home." And I'm just like, "Mom, I mean, I see him all the time at
> school. You're never around. He comes into my apartment."
>   Then she just gave me the look, like, whoa. And then the next day
> she's like, "He comes over to your apartment? No, that's not right."
> "What's not right about it? He's one of my friends." She's like, "No,
> that's not right. Things can happen." I'm like, "Mom, if things are
> going to happen, they're going to happen."
>   I would never say anything like that. I mean, you just don't say
> that. But then I'm not interested in him, and I'm trying to explain
> everything to her. And then I ended up saying something like, "I under-
> stand that you feel that way, but I don't agree." And that just ended
> it right there. That was like the first time I took my stand, different
> than hers. But I feel like I'm growing up, and she needs to know me,
> that I don't agree with everything. 'Cause she's just going to get hurt
> later on.
>   So, I guess that that was pretty much it. I was sick of, like, lead-
> ing this double life, you know. I'm trying to develop a solid view of
> who I am, and to constantly, like, say one thing and do the other, or
> hide. I was like, "I'm twenty years old. I'm sick of this."

Vaidehi recognizes this new openness with her elder daughter.

Have you seen any changes in Anar since she went away to college?

I would say yes. And that is also natural, I think. Because she's away from home, so when she comes here, she doesn't want to behave the same way as Mausami. Mausami and I can have so many arguments, more often than Anar and I can have now. I and Anar, we argued more before, but not as many now. But I think we are more open now than before.

Like she likes to know, "Mommy, what do you think about this? Give me your ideas." And she would listen to me. Of course, she would tell her ideas also, but now she is asking more, "What do you think about this?" Or sometimes without her asking me, I just tell her that that's the way I think, and "I shouldn't feel it went by without me letting you know. I don't want to see you hurt because of that. It's up to you how to behave, but it was my responsibility to make you aware of that. That's how I feel, and if you like to consider, that's up to you." And she does consider that.

Do you think she's becoming more open with you about how she feels about things?

Yeah. I feel that she's much more open. As open as I am with her. I feel good when she says, "Mom, I can't sleep, I want to come over and sleep next to you." It makes her feel good to be with Mom. And when she is there [at college] and she cannot sleep, she calls me. And I talk to her for a while, and I tell her, "We are together. Tell me anything. I can help. I always like to help. If we cannot do anything about it, what can we do? So just pray for the best." So after she talks to me, she does let me know that, "Mom, it feels really good."*

While Anar's openness with her mother is a recent development, she sees her younger sister being more open at an earlier age. Subjects like boys are still sources of deep disagreements between mother and daughters, but in Mausami's case, Anar feels they are more openly discussed. But, at the same time, she feels that her sister has been more receptive to her mother's ideas, her Indian background, than she herself ever was.

I think my mom's influence is really strong in her. She's so stuck on, you know, "Mom feels this way, and I know it's going to be good in the long run." But that's really frustrating for me right now. And I don't know if it's just because she's incredibly mature for her age, or it's that she doesn't understand what my mom's trying to get across

---

* Note here that Vaidehi links this new openness between mother and daughter, one which clearly brings differences of opinion into sharper relief than they ever were before, with a continued closeness in the relationship. The intimate bond, evident in sharing a bed and late-night phone calls asking for advice, reassures Vaidehi that the new open communication does not threaten the mother-daughter bond. From Anar's point of view, this new openness enables her to feel more comfortable with a bond that was once a source of ambivalence. Once duty connected her to her parents, but heart drove a wedge between them. In beginning to be open about what's in her heart, Anar is finding that duty and heart may not be so incompatible after all.

to her. I don't know which one it is, but it seems like she has a really strong awareness of that. And she's very curious, too. Like my mom does *bharata natyam*. My sister took it for a while, but she'll sit there and watch my mom, and want her to explain everything to her. Whereas I'm just like, "Yeah, this is nice. I'm glad you're getting this exercise, Mom."

I feel like she does what I think I should be doing in a lot of ways. Just like in growing her hair. My mom said, "I want you to grow your hair. You can't cut it until you're thirteen, because I want your grandmother to see this." And she just does it, and has a little bit of trouble with it sometimes, but will still do it. Whereas I'd probably really make a big deal. I'd be like, "I'm not doing this. I'm going to cut it on my own." Which I did. I was like cutting my own hair, because I didn't want to grow it.*

In Mausami's description of her life with her mother, the sensitivity toward and appreciation of her mother and her mother's background is apparent.

On Friday night, my mom and I spend time together. Like we'll go out clothes shopping together. Anything, just to do something together. 'Cause we're both so busy during the weekdays and stuff. It's just a time to relax, really. It's just like I feel closer to her, 'cause she's like always . . . with the phone, "You're on the phone, you're on the phone." Or, you know, "You haven't been spending time with me because you're doing your homework." You know, stuff like that. But, like, we're sitting on the couch, and it's like TGIF time. There's four shows that come on every Friday, and we watch those together. And then maybe we'll go out or something. I just feel like there is something between us, that I live here, and she sees me . . . that's what it feels like on weekdays. I'm home, I eat dinner really fast, and then I run upstairs and do my homework, you know. On Fridays, it just feels like we have a mother-daughter thing going. A lot of times, it feels like I just live here.

What kind of things do you talk about when you have conversations with your mother?

We talk about my dad a lot. She likes to talk about that. I feel comfortable with talking about him. We talk about, like, how she was. She likes to ask me how she was after the accident. She asks me "How were you?" and stuff. But I don't really remember. I just remember feeling so lost, like nobody told me. I didn't realize that he was gone until I was like seven. You know, it didn't click. I didn't really understand anything. Everybody was coming, visiting my mom. My sister was totally freaked out about everything. So I was just like a little person sitting in the

---

* Note the way Anar is using contrasts between her sister and herself, and similarities between her sister and mother as a way to work out the identities of family members.

corner, just not knowing what's going on, and just lived with it. And then finally, when we went to India, I went, "Oh, I get it."

She tells me when they met, when they were engaged and everything. She tells me things like that. How I was when I was a little kid. How he dealt with me. Stuff like that, about him . . .

You mentioned earlier going to the temple. Do you go to the temple sometimes?

Yeah. We go there a lot. For someone's birthday or when we feel like it. But I like it. It's just the time that I feel cultured. Sometimes I feel like, "Gosh, my mom knows so much about everything and when I'm going to be a parent, my kids are going to be so lost."*

Does she try to explain things to you?

Yeah, she explains a lot. Like on channel 26 every morning. [Half-hour episodes of a dramatization of the Indian classic *Ramayana* are broadcast daily.] She wakes me up. Well, it's good to wake up on days I have band, but . . . other times, I just feel like, "Can't we tape it?" But when I'm sitting there, I'm like, "Well, what does this mean?" And she'll explain it to me. So I think that with watching that, I'll be able to explain things. But I'm still concerned about when I'm a parent. What am I going to do? I won't know anything, you know. She knows stories, like little stories. I'll just know the basics, but she'll know, like, little inside stories, and she'll explain them to me. But that's my only worry, that what kind of parent am I going to be?

Mausami also perceives a difference between her own relationship with her mother and that of her sister.

We're different, a lot. She's . . . I don't know. We're just . . . our personalities are going to be different. I think it's just 'cause right now, my mom and I are spending so much time together, 'cause [Anar's] not here, you know, so I'm like an only child now. So it's kind of different that way, too. My mom is cooking things, you know. My sister, she can't cook. In her apartment, we ate out every night. [Mausami had just returned from a weekend visit to her sister.] And I'm like, "Oh, we could just make this." That way we're kind of different. I have a different background with my mom than she does. That way we're just totally different.

Here we see Mausami positioning herself in relation to her sister and her mother. Anar sees Mausami sharing more with their mother than she her-

---

* Here the contrasts Mausami draws between herself and her mother are moving us away from a focus on social relationships and toward a focus on Indianness. In addition to the particular concern the Nagar's have with social relationships (their idiom), their Indian heritage also plays a role in the construction of their individual and collective identities. In both cases however, speakers consistently negotiate these identities through the distinctions facilitated by references to similarity and contrast.

self does. Mausami sees herself as different from her sister, in terms of their relationships with their mom. Again and again, when family members talk about themselves, they show a sensitivity to social roles—daughter, mother, sister—both as abstract or reified roles that entail certain obligations and as very particular lived relationships that help each person to define herself in relation to others.

This tendency is evident as well in Vaidehi's assessment of her daughters. I asked Vaidehi if she felt there was any difference in the way she raised the two girls, to see if the differences the two girls perceived concerning their relationships with their mother were equally visible to Vaidehi.

> Pretty much the same. But sometimes to Mausami, I'll say, "When Anar-ben was little, she would do . . ." "But I'm not Anar." So it's kind of hard. Sometimes Anar also was thinking that, "You like Mausami better." But now Anar, when she sees Mausami, she says, "Mausami is good. I wasn't like that." So I say, "No Anar, you are also good." She says, "She knows a lot. Better cooking and behaves in a certain way. I wasn't doing anything." "Anar, that's all right. You weren't in the same situation. Right now, Mausami and I, only two of us are living here, so I have more chances to teach her how we ought to do, what we ought to do. And when you were at that age, my in-laws were with us. And it was also after Daddy died, minds were also not functioning same way. At that time, when there were more people in the house, we cannot just play with the food. I just wanted to finish at that time and get over with it. Rather than, right now, Mausami takes longer time to roll the rotis, it's okay. And if they're out of shape, that's all right, too." So I understand that I didn't have as much chance to teach Anar as Mausami.

As the Nagars discuss their relationships with one another, we see both the continuation of their family idiom (an intense focus on social relationships as a lens through which to interpret experience in general) and the use of comparison (attention to difference and similitude) as the mechanism through which individuals and the family as a whole construct their identities. There is a set of intersecting comparisons that position each family member in relation to others, but also a sense that the family as a whole has a certain character that differentiates it from "typical" Indians. Particularly in discussing relationships with relatives, Vaidehi and Anar come together in their assertions that their family doesn't believe in inherent inequalities between men and women. While other families will have different preoccupations and focus on comparisons of different features, this process of comparison is at the core of the process of assimilation. It allows people to create the identities that position them within their social worlds.

The next section of dialogue explores more directly what is Indian about the Nagars. While earlier sections focused on the nature of this family's idiom (which in part was seen, at least by Anar, as having roots in an Indian way of thinking) and the universal aspects of the process of adjustment, here the family addresses many of the "typical" issues that preoccupy Indian immigrant families. In their concern over these issues, their connection to the larger Indian community is forged.

The feelings the girls have developed concerning the parameters and potentialities of interpersonal dynamics have developed in the atmosphere Vaidehi has worked to create in their home. As Anar points out above, most of her sense of how one should behave has developed out of her exposure to the subtleties of behavior she has observed. From Vaidehi's perspective, she does try to create an atmosphere in which Indian culture and values are the guiding force. In the passage below, however, the difficulties Vaidehi has faced in creating this atmosphere are apparent. Of particular interest is the way in which "atmosphere" has not been equal to the task of socializing her children in America. The need to supplement atmosphere with explicit explanation (i.e., to answer the children's perennial "Why?") has been a struggle for Vaidehi, as it has for many Indian parents.

So tell me a little bit about what it's been like raising the children here.

It's a little hard because we don't get the atmosphere here. But we try to create atmosphere in the house, and try to attend other Indian community programs.

It's mainly, I would say, if it is a religious occasion, everybody around us is from the same religion, with the same background. So they all have the same kind of feeling that you would have. And when children are raised in India, you don't have to tell them that this is how we should do, or this is how we should behave. They just grow up in that atmosphere.

What's been important in creating that atmosphere around the house? American culture is there banging on your door all the time. How do you try to create that atmosphere in the house?

American culture doesn't bang on my door. Because they are going to school, where they are not going to learn anything from Indian culture or Indian religion. They don't have any idea about Indian culture and religion. I haven't been to American culture except at work, but I don't have any knowledge about Christian religion or this culture other than what they come home with—the songs and the stories. But, I mean, I don't have any rejection about what they learn, about American language. Only thing that I'm doing, I've also good meaning, so I want them to learn, too. I'm very happy with the way I have grown up with my religion and my culture.

Do you think that your daughters have the same feeling inside them that you have inside you? About your culture?

Not same, but they do have good feelings. Some of our cultural aspects they don't like. They're not, what to say, I think they just cannot justify, "How can this be done?" Like, I would say one thing, that they just respect elders more in India than kids do here. They argue a lot with parents. They say, "Why? But why?" I never was asking. Not that I was not smart to think "why," but just didn't argue with them. What they are saying to do, it's not going to hurt me, so must have good meaning. So I was just doing it.

These kids ask, "Why?" and I have to come up with some answer. Long time ago, it happened. That we respect money, goddess of wealth, and money shouldn't be under our foot. We shouldn't touch money with our foot. God we just don't touch with our foot. So once Anar bought shoes. They were called penny loafers. She just said, "Mommy, can I buy penny loafers? They are in fashion." I said okay. I didn't know. And then there were some holes on the side, and she said, "Now I'm going to put pennies in my shoes." So that is something, no. No. No. You cannot put money in your shoes. I said, "No, Anar, you can't put money in your shoes." I think once she was going out, and she put money in her shoe or something.

Yeah, that's a common thing that kids do.

Which I don't agree. So I said, "No, you can't put money in your shoes." And she just said, "But why?" "No, I told you not to do that, so don't do that." My husband said, "'Cause it's not our culture." So I don't know what else I would have said. Can't just do it. Many things like that.

In describing her life with her daughters and her concerns while raising them, Vaidehi focused on creating a certain atmosphere in her home built around the more obvious components of Indian culture (religion, food) as well as more subtle elements, such as the particular style of interpersonal dynamics. In the incident described above, Vaidehi clearly explains to me why her daughter should not put pennies in her loafers but resists giving such an explanation to Anar. This episode clearly taught Anar more about interpersonal dynamics ("Don't ask why") than about religion.

Other concerns typical of Indian parents had not been spontaneously discussed by Vaidehi. So I asked.

Has education been important?

Very. I told my Anar. "Anar," I told her, "when I was going to get married, before I knew about my husband, at a certain age maybe that idea comes in your mind that you will get married. You hear other girls talk about that, too, what kind of husband. My friends were talking about rich husbands and then I was also at that time thinking that my husband should be very educated. Handsome, too. But very educated. Education was more important than actual money. If his father was very rich but if he didn't go to school, then it wouldn't please me. It wouldn't make me excited about him. Because I was feeling, if my husband would be educated, no matter what kind of situation may come during the life, if he had education, he could always come out ahead. Lump-sum money if he had, that could be gone. But because of his education, we could always come out."

So are you hoping that Anar will go on to more school? When she finishes?

I hope she could study as much as she wants to. Of course, she should communicate with her husband if she gets married before she finishes her education. Because after getting married, whatever both of them do, it should be joint venture. Should not be just his wish or her wish, because both are concerned. At least, I want her to be graduate, then I hope she gets married.

What kind of person do you hope she'll marry?

I hope it's someone, of course he should be Indian, and he should be as caring as she is. I think Anar is a very gentle and caring person. I often talk to them also, "Life is a commitment. It's not like trial and error. You get married, you should be married for life. Even we were married for life after death, too." That's how I believe. So life is commitment, and, of course, arguments are going to be there.

But still, what I'm afraid, that won't happen to her necessarily, but you always think of that thing, too. When you see so many people fighting, then separating. So many of their friends' parents are divorced. Fortunately, our marriage was so good, but unfortunately, we didn't have long time to live together to show our children our happy marriage. Anar, she did have good time until thirteen years, but still at fourteen she didn't have. Mausami, she was six when Raghav died. So both parents living together, they haven't seen it that much.

'Course I talk a lot about him and our marriage. We are living as if we, like four people, like a complete family together. Even though he's not with us, he is always there with us. But I still feel that it could have been different.

It is very hard to, I wouldn't say hard, but it's not as much fun to raise kids all by myself. I remember, like, to live with two parents, go whole family out together. In the beginning in the years '84, '85, I was kind of scared that if bad things happen, I will be accused, "Mom didn't take good care of them." But it didn't happen that way, I did take good care of them. And I presented both of us to them, instead of just myself, or just himself. I presented both of us.

Anar's perceptions of her mother's expectations for her are sensitive to the meanings of concepts like "family" and "education" that are the cornerstones of Indian parents' talk about their children. In the excerpt above, my questions about education clearly revealed a contrast between my assumptions about what I was asking (i.e., about the girls' own education) and the contextualized meaning Vaidehi ascribes to education (i.e., as a family rather than an individual matter). Anar's understanding of her mother's aspirations for her, however, clearly take account of the shades of meaning that are somewhat at odds between mother and daughter.

Sometimes I talk to her and, you know, tell her about how I want to go to med school. And she's just like, "Well, you know, the most important thing is raising a family." And I'm just like, "What're you talking about?! You know, like my career comes first." And she's just like, "No, you know, I think it's important." It just surprises me. I'm like, "I thought you were a woman of the '90s, you know, like you're in a job, your career, you manage this house. I thought you'd understand that." But no, that's something that she really believes.

And that seems strange to you? Like when you were a kid, you felt they were always encouraging you. [My comment here refers to an earlier conversation we had had. Anar had talked about how her grandparents always expected her to be number one in her class.]

Yeah. I guess they're encouraging me to a point, but then when it comes to, like, hard-core reality and having a family, they want me to fit the mold. So . . . I don't know, it's really confusing, the messages are confusing.

Like, I pretty much decided that I'm thinking about doing medicine, which I don't know anymore. But I'm staying with my concentration. I'm picking out mentors within the university. Like, I'll ask for women that can help me, you know. I want to see how they handled their careers, and juggle everything.

Medicine is a very popular profession for Indians. But that's not something that you felt from your family? Like, "You have to be a doctor"?

I always felt like I'm supposed to be really successful, but I don't know if it was, I guess I did feel it, but it's really hard to say. I remember them talking about it all the time, you know. "Oh, she's going to be a doctor," or "We'll have a doctor in the family now," and stuff like that. They're always saying things like that. But not really like a pressure.

Or was it just that you've always felt you loved medicine?

No . . . no, that's not it at all. It's really strange, because my mother did her undergraduate work in psychology. I'm so interested in psychology and sociology. So sometimes I stop myself, and I'm like, "Well, if I could do anything, and I wouldn't have to worry about what I do?" And I'd be like, "Oh, I just want to probably just become a sociologist and do research." But then there's this other side of me that's like, "Well, how would that be seen? How prestigious is that?"

Both Vaidehi's dismay with her daughter's constant inquiries and Anar's concerns over the prestige of possible career choices connect the family to some of the fundamental concerns of the Indian community at large. The family's Indianness, however, also has ramifications internally. In addition to negotiating identities at a general level, each daughter faces the task of what to do with her Indianness.

What had originally intrigued me about the Nagar family was the particularly psychological interpretation Anar gave to her experiences as a person of Indian origin. This may stem from the way Anar perceives her own and others' Indianness. Exemplified by her dhoti- and sari-wearing grandparents, the outward signs of her Indian heritage were sometimes an embarrassment (as they are for many of the second generation). But it was the inner Indianness, the ways of speaking and acting for which she was praised by other Indians, that fueled her "two people" theory.

True to her mother's characterization of her, Anar does seem a "very gentle caring person," even if she does not share the soft-spoken demeanor of her mother. And, as Anar herself says, she admires her mother because she is "just a considerate person." It is clear that Anar deeply values caring for others. However, for Anar, the value of being a considerate person is grounded in interaction. When you give respect, care, and consideration, you expect to receive respect, care, and consideration in return. Being caring is about building personal, particular relationships.

Yet in the Indian context, the praise she receives for being a "good girl," originates in a very different understanding of what it means to be a "caring person." In the Indian context, Anar's behavior is admired because it fulfills her duty as a child, as a female. Anar finds this motivation not just unsatisfactory but suspect. She dislikes the person who "plays the role" out of duty, and she is ambivalent about the praise received for that behavior.

This has contributed to Anar's "two people" theory. Precisely because much of what she found admirable about herself (being a good student, trying to be a considerate and caring person) was also admirable in an Indian context, she often had the luxury of pleasing both herself and her parents. Still, she was aware that there was a fundamental difference between the person who got good grades because she enjoyed learning and the person who got good grades out of filial duty. It was Anar's ambivalence toward the "dutiful daughter" she knew she was that set the stage for her sense that she encompassed two competing personalities.

Anar understands these competing personalities all too well. In her comments above, she clearly knows what each type of person "should" do. However, with the exception of her recent attempts to transform her relationship with her mother, she has rarely strategized about how to reconcile her two personalities. The difference Anar sees between the "dutiful daughter" and the "strong, assertive young woman," between Indian and American, is dramatically symbolized in the ending of Anar's story about her friend Dave, whom she had wanted to visit her home.

So Dave didn't come?

No. I mean, it really made me sad that my friend couldn't come up. 'Cause he's a big part of my life, and he's one of my good friends. And she's [her mother] a big part of my life, that they could never, ever, meet and talk. Just because he's male and he's white. So . . . like that could never happen. That really hurt. But I didn't know what to do about it.

So it's more than just that you would be alone with him, it's also that you feel that she could never relate to him personally?

Yeah, I don't think she ever could. I don't think *he* could. Like, he can't understand why she's reacting the way she is. Especially because I've been to his house. I mean, you know, so it's not equal. And I usually don't try to make a big deal about it or explain it.

In contrast to Anar's own reaction to being raised in America and being of Indian descent, she sees her sister dealing with these issues quite differently.

My sister's a lot different, though. She tries to explain to the people why. She'll say things like, "My mom was brought up in a different culture, and this is the way she thinks." Well, my sister's a lot different than me. I've always been like, "Well, whatever, I don't want to deal with it." There's no reason to talk about it.

But she takes such a different approach. Like, if a boy calls her, she'll explain it to him how he can't call here, because my mom gets really upset, and my mom won't let her talk to him or anything. I would never do that. I would never explain to the other person, I would just handle it on my own.

True to Anar's analysis, Mausami has dealt with her Indianness quite differently. Mausami is not "two people."

Do you think about it? Do you think about being Indian?

Sometimes. I only think about it really when people are made fun of, at school, I think about it. Or just when we have any functions. Then I'm really, "Wow! I'm Indian."

But I don't even really think about it. I just say that this is my identity, and I have to live with it. I was born Indian, and I'll die Indian. Can't change it. Whenever I think about it, I just think of it as my identity, you know. Just I'm Indian. My family's from India.

When they come here, a lot of my friends are really curious. When they go into the kitchen, and there's like a little temple in there, they ask me, "Well, what is this? What is this?" And I'll tell them. And they think it's neat, you know. Like my friend Karen, when my sister gets married, she's really excited to come. She really wants to come and dress up and everything. And she likes to eat Indian food. I like that when people are curious about things.

When problems relating to her Indian heritage do arise, Mausami's ways of dealing with them illustrate the high level of comfort she feels with her ethnic heritage.

My teacher and I, we disagree on a lot of things, like just pronunciation. I told her, she's like, "Well, this is what it says in the book. So I'm going to go by it." I'm like, "Yeah, but I'm here to tell you. If I wasn't here, or if nobody was here to tell you how you really pronounce it, then you could just go ahead and say things." It really bothered me. There's a king, she kept saying "Osoka," and I knew it was King Ashok. And I just told her, even in the book it didn't have the little dot over the s . . . And I told her that there's supposed to be. She's like, "Well, the filmstrips go by this, and the book goes by this. I can't teach all my classes this." I'm like, "You teach your classes so many things, every day . . . you can't just explain just one word, and it's a big thing, you know." There was a whole chapter on it in the book, and she kept saying it wrong. It really bothered me. She hasn't just done it about India, though. With anything we've learned. And that's why it doesn't encourage the students to learn about it, either.

Similarly, Mausami's peers must contend with her strong and confident character.

I see that a lot, that they just use it as an excuse. Oh, you're Indians, you're bad. I don't get it. They also associate Indians, they're totally intelligent, totally smart, and always being lawyers and doctors and engineers. I just don't get it. They always say, "You stupid Hindu," right? Then they say that we're really smart, and we're going to grow up to be doctors and lawyers. I just—does that work?

We have some close friends that are now in my school, that are sixth-graders. They're Indian. And they always tease those kids, constantly teasing them. Like, "Come on, let's go fight," and stuff like this. They're like, "You're just such a wimp, I'm gonna fight you." I'm like, "If he's such a wimp, you're going to fight him? You know, you're just insulting yourself, really." And I say these things to them. And then they're, just because I'm Indian, and so is he, "Oh, you're defending your own kind." I'm like, "No, if it was anybody else, I'd defend them, too. It's not right what you're doing."

It sounds like you stand up a lot for what you think is right, and you speak out. You're very forthright about things. Does that ever cause problems?

Sometimes. That's what people know me about. At school, I'm known for talking, I'm known for standing up for what I believe in. If I'm upset about something, I will tell them. You know, I don't see that I should hide it, or that I should live with it, because I shouldn't. It's my right as a person to tell people how I feel. And people say, "Oh, don't lecture me. I'll listen. I'll do what you tell me to, just don't lecture me." Sometimes, I might carry it too far, but if I'm upset about something, I think people should know. I just think they should know what they have done. And I think I should be able to tell them, and not be scared, like, "Oh no, I'm going to lose a friendship." Because they're not worth it if they don't understand me.

While Anar's sense of self, her sense of her Indianness, is problematic, Mausami's does not seem so. Although Mausami has a greater curiosity about and appreciation of her Indian heritage than her elder sister (she wants to share her cultural heritage, while Anar wishes it to go away), her personality seems to me less Indian. The caution about speaking one's mind in all situations that Vaidehi values and has tried to pass on to her daughters seems lost on Mausami. As she says, "It's my right as a person to tell people how I feel." Vaidehi acknowledges this difference in her girls.

> Well, I think you are right. Mausami is doing that, and sometimes even when family is getting together, she doesn't like certain things, she just stands up and tells. I say that your point is correct, but I wouldn't have done that.
>
> We went to my sister-in-law's house. My brother-in-law was getting mad at his son. And Mausami was trying to take [her cousin's] side. My brother-in-law was really mad at him, and she was saying, "You should listen to him. And you should watch him. You should give him encouragement." So I said, "Mausami, what you meant was good. It was good for him. But you cannot change a person. What you could have done, just sit at Rahul's side, rub your hand on his back. You should not teach him to talk back to his father. And you shouldn't have done that, either." She says, "I cannot take it. He was wrong. He was wrong." "But do not do that because older people, they are not going to like it. They are not going to think that Mausami is a nice and quiet girl. They will think that she is talking back. I don't like that type of feeling for them to have for you like that." But she does seem that way.
>
> In the school also, some kids are not treated well, she stands up for them. In a way, it's right that if another child is beaten up, if nobody will stand up . . . but how good will it be for her?

Do you think it is just an age thing? Did Anar do that when she was Mausami's age? Talking back, being so assertive in terms of standing up for what you think is right and letting everybody know what you think is right. Or was she always more reserved in that respect?

Oh, yeah, she was. Of course, she was always talking back to me. But to other people, she wasn't talking back. I think it is different personality. I don't see one is good and one is bad. Of course, I don't like it. As I am not too aggressive, I don't like them to be very aggressive. Sometimes they could get in trouble. Maybe someone can hurt them because of that. That's what I wouldn't like to see. That's why I ask them not to be so aggressive, even though your ideas are right.

At the same time, what I have experienced because of my in-laws talking so much to me, and I wasn't saying back. I mean, that didn't improve me, improve my situation. Maybe all the good they can think of is that I didn't talk back to them. But other than that . . . because sometimes even though ideas are so good, they shouldn't take it out. Sometimes it is good to say it out, and sometimes it's not.

Vaidehi's theory about why the two girls behave so differently has to do with their "different personalities." While this is certainly true, other factors are at work as well. Anar feels like two people because of her conception of Indianness, which she defines in terms of interpersonal roles and relations. Her ambivalence toward the "dutiful daughter" is at the root of her feeling of duality. Mausami, however, *doesn't* feel like two people, because for her Indianness is about the material manifestations of ethnicity. It is about cooking and eating the right foods, knowing the rituals and the customs, and seeing the roots of ethnicity in accidents of geography: "I'm Indian. My parents were born in India."

Why have the two girls defined Indianness so differently? There are several possibilities. One is that Mausami, at age twelve, is just too young. She hasn't reached the teenage years, when difference between one's parents and one's peers (in this case complicated by a different ethnic heritage) become salient. As she moves into adolescence, she may in fact come to see her differences with her mother as more problematic. She may yet become sensitized to Indianness as something not only outwardly ethnic but also psychologically meaningful.

Another possible explanation lies in the different family lives of the two girls. As all the family members suggest, much of Anar's childhood and adolescence happened on the fringe of familial attention. Vaidehi was not able to spend as much time teaching Anar about custom and ritual. Anar was expected to attend community functions and partake in family rituals but not necessarily to understand why. In contrast, Mausami has been exposed more methodically to the most obvious aspects of Indian culture.

Mausami's familiarity with stories, rituals, and customs undoubtedly enables her to share her knowledge of her culture. Anar, while very knowledgeable about what she should do, is less knowledgeable about the meaning behind Indian symbols and rituals. When I chatted with her at the youth program at the temple, she confessed that she didn't know much about the god she was assigned to explain, other than what was printed on the paper the organizers had given her. With this difference in familiarity, one might expect Mausami to latch more easily onto material culture to express her Indianness.

In addition, the changing climate in America regarding ethnicity has helped Mausami feel more matter-of-fact about her ethnic heritage than her elder sister. When Anar was in grade school, ethnicity separated students. She still feels "weird" when her Indian friends and her "white" friends (her "school friends") meet. In contrast, from a very young age, Mausami had been exposed to a multiplicity of ethnicities at school, and ethnicity in some sense had become a mainstream concern.

This changing attitude toward ethnicity in the educational system is now affecting Anar, who says it has helped her to begin to integrate her two selves. When she arrived at her dorm freshman year in college, there were smiley faces on all the doors with the names of the new occupants. She drew a *bindi* on her smiley face. In doing this, she said, she surprised herself. Before, she would never have done that. Now, she wanted people to know she was Indian.

She attributes this turnaround to the "diversity credo" of the university. In her first semester, she took a course on ethnic identity. She was active in the Asian Students Coalition. (Significantly, she did not become involved in the Indian Students Association. She says that with the Indian students, she felt she was always being judged about whether or not she was fulfilling the role appropriate for an Indian woman.)

In all the families I studied, there seems to be a basic need to process this difference, to think about one's Indianness, in relation to one's peers. In sharp contrast to the public rhetoric of dual lives, it is not enough to be Indian at home and American at school. Somehow, one's Indianness, what marks one as different in the world of school and work, needs to be processed in that environment. Mausami could ethnicize her heritage, just as her Filipino friends and her Korean friends could. The whole class could study India together.

For Anar, until college, that opportunity didn't exist. Therefore, she developed two sets of friends, her Indian friends and her "white" friends, for her Indian self and her American self, which usually overlapped but sometimes collided. Anar's psychological theory of Indianness may be changing as the social climate around her gives her more options. She is exploring her Indian identity as an "ethnicity" at school and trying to be "herself" in her relationship with her mother, no longer presenting her particularly Indian self in that context.

For the Nagars, one's particular life experience plays a major and ongoing role in what one does with one's Indianness—the way being Indian becomes incorporated into one's identity. Vaidehi, having grown up in a traditional Indian setting, simply *is* Indian. She continues to express her Indianness unself-consciously in the way she talks about herself, her connections to other people, and her expectations for her children. She rarely offers an explicit interpretation of her social world as "Indian." It simply *is* her world.

Similarly, her daughters have both been shaped by their life circumstances—living in America, living in particular family arrangements, attending school at distinct historical moments. Creating and maintaining an ethnic identity is an ongoing process in which one is constantly reprocessing what has come before. This notion that historical particularities are paramount in understanding the intergenerational flow of Indianness will be important in understanding the other four family portraits as well.

A second lesson we can draw from this portrait of the Nagars concerns their family idiom. Vaidehi and Anar, in particular, show a deep sensitivity to interactional dynamics—how one speaks, to whom. For both mother and daughter, this sensitivity entails a perpetual dilemma. In interactional settings, should one perform one's appropriate role, or should one speak one's mind, present one's "true" self? It is a dilemma between duty and heart. Even Mausami, who does not seem personally to be caught in this dilemma, participates in the overarching family dialogue through her declarations that "heart" is paramount: "It's my right as a person to tell people how I feel." Like the Nagars, each family in this study has a particular way of conceptualizing itself, which is expressed through their peculiar idiom. Family idioms become the basis for constructing a collective, shared *family* identity.

The interaction between the centrifugal effects of the particular histories and personalities of individuals and the centripetal pull of a familial idiom guides the trajectory of assimilation for each family. We also have begun to see the role played by comparisons—people's repeated references to difference and similarity—in the process of working out individual and familial identities. The portrait of the Iyengars illustrates the same constellation of forces, but, as one would expect, the path of the assimilative trajectory is significantly different.

8

The Iyengars: Historical Indians

Lakshmi: If we had given more Indian culture, Bob wouldn't be walking around in a leather jacket.

Shivan: You are always going to have doubts even if you did not have a second culture involved. Maybe if we had taught him more Indian culture, he would have turned out slightly different. But maybe this way he's going to get assimilated a hell of a lot easier into the society in which he is going to live. A lot better than we have been. He's more comfortable, at ease, with it. That's the life that our staying here has made for him. And if this is the norm for kids his age in the society, why should I . . .

So long as he doesn't get in trouble. So long as he doesn't become destructive. I don't know that it's particularly important for you to hang on to . . . one thing we have is he appreciates that there is a different culture involved. Its value. It should be appreciated like any culture. So that's all I can expect.

It's not exactly like we were orthodox Hindus or Indians anyway. We have led a fairly Western life.

Lakshmi: Some of my friends in India who went to high school with me—look at their kids. They grew up in India, and they may speak a local language, but they are not any more Indian. I think the next generation is sort of becoming more or less uniform—jeans and Coca-Cola and rock music. So from that angle, I feel like maybe we couldn't have done anything that different.

But on the other hand, we had something that we clung to. I don't even know how to explain it. I can't say I'm Hindu, but I can say that there's something—a mixture of Hindu, Indian, philosophy, whatever, that is my pillar, in a sense. And I wonder if our kids have that. You need something that gives you inner strength. And that comes from your upbringing.

Shivan: That issue has nothing to do with whether you are an expatriate or not. That issue has to do with the fact that we were basically agnostic. We chose to have religion play an extremely small role in our life. Certainly an extremely low-key role. And so the kids didn't have that kind of thing as their backup, you know, bench strength. And that's got nothing to do with moving from India to here. That would have been the case if we lived in India. And that would be the case if we were American, born and brought up here.

That's a function of that particular choice that we made. And that point, I'm not sure we did the right thing. That point, very definitely, I wonder. And ultimately, when you're going through serious problems, when you need an anchor to hang on to, for just sanity, not because God's going to come and solve something for you. But it just gives you the ability to cope with the situation. We haven't created that. Maybe it'll automatically come.

You know, I'm sure they pray to "God" just before their exams.

I am sitting at the dining-room table with Lakshmi Iyengar and her husband, Shivan, discussing the upbringing of their two teenage boys, Bob, fifteen, and Michael, twenty. In this dialogue, and throughout our conversations, Lakshmi and Shivan struggle with a genuine ambivalence and uncertainty about the role that "Indianness" plays or should play in their lives and the lives of their children. In other families, the dilemma about letting Indianness go in the second generation is grounded in a strong sense of parental Indianness. Deviations from the Indian way of doing things in the second generation are seen as compromises made necessary by residence in America. Similarly, changes in parents' own behavior (in customs of dress, food, etc.) are rooted in environmental necessities. These changes do not challenge their view of themselves as Indians. For most parents, Vaidehi Nagar among them, Indianness is also deeply embedded in their personalities. There is something about the way they see the world that is peculiarly Indian. They are Indians living outside India.

For the Iyengars, however, an uncertainty about their own Indianness complicates the issue. The Iyengars see their Indian heritage as simply a *part* of themselves, an artifact of the location of their birth. Had they been born elsewhere, one still might meet the same Iyengars—they would talk about different experiences, but they would still be recognizable as the same people. They construct themselves as *historically* rather than *essentially* Indian. It is their history rather than some core essence that marks them as Indian.

Constructing themselves as historically Indian, however, does not totally obscure a subtle Indianness that they still retain. The kind of care they
demonstrate in their attention to familial relationships is highly reminiscent of the familial connectedness that exists in all the families that participated in this study, though the Iyengars themselves are not sure whether
their concern with and attention to familial relationships is particularly
Indian.[1] The centrality and intensity of familial relationships were from my
perspective remarkable features of these families, features I will discuss in
greater detail in chapter 12.

Like the preceding portrait of the Nagars, this portrait of the Iyengars
includes the parents' recollections of their own upbringing. In comparison to the childhood recollections of Vaidehi Nagar, both Lakshmi and
Shivan tell very elaborate stories about the importance of their upbringing
in forming the persons they have become. To explain who they are, they
need to explain their history.

These childhood recollections are also important for understanding the
present-day family. The importance of familial relationships is revealed in
both parents' extensive contact with and recollections of their extended
families. Further, both parents speak about the importance of their formal
educations to their development as people. Familial relationships and education are "issues" that will be recycled in their children's discussions of
their own development. This recycling of issues is an example of the
intergenerational dynamic which ensures a certain degree of continuity
between generations and allows the family to jointly develop an idiom that
unites and defines them. At the same time, however, the way relationships
to parents and the role of education in one's development are conceptualized by the Iyengar boys illustrates that tendency to contrast oneself with
parents, siblings, and other Indians as a way to stake out a personal identity.

I came to know the Iyengars through a referral from a relative of theirs who
is a colleague of an acquaintance of mine. I knew nothing about the family
other than that both parents were Indian, they had at least one child older
than eighteen, and they had been living in the United States for at least ten
years—the initial criteria for eligibility that I used to choose my families.

I first visited the Iyengars' spacious home in an upper-middle-class,
integrated Chicago neighborhood a few days after Christmas. Their Christmas tree was still up, topped with the Devanagari alphabet symbol (the
alphabet of the Hindi language) equivalent to the sound "*om*"—a syllable
used in meditation and Hindu religious ceremonies. The living room and
dining room, the only rooms visible to a casual visitor, are comfortably, if
sparsely, furnished. There is a grand piano in the living room. Indian batiks
and metalware are scattered throughout, as are artifacts of other countries
and cultures they have visited.

The text that grounds this family portrait is the continuation of the
conversation quoted above when Shivan, Lakshmi, and I were discussing
child rearing. It was in this conversation that the dynamics of family inter-

action and the role their Indian background plays in these dynamics are most clearly articulated. Interspersed are excerpts from the individual life-history interviews with the family members. These individually constructed lives provide a context and lend a richness to Lakshmi and Shivan's talk about their kids.

Even though they may not have religion per se, do you think you've tried to give them some core values that'll help them in those kinds of crises?

Lakshmi: Oh, yeah. I think very much. I mean, I can speak for myself. In this particular area, I think, we're [speaking of herself and her husband] more similar than dissimilar, you know. We have very strong values of responsibility to each other and to other human beings. And about rude and crude and ugly behavior. You should be accountable for what you say and do. So that part of it is there.

Then the other thing is, we try to do a lot of stuff together. Over our twenty-some years of marriage, we've spent less time with each other alone than we have as a family. And the kids know that that's a very important thing. We take family vacations two or three times a year. And it's a big issue that our older son sometimes has suggested he couldn't come and it's a big burden on him.

Shivan: What "suggested"? Not suggested, he's actually not showed up a couple of . . .

Lakshmi: Once. He only succeeded once.

Shivan: We also try to dangle bribes in front of him by picking the locations that he would dearly love to go. And now he's got a tough choice to make. So we work it out.

Lakshmi: We are very clingy to our Michael.

Shivan: She more than I.

Lakshmi: I'm not ashamed to admit it. I'm very happy that our son might be coming back [i.e., transferring to a local college]. I expect to keep their rooms exactly the way they want to forever and ever. Those are maybe, I don't know if they're Indian values or immigrant values or just our values.

Shivan: I think the sense of family perhaps has a strong carryover from our background. For example, her family's going to descend here in May. And I have, in some conversations with my American colleagues, found that they make statements like, "Oh, boy, you must really be hating the fact they they're going to come and camp on you for six months. You must be fighting with your brother to make sure that they go and stay there for their fair share, so you are not burdened."

We will fight, but it's the other way, saying I want them to stay more here. It's very different, that family thing, I find that they sometimes don't seem to be able to come from quite the same point.

Lakshmi: But I think that also relates to the issue of drawing lines, you know, which I think the kids, I feel pretty good as they are coming out, that they have absorbed. There is a line between what is mine and my rights and my money and my time and my privacy and where can it overlap with other people. In our family, we've tried to say, "Hey, we're a socialist family, and the guy who needs it gets it."

There are no equal transactions. And I don't even know if it's desirable. You know, why should it be a goal? So from that angle, the kids never resent having my or his relatives or friends. We've tried to say that you can bring your leather-wearing, metal-dangling friends over as much as I have mine.

Shivan: An extended family, something that's a fairly normal thing for us, a fairly commonplace feature in India, appears to be less of a commonplace feature here. Therefore, I have to infer, but I can't prove it, that that's one thing maybe our attitude is shaped and our values are shaped by our background. Maybe those values would have been different if our background was not what it is.

Lakshmi: If you look at what's important in the values that you impart to the kids, while I may be a little disappointed that neither of the boys speak or can read or write any Indian language, I wish they could appreciate Indian music. But on the other hand, in terms of the value system, I feel like both the boys have good humanistic values, whether they're Indian or whatever.

Shivan: They may be an Indian version of the humanistic values, more than an American version. I don't think fundamentally they're very unique.

The Iyengars' values, the values they are trying to pass on to their kids, are very similar to the values identified as important by other Indian parents—the importance of family in particular. However, where other parents are quicker to identify their core values as Indian values, the Iyengars are more equivocal. They are not sure, it seems, of the extent to which their values are rooted in their Indian background. Shivan tries logically to deduce the probability of an Indian origin for these values by comparison of his attitudes to those of his American colleagues. He offers, though, that he has to "infer but . . . can't prove" the Indian origin of these values. Lakshmi takes Shivan's equivocations further, claiming that these values result from the underlying socialist orientation of the family.

To whatever degree these values may be "an Indian version of humanistic values," the Indianness seems to derive from the Iyengars' own experiences of family in India, rather than from an essentialized "Indian culture" which claims that family is important to Indians. In Lakshmi's rather nontraditional upbringing and education, the experiential origins of her talk about "good humanistic values" and the importance of familial relations are clearly evident.

I was born in 1947, which is the year of independence. ["One of 'Midnight's Children,'" I interject.] Right, absolutely. I read the book, and I could see a lot . . . I was born August 28th, so it was a few days after independence.

My father's family immigrated from what is now Pakistan to India, and my grandfather was a chief engineer at the electric plant in Udaipur [in northern India]. So I think he moved up there by '48, but it was very traumatic because my father's family didn't want to move from Hyderabad [now in Pakistan]. They had lived almost all their lives there, and my grandfather had been chief engineer at the power plant and was very well established and respected in the community and so on. My father still has a lot of visceral feelings about partition. He just thinks that one day it should all be one.

All my father's family, they were South Indians. Same caste and creed and blah blah blah. So it was normal for my father's parents to come south every year, to look for brides for their sons.

My maternal grandfather was a registrar in the high court in Madras [South India]. You know, educated and quite reasonably . . . professional families. They're not business families.

He had a very important role in my life. He was a patriarch of the family. Since I was the eldest, first granddaughter, I lived a charmed life until I grew up.

Around 1950, when my brother was born, my father quit the job he was in. Or rather, they had a great parting because he was a staunch nationalist. Before he got married and so on, he had been in the freedom movement. A very staunch nationalist. And this company was a British company, and they had separate bathrooms for their Indian employees and for the Western employees. And he made an issue of it, and he was asked to resign.

So after he resigned from there, and he was jobless, and he was working in odd jobs. Worked for my grandfather in his company for a little while, and basically was severely unsettled until probably '53 or so.

But since he was severely unsettled, my mother and brother and I, and my dad, lived in a joint family. My [paternal] grandfather's house. My mother and the two kids spending large sections of time with her parents down south.

And I spent large sections of my time with my maternal grandfather, whenever there was any unsettledness. From 1952, I was with my maternal grandfather, and I was going to school in Madras. He moved to Delhi, because he got a post with the supreme court. I moved with him to Delhi. My mother left me with my grandfather.

My maternal grandfather was an education buff. Reading a lot to the kids. He was just a real grandfather. They figured it was a good deal for me to grow up there. And it was. Because I was the only child in that household. So between, like, 1950 and '58, I spent with my maternal grandfather.

From '52 to '58, I was in Delhi. And there it was a nuclear family. 'Cause in Madras, even my maternal grandfather was the head of joint family. His sisters, who were widowed or, you know, it was just a household with lots of comings and goings. But in Delhi, it was a nuclear family. It was my grandfather, my grandmother, my aunt, and myself.

My life in New Delhi was really great. Because my grandparents were very lenient and at the same time very watchful. My grandfather was constantly watching over my education. I remember it being both fun and a pain. He'd wake me up at four or five to study. He would read books and stories. Everything ranging from folktales in English to . . . mythological stories. He was a great reader of the *Upanishads* and the *Ramayan* and the *Mahabharata*. But from a stories point of view, not religious. He was agnostic. He didn't believe in organized religion. So he would tell me a lot of stories with some kind of moral or idea that came across rather than any religious implication. So I remember all that with very great fondness and excitement.

And Nehru was really big in Delhi. We lived, initially, opposite the home of a minister called Maulana Azad. I remember that Maulana Azad had this grand yard. And he would have flower shows in February. Us kids just loved going there. We'd sneak in and out of the flower show all the time. Nehru would come there, and he would talk to the kids or, you know fondle the kids, and it was a big deal. To some degree, if you've read *Midnight's Children*, there was a sense of being charmed. Because you were born an independence person. There was a sense of nationalism, greatness of India, and all that kind of stuff. Nehru was a very important part of Delhi.

And another thing that I participated in very religiously and regularly was going to Nehru's home on his birthday, which was declared Children's Day. We'd all wait for him to come out, and they would garland him, and he would say a few words. He was a very friendly and warm person, and that came across. He would look the children in their face and talk to them. Just maybe pat you on the cheek, something very . . . today, you know, we're cynical. You may think, "Oh, big deal," but it made a difference to you at that time. He was very friendly, and there were crowds and crowds.

My grandfather was not somebody who sort of believed in all this hype, but somehow or other, he sent me to these things, which was kind of peculiar, now that I think back on it.

So my life in Delhi I remember with great joy. I don't remember any conflict or unhappiness. School was easy. I was always, like, doing slightly worse than I could. I could do a little bit better. All my grade reports, I remember everybody saying, "If she put a little more time on it, she could do even better." But that didn't matter to me. It mattered only to the extent that my grandfather would say, "Come on, you could have done better." I was in the top few percent of the class.

Never at top, just the top few percent. And that always bugged everybody in our family.

In '58, my parents came back from Germany, and they set up house. And for the first time, my parents felt that, "Okay, we're going to be a family now." So my brother and I moved into Bombay, and then we went to a convent. My dad and mom were very keen that I learn all the cultural things of music and dance and so on, so they tried to put me in different programs and . . . mixity, the life was crazy. They had a tiny apartment. They felt that my education was slipping. Trying to get us to these activities was a real hassle. So my dad decided that we should go to a boarding school.

Most boarding schools in India at that time were very British snobbery. That was something that really bugged my grandfather, who was quite—and my dad, too—was quite nationalistic. But at the same time, they didn't want us to go around with dots and saris. They wanted us to have an open education.

Boarding school played a very, very important role in my life. Those five years were crucial. I learned a lot of the cultural things. Like, I did *bharata natyam*, and I played the vina. I took part in dramatics, I took part in every single thing they had, from, not so much sports, but from sports to cultural activities to debating. They had a lot of activities. You could do as many things as you wanted.

They had lot of discussions of world events and philosophies and how to think about yourself. It was great. And still, most of my friends from school, I'm still in touch with them. They're all over the world, but we stay in touch.

In Lakshmi's childhood, we see the importance she places on both the experience she had with her extended family and her educational progress. These experiences are vivid and concrete. In contrast to Vaidehi Nagar's more tentative discussion of her upbringing, the specificity of Lakshmi's story supports her own and her family's views of themselves as the products of history. Her educational experiences in particular are atypical and have very specifically contributed to her outlook. We see the roots of the dilemma the Iyengars will face in overseeing their sons' educations. Should education serve practical ends, or is it a search for personal fulfillment and an opportunity to broaden one's horizons?

Shivan's early life also is marked by a certain breadth of experience that is fairly unusual. While his family is not so nationally prominent, his nuclear family at least was mobile on a national scale. In addition, his great-grandfather's socially conscious philanthropic activities set a tone for the family and its contact with others that was certainly a departure from a traditional caste- and community-bound pattern of concern.

I was born in 1942, in July. And 1942 was the middle of the war, and there had been some shelling of Madras from submarines of the Japanese. My grandfather sent the family away to the interior to be away from that. So I was born in one of the interior towns.

He had some friends, and they organized care for my grandmother and my mother and so on. He was a judge in the British judicial system that was in India. It was a fairly powerful position, and so he knew lots of people. He was able to, I guess, take advantage of that.

And also my great-grandfather was a lawyer, and he was extremely famous and well known for both his legal work and for his philanthropy in the south. In fact, I occasionally run into real old people, and when I get to talking and I say I'm so-and-so's son, they say, "Oh, you're so-and-so's great-grandson." The saying goes that there was never a night when there was not fifty-sixty people eating at his house, who were essentially poor people. And he would find bright young kids and essentially say, "Fine, you can stay here and eat here," and put them through school and that kind of thing. So he was extremely well known.

There are lots of people who were more than happy to help out in the situation.

My father's side of the family is kind of sketchy because my father lost his father when he was very young. He was brought up by his mother, who was helped by her brothers. So most of what I remember is some familiarity with that side of the family, but most of the interaction was with the mother's side of the family.

The earliest I remember is . . . I must have been five or six years old. My father was in the government, in the tax department. I remember that my father was posted at a place called Guntur about two hundred miles north of Madras. And it was awfully hot. We used to have help around the house, and you had somebody who . . . I mean, you didn't have ceiling fans, and . . . the *pankha*,[2] and they put water on it to provide . . . to cool down the thing, and I remember that. And I remember for some reason, I remember Independence Day.

I remember Independence Day where my cousins . . . my mother had two brothers, one of whom died . . . with one daughter. The other one, we think, is dead. He kind of disappeared a few years ago. He had five kids. And those kids, we grew up with them. They were visiting us in Guntur when all this happened, and I remember it. We didn't know what it was, I guess. But it was exciting, and we took the flag and ran around in circles on the roof.

Then my father kept moving around. We went from Guntur to Tanjore, which is south of Madras. I remember, before that, actually, I used to stay with my grandfather, and he put me into elementary school, and he started teaching me English and so on. I remember that if I didn't do the work, or goofed off, he'd catch me by the ear and twist it, and that was absolute . . . so you did the work, otherwise your ear got awfully hurt.

Then I spent a summer with my grandmother. I was extremely attached to them. At the end of the summer, it was time for me to go back to where my parents were. I was extremely unhappy, and I was unhappy enough that three weeks later, they told my grandmother to come and stay with us for a couple of months, so I would get used to the idea. When she left, I remember I was in school, and I was watching for the train. The train line ran by, and I knew which train she was on. I still remember for some reason watching the train go.

Then, really, the first major move happened when my father was posted to the north, to Calcutta. That was the first time anybody in the family had left the south.

I entered school. There was this teacher who taught Hindi who was particularly nasty. One day, something happened, and he got mad at me and slapped me real hard a few times. Hit me on the temple. And I got really shook up. When he realized what he had done, he was probably the most scared man on earth. He was awfully nice to me and insisted I go home with him, and he gave me food to eat, and he made me feel comfort, saying, "I'm sorry, I shouldn't have done this. You need any help, just come to me." Being a normal thirteen-fourteen-year-old, I milked it.

I didn't do too well in school. I used to goof off a lot. I did well in most subjects, but Hindi, I got thirty-five out of a hundred. Just barely enough to pass. Otherwise I'd have flunked. You had to pass every subject. You could not flunk any subject for you to go on to the next level.

What happened was that the good school that I wanted to get into, the top college, was called Presidency College, I couldn't get into it. My grades weren't good enough. Then there was a very good Jesuit school called St. Xavier's College. And my father talked to somebody in his company, who talked to the chief admitting officer there or something, saying, "Hey, why don't you make an exception in this case? The kid is good, from a good family," and all that sort of thing. So I got in.

And I guess I continued to goof off. At the end of the first year— it was a two-year program—at the end of the first year, summer holidays, my cousins were there. They had come to visit us. When we were in Calcutta, every summer, either we would go south or they would come north.

I remember those train rides. They were long. Since we were five kids, husband, wife, seven, it would be a six-berther or seven-berther bogie, which was like this room on wheels. Slightly narrower. Bathroom with shower and fans. You essentially spread out and lived there for two days.

My great-grandfather's, one of his many good associates' son was in a town called Rajahmundry on the way. And when this gentleman found out that we travel like this, he'd want to find out, and when the train came to Rajahmundry, he would come to the station with food, and they'd bring huge baskets of some of the most delicious-tasting mangoes. Because his father was essentially put through school by my great-grandfather, so he felt a sense of loyalty.*

So . . . summer is hot and humid in Calcutta. Just beginning to get to be the beginning of the rainy season in June, and I guess the grades arrived. And it was pass in all subjects except in English, in which I got extremely high marks. So my dad essentially called me over and said, "We got some decisions to make. I got five kids to educate. Either you take it seriously, or I still have this plot of land in the village, you can go farm it. I can't afford to waste money if you're not interested in doing something with it."

I guess that, in some respects, was a seminal moment in my life. Until then just getting by was okay. That somehow got to me. And the next year, I guess, I did nothing but really study. At the end of the year, we were going to take the university exam. Now, this is Calcutta University exam. And depending on how you did on the university exam, either you went on to other things, or . . . it helped you in how you got into engineering school or medical school or things like that.

And so I wrote the exams, and I thought I had done well. Then, about a week later, I convinced myself that I had really blown the chemistry exam. And it takes about three months for the results to come out. So you go through a lot of hell. You have no way of finding out. You think you have blown it.

I remember the day that they were going to announce the results. The way they do it is, when they announce the results, the newspapers print them out. Actually, as they get the results, they announce them over the public address system. So there is this mob in front of all the newspaper buildings, each office, to listen to them.

I went there, picked up a newspaper. They're printed by first class, second class, third class. Then there are people who flunked. And when I got the paper, I looked at the second-class section, 'cause I was absolutely sure that I was going to be in. And my number wasn't there. I looked in the third class, my number wasn't there. And I convinced myself that I had flunked.

I took the long way back home. When I got home, my father said, "What happened?" I just gave him the newspaper and went out, I guess locked myself up. A few minutes later, he came in and said, "Why didn't you tell me you did so well?" I had gotten first class.

But in some respects, I think that what happened was that my father telling me that by working hard and getting something for it, kind of shifted the plane that you measure yourself against. One, you said, "I can do it," and two, you were not satisfied unless you did it. And from then on, doing well in school became very important.

---

* Although Shivan's story about summer vacation is a digression, the elision of "family" and "education" stories demonstrates the salience and interdependence of these two themes in Shivan's life.

As Shivan said, there was a point in his life where "doing well in school became very important." This is something that the Iyengars, along with most Indian families, stress with their kids. But doing well in school introduces a host of other issues into the Iyengar family dynamic. It is tied to issues of individuality and personal desire. To what extent should the boys be allowed or encouraged to explore their particular talents or propensities, which may lead them in directions that are less conducive to academic and professional success? The Iyengars struggle with this dilemma. They try to balance what they see as a tendency toward conservatism with a desire to foster a breadth of experience in their sons (reminiscent of Lakshmi's education at boarding school).

Is it important to you that they get straight A's?[3]

Lakshmi: Yeah.

Shivan: Oh, I'd love to have them get straight A's, but I haven't had that experience yet.

So what happens then they get B's?

Lakshmi: We talk about it. Well, you know, Michael was not a problem. First of all, he didn't grow into the social environment quite as quickly as Bob did. So he would slip a grade here or there, but in general he got A's. And he did very well.

Bob is just the opposite. He doesn't feel grades are important, and everything he does is a statement. He tries to convince the teacher that his point of view is right. If somebody's asking a certain question and is expecting a certain answer, why the hell don't you give it and get an A? But if you want to go and tell them that the question they're asking is wrong, and the answer they're expecting is wrong, and that your framing of both the question and answer are the appropriate ones, and you go with a leather jacket and boots and metal, you are going to be picked on.

The counselors have so much as said, "If Bob decides to change his approach, he's a very bright boy, he knows the subject." This is repeated again and again. So he gets B's and C's, and it's an issue.

Shivan: And it is not just grades. Till he figures out how to deal with the outside world, there are a hell of a lot more of them than there are of you. And they'll always beat you down. You have to learn. You have to be comfortable about saying, "I don't have to flaunt my values in front of somebody else to prove to them, or prove to myself, that I can hold different values." If you have different values, you don't have to demonstrate them by your exterior. Whether you believe something is good or bad is not demonstrated by whether you wear a jacket and the black thing and long hair. If your whole value system is proved by your exterior, it's a very shallow value system. But those are the kinds of difficulties that we have, and, believe me, it keeps me awake at night.

And it's got nothing to do with being Indian or otherwise. It just is that fact that I see a bright kid who is essentially hurting himself.*

Lakshmi: He says, "I can't live with myself if I do that," you know. They were studying the Bible, okay, and they had a special project on the Bible. So what does he do? He wears an agnostic T-shirt, writes a very nicely composed rock piece, and performs it with the boots and the leather jacket and this whole thing. And this woman is a devout Christian who's teaching the Bible. So what does she do? She says A on artistic merit, A on content and understanding, C on performance. Or something, you know, the whole grade he got was a B. He hurt himself.

He said, "I'm not going to win against the system."

Shivan: And he is right. He is not going to win against the system.

Lakshmi: This has nothing to do with being Indian. Parenting problems.

Shivan: In some respects, I think kids have it a lot easier in India 'cause there's a lot more regimentation. It forecloses enough options from way back when you're young, they're not an issue.

Lakshmi: They're not an emotional traumatic issue. Bob says, "I'm selling myself." I mean, what is the big deal, you know?

Shivan: And maybe if we had raised him with a lot of that Indian culture and that narrow focus, he wouldn't have faced it. But regardless of what we did, his kid and he would face it.

What is at issue for the Iyengars is not really whether or not their sons are getting straight A's but rather whether they are living up to their potential. Bob is capable of doing better in school, and that is what is troubling to his parents. What is particularly troublesome is Bob's insistence on being different, not wanting to work within the system. While other Indian parents might object to Bob's behavior simply because of his non-traditional clothing and his lack of respect for authority, the Iyengars' objections revolve around Bob asserting his individuality, playing up his difference. I sense that if Bob had been able or willing to "work the system" and bring home A's, clothing and styles of interaction with teachers would not have been issues for the Iyengars. Although the Iyengars don't see this concern as particularly Indian, perhaps it is connected to a separation anxiety that is rooted in a traditional pattern of continuity in Indian familial relationships.

* As we resume the conversation, we see again the expression of uncertainty about whether particular aspects of their family experience are Indian. In addition to marking the Iyengars' resistance to seeing themselves in essential Indian terms, these recurrent references to what is Indian also mark the use of prototypes to carve out individual and familial identities. It is also worth noting the way Bob and Michael are contrasted to each other as a way of articulating family experiences.

Coming of age and asserting one's separateness from one's family seem to be, for most families in this study, a slow and careful process—a process that, in fact, may never be complete.[4] Bob's developing independence seems to be much more along "American" lines.[5] In his strong assertions of individuality, Bob seems to be staking out his own territory, preparing himself for a life very different from that which is envisioned for him by his parents.

My conversations with Bob reflect this. In some ways, they were very similar to the talks I had with Mausami Nagar. I think largely because of age, my discussions with these young teens were very much directed to their immediate concerns and life experiences. Bob does not specifically address his own development or his sense of where he is going. Nonetheless, many of Bob's current concerns reveal the kind of concern with individuality I am suggesting.

And then sixth grade, we got our first exchange student, who was Nadar Rittner, who's from Germany but he's Iranian. It was a rather strange mix having Americans from India and a German from Iran. We had some fun with him. He's the one who made my brother insane.

He wasn't insane before?

No, before that my brother was a very nice little boy who had a computer. The most illegal thing he did was pirating games. And jaywalking. That's okay, but that's not exactly a life of excitement. I mean, but Nadar actually got him out of the house once or twice, so he actually learned how to have fun. He went to a couple of school dances.

Then . . . last year was it? Yeah, last year . . . not much happened between sixth and eighth grades. My grades slipped a lot, but . . . no big deal. And then last year, my grades slipped more, and I joined the theater in school.

That's pretty much a lot of what I did. For the past four shows, I've acted, and this is the first show where I'm not acting and I'm being tech director for the show.

Did your family come to see you?

Yeah. They've been coming and seeing all the . . . and asking me why I can do so well at those but don't do this great at school.

So it's a concern for your parents?

Yeah. School's a big concern with everybody. Everybody except him [the dog, who was sitting at our feet] and my friends.

What about with you?

School, I mean, I'm happy if I get a B average. These guys, of course, are only happy if I get an A average. My aunt just wants me to work hard and do the best I can. My brother understands.

Sometimes I study. I do basically what I've got to do, 'cause after that you'd go insane. I mean, this week, so far this week, let's see, Tuesday, I had a paper due and a test. Monday, a teacher said, "All right. Pop essay due Wednesday, and this is the topic." And we just started the topic on Friday. So, of course, nobody had read the packets he handed out. Today, I was supposed to have another paper due and then two tests. But there's something called the Workload Committee in our school which says no more than two big things in a day. Which means you can only have a paper due and a test on the same day, or two tests or two papers, and you can basically decide. So I declined to do my English paper. I did my music theory test and math test. Music theory test I didn't even have to take today, 'cause the Terra assembly took it over.

The Terror Assembly?

Terra. We have an environmental group in our school.

Oh, like terra firma?

T-e-r-a, not terror. So it was an assembly today.

Beyond that, my weeks are pretty crammed in school, and if they're not crammed in school, they're crammed in theater, and if they're not that, then I cram them with music.

My music is really, really big. I write mainly hard-core trash, punk, and stuff like Slayer, Metallica, Megadeth, that kind of stuff. But then I also write some blues stuff. I'm kinda varied. When I play with my brother, I do lots of blues and rock. When I play with the guys in the band, we just play hard-core skin songs, and punk, whatever.

Some of the Iyengars' frustration in dealing with their younger son is mirrored by his frustration in dealing with them.

"You watch too much TV. You spend too much time on music. You spend too much time in the theater. Broaden your interests. Read more books. Join the track team. Join the swimming team. Join some physical team. You should work out more. Cut your hair. Get new clothes. Dress nicely." I think this is nice [referring to the jeans and Megadeth T-shirt he was wearing, which were neat and clean]. So . . . a lot of things.

So do any of these things they're saying make any sense to you or not particularly?

I mean, some of 'em do. I mean, I understand their reasons, but some of 'em just don't make sense. Like "Change your taste in music" was once called. And "Spend more time playing piano." But I play guitar; that's an instrument, too.

"Spend more time studying" I can understand. But they always say, "You do the bare minimum. You study, then once you've done enough, you stop. You should do more than's expected of you." Then that will be expected of me all the time. Then I'll have to keep piling on more and more work just to do more than's expected of me.

Michael, the elder brother, confirms the other family members' perceptions of the differences between the two brothers. Just as Lakshmi and Shivan note the different problems they have faced with the two boys concerning grades, and Bob notes his brother's relatively recent "insanity" in comparison to his own more long-standing "insane" self, Michael notes that his younger brother is "different" despite facing some of the psychological issues he himself had faced. Again, what we are seeing is the use of contrasts among family members to work out the unique identities of each.

A lot of the things I went through psychologically, he's going through. But he's different. I studied a lot in school. He's more into arts, and he's a lot more socially active than I was. There's different things, they manifest themselves differently. So he has more trouble with my parents than I did.

Did you see him when he walked by? He's into all sorts of punk music and wearing leather jackets, and he's got a skull earring. He wants to go to flesh metal concerts, and my parents don't want him to go to those. And he makes a big deal about it because he wants to go. He's a punker already, and they're worried he's going to go and become a gang fiend or something. They see the tendencies toward that side, and they're more worried about that than they would have been with me, because I watched a lot of TV and I did a lot of computer stuff, so it wasn't really an issue.

I don't think he's on his way to gangland, but I think some of his friends aren't the best people. A lot of his friends do drugs and stuff, and I don't think that's good, I don't think that's a good influence. But I think he's a pretty smart kid, so he's not going to . . . I see where it could happen, but I think the biggest problem is just that he's . . . kind of . . . he's extremist in the way that he's not willing to compromise. So when he comes and asks my parents for something and they don't want to do it, he's not willing to compromise. So he just makes a big scene, then he gets into trouble. That's, I think, the biggest problem.

Michael, however, has his own set of disagreements with his parents. These days, the major disagreement concerns his choice of a college major.

The newest thing is, I've always been good at science and math, so I figured I'd do engineering when I went to college. But now I think I want to go to law school instead. So I'm thinking of changing my major. But my parents want me to finish engineering and then go to law school. I want to change to political science or something and go to law school.

I don't like engineering. Since I'm not going to be an engineer, why should I put myself through a lot of stuff that I don't like when I enjoy doing political analysis and stuff?

Ultimately, who makes the decision?

I guess I do. They won't force me to do anything. It'll be debated back and forth before a decision is made. I can see both sides of it. I'm feeling I want to do one thing, and I'm trying to figure out if I want to do that because it's easier or it's what I want to do, or what would be best. I'll have to figure it out.

There's always been a big emphasis on grades. There's always been a lot of pressure to get straight A's. If you get a couple of B's, they say you've got the talent and you shouldn't be getting these grades, study harder.

Is that important to you?

Yeah. I think you should try to get straight A's. But I'm saying that, like, when I was in high school, sometimes if I got a B, I'd feel really, really bad. I'd come home, and I'd have to try to explain it to my dad, I got a B instead of an A. And looking back on it, I don't think that . . . that much pressure . . . well, I mean, it's good to teach the kids to go for straight A's, if you believe they can do it.

I remember one time, I got my first B in high school, and I was coming home and trying to explain to my dad why I got a B. I was feeling so bad, like I disappointed him so much. That was bad. I think that there was a little more pressure to get straight A's or be the number one in school. More than a lot of other kids had. I don't know if that's just my parents—because they've always been successful.

Now it is still a big issue, but not as much. When you're a kid, what your parents feel is what you feel. So now I realize that they might not always be right. While I still feel if I get a couple B's when I could have gotten all A's, I feel really bad, and I try to explain to my parents that I could have gotten the A's. So I feel really bad about that, too. But it's not as bad, 'cause I know if I tried hard, I know when I've worked in class and when I could and when I couldn't have gotten better. I feel less bad about it personally, but they still think I should be getting straight A's.

While Bob is the "extremist" and Michael has been more sedate, both boys have had their disagreements with their parents, over grades and over life choices (be it punk rock versus classical music or political science versus engineering). One thing that is striking to me is that neither son discusses his disagreements with parents in terms of the parents being Indian. This is in sharp contrast to the ubiquity of her mother's Indianness in Anar Nagar's adolescent traumas. Her mother's Indian point of view was always an issue and sometimes blocked communication altogether. Disagreements in the Iyengar family are rarely over Indianness. "Philosophy" seems paramount, whether disagreements are between parents and children or between parents.

In addition to the issue of grades, career choice is important to Bob and Michael's parents. However, unlike their consensus on basic values, Lakshmi and Shivan do not totally agree on the guidance they should give to their sons concerning careers.

Lakshmi: To be honest with you, even though we like to say, "We want you to be happy, we want you to set your own goals," we also have goals for them.

Shivan: [I want them to be] successful in terms of being able to meet all of their desires and successful as good human beings. And if their desires require them to be rich, for them to satisfy their desires, I hope they're rich. If it's not, I hope that what money they have, they'll give it to other people who need that money to achieve their desires.

Lakshmi: Yeah, I hope that, in today's world, forgetting whether they're Indian or American, and this is one of the areas where we have some, at least I have some confusion again. If we had brought them up as sort of typical Indian immigrant families, we could have given them a real clear sense of what they should be when they grow up. Doctor, lawyer, engineer.

And we did some of that, because we really emphasize academics a lot. When they come home with C's, we don't like it. When they come home with A's, we say, "You could do better." So that's definitely a very important part of it.

But we haven't done it with the same sort of conviction that makes them chase it with the same conviction. So they end up having mixed signals and mixed results. Because, you know, we say we value extracurricular activities, you should be well rounded human beings, and you should have a social life, and all the things that make you be a well-adjusted human being. So I think we have given mixed signals there.

So one of my fears has been sort of saying what I'd like them to do when they grow up. My fears are that, you know, under the worst of circumstances, there's going to be these zillions of young kids today who are unsure of what they want to be when they grow up, and they try this for a little while and they try that for a little while. And that's something that we're very nervous about. So we sit and talk to them a lot about it.

And the other thing is that, you know, I really would like to see them do what they're doing well and with total commitment. And I think if they did that, they'd be very successful. Because if you do something well and with total commitment, you're bound to get enough money to do it, you're bound to make yourself happy.

Shivan: If you want to break rocks, you do it with total commitment . . . ?

Lakshmi: Well, within the realm of possibilities, you could be a good musician . . .

Shivan: Society puts values, right or wrong, on certain kinds of activities, less value on certain other kinds of activities. All you have to do is to turn around and look at newspaper articles on teacher contract negotiations and in the sports page what they are paying the most recent baseball pitcher. That's a value system that's been very clearly established. That automatically denies the thesis that if you are the best at what you are in your chosen field, you're going to have as much opportunity to make a living as if you had picked a different field. Here it seems to be a two-variable function. It depends on the field you have chosen and also how good you are in that field.

So, in terms of what do I hope, I hope they pick the right things that will permit them to lead a decent life. That's to be able for them to provide for their desires and expectations for themselves and for their families.

Have you tried to give them any guidance in terms of what career might be preferable, or encouraged, versus other careers?

Shivan: If I have, I have not succeeded. I tried to talk to both of my kids about the fact that a medical profession might be an extremely interesting one. Not necessarily in terms of practicing medicine, but even if it is a research-type thing, because it's something I have always . . . all of us in one way or another seem to be involved in the health-care business. You look around saying here is something you have a nice foundation of being able to make a decent living, at the same time make a difference. A lot more than selling soap.

But one session with the fetal pig was enough. No way. And that was that. Did I really push hard? No.

Lakshmi: In this area, we have slightly differing . . . I mean, I'm more optimistic about being able to make it. And the kids really have a problem with this conflict because, you know, push academics but also the social life and everything else. We say, "If you can't make money, if you're poor and you're hungry, you can't produce anything that's worthwhile. You can't be creative." On the other hand, you know, I kind of tend to say, "If you do what you do well, you can be successful."

And Bob has often said, "I want to be a musician." And I said, "Well, you know, if you end up being a musician, at least as long as I'm alive, I'll support you."

Shivan: We don't have a slight difference of opinion here, we have the most contradicting views. To the point where I think a reconciliation of these views is . . . I have given up. Because I don't think there is possibility to reconcile.

Lakshmi: We grew up in India, where you don't have the chance to futz around. When you're taking your high school graduation exams, you focus on a certain group of subjects which excludes other groups of subjects. Then, when you go to college, you know, if you go to engineering school, you go to engineering school. If you go to medical school, you go to medical school. It's not like here, where you can get basic liberal arts or something and then you can change. If you do engineering, you can't become a doctor later on.

But you take Michael, for instance. He thought he was all set to be an engineer, and now he wants to study political science. I don't know if he'll end up being a lawyer or what, but it certainly created significant trauma in us that he wants to change. And, you know, while we didn't force him to change or not change, we did have a very serious talk with him to say, "This is a big decision."

So, what's so scary about the prospect of changing to political science?

Lakshmi: For one thing, I'll tell you, it shows a lack of intellectual discipline. And commitment, you know.

Shivan: Finish something that you start with.

Lakshmi: And really think about what it is you want to do. Because today, I can say I should have been a doctor. And I can say, "Fine, I'm going to go back to medical school and become a doctor." And maybe it's a perfectly wonderful thing for me to do. But, you know, there are consequences, not just on myself but on the people around me. And this is where I come back to, you know, values and everything else. If you decide you're going to futz around, there are consequences to this. On every aspect of your life.

Shivan: But there's also something else, and that is that it's very easy for you to say, "I'm going to do this." You get into it, and the first time you hit some difficulty, you say, "Hey, I really have to work at the thing. It's not as easy as it looks." Saying, "I'm going to change." Because that looks easier. Sooner or later in life, you're going to find yourself in a position where you're going to have to dig deep and just do something whether you like it or not, and try to do it well. And this flipping around raises a question, saying, "Hey, are you learning that skill?"

And what we told him was, "Hey, you want to switch? Switch. But finish what you started. You want to be a lawyer? Finish what you started, and then go into a law program or anything else. But finish something that you started. It doesn't matter whether you like it or not. And, actually, people will be looking for that skill. You are demonstrating that you can do well in a challenging environment, even if that environment was not what you were defining as ideal. That says you have the ability to buckle down and deliver. Get through it if you have to."

The Iyengars' concerns with getting good grades, doing what one does well, picking a career to maximize one's options and secure one's lifestyle, finishing what one starts, are all emblems, as Michael rightly points out, of the Iyengars' own successes in their education and careers.

Shortly after their marriage in 1969, Lakshmi and Shivan came to the United States to pursue advanced degrees. Shivan switched from an original plan of pursuing a Ph.D. in engineering to an M.B.A. program at a top university. Lakshmi went on to complete her Ph.D. in physics. Since completing his M.B.A., Shivan has been employed in management in a large medical firm. After a series of positions as a computer analyst and computer services director, Lakshmi has started her own consulting business, with a burgeoning business in trade with the former Eastern bloc. They are both ambitious, motivated, and dedicated to their careers.

Although the Iyengars' emphasis on success is consistent with a similar emphasis in other families, the Iyengars themselves do not see this emphasis as particularly Indian. In relation to their troubles with Bob and grades, Lakshmi explicitly says that these problems are simply "parenting problems," and both claim that they have "nothing to do with being Indian." Similarly, their treatment of their disagreement with Michael over his change of major is prefaced by a discussion of the way it was in India regarding career choices (i.e., that one just went along established tracks with limited choices). The subject of Michael is introduced after this discussion as a point of contrast: "But you take Michael, for instance. He thought he was all set to be an engineer, and now he wants to study political science." Their arguments in favor of Michael sticking with engineering center on the value of "intellectual discipline," not on the Indian values of more or less prestigious careers.

When the Iyengars and their sons do talk about things Indian, it is with a certain detachment or objectivity. Indian culture is composed of specific skills, interests, and obligations. By virtue of their particular histories, the Iyengars have access to these cultural attributes. One can imagine that others may gain similar access through dedicated study or particular experiences (such as living abroad) that establish links to India. This objectivist view is evident even in Lakshmi and Shivan's early experiences as Indians living abroad. Lakshmi comments on their early days as graduate students.

> I showed off our culture. We didn't really feel a need to either integrate or not integrate. Now we think about some of those issues, but at that time we were just a few Indians.
>
> I always wore a sari, and I had my hair up, and it was long. I was not at all uncomfortable. In many ways, I am uncomfortable today if I dress in conventional Indian dress.
>
> I performed my *bharata natyam* in functions. A local television station had a cultural program. In those days, it was unique. Exotic. That's the word. I was very exotic. But I didn't feel exotic. I was happy to share my culture and background. But even in India, we had been used to listening to Western music and Indian music. And even here, we were used to listening to both. My husband was and is a connois-

seur of Western classical music. I didn't feel like I didn't integrate. But at the same time, I didn't change myself in any way.

Were most of our friends Indians? This is true. But we had some Western friends, too. Okay, let me put it this way. I think that, you know, we had several Western friends, but I think we felt that it was natural for us to be friends with all the Indians who were there. That it was in some way our responsibility. So even if they were not our . . . in other ways would be good friends, just because they were Indians, we socialized with them. But in my classes, some of my American friends were closer friends to me than my Indian friends.

Their early connection to other Indians was simply because they shared a certain background, not because they themselves felt more comfortable with other Indians. Similarly, Lakshmi's dress and *bharata natyam* performances resulted from what she happened to know rather than any ideological commitment to Indian culture. Shivan concurs with Lakshmi's feelings that "to integrate or not integrate" was never a very pressing issue.

Sometimes we sit back and say, "Hey, you know, we really are not part of this Indian community." And you ask yourself, are you part of the American community, and say probably. I don't know. As much a part of one as the other.

We had some good Indian friends. But it was more because either we knew each other before, or I was into cricket and those guys were into cricket so we played cricket together. But if we had found Americans who had the same interests, it would have been the same way. It was commonality of interests that brought the friends together rather than the nationality.

In recent years, this feeling continues.

Lakshmi: Well, actually, you can divide our life into sort of two segments. There was a suburban segment, and there's a Chicago segment. In the suburban segment, we had a lot of Indian friends. We did a lot of Indian socializing. And we threw parties for Indians that had twenty people and thirty people. And, you know, Divali celebrations. But it wasn't "Indian."

Shivan: They just happened to be our friends. These are some of the guys I went to college with, that I ran back into here. We played the same kinds of games. We were part of the same teams.

Lakshmi: Even today, it would not be fair to say that . . . supposing we had a New Year's Eve party this year. I would have to say maybe at least forty percent of the people would be Indian.

We haven't participated in any organized Indian activity. So, you know, we don't organize or create an Indian activity. But it would be wrong to say that we don't have an affinity for Indians. You just have affinity for the people you've grown up with.

Despite this lack of concern with their status as Indians in America, issues of cultural change have arisen. Lakshmi, for instance, attributes her initial difficulty in getting a job to her Indian attire. She "found that people just focus on your cultural life rather than on you." When she cut her hair and went to three more interviews wearing a "real stupid looking polyester pantsuit," she landed all three jobs. However, the Iyengars see the adjustments they have made as more instrumental than morally troublesome.

This interpretation of the Iyengars' adjustment dilemmas is further reinforced by the way they frame their own attitudes toward cultural change in contrast to those of the Indian community in general. Just as Vaidehi Nagar and her daughters spoke of their commitment to certain egalitarian values in their hearts in contrast to typical Indian beliefs, the Iyengars use the prototype of Indians to define their family's idiom and the pragmatic approach they have taken to the process of assimilation. In the following passage, Lakshmi in particular articulates her family's commitment to cultural eclecticism by contrasting it with the attitudes of cultural chauvinism she feels characterize the Indian community.

Lakshmi: If I were to get up on the pulpit, I would tell the Indian community, you know, you guys are absolutely, I mean, they're bastards. They just want to take the economics of the situation, and you don't want to melt in. And the supercilious attitude that . . . they are superior. Our values are superior. I think this thing has to fix, because what they're giving their kids is, you know, when I hear a twenty-year-old child mouthing the same things 'cause he's heard it from his father. Then I say this kid is doomed. And our community is doomed.

And when a guy stands for election and says, "I'm an Indian, and I'm going to stand for election as an Indian," then I say, "Go back to India." How can a guy stand for election as an Indian when he has a constituency that . . . it's segregationist.

And that is one thing that our kids have not picked up. That they are not segregationist. And, you know, it's most wonderful when my mother comes, and my mother is very attached to Michael. Very first grandson and whatever. I don't know what it is. But anyway, she will sit down, and she'll talk to him about, you know, she's really worried. "Why doesn't he have Indian girlfriends? All the girls who come here are white" and blah blah blah.

He said, "No, Grandma, I have black girlfriends, too." His prom date was a black girl.

My mother died, you know. He brought his date over, he hadn't told my mother. And I said, "It's not fair you go to the prom and I don't see both of you nicely dressed. So they came over, and my mother died. And, you know, she was like, "My grandson is so handsome." And I said, "The girl's very pretty, too." So she tries to talk to him, and, you know, it's interesting for me. Then I feel really good that we've given them a good set of values. I feel really good because he can calmly try to tell her what he's interested in, in a girl.

It's interesting that in the last four or five years, my parents have started to come around in their thinking. That, you know, whatever color their granddaughter-in-law's going to be, it's going to be okay. Because all his friends come, they go, you know, "Oh, Grandma . . ." It's very difficult not to love charming kids.

Lakshmi and Shivan's pragmatic approach to cultural attributes is echoed by their sons, demonstrating again the power of parents' experiences and outlooks to shape an overall tone for the family. The elements of Lakshmi's and Shivan's lives that remain Indian are rooted in the simple fact of their having been brought up in India. Their sons have been similarly shaped by their American upbringing. Any interest in India and their own Indianness is limited to an interest in the material aspects of Indian culture, if that.

When I was talking to Michael about his friends when he attended a Montessori elementary school, I asked if any were Indian or the children of immigrants.

I don't remember there being any children of immigrants. There was an Italian kid, but he wasn't really Italian. A couple of black kids and stuff, but that's not really immigrants, either. So I think I was the only immigrant kid. But I never considered myself an immigrant kid, because I always lived in America and grown up, so I was as American as anybody else.

Later, when I asked about his friends in high school in a less intrusive fashion ("Tell me about your friends"), he responded by discussing their ethnicity.

Couple of white kids. There's a couple of Jewish kids. Couple of Oriental kids. They're all Americanized. I know a couple of Indian kids, too, but they're all Americanized, too. One girl speaks Tamil. I don't know, she speaks it at home. But she's still pretty Americanized. So I don't feel that any of my friends are more or less . . . they're all pretty much like me. Immigrant friends, which their parents are immigrants or whatever, they're pretty much Americanized.

Michael said that visits to India are the way he got most of his contact with culture.

[We went to India] about every other year, every other summer. It was really different. At that time, I didn't notice any, like, culture or anything. So it was just a different place. It was like I was on vacation, visiting another country. Like my family all got together, and we went to Japan or something. It would be like that.

My mom had millions of cousins, and my dad has a lot of brothers and sisters. So we'd go play cricket.

The other way that I got most of my culture was they had these comic books. Tales and legends and things like that. I was big into those. I don't know where they are now, but I had huge collections of these Indian comic books which told all the legends and history and stuff like that. So I know a whole lot about that. That's probably where I got most of my knowledge of Indian culture was from stuff like that.

It seems to me that our life was pretty much like the life of a regular American family, except the food we ate and maybe some of the books I read. While they kept me in touch with Indian culture, they didn't do anything special.

I feel like I'm as much American as I am Indian. I've grown up here and lived here so much. I'm probably more American than I am Indian, it's just I have a pretty good knowledge of India as a country, its culture and stuff.

I asked Michael about his thread ceremony, which marks the transition to adulthood for young men.

I had that. The thing is that I'm not really that religious. I don't subscribe to any particular belief or anything. So, when it was done, it was done more as a ceremony that my grandparents wanted to have done. My parents aren't religious, either, so they went along. I don't know whether they believed in it or not, but they went along with it because my grandparents wanted to have it done.

I got dressed up in traditional clothes, and they had a priest come that said all kinds of things. It was in my dad's parents' house. They'd, like, draw designs on the ground, and my dad had to come and whisper things in my ear. Supposedly passing on the knowledge of the ages or something. It was both for him and me just ceremonial.

There were things I was supposed to say back. It wasn't that much I had to say. And also there were people giving me cues and stuff on what to say as it was going on, so it wasn't that hard. And then they poured water on me. It was supposed to give me a bath, cleanse me, I guess. I ate some little bits of food here and there that were brought by people. It takes a long time. It took like a whole day. It's mostly just like different things, like my parents come and say things, and I sit in front of, like, a ritual fire, and the priest does things.

I also asked Michael about his involvement in Indian organizations at college.

My parents always ask me why I didn't join that. I just didn't. I think actually it's a little silly, 'cause most of the kids who are Indians at the university are not immigrants themselves, but they've grown up here. I don't see how they need an association to keep their . . . I can understand it if they're all immigrants and if they get together because they want a place where they can come and talk in Tamil, eat Indian food, and stuff. I just think it's kind of silly to sort of set them aside from everybody else as being Indian students when they're all pretty much American.

You can sort of look around the house. We've got some Indian decorations and stuff, but it's a lot like a regular American house. I don't think my friends ever thought of me as being particularly Indian, just as being another kid. I was never teased for being Indian or anything.

I haven't really lived an Indian life. Like you say, in India it's what they do, but I've lived a lot more of an American life. I've lived my whole life here. My parents have tried to keep us as regular kids as they could. Like, if kids were really different . . .

Like, I remember there was a Sikh kid in high school for a year, my first year in high school, and he had . . . not a turban, there was like a little baggie on his head. So we used to call him the kid with the bag on top of his head. He got teased sometimes about it. They probably didn't want us to get teased about being different, so . . .

Do you ever miss that? Do you ever miss not having a stronger sense of . . .

Not personally, because I think I have a strong sense of me, just who I am. I don't need any external sense of being anything, 'cause I'm . . . I think I have a pretty strong identity as to who I am. I'm pretty secure in what I can do, and who I am, and my friends and everything like that. I never felt that I needed anything extra to define "me." I think that probably my kids are going to have even less of an experience with Indian culture than I did. I'll probably give them some of it, because it'll be important to my parents and grandparents. But personally, to me, it wouldn't . . . to me, it's not that big of a deal. I'll show them some of the culture, like legends and things like that, because I think it's interesting. But not because it's particularly significant. I consider myself as American as the people down the street.

Bob talks about his essential Americanness in much the same way as his elder brother, but he seems to lack even the tourist's curiosity that Michael feels toward India.

So let's talk a little bit about being Indian.

I can't really say I know, 'cause since I was born, I've felt like an American. Most of my friends have thought of me as an American, and nobody really cares, actually. I mean, I've grown up with an American accent. No Indian anybody plays hard-core guitar, screams in a death grunt when he sings. So I'm considered another one of the guys.

On one occasion, Lakshmi did express at length some desire to pass on something of an Indian sensibility to her children. Even here, though, her ambivalence is clear.

I don't know. If you meet my kids, you . . . we haven't been . . . maybe because we don't have daughters. Somewhere in the middle, I tried to take our older son to Sanskrit lessons. Then I gave that up as a lost cause. Because I personally didn't feel comfortable with the other people who were there, and forcing my kid to be comfortable with the other people who were there was really stupid.

They're very, very religious, and very Tamil. Not even Indian. That's something that really bugs me about some of the immigrants here. They're more sectarian than they would be if they were in India. Many of my classmates in India, their kids don't speak Hindi, either. They speak whatever language their servants and their community do, but English is their mother tongue. They feel about religion the way we do—which is mixed.

I feel like we sort of have to have a more open view of all cultures and religions. My son's classmates were all Jewish and black. I think our kids are fairly well integrated. They have problems, not because they're Indians but because they're teenagers. Sometimes they'll come home and they'll say, "You don't want us to do thus-and-so because you didn't do thus-and-so, but you grew up in India, not here."

Like our fifteen-year-old son, I was talking to him about this, some of his friends and their promiscuous behavior that I just didn't feel was proper. Forgetting the fact . . . I said it's not proper in any country. Go to Sweden, and I don't think it's proper. His response was that it's perfectly proper in today's American society, and it's normal, quote-unquote, and our response of shock is because of our Indian upbringing. Even that keeps getting thrown here and there.

And my parents feel their grandchildren should marry Indian girls. I figure there are some Indian girls I would just not want him to marry at all, and there are some Western girls that I would say, "Hey, you know, she would make a good wife for you. You'd do well together."

We do visit the temple. I take the kids to the temple. Again, I try to go there on the weekday when there's not so many crowds there, some of the fanfare gets to me. I don't know why. It's just, I think, Hinduism is more for personal internal religion than social religion, and I think that what people are doing here is making it more social than it is even in India.

We have a little corner [in the house]. I've always had a little corner with the deities and the lamp and so on, so it gives some atmosphere for all of us. At least for me, in those few seconds, I can think about whatever I want for my life today. Then I try to tell the kids to notice it if nothing else.

Do you think they do?

Yeah, I think they do. I think they notice it, but they don't necessarily believe it. They would be very quick to say they don't believe it, but I prefer not to talk about it because then, you know, you establish a view. But they'll complain about going to the temple, but I say, "Hey, do it for my sake."

My cousins and my relatives just wonder what I'm doing. I'm not sure what I'm doing, either. But at the same time, I feel it gives them something, too. That they belong to something. My kids sometimes say I'm a hypocrite. My husband's totally neutral about it. Whether we're Indian or non-Indian, it begins and ends with me.

On the one hand, I want something culturally, you know, some identity forming, something, I don't know what. I can't even describe it. But on the other hand, when an Indian family sits and says, "This is good about being Indian, and this is bad about being American," or vice versa, I just know that this kid's going to walk through the door and say, "Dad, this is my new husband." And he's going to choke because this kid's going to be white and blond. And all the characteristics that he categorized, you know, are going to be in her mind, but she's going to be in love with this guy.

I have mixed opinions. Maybe we brought up our kids too liberal. Maybe they're going to be all unhappy.

Lakshmi and Shivan Iyengar, I think, more so than any other parents I studied, are genuinely ambivalent about Indianness and the role that their Indian heritage should play in their lives. For other families, Indianness is either the unquestioned core of family experience, as for the Nagars (chapter 7), the Kumars (chapter 9), and the Shankars (chapter 11), or a part of life that has clearly been subordinated to alternative identities, as for the Shenoys (chapter 10).

At the same time, however, I think the Iyengars' ambivalence has given their family a certain strength and stability. Precisely because Lakshmi and Shivan question the value of an essentialized Indianness themselves and are open with their children about their uncertainties, their sons have not felt the need to come to terms with their Indianness in their own lives the way the Nagar girls have, for example. For Michael and Bob, the fact that they are of Indian heritage has not compelled them to broadcast their ethnicity, to seek out Indian friends, or to ruminate about the place of Indianness in their developing identities. Each is comfortable being just another one of the guys.

Aside from their parental example, however, the Iyengar boys' way of dealing with an ethnicity that has the potential to mark them as different from "the mainstream" has been shaped by the community in which the family has lived. Their neighborhood and the school the boys attend are both very well integrated and politically progressive. The Nagar girls, in contrast, have been raised in a much more homogeneous and conservative community and were forced by that context to pay attention to their Indianness.

Another element of the Iyengar family's story that I think deserves comment is the developing individuation of their sons. It is in this area that I think the Iyengars do have expectations and values deeply rooted in their own Indian upbringing. Lakshmi and Shivan themselves discuss their attitudes toward family—the notion of an extended family, in particular—as perhaps Indian. They are comfortable in a household "with a lot of comings and goings." In their life in America, however, this extended family concept has encompassed extended stays not only by their parents and relatives but their children's friends and a series of European exchange students.

This Indian aspect of their lives extends beyond the surface organization of the household to a deeper attachment to their sons. As Lakshmi says, "We are very clingy." She expects to keep her sons' rooms intact forever. I think they also expect a continuation of their sons' integral place in the family. The Iyengars want to retain an emotional and social bond with their sons that is not so common in Christian, European-origin families in their economic class (what the Indian community perennially refers to as "the mainstream").

This fear of separation is at the root of their arguments over Bob's involvement in heavy metal, and even at the root of their concern about Michael's change of major. Both parents, on different occasions, have expressed a distrust of this "individualism" that pervades American culture. As their sons try out their wings, begin to pursue their own desires, that individuality threatens to leave them "isolated, lonely, and unhappy" and to break the familial bonds the Iyengars have strived so hard to preserve.

If there is some deepest Indianness that persists in all families of Indian origin, I think it revolves around the balance between individual personhood and familial bonds. While Michael and Bob seem true to their own self-description, pretty much Americanized, I cannot say whether or not they have truly diverged from the kinds of intense familial bonds that I see in the other Indian families described here. Even in the most highly "Westernized" Shenoy family (chapter 10), the parental bond has persisted, often to the amazement of the Shenoy children themselves, now in their late twenties.

Thinking back to the portrait of the Nagars, and to the suggestions I made concerning the way that family's experiences could help us understand something about the processes of intergenerational change or assimilation, it is clear that both the importance of particular histories and the notion of a family idiom apply equally as well to the Iyengars. Vaidehi Nagar had a very different upbringing and is a very different kind of Indian from Lakshmi or Shivan Iyengar. The particular experiences of the parents in these two families molded what they have tried to accomplish in raising their children. Vaidehi has tried to create an "atmosphere" in her home in which both Indian material and social culture are available and positively reinforced. Each of her daughters has been influenced by this presence, although Anar has been troubled by the social aspects of Indianness and Mausami more engaged with the material aspects of her heritage. Similarly, just as Lakshmi and Shivan are "historical" Indians shaped by their relatively liberal upbringings, their boys are "historical" Americans. As they repeatedly pointed out, they have been born and raised in the United States.

That, coupled with the liberal outlook of their parents, has shaped the persons they have become.

This notion of historical ethnicity is what I would identify as the Iyengar family idiom. The Nagars talked about their life experiences in terms that led me to see "heart" and "duty" as recurring themes in their understanding of their lives. Social relationships, determined by age, kinship, and sex, were played out in terms of heart and duty—the dictates of one's "inner self," and the demands of propriety. For the Iyengars, while they, too, have concerns about social relations, particularly about maintaining strong relationships between generations, the dominant idiom coloring most stories and experiences they chose to share concerned their notion of themselves as historical accidents. Their formative environments are incidental. Growing up in India versus in the United States did not make parents and children fundamentally different kinds of persons. At most, it left a residual of "affinities" which affected subsequent choices of friends and lifestyle. And, as with the Nagars' use of heart and duty, the Iyengars' sensitivity to historical accident gave them a common language through which the family could both share a certain experience (creating a kind of familial bond) and make sense of the change processes that were taking place across generations.

Finally, we see repeated by the Iyengars the use of comparison as a tool for staking out familial and individual identities. As a family, they are not like other Indians. They do not share a view of Indian culture as superior. They do not want to push their children into suitably prestigious careers. As Michael and Lakshmi both report, no one wanted the boys to feel "different" from their peers. As individuals, they are different from one another. Lakshmi and Shivan differ in their ideas about suitable careers for the boys and in their interest in passing on any sense of Indianness to their sons. The difference in temperament between the two boys is evident from everyone's perspective. Like the Nagars, then, the Iyengars use this process of comparison to define and identify themselves.

9

The Kumars:
Compromise

The Kumars are practicing Christians who emigrated from Hyderabad, Andhra Pradesh, in the late 1970s, with three children in tow. They did not come "for a few years" with the idea of returning to India.[1] Unlike most Indian immigrant families of the late '60s and early '70s, Ravi and Ratna Kumar were not a young couple whose emigration was contingent upon a decision to break away from their parents in India. Instead, Ravi's mother, widowed for six or seven years, had been the first in the family to move to the United States. It was she who encouraged her four sons in India and their families to join her there. Within a few years of Ravi's mother's immigration, the entire family had been reunited in Chicago and lived together in the apartments of a three-flat.

Although they have not escaped the parent-teenager conflicts that characterize all the families I studied, the permanence of their immigration decision has allowed the Kumars to anticipate and prepare for the difficulties they knew they would face in raising their children through adolescence. Other families thought that by the time the troubled teens rolled around, the family would be safely back in India, where (they assumed) temptations would be fewer and options would be limited. The Kumars, in contrast, have been preparing for the imminent teenage crises since before they arrived.

This aspect of the Kumars' particular history provides another example of how biography shapes behavior over time and ultimately guides the processes of assimilation along certain paths. We cannot, however, simply look at the intended permanence of immigration as a variable related to other indices of assimilation (the degree or content of parent-child conflict, for example). Rather, we need to examine in detail the way the Kumars *use* their particular situation to ground discussions and develop strategies to cope with intergenerational issues. It is the *process* whereby the anticipated permanence of their immigration *affects* particular assimilative outcomes that is of interest, rather than correlations between initial intentions and particular outcomes themselves.

The process of adjustment in this family has also been greatly influenced by its Christianity. For the Kumars, their identity as Christians is of equal if not greater importance than their identity as Indians. Furthermore, unlike other families for whom religion is important, the Kumars seem to view their Indian and Christian identities as separable (although they see them as sharing many fundamental values in common). In other families, a single "cultural" identity encompassed both religion and national origin. I will argue that this separable Christian identity, one they can share in common with at least a segment of the non-Indian-immigrant population of America, has shaped the way they view their process of adjustment, particularly the view of the Kumar children—the second generation.

I came to know the Kumars through their church. They belong to one of the many small Indian Christian churches in Chicago. During my fieldwork in the Indian community's organizational network, I had come in contact with leaders of these Indian Christian organizations. I wanted to include at least one non-Hindu family in this study, so I asked some of the leaders if any families they knew would be willing to participate, and I was introduced to the Kumars.

The Kumars live in a middle-class neighborhood in Chicago, made up largely of small detached houses. One of the larger homes on their block, their home has been expanded to include enough bedrooms for each of their three children and the occasional guest. On the first floor, one enters a cozy living room and dining area filled with family photos and Indian knickknacks. In contrast to the rather formal display of Indian artifacts in some other homes, the Kumars' things are much more informal and have a folk art feel to them. The atmosphere is very cheerful.

Ravi and Ratna both grew up in major cities in southeastern India. Ravi was the eldest of four brothers, and Ratna was the fifth child. At age four or five, Ratna was given by her birth parents to be raised by her father's sister and her husband, who were childless. So Ratna actually grew up as an only child with her aunt and uncle, whom she considered her "mom and dad."

Ravi and Ratna's marriage was arranged by the families shortly after Ravi's father passed away. Ravi says that his mother's health was failing, and she wanted to see Ravi married before she died. At the time, he was nineteen years old. After his father became ill, Ravi stopped attending college full-time and took a clerical job. He continued to go to night school, eventually getting his bachelor's degree.

Ratna recalls her family's reasoning in arranging her marriage when she, too, was nineteen.

Oh, that's a story. It was an arranged marriage. Actually, I did not even know my husband or his family. We went to somebody's engagement, and there his aunt saw me. She invited me to her house. On the same day, he, my husband, and his mom showed up there. They were looking for somebody for my husband to get married. He was around twenty years or so. Then I guess they were interested in me, and so they proposed to my father, you know, I would like this match? So, of course, as all girls would say, they don't want to get married now. Anyway, he [her father] convinced me and said, "Yes, you have to get married. It's better." You know how in India, they usually say, this was what my dad's logic was—they had no girls in the house, my husband's family was all boys. So they thought I'll be the oldest daughter-in-law. 'Cause he's oldest in the house, my husband. So they said, "You'll be the oldest." Oldest has a certain place, so I would be given all the responsibilities, and the special treatment would be there. So that's how they told me. I got engaged on May 1. See, actually, I met him on March 31, I remember then the engagement was May 1, and I got married then the 11th. It was all in one month and ten days.

After their marriage, Ravi and Ratna resided with Ravi's mother and brothers. Part of the marriage agreement had been that Ratna could continue her education. She was a high school student when they were married. Ratna describes her mother-in-law as very supportive of her continuing her education. She continued in school, completing her intermediate and then her bachelor's. During this time, she and Ravi had their three children. Among the ayah, or nursemaid, other household servants, and Ravi's mother, there was always enough help available to allow Ravi and Ratna to work, continue their educations, and start their family.

After her immigration, Ravi's mother started urging Ravi and Ratna to move to America. Their main concern in making the decision to come was the impact life in the United States would have on their ability to raise their children as they wanted. Ravi and Ratna had each briefly visited the States after Ravi's mother moved. During their stays, they became aware of the different mores and lifestyles that their children would be exposed to if they emigrated. So, before they decided to come permanently, both agreed that they would have to make some compromises with regard to how they would be able to bring up their children. Ravi recalls:

Back in India, before we came, we said there are things we have to compromise. Some things. What are our limits? How far we can go? How much can we compromise? What are the things we cannot compromise? Then we decided, we can compromise to certain extent. But again, we said, you know, something can happen where it is beyond our expectation. We don't even know what it is, until it happens. How do we handle? Then we said, we'll have to take that chance.

See, actually, they are in college right now. They don't drink. They don't smoke. They don't do any drugs. And no sex. That's a great accomplishment in college and afterward. That means we know that it's going good, our relationship. Working and doing everything like that, compromise and adjusting and understanding.

Ravi feels his kids are doing better than many other Indian kids. He attributes some of the problems he sees with other kids to their parents.

Well, in other kids, some kids, I say, they have problems with parents. Because I think it is something wrong with the parents, too. They are too strict, or they are not compromising. Or they think, with good intentions only, they think that changing so much is not good for them. So what they do is, they are so strict, they [the kids] break open. And then they really get into trouble. And they do some things which are not beneficial to them.*

Although the Kumars approached the task of rearing their children in the United States with the idea that some compromise will be necessary, this does not mean that the compromises have been easy. The issues of hair and clothing styles are among the least serious of the family's disagreements but nonetheless illustrate the Kumars' search for workable compromises and the feelings that attend that search.

The second daughter, Anu, age twenty, describes her view of the hair and clothing issue.

Oh, sure, you go through stages of crisis. High school clothing. My father didn't like me to roll up my pants. And then my hair, he hates my hair. Even if I had it straight, he didn't like it, 'cause I'd leave it open, and he didn't like the way it looked. 'Cause it looked too fine, you know. That's what guys look for when they go rape people. So I'm like, "Okay, Dad." Finally, he gets used to it, and then I go do this. [She now has a permanent.]

Ravi's account of the same issues corroborates Anu's perception of her father's struggle to feel comfortable with these changes.

Well, now they started going to teenagers. Once they started going to high school, lot of competition is there. Lot of peer pressure. I mean, from fashions to eating habits, their talk. And everything slowly started changing.

---

* Ravi is using the standard techniques of comparisons to prototypical Indians to distinguish or delineate the identity of his family. Implicit in this passage is a comparison of his kids to other Indian-origin kids and a comparison of his and Ratna's willingness to compromise to the rigidity of the prototypical Indian parent.

And now we started worrying at that time, you know. They used to come home, and their talking was different. Still some words I don't know the meaning of it. But I know it's not very bad, not vulgar. But it is kind of disrespectful. So whenever they . . . "Oh, stupid." A casual thing, but you know, for us, why do you call a person stupid? That was a great shock even to say that.

Slowly now we started realizing, okay, maybe that's just casual way of doing. But if we say to them, "Stupid," they get mad. I asked them how come? I just wanted to see their reaction one day, and I said, you know, "Hey, you stupid." And my son got so angry. It was in the car. He actually got out of the car. "Wait a minute. You talk to your sisters and call 'You stupid' and all these things, and when I say it, why are you getting so upset?" "No, Daddy. You shouldn't say that." I mean, it's a matter of fact for them. It's a casual thing. It's okay between them, but me calling them, that is a real insult. So then I realized. Now, even if I say something, they'll correct me. "No, Daddy, you shouldn't say those things." You know, like that. So that's some small instance. For each every small thing, it was a decisive moment. I mean, now we know we are really culturally changing. We know that, we can't resist it. It's foolish to resist.

Did you try initially to resist it?

Well, it was for me like an emotional block, you know. I mean, it's hard for me to get out of that thing first. Even for my wife also. Even for my mother, my brothers, everybody. It was very difficult thing, you know. Then we realized no matter what we do, there will be some changes. But the changes, whether it's good or bad, we have to decide. Rather than blankly say no for everything. So we realized that, and we said, "Okay, but don't go beyond this limit." We used to set up parameters there. Don't go beyond that. And then don't go beyond this. Cutting hair. Don't cut too short. For Indian woman, the beauty lies in the hair, the long hair. So they never cut it.

Now they wanted to have perm. First I said, "Don't do it." I was against doing that one. I know these perms, chemicals and other things. But then she went and did it, and she doesn't like it. Now I told her again, "Don't do it. Leave it as it is. It can grow out of it. It won't last long. You don't put again, chemicals again." She said, "No, Daddy, I don't like it. I must go and do it." Say, "I told you first not to do. You went and did it. Now I say again don't do it. You are going to do it again." Then afterward, "Okay, I will leave it alone." Really discuss. Don't do anything without consulting us sometimes. But most of them, they do it on their own. They know now what is good and what are the limits and not permissible.

Issues such as going out at night and dating caused more serious arguments, but the tenor of the process of compromise is the same. Parents and children discuss quite vigorously and come to some compromise. Unlike other parents, however, Ravi and Ratna seem to be as interested in discussion and compromise as their children. In families such as the Nagars (chapter 7) and the Shankars (chapter 11), parents described arguments with children as onerous and unpleasant. They were unhappy that children were always asking why and not simply letting their parents have the first and last word. Children, they felt, should realize that parents have their best interest at heart and accept the wisdom of parental decisions and advice. For the Kumars, although the process of discussion and decision was often painful and heart-wrenching, in general they felt good about the outcomes of the process. Parents and children reached a true consensus, and this allowed the Kumars to have confidence in their children's behavior even when they were out of sight.

Anu described her approach to her parents on the subject of dating.

> I couldn't hide it. I didn't want to be like the other Indian kids, where they lie. I couldn't do that.
>
> I remember I asked them, we went out for breakfast one day, and I told [my father], "I want to go out with this person, just on a date, you know, nothing else." And they thought about it, and they said, "Well, okay. You know we trust you and everything. You know your limitations and what we expect. So, see how it is."
>
> And so I started dating. It made it more difficult, but I knew I had to deal with it honestly, you know. I just couldn't live with it if I just lied and did all that and sneaked around and said I'm going here instead of there. I just couldn't. And they were really nice, because he came home and met my parents and everything.

Her father reveals more of the give-and-take of the decision process that lead up to Anu's dating experience.

> So the next thing was dating. They asked me, "Daddy, if somebody asks me," it started in high school, actually, "If I date, what is your opinion?" I asked her, "What do you mean by dating? Dating can be different meanings. In what sense you are asking?" "If somebody comes and asks me for a dance, or for a party, or for anything like that." And then I asked them, "With what intention he's asking you? There are so many intentions behind, in asking, for a genuine friendship, or just to show up, or just for some other purpose." Then she started thinking.
>
> It's an education process for us, and it's an education process for them also. They go through that one personally, but we have to stand back and watch and learn and then advise them. We didn't know anything, so we start researching. We had to go and read some things. Even talk to other friends. How did they handle their children? What is the meaning of this? In the church, we used to discuss about these things. What is this dating? What do we have to do? So at least we get some feedback from other sources also, before we could answer them. I must

not have been knowing anything about dating, because I never went through that period. So I had to learn myself, on all those things.*

Then I told her, you know, dating, if he really wants to be a friend, okay, that dating is all right. And beyond that, I don't think you are in an age you can go beyond that one, for any intimate relationships or anything like that. Sex is not permissible. Even kissing, I told them. That is beyond our limits. Then, after high school, they had a little bit of struggle and that and this. But the serious thing started when they went to college.

Now the real serious things, really they started calling home. All the boys. Slowly, one day, she came and said, "Daddy, we have a friend. He's asked me to come out on Saturdays. Weekends, Fridays, like that. What do you say?" I said, "Not on Sundays."

We had to talk, children, me, and wife has to sit and think, because we've never gone through. So think think think. We break our heads. That was the worst period of our time. I mean, in controlling our children. Because now she is becoming little bit independent. She wants to break open and move. I said, "Okay, everybody has to do that one time or other. No problem. But I'll give you an example. These are all circles. [He draws a Venn diagram on a napkin.] Nobody's independent. Everybody's dependent on something or other. Financially, emotionally, any way you put it. This is our circle, you are here. You think you want to be independent, and you move out. Okay, you break open, and you go into some other circle. But you are going into some other sphere of influence. If it's a boy or a boyfriend, you are going to his influence. Or you're going into some other influence. But you are not independent. You got to choose which influence you want. Good influence, bad influence, which is beneficial to you or not. I do not want to stop you from moving out if you want to move out, but as long as you are here . . . you grew up with us, with the family, we're not going to harm you or give you wrong advice. We give good advice. But you want to go away independent, go. No problem. But think before you go where you want to go."**

---

* Ravi's comment here reveals the importance of parents' own experiences in shaping the issues that arise when they raise the next generation. Had Ravi and Ratna themselves had relevant dating experience, Ravi implies that these would have become the models upon which to base advice for their children. It is only when these natural models fail that parents must search for alternative authorities on which to base advice.

** Ravi's description of the relationship between a person and the people around him or her, and the ultimate impossibility of true independence, coincides with the interdependence of individuals characteristic of an Indian worldview (see chapter 2). Like Vaidehi Nagar's explicit discussion with her daughters concerning the proper order of relations with grandparents (in particular, the sense of connection to her husband's parents she tries to instill in her daughters even after her husband's death), Ravi's talk with Anu about interdependence exemplifies the rather exceptional moment when parents attempt to explain to their children what the social world looks like through their Indian eyes. Most of the time, pieces of the Indian view of the social world inform the issues that arise between par-

Ravi commented on the entire process of reaching a compromise.

> With my parents, you know, we used to talk, but we used to listen a lot. More than talk. Now it goes both ways. They listen, and they talk also. So it is to and fro. That is the difference. Now, if they don't like it, they will tell you on the face. But with my parents, we had to be very subtle in telling them. Even if you disagree. Very calmly, very gently try to put it. Now, they tell it blankly. For us, it is a shock, I think. But at the same time, we realize, you know, this is the way it is. I guess we are compromising some things at the same time.

Minakshi, the eldest at age twenty-one, expresses the appreciation that I think all three children feel toward their parents' efforts to understand them and their lives.

> I really pity my parents for what they have to go through. I mean, because if I want to do something else, and they're just not used to that way . . .
>
> Like going out once a week. I mean, "Why do you have to go out every week?" They do let us go out, but curfew times, they have big debates about that. I consider my parents the most liberal. You know, compared to all the other families in our church.* And I think they go through these feelings of guilt, saying, "Are we doing the right thing? Are we giving them too much freedom?" I think they go through that every single day.
>
> It's hard for them to completely let go of their authority on us, because, you know, in India, the parents can even tell them what to do when they're forty or something. And they know it's different here. It has helped them, because they, too, sometimes resent my grandmother telling them what to do. My father would be like, "I'm forty years old." So I think he understands how we might be feeling.
>
> I think that also most Indians will adjust very easily, because they're very materialistic. I think the entire Indian culture in a sense is very materialistic in the sense of wanting good jobs. They want to get up

---

ents and children but are not made explicit. (For example, when Lakshmi and Shivan Iyengar argued with Michael about changing his major, their objections were in part a consequence of their desire to see Michael as an integrated part of the family unit, even as he moves into adulthood and begins to think of his life as his own. All that was made explicit, however, was their sense that one should finish what one starts to demonstrate one's intellectual discipline.) The second generation, then, confronts their parents' Indian worldview usually implicitly but sometimes explicitly. It is interesting, though, that Anu's description of the dating decision leaves out this explicit rather theoretical argument. The same is true of the discussions I had with Anar and Mausami Nagar concerning their grandparents. Explicit attempts to explain Indianness do not influence children nearly so much as the examples of Indian views that remain implicit in a wide range of more concrete discussions of dos and don'ts.

* The Kumars' church is one of the small Indian Protestant congregations. So Minakshi's comparison here is between her parents and "other Indians."

in the social stratum of everything. And they're willing to let go of their culture, more than, more than, let's say, Polish culture, where they're not willing to let go. They're willing to pay that price. I see that in my parents. They are willing to let go of parts of their culture to make it in this culture, in this society.

It is noteworthy that Minakshi juxtaposes the cultural changes connected to intergenerational issues within the family and the cultural transformations that her parents themselves have gone through in their attempt to "make it" in American society. This juxtaposition introduces a second overarching theme in the Kumar family's talk about themselves. In addition to this concern with compromise and working through difficult parent-child issues, the ambition to advance professionally and materially has been a cornerstone of the Kumars' lives in the United States. It is not that the parents were possessed of a relentless drive to succeed when they came. (In fact, they talk about their main motivation to come as reuniting the joint family.) Rather, their growing appreciation for the opportunities and possibilities that were and are available to them has fueled their eagerness to take advantage of those opportunities.

The early years in America were difficult financially for the family. Initially, Ravi moved boxes at a warehouse and Ratna was a clerk at a toy factory. Ravi, however, was dissatisfied with his opportunities for advancement. Already burdened by the cost of sending his children to parochial school and anticipating the cost of college years down the road, Ravi searched for alternative employment.

Rejecting other equally "dead end" jobs, Ravi eventually entered a two-year training program to become an X-ray technician. During his training, he worked weekends keeping accounts for a downtown hotel. Just as he finished and secured a job, Ratna was laid off.

> That was a real shock to us. I didn't realize laying off like this. It's not good. I mean, we are planning to send our children to college and school and other things. When they are in school or college, if you are laid off, then what happens? Children's education is disrupted. Our life is disrupted. Everything is a mess.
>
> We thought another job will solve it. Then we thought again, "No. No. This is no good. Again you go there and work. Again you'll be laid off. Again we'll have to go through the same process again. Why? So why don't you go to school?" So then she decided that she will go to nursing.
>
> And then we had real decision time, because now, by the time financially we are more strapped for money. And then we had to look for future. So then we all kind of joined together, we sat and we talked and talked and talked for a long time. Whether to go to college, and even me going to school, also we had the same process. All the family sat. All my brothers, my mother, and everybody sat, and we talked and talked and talked. See, we talk a lot, when it comes to decision tim-

ings. When I went to same process, at that time, my brother said, "Go ahead and do it. Anyway, if worst comes, we're all there to support you."

And the same process again, with my wife, we had to go through. Then we sat, and by then, at least now, I am working. I know for sure I won't be laid off. But again, it was a financial thing. My mother and my . . . they didn't give us any money, but at least that moral support, you know. "Well, should anything happen, we are there. Go ahead." That type of a confidence.

Through their own financial and professional struggles, the Kumars have come to view financial security as the number one priority in terms of their children's careers. I asked Ravi what he would like to see in his children's lives in ten years. In addition to stable and close family lives, a secure career was also important.

I wish they study good and have such financial background that their children don't have to go through hardships. That they can go through their education period without worrying too much from what is the next day going to be like.

Career, you know, I tell them that there are two things. See, one thing is, you have to have your own financial stability, so that you can stand on your own feet, not depend on anybody for anything. I told them not to depend on your husbands. You have relationship with your husband, good relationship, but financially you have to stand up on your own feet. Because I have seen many of my friends, women depending too much on men. Particularly Indian women. Should anything happen to him, accident, he dies, then she's stranded, without anything, without any financial support, and the children will suffer. Whole family suffers.

So that's why, when I got married, the first thing I said to her, that was our understanding, that she be independent, no matter what happens. You have to have your education, you have to stand on your own feet. Educating herself, financially getting a job, and independent, everything. Same thing I tell my girls also. Whatever happens, you have to stand on your own feet. You never know. That's one thing, financially.

At the same time, you know, sometimes you go for financial things, you have to find a job, very security, financial security. But that's not the thing she would like to do. You would like to do something else. So I said, "You get something, job, and get yourself financially secure, and go and do whatever you like to do." My Anu likes to write, read, she likes literature. I mean, okay, just go. You like it, you do it. But is that going to support you financially? No. So what you do, you find a career or job, just to support you financially. With Minakshi also, I tell her, you may not like sometimes, I too don't like certain jobs. But financially we have to do it. To stand on your own feet, you have to go for financial security. For that career which will give you that. I tell her.

This message has been successfully received by all three children. Minakshi, the eldest, is a biology major headed for nursing school. But, she confides:

> I have different ambitions and dreams for myself. According to me, they might be good ideas, good ambitions, but to my parents, who have been raised differently, with different kinds of values, it's not going to be that great to them. If I wanted to be famous, or excel in drama, or playwriting, or something like that, they would be like, "That's nothing. Anybody could do that." Because to them, anything in the sciences is great. To me, it would be a great accomplishment, and I would take pride in myself and say I've done something. But they wouldn't feel that way. Because it's not what they value.
>
> Hopefully, I'll get a career, and part-time I can do exactly what I want to do. Writing, directing, or something. I feel that's where my talent lies. That's what I would be taking pride in, so . . . I mean, I want to make my parents happy, too. 'Cause they've done a lot for me, sacrificed a lot for me. And I do want to take care of them, when they get older and everything. But I should also be able to use what good qualities and talents I do have to the best of my ability.

So was it ever an issue? Did you ever say to them, "What I'd like to major in is theater"?

> Yeah, but they would always say something like, "Well, there's no job security." That was very important to them, job security. 'Cause when my mom was here, she got laid off. That's what made her go to school. And they realized the importance of having a profession that has stability. Especially if you have a family, and people relying on you and everything. After you have a secure job, you can do anything you want to do, part-time, on the side, as a hobby. That was very good advice. I think it's better this way, for security and a job, as well as pursue your interests. I think that's good.

Anu, too, understands her parents' desire for her to achieve financial stability in her career. But she, like her sister, finds her interests and talents in areas that from her parents' point of view do not lead to financially secure careers. I asked Anu what she was studying in college.

> Now, I think I switched my major four times already. Three times . . . I keep switching. After I came in here, 'cause my parents said go into therapy, because that seemed . . . because I stink in math. There's nothing you can do to make me get better in math. So, there was nothing else I could do, actually. I listened to what they said, 'cause what do I know, coming out of high school. I went into therapy. Then I started

taking the bio classes, and this and that, and I said, I don't like this, I hate this, you know.

Actually, I always wanted to do something in English or broadcast journalism. My parents said, "You can do whatever you want after you graduate, after you get your bachelor's. You can go back for this, as long as you become independent financially in every way, stand on your feet.* Then you can support yourself and go back and be whatever you want." That seemed like a good idea.

I mean, we came from India to get a better life here. Which is the main goal and the purpose we did it for. They want us to use the advantage we have of an education here. My parents did that. Because they started all over again. And we have an advantage in having an education here.

So I guess because we weren't middle-class, we were lower, in India, lower-middle-class, my parents want us to be very well-off. But see, I think they know I can't by myself become . . . well, see, for each child it's different. Even if I'm in the middle class, if that's the best I can do, that's fine. But then also you have to remember how Indians think. As long as you get married to a husband, he can bring the income right back up, you know. And that's fine by them.**

While all the children have heard their parents' message about career, ambition, and financial security, each child also confesses an inability, unwillingness, or lack of interest in devoting as much energy to his or her own career as their parents have to theirs.

The Kumars' son, Raj, always had career goals that matched his parents' image of a financially secure profession. Originally, he had planned to pursue an advanced degree in bioengineering or attend medical school after completing his B.S. in engineering. Lately, however, Raj has decided that this plan "might be a bit too much for me. Not that it would be difficult, or anything like that, but just that I'm not that interested. Then sometimes I feel I should, but I get lazy."

Raj referred to his laziness on other occasions as well. We were talk-

---

* Listening to what Ravi and his daughters have to say about educational and career choices, the similarity in language is very evident. To "stand on your feet," to ensure "financial security," and "job stability" are the goals driving career decisions. The overwhelming continuity between parent and children in the way they frame career issues illustrates quite clearly the importance of a family idiom in mediating familial interactions. By adopting this common language, children create a mechanism for demonstrating connection to their parents while at the same time providing a foil against which differences can be highlighted. The girls' expressions of their own career aspiration, which are driven by personal fulfillment rather than financial security, are rendered less threatening through their incorporation of common familial language into their statements. There is a subtle balance between connection and differentiation achieved through the family idiom.

** Anu flags the way Indians think to explain her parents' attitude toward her financial potential. Although she is comparing her parents favorably to these prototypes, one senses that their similarities are paired with her own differences.

ing about his father's role as disciplinarian when he was a kid. I asked what issues resulted in discipline.

> Let's see. Mostly school. I used to do bad in school for some reason. And he used to get upset because he thought I had a lot of potential but I never used to make use of it. That was the major thing.

How did you feel about that?

> Well, I thought he was right. I used to watch a lot of TV when I was a kid. But I never tried. I just kept going with my life. Just taking it one day at a time. Not thinking about the future. That's my whole mental idea. And all through high school and grade school, I used to get yelled at about that.

Do you still feel the same way, or do you think your attitude has changed?

> Well, when I started college, the first year I was doing okay, but then I slowly slacked off, and I wasn't thinking much about school. I was thinking more about friends and different things like that. And that's when I started going berserk and doing bad in school. But then, right now, I'm getting back into the school aspects. I'm starting to think more and study more. But I do get lazy sometimes. I'm very lazy.

Anu talks about a similar lack of ambition but uses "guilt" rather than "laziness" to describe her feelings. I asked what her family did (i.e., what jobs they held) in India.

> My mother was a clerk. My father worked in a department, it was a mechanical something. And the thing was, my father didn't have a chance to go on for his education. He wanted to go into math, and it's just that you don't have the opportunities to do that, so he never got a chance. So he always wants us to do that, you know, to use whatever we have. That's why they'd rather just support us and put us through school, so we can get that chance. Neither of them could have it.
>
> I think most of the Indian parents, that's why they stress education so much. They know what kind of life you can have, that they had over there. And, like, you can use the opportunities here, you know, because America's a pretty good country, actually.
>
> Sometimes I feel guilty when I do miserable in school, you know, because you have a little added pressure, because you start thinking about all this. You understand what your parents are trying to tell you, which makes it more difficult. Because if you have your values and you don't listen, you could do what you want. But then, there's this other side. If you understand them and you love them, it makes it more difficult.

Minakshi shares a similar feeling. We were talking about the cultural compromises that her parents had to make in order to "make it" in American society, and she had just commented that these adjustments are made easier by the fact that Indian immigrant culture itself has a strong drive to succeed.

> They want to be wealthy, well-off, you know, upper-class. That's their goal. And they're willing to do anything, I mean, not anything, I'm not saying . . . they're very ambitious, is what I'm saying. At least, that's with the first generation.
>
> And it's so sad, because the second generation is not having the same feeling, 'cause they're already into the [American] culture. They're so diffused. They have no ambition to take on their parents' dreams. Because, you know, they don't see it. They don't understand what they don't have and what they have. But my parents still remember them. That's why they want a better life for us, and they want us to be great.
>
> I hear them saying all the time, "If we were here at your age, we would be going to school and becoming this, becoming that." If they had all these opportunities. And sometimes I honestly wish that they did. 'Cause I think if they did, they would do a lot more than what I'm doing. 'Cause they have what it takes. They have that ambition, to make it here. That I don't have as much as they do.
>
> I really admire my mother. She's a very ambitious woman. It was amazing. She was just like a secretary or something when she came here, went to school, became a nurse, and . . . . it's like there's something that's fueling that desire in her to succeed.

The degeneration of ambition that the Kumar children talk about is matched, in Minakshi's mind, by a cultural degeneration.

What do you see in the future for your children?

Well, I feel sorry for them . . .

Why?

'Cause I think it will be even worse, you know, nothing gets better. In generations, when you start off with first generation, first, second, third, I think it always goes down, it never gets better. In everything, in status, in morals, culture, everything. For example, my grandmother, the culture that she has is so rich and so complete. As opposed to my parents, they did accomplish their own, and in a different way, but I feel it's a step down from what she has done. And I feel I'm a step down from what my parents have done. You know, I don't feel as though we're getting better.

And I feel that a lot of the Indian people here are like that. You get kind of relaxed with the stuff that you do have. Of course, I'm going to be better educated than my parents. My parents are better educated than their parents, but that's not necessarily what makes you better. Holistically. I mean, it's your culture. It's your morals. It's how you fit into the society around you, and what you give to the society as well. And I feel the richness of it is just . . . I'm sure it'll make it up in something else, but I think that's what's being lost . . .

This feeling of loss and inadequacy, which all of the Kumar children express, is reminiscent of feelings expressed by Anar and Mausami Nagar and Michael Iyengar. Anar worried that her choice of professions might not be "prestigious enough," and Mausami wondered what kind of a parent she was going to be when she compared her knowledge of Hinduism to the much richer knowledge of her mother. Michael Iyengar felt his parents' extraordinary success in their careers was something he might never be able to match. All these are instances of the status anxiety that festers among members of the second generation in the families I studied. The subtle differences in the types of status anxiety expressed will be fleshed out in chapter 12. At this point, though, it is important to note the emergence of this pattern.

While children in all these families express some sort of status anxiety, the overwhelming consistency in the way the Kumar children express this anxiety points to a particular dynamic that guides this family's change process—a dynamic that attempts to manage three identities rather than the usual "Indian" and "American" pair. Minakshi generalizes the inadequacy all the siblings feel regarding their careers into a larger issue of cultural drift. Her feeling that the "culture" of her generation is a step down from that of her parents and grandparents is in part a product of the particular way the Kumars have chosen to emphasize their various identities.

In the parental generation, a core Christian identity is contextualized within a broader Indian framework. For the second generation, however, Christian identity becomes separated off from the Indian context and floats around somewhere between Indian and American. This lack of alignment between various identities spurs the Kumar children's sense of cultural diffusion and the lack of coherence and purpose in their lives.

When I asked Ratna if she had tried to pass on anything Indian to her kids, her reply shifted the question of Indian traditions and values to Christian ones, while maintaining that there is a substantial commonality in Indian and Christian values and sensibilities.

> Yes, we have. A lot of it, we have. Respecting the elders is number one. And keeping the culture that we have. Dressing appropriately, for one. Then character is very important. Not to blemish it in any way. So . . .
>
> Actually, I think we're more, I wouldn't say cultural, exactly, as it is following the Christian principles. That's what the whole thing is. Because in India, even a Hindu also has principles, as a Christian. Like not telling lies, no robbing. Just following all the Ten Commandments. And most all of that, I think, even the Hindus do, 90 percent of them.

The children, too, see their Indian values as inextricably linked to their Christian ones. I asked Minakshi how she felt about being Indian versus being American. She, like her mother, brought in Christianity as a central identity. There is a generational difference, however, in that Minakshi uses Christianity as a bridge between Indian and American, while her mother presents Christianity and Indianness as a unified set.

> I take pride in being an Indian. And my family history, I do take pride in the stories that my grandparents and my parents tell me about India, about our family. I also take pride in a certain amount of culture. Not all of it. In the good of the culture.
>
> I think that's one culture [i.e., Indian culture] that has tried to at least put religion and culture together, in a sense of morals. I think it worked a good balance out. 'Cause they tied so much morals into the culture that you wouldn't even consider it religion, really. And it even is diffused into the Indian-American Christian culture. A lot of the morals that we have are like Indian morals mixed with Christian morals. It's very similar.
>
> But I think if you're going to percentages or something, I would consider myself right now (it'll probably change by next week or something, it's something you experience all the time, you change all the time)* around 40 percent Indian and 60 . . . actually, I can't even say 60, I would say 40 percent American and 20 percent I don't know. I think mixing both of those together, you actually come up with a new culture all of your own. So I think that 20 percent would be that new culture. I can't even say 60 percent American. I'd have to say 40 percent American, 40 percent Indian, and that rest would be like a combination of both.

Despite the fact that Minakshi sees Indian culture as sensitive to the same values as Christianity, she does see a difference between the contact with American culture that she as an Indian Christian has experienced and that contact as it would be experienced by an Indian Hindu.

> I can see differences between me and any other Indian person from a different religion. Most of the Indians that do come from India are Hindus. They have a bigger group, and so I think that will help in diffusing the culture less. And Christian Indians don't have that. 'Cause we're small groups and little, little churches. I think the Indian Christians have less of a culture than Indian Hindus, or even Indian Muslims, because we're fewer people and we don't really stay together or anything. You won't see any Indian Christian associations, where everybody comes.

---

* This comment is very telling. My overarching argument has been that assimilation should be studied as a social process rather than through a comparative analysis of the way different individuals, generations, or ethnic groups reach various signposts along some relatively standard trajectory of social change. Here, Anu herself recognizes that the way she conceives of her position in the social order changes constantly. What demands study, then, are the interactional and social-psychological processes that produce these fluid shifts. These are precisely the processes that these family portraits articulate.

But religion has helped in a sense. It has helped in the sense of adapting to this culture more than anything else, more than I would say for a Hindu person. Because I think my parents have stressed religion over culture, with the morals of the religion, more than the culture. Which has been easier. It's easier for us to adapt to this culture with that than a cultural thing. That would have made it more difficult. 'Cause it's like you're not supposed to do this, because it's just not done that way. You can't live in an Indian culture in America, because this entire culture is American.

But you can incorporate your religious views and your culture easier to the American system, I think. And that has helped me, you know. Just see what's good, what's bad, and am I keeping a lot of the culture within me. That has been a good balance for me, at least.

Anu sees Christianity as playing a similar bridging role between Indian and American cultures.

The thing is see, okay, I can't be a true Indian or a total American. I can't be a true Indian because I can't like all of its music, and I can't like all the culture. I can't be all American because I can't exactly . . . to this day, I have not gone to a rock concert. That's really why I can't become a best friend with an American person, because she'd have those interests, or he'd have those interests. So as far as music's concerned, I feel like I don't belong in either this group or that group, an Indian or an American, right in the middle.

Even my personality, it's right in the middle. I can't totally disagree with American, I can't totally disagree with the Indian. You can be an Indian and still do the things that are wrong. And you can still be an American and do the things that are wrong. So I'm right in the middle, which would be my basic Christianity. I follow that. The way I figure, I don't think I respect American culture or Indian culture that much, I only respect Christianity.

The family's choice of Christian rather than Indian identity as their anchor goes a long way to explaining the children's feelings about the intergenerational degeneration of the fullness of life—as Minakshi puts it, the degeneration of "status, morals, culture . . . everything." By focusing on Christian identity and values, as Anu points out, their adjustment to American society has been eased. Coupled with a genuine parental openness to discussion and compromise, the strong Christian identity and involvement have made the teenage years of the Kumar children relatively less traumatic than those of some of their peers. Because of this, the Kumar children do not experience their own cultural transformation as a proactive process, the process of taking two cultures and transforming them into a specific, unique amalgam (the way, for example, Anar Nagar talks about reconciling the "two people" she has become; Mausami Nagar becomes an advocate for the "correct" incorporation of Indian heritage into class content and interpersonal relations at school; or Bob Iyengar sings in a death grunt the way "no Indian anyone" ever would). Rather, the Kumar children interpret their own experience as a diffusion of "culture." "Culture" is becoming formless, shapeless, background noise.

As Minakshi says, the 20 percent of her identity that is neither Indian nor American is just unnamed—"that new culture . . . some combination of both." Similarly, when Anu talks about not being either totally Indian or totally American, about being "right in the middle," she, too, invokes a cultural no-man's-land as her own. Christianity fills in some of that gap, particularly in terms of values, ideas about right and wrong. However, when it comes to the material aspects of culture and the materialism they see on the parts of their parents and grandmother, the Kumar children see their own interests as diffused, not integrated into a complete identity that one can be proud of. They do not see themselves as eclectic in their tastes or appreciative of a wide range of worthy, fulfilling career pursuits (as, for example, the Iyengar boys feel about their interests in music and political science). Rather, they see themselves as drifting away from the singularity of purpose and cultural unity that their elders bring to their lives.

The Kumars' story adds two important elements to our understanding of the experience of Indian immigrant families. First, the Kumars demonstrate quite dramatically, in recounting their processes of discussion and compromise, the impact that parental attitudes toward immigration can have on family dynamics. Even before their immigration, the Kumars knew that living in America would require them to make adjustments in the way they raise their children. As Ravi told me, "there are things we have to compromise." This realization, coupled with an established family pattern of discussion, debate, and mutual decision making which preceded any considerations of emigration[2] (part of the Kumars' family idiom, if you will), has placed their children's maturation on firmer ground than is the case for some of the other families profiled here. This aspect of the family's behavior resonates with the dynamic that has evolved in the Shenoy family (chapter 10). Although the Shenoys are very different from the Kumars in their background and concerns, there is a similar solidity built through very serious and contentious dialogues between parents and children—dialogues to which both parties have a genuine commitment.[3]

Another aspect of the Kumars' story, which also likens them to the Shenoys, is the way they have used multiple identities in the adjustment process. The Kumars' identity as Christians has complicated their effort to come to terms with Indian and American cultures, experiences, and contexts. For the children in particular, their status as Christians has given them a leg up into the "mainstream." At the same time, however, it has made them view the experience of their generation as a diffusion of ambition, status, and culture. I don't think the Kumars' Christianity has actually lessened the difficulty or angst associated with their adjustment in comparison to other families with comparable levels of dissimilarity between their lives in India and their lives in America (e.g., the Nagars and the Shankars).

However, the existence of this "third identity" has shaped the way they think and talk about their experiences. In this respect, we will see a similarity in the way a different "third identity" has shaped the interpretive process among the Shenoy children. These third identities function as another prototype (in addition to Indian and American) against which individuals can make judgments of similarity and difference. As the critical prototypes expand in number, the process of differentiation becomes more muddled, leading to this persistent sense of cultural drift for children situated in these more complicated arrays of models for identity and behavior.

10

The Shenoys: Alternative Identities

After our first interview in her home in a very wealthy Chicago suburb, Durga Shenoy took me to lunch. When she had asked me to join her, I had told her that her offer was very kind but that I had already taken up enough of her time. She told me that at this stage in her life, she felt it was important to take off a few hours and go out to lunch when she felt like it. After a tour of her office and a quick check of the stock prices, we were off in her Mercedes.

Durga is direct, honest, and very genuine. She is sure of herself and eager to pursue her many projects and interests with the full force of her energy. While I would not say she is the anchor of her family in the sense of being its emotional core, I do think her personality reflects the general emotional and social tone of the family as a whole.

The Shenoys are the most senior of the families profiled here. Durga and her husband are in their mid-fifties, and their three children range in age from twenty-one to twenty-eight. Each family member is a capsule of energy, vigorously pursuing whatever his or her current interests happen to be. In the Shenoy family, there is a higher level of individual autonomy than I observed in any other family. The individual Shenoys seem so autonomous because each has his or her own very personal story to tell. Each person has an idiosyncratic point of view, and during our conversations, each wanted to make sure I knew what that point of view was. I think they see their family life more as a vibrant coexistence of strong individual wills than as an integrated life as "the family." The family idiom that has developed stresses individuality and differences among family members. For the Shenoys, not only is differentiation the central dynamic through which individual and familial identities have been shaped, but difference is also a key component of individual and familial identities.

Despite the high degree of autonomy in the family, there are still surprisingly strong bonds among members. I will return to discuss the nature of these bonds and their relation to the identity choices that family members have made. First, it is essential that one gets to know the family in all its diversity.

I got to know the Shenoys through one of their daughters. I had been interviewing members of the second generation about their generation's organizational network. One young man mentioned a friend who, in his opinion, was not Indian at all and suggested that I talk to her for a different perspective on the second generation.

I contacted this young woman, who turned out to be Padma Shenoy, the second daughter and middle child of the Shenoy family. In the course of our more general conversation about the second generation and her experiences in second-generation organizations, Padma's description of her family intrigued me. They seemed like no other family I had yet met. After our initial interview, Padma recruited her family to participate in this study.

As I suggested at the end of the Kumar family portrait, the Shenoys, like the Kumars, have a "third identity" that has affected the way the family understands its experiences. In the Shenoys' case, however, "third identity" is perhaps a misnomer. Unlike the Kumars, who clearly talked about being Indian, being American, and being Christian as three distinct aspects of their amalgamated identities, the Shenoys' third identity is based primarily on a certain philosophy of life they have developed. Originally, I called it a class identity, but Durga in particular disagreed. She explained that it was more complicated than that. The nature of this third identity will unfold as the Shenoys tell their stories. Being Indian or being American is only rarely discussed, and then usually in terms of how the nuances introduced by these two identities are dealt with from the point of view of their overarching philosophy of life.

Yet just as the Kumars' Christianity led the children to a particular experience of intergenerational change, one more linked to a sense of cultural diffusion than cultural transformation, the Shenoy children's exposure to their family's philosophy of life has led them along an ever-branching path—each child moving off in his or her own direction. The status anxiety expressed by the Kumar children is mirrored by the Shenoys' expression of a similarly clear and consistent anxiety. The roots of these anxieties lie in the sense of diffusion that accompanies the management of these third identities.

The Shenoy home is very gracious. The colors are soft, and there is a mixture of French and modern-style furniture. The formal living and dining rooms on the first floor are quite large. When I visited, I was received in the more intimate spaces toward the back of the house: a comfortable family room with fireplace, lots of light, and a large array of family photos; a well-organized kitchen; and a well-groomed backyard. On one occasion, Durga prepared lunch and we ate in the dining room with its lovely Impressionist wall murals.

We begin with Durga and a rather lengthy description she gave of her childhood. Unlike most of the people I interviewed, Durga chose to share very vivid and detailed memories of her early years. I include many of them both because I find them fascinating and because I think these early experiences have made Durga into the independent, strong-willed woman she is today. Reading Durga's story, we are again reminded of the importance of history. The active, strong-willed approach to problems demonstrated by Durga's mother and her father's interest in giving his children hands-on active learning experiences are both elements of Durga's upbringing that she has incorporated into her own adult life and her approach to raising her own children.

> I was born in the mid-'30s under the star of Virgo, as they tell me, in a very small village in Punjab. I have some hazy recollections of my very young days. I remember playing with peacocks, 'cause my parents found that I loved animals, so they had bought a couple of peacocks.
>
> Once my mother decided that she was tired of getting the servants to go far out in the village well to fetch the water. In those days, obviously, there was no running water. She was one of these people who took the initiative herself. And so what she did was, my dad had gone away on a medical tour as a doctor, and she just went out of the house and drew a circle somewhere outside in the compound and asked some people to come and dig a well. She had no notion that just because you dig a hole doesn't mean there's going to be water. You're supposed to have someone come and test for water and things like that.
>
> So when my father came home, I don't know how many days later, two or three days later, the hole was already pretty deep. He really didn't know what to say. But luckily, water was struck during the well digging.

As she discussed how her parents met, Durga digressed into another story that emphasized her mother's character.

> It was an arrangement. My mom was probably seventeen, something like that, when she was married.
>
> My mom was a rebel in the family. She didn't like the schoolteacher who favored certain gift-giving students. She always put up a big fuss. And she would influence the younger sister all the time. So these two young girls, my mom was the ringleader, and she would have this big fuss about how she hated the school.
>
> She just refused to go. So she put up a big hunger strike. She wouldn't eat. So my grandfather had to consult all members of the family. "What should we do with these girls? They are not going to school, and they are on a hunger strike."

Their uncles and aunts put up a strong protest, saying that girls should never be sent away to school and so on. But my mother stopped eating. That was it. So, finally, my grandfather had to send both the girls to a girls' boarding school. This was a very big break in the rest of the family, because none of the other girls had been sent away to school.

During the last year of high school, my mother was married. Once she got married, she talked her father-in-law into letting her complete her education. The family sent her to medical school for one year, which was totally unheard of in those days. And then, because her father-in-law got really ill, as she was the oldest son's wife, she had to come home and take care of him. So at that time, that was the end of her medical school education.

Within a few years, Durga's father went to East Africa to help with Britain's war effort there. The story of what happened to Durga's mother and her children in his absence again illustrates Durga's preoccupation with her mother's character.

So now my dad goes off to Africa, and I remember my mom moved us to her dad's place for a while. She found that because she did not have a husband, that her husband's side of the family really didn't want her around. I mean, they just were not that happy. Even though my dad was sending money from Africa.

In the meanwhile, it looked as if my mom's side of the relatives weren't really that happy to have her, either. This married woman with four children was too much of a burden. They didn't know if her husband would ever come back. There was quite a bit of tension, and not wanting all these four kids around.

She decided that it was in her interest to go back to school and get some sort of a training and education, so that she could work and earn a living just in case anything happened to my dad. At that time, she broke up the whole nuclear family of ours. I was farmed away at one of the uncles and aunts in Delhi, and she put my two brothers in a boarding school, and she put my sister, who was just a few months old, in this orphanage right near the Delhi train station.

It was very hard for her to get back to school. She managed to get back to Lady Harding Medical School, for nurses and midwifery training. Because part of the training program was you had to live on the premises, they didn't want any children around. That was the reason why she had to farm out the kids.*

* Durga's stories about her mother focus on incidents in which her mother's strong will is paramount. Whether it is a hunger strike to force a change of schools, the digging of a well, or the difficult return to school for a married woman without family support, Durga's mother, in Durga's eyes, exhibits the strengths of character that are so much a part of Durga's own personality. As with the Kumars, where the elder generation's collective "talk, talk, talk" about critical life choices is followed by Ravi's similar behavior with his own children, Durga's recollections of her mother's approach to life signal a pattern that has been incorporated into her personality and that she has tried to pass on to her children.

All that separation from the family and so on I'm sure had a lot of effect on the kids, on all four of us. I remember being farmed out to various aunts and uncles.

I'm telling you this was when I was maybe seven or eight. My mother had tried very hard for me to go to school in one of the convent schools. At least in our people, it was just very important to have good-quality education. And even if we were not Christians, the idea was send your kids to the best education that was available.

But I also remember my discomfort when, for some strange reason, there wasn't that organizational setup so that my aunt would wake me up in time, bathe me properly, and dress me properly, send me out to the bus. There were times when I got to school late, and I was unwashed, and my eyes were gooey and sticky. I remember the convent sisters being unhappy that I was not properly looked after and disapproving of my unclean appearance.

And then I remember I got very ill. Looking back, I get the feeling, probably, most of it was psychological. Because my aunts and uncles weren't happy to have me. They very distinctly mistreated me, you know. Not feeding me properly, having me live in the servants' quarters, things like that. All I remember is feeling very unhappy, and every time my mom would come, I would say, "Mom, gee, I really don't want to live here. Take me with you. Why do I have to live here? Where are my brothers? I want to be with my dad."

Those hurts didn't go away for many years. My mother, however, didn't want to take any sides. She just totally didn't want to accept that the family was mistreating me.

Eventually, Durga, her sister and brothers, and her mom made their way to her father's post in rural Africa. Durga's memories of life in Africa also stress her educational experiences.

The other thing I remember is my dad was the government hospital doctor. And one of his jobs was to every day look at all the meats that were going to be cooked for the hospital staff and patients. All of that meat had to come to the house. He would stand there and inspect it. And we as kids would stand around him, and I remember learning what liver looked like, what gizzard looked like, what necks looked like, what diseased liver looked like, too.

There were many such things where education took place through visual connection. This was a routine that went on every day.

One of his jobs was to go into the Kalahari desert. He would have to make various stops in various villages where the British medical system had established these small clinics. I remember going to these places and observing he had a lot of respect. He would say hello to the chiefs, and then people would come, and he would dispense treatment. I would sit with him and watch him do that.

After a few years, Durga's father was transferred. He became the doctor for a prison in the colony's capital. During their early years in Africa, three more sons were added to the family, bringing the total to seven children—five boys and two girls. In the following excerpt, Durga reflects more on her educational experiences. We begin to see the shift from the early hands-on educational stimulation provided by her parents to the self-possessed drive for intellectual stimulation and academic success that has characterized her adult life. Later on, Durga also begins to describe her growing sensitivity to family relations and to the way gender and education figure into the lot of women in the family context. A general intellectual curiosity and a serious focus on the politics and dynamics of interpersonal relations are the two main characteristics through which Durga has influenced her own children. The Nagar family also had an acute sensitivity to the dynamics of interpersonal relations. However, in that family, the focus was prescriptive—how people *should* be interacting with one another. In the Shenoy family, the attention to interpersonal dynamics is much more analytic. Durga, in particular, is extremely engaged in figuring out "what's going on" in relationships.

So . . . let's see now, I'm fourteen or fifteen. In the meanwhile, the struggles go on. My mother decides that she really prefers to work. And so what happened is that she was able to get a job as a health visitor. Her job was to provide prenatal counseling and early child care.

Then my family decided that they wanted to go to India for a visit. Somehow my mom and dad thought that in Africa, the schools for Asians were not really that great. And they didn't want to send me to a boarding school in England. A lot of Asian families were doing that. For me, they found this Indian girls' boarding school. It was a totally foreign experience for me. All the schooling was in Hindi language. Because it was a transitional period, I had the special permission to write all my exams in English. So here I am, fourteen, in all of these classes all day. Everything is being spoken in Hindi. I was totally behind in my work. And then, just being in the boarding school and interacting with all the other girls. Not really having much of an idea what was in my self-enlightened, self-interest . . . which was to sit down and clam up on the books. I wasn't doing any of that [laughing].

So, my grades were not the greatest. And I had come from Africa with very decent grades. I knew this was going on, but I remember not having the sophistication to talk about it. To say, "Okay, let's find a tutor." I didn't have any of that. I just knew inside me that I wasn't doing well in school. And I was totally petrified of flunking. The thing that saved me was that the final exam of high school is set up by the state. You are given, if I recall correctly, almost three months of preparation leave for final exams.

So, those three months, I remember, I collected all my textbooks—math, Hindi, history, English—and I proceeded to start working on each text from chapter one onward. Suddenly, I was understanding everything, and I wasn't behind anymore.

I think all my teachers expected I would fail. I didn't know this, of course, because they were all too polite to say anything to me. But when the results came, and they all publish in the newspapers, I had passed. So I was just totally so pleased.

Then I did my two years of college in the same school. And now I was more organized. I remember being pretty active in our student groups. [There was] a group of five of us. We had taken a vow to be the best friends, to be very truthful to each other. We were called the five Pandavs. I don't know why we took those male things, but we did.[1] We were the five Pandavs, and we proceeded to be that way. No one could break our friendship, and there were people who tried to do that.

We made all these vows that if anyone gossips against us, we should always talk to each other for verification and be truthful. We would expose anyone who was trying to break up our friendship by just coming out and explaining whatever the real problem was. The idea was to go after the truth. It worked beautifully. We became very good friends. And even when I came back to Africa, I came to the States, we carried correspondence for many, many years.

So now I finished three years of college, and during those three years, the school system was very much like the British, which is every three months you had three weeks off. And so those three weeks, I would farm myself out to different aunts and uncles. And looking back, the benefit of that was you kind of saw at close hand some of the family problems. These problems were really one of male domination over the females.* I remember participating in trying to resolve the problem of one of my aunt and uncle's household.

This cousin of mine, who was several years older than I, was always very irritating. Constantly causing problems. My aunt had her brother and his wife with their children who had come and visited. So my aunt had been spending time being a hostess. And somehow, this older cousin was extremely, extremely jealous. I remember sitting with my aunt, this is teatime at four o'clock. My aunt had prepared this huge kettle of tea, and she's pouring the tea. My cousin was so angry with her. The fight was about her giving attention to her brother, and doing all these things for them. He poured this boiling water over her hand. It was all covered with blisters.

When I saw that, I was so angry. I didn't say anything to my cousin, but I got my cousin's younger sister to write this three-page letter as to what was wrong. This letter was sent to her dad [who was away on business], saying that your presence is required here to handle this problem. Maybe this cousin should be sent away to boarding school, and things like that.

* Perhaps spurred by her recollection of friendships at school, Durga digresses a bit from the story of her education. This digression, however, introduces another facet of her experience that has been critical in her interactions with her children. We begin to see the analytic intensity Durga brings to her assessments of social relationships.

I dictated the whole letter to her, and she sent it off. And sure enough, within a day or so, my uncle was there, to see what was the problem. So throughout all of this, basically, what I saw was that my other older cousins and my aunts, who had professional degrees, had a lot more respect. Even there, I saw that there was this burden of running the family. It had a lot to do with how you interacted with the main household head. When I saw that anyone with a degree in medicine or law, somehow their status was much better, but still some family problems existed in any case.

But I also saw at that time, I had this cousin who was the principal of this school. While she was finishing up her education, she kept on turning down all the marriage proposals. Now, she was in her thirties, and all the looks were not of a youthful young woman to be married. Suddenly, she wants to be married. So, as a kid, I'm observing all this, and I'm saying, "Oh, well, just being educated and earning your living is not the whole story. There is the need to have a family, and also to have a good marriage."

Durga continued this conversation with a story about her admission to medical school. Just as she was about to enroll, her father wrote her urging her just to finish up her B.S. and not pursue an M.D. in India.

And I think, now I look back, I think maybe for homesickness reasons, I decided to go back and finish my bachelor's in science. The reason was I had been in India for four years, I hadn't seen my family, but still did not have the sophistication to write to my family and say, "I miss you guys. I want to come and visit." I didn't say any of that.

It was just an unsaid, understood kind of a thing that I'm the oldest of the seven, and it's pretty expensive to go back and forth, and therefore I'm expected, for saving money, not to visit them. If I went to medical school, that would be another five years. So the level of communication was pretty mediocre. There wasn't the back-and-forth exchange and dialogue. And the only thing was that my parents did get my brothers to fly over there to visit them. But they didn't get me to go and visit them. So there was that feeling of hurt also, at that time.

So anyhow, I decided I'll listen to my dad. I think maybe that was an excuse, when I really look back on it. That was an excuse to go back.

Upon her return to Africa, Durga taught high school and began to be introduced to suitable young men. These introductions made her quite uncomfortable, so Durga began looking for opportunities to go back to school. She received a Fulbright fellowship to come study in the United States.

Despite Durga's contention that her desire to continue her studies was a strategy to stave off any impending marriage, her initial experience in America reveals that the opportunity to study abroad was more than that. In the excerpt below, Durga's curiosity and self-confidence are evident. She was excited by the new environment and actively sought to participate in it as fully as she could. This attitude toward her initial U.S. experience contrasts sharply with that of Vaidehi Nagar. Although Vaidehi "wanted to know more Americans," her unfamiliarity with her surroundings and a shyness in her personality resulted in a rather limited range of exploration. She spent most of her time with an Indian immigrant neighbor and ventured out little beyond her immediate neighborhood. Durga's initial experiences are much more similar to Lakshmi Iyengar's. She, too, came as a student and developed a close relationship with an American host family. Initial experiences set a tone, or comfort level, that shapes the way Indian immigrants conceive of their own difference from the American mainstream. The difference of parents has a profound effect on the second generation's experience of its own difference.

I caught one of the Queen Elizabeths, Queen Mary, or something. One of the ships. I'm all by myself, and everybody's asking, "You're traveling alone, all the way to America?" "Yes, I am," you know. I'm feeling very confident. Because in India, when my parents left me, I was fourteen, and I finished my last year of high school, four years of college, I'm nineteen by that time. And I had to take the train to go and see my family. I mean, in those days, the way you looked after yourself was, you never left the luggage to go to the washroom in the train station. You always checked into the women's compartments, and you covered yourself very nicely and watched on all sides so that nobody would come out there to pinch you. And now I'm coming to the West, when I am finding things are safer. I'm not scared at all. It's not as crowded.

There was a six-week orientation program at University of Kansas for fifty-one students. Part of the tour was to go and see a GM factory, and see exactly how a car is made. I was totally floored. I had never seen anything like this. It was just so beautiful to me, it really was beautiful. When we went to the villages in Africa, the mode of transportation in the villages was still very primitive—bullock carts. And I come into Kansas City, and they're producing cars on an assembly line in I don't know how many hours. It was totally astounding. So creative. Then one weekend, we were taken to a small "village," you see. And my conception of village is a village in India, a village in Africa. That's a village. They say, "Okay, we're going to take you to a village." And they farmed us out to different families. I said, "This is not a village. They have a television. They have electricity. They have running water. They have tarmac roads. What village? They have everything here."

So then I'm being explained, this is called urbanization. Part of the tour of the village was to go and look at a dairy place, where we went and saw the milking of the cows. It was all automated. And then we saw the cheese being made, and all of us agreed this is no village. We could not see a village! Such a contrast from the villages that we were used to.

When I reached the university, I think I was the first Indian woman. That's where I met my husband-to-be. He had come from India as a foreign student. We started off with an argument, because he asked me, I was wearing a sari, and he said, "Are you from India?" I said, "Why do you think I am? Just because I'm wearing a sari from India? I could be from Burma. I could be from Fiji, all kinds of places. There are Indians all over the globe." So he was kind of miffed about that.

In my second year at University of Arizona, my husband and I were married.

How did your families feel about that?

Well, as I said, when I was growing up, my dad was not an orthodox Hindu. When I was younger, he would say that I would get to choose the man I wanted to marry but that he would recommend or try to see that the same religion—which my husband is, the same religion.

But they did put up a big fuss about the one fact that my husband had a disability. When he was ten years old, he had met with an accident and lost his eye. So they were worried about that. How could he take a wife? And things like that. The other thing was that, like typical Indian families, which I'm sure you've met also, they also thought it would be good to marry someone who had a profession. By profession, they meant a medical profession, a legal profession, and so on. And I just didn't go along with that. So I just told them that that was not acceptable to me. So that was it.

Durga's husband was not nearly as complete and dramatic in his recollections of his childhood as his wife. However, he seemed to share the self-possessed assurance I found so evident in Durga. There is definitely a no-nonsense, tell-it-like-it-is tone in all the family members' talk about their lives.

Well, where do I start? In terms of family, my father and mother were sort of the core in the household. And one of my father's brothers came in because he was sick, and he came with his whole family. Another brother of my father, who was a headmaster at a school there, he was unmarried and he stayed with us. So we had something like over forty people under one roof, in the house. And then, of course, some other relatives would come just for the meals, at night. All the women cooked. And, as you women might complain, it was sort of man's world. We didn't have to do anything. But everybody was treated fairly, sort of, by the older people.

My father was the only one who worked, plus my brothers . . . few of them. The money was put into a pot. It's not in the same fashion that I do. It is some kind of a joint property. I believe in private property having come to this country and sort of having known . . . but anyway, I still send money home to all members of the family who I believe, you know, are in need.

We were what I would call lower-middle-class people. Not really wealthy, but we were well-off in the sense that we had a home of our own and we had some private land. It was sublet for farming. I don't remember when it was that the Indian government tried to national-ize, I mean, give it back to the farmers. We lost all the land without any compensation. And our family did not really go after getting com-pensation in any way, because we sort of go through a rut in the vil-lages where you don't really know what you can and cannot do. So that's the family.

In terms of the religion, we are Hindus. Religion was a tremen-dous influence, and yet it was not like a formalistic type where you go to church every Sunday. It was a basic thing. Each one of us tried to copy some particular one that we were impressed with, in terms of our deities, who all had a story.* The various Vedic principles were also emphasized by the parents. When you violated in the sense of, if you sort of beat up somebody, then you should not. There was tremendous respect for the elders. And, however much you disagreed with your older people, even if they were not related to you, you never sort of said bad words against them, or ever dared to hit them physically.

So that was the overall religious influence. So I told you about the family, religion, and what else would you like me to talk about?

Were there any particular family members whom you had close relation-ships with, who you would say were major influences on you personally?

Yes, we were six brothers and two sisters. My second eldest brother is a professor. He went when he was very young to Madras, which is on the east coast. We are from the west coast. And he got his Ph.D. in chemistry. He was sort of always involved with research, teaching. He was loved by his students. He had a tremendous reputation in the whole town, even outside the academic establishment. And so he was a tre-mendous influence. My oldest brother was a great influence in the sense that even though he was a teacher in the high school, he was a vora-cious reader. He used to read people like Dickens and Goldsmith and Johnson, many others.

* Shenoy is suggesting here that as part of their religious sensibility, he and his friends tried to pattern themselves, in character and action, after one of the deities. This use of deities as personal models echoes the use Durga and her friends made of the five Pandav brothers. Both Shenoy and Durga, then, exhibit in their early lives a commitment to action as a path to God. Living a particular kind of life is a religious activity. In Hindu philoso-phy, however, right living represents only one of the paths to God. Devotion (worship) and knowledge (the study of philosophical principles) are the other paths. Thus, Durga and Shenoy share an action-oriented, this-worldly approach to religion. It is important for them that their philosophy of life translates into concrete actions. We will see this orienta-tion again in the way they advise and interact with their children.

Specializing in English literature, in some fashion, was considered one route to sort of success in our society, because all of the plums or rewards of the society were to be had by competing in the examinations which the central government used to have. Indian Administrative Service, or Indian Foreign Service. Not only was that the immediate passport to secure a very high level of earnings, in relation to the average in India, but it was also a way by which you get into the power structure. Because then you get to be the head of various village governmental structures, or city structures, or central government. So, trying to learn English and do well in school was one method by which you could hope to competitively win in this examination. And that was our major goal, in families of our sort.

We were essentially, my family was in our Indian caste system, were Brahmans, and hence you specialized in knowledge activities. So this was quite suitable for us, if we sort of took pride in the objective to achieve, then we had it sort of made.

School was very important, as I said, because of these exams. So much so that when I became the school valedictorian, even though my first prize was just an Oxford dictionary, I sort of cherished it. And the whole village sort of looks up to you. So I guess I must say that school was extremely important, was the focal point.*

Shenoy's initial reaction to the United States reveals some of the awe for material conditions that so characterized his wife's response. Shenoy goes on, though, to see in these differences opportunites for himself. He begins to reveal the ethic of material prosperity that is central to this family's character.

One thing I can say is that everything was on a bigger scale, more mammoth scale. It was a dream in the sense that many of the things that probably would never have been within my reach in India looked extremely easy, easily solved. Such as having a nice home, nice car, traveling, getting to do wonderful jobs in any kind of occupation you choose to specialize in. That kind of a thing was sort of a tremendous break from India.

After finishing his education, Shenoy flirted with the idea of returning to India to take advantage of the new government-sponsored opportunities to develop manufacturing concerns. As he investigated these initiatives, however, he found that without connections, opportunities were few.

---

* Education was important to both Durga and Shenoy. (Mr. Shenoy, like many South Indians, has no first name as such. People address him simply as Shenoy.) For Shenoy, however, education was formal education with the instrumental goal of achieving a high position in public life, in government service. For Durga, formal education was couched in a broader commitment to hands-on exploration of the environment and a commitment to use knowledge for service to others (as exemplified by her parents' medical careers). Nonetheless, for both, education was connected to public, community life. Again, knowledge translated into action.

*When you decided you weren't going to go back, was that at all a diffi-
cult decision for you?*

Oh, no. No. In fact, by that time, I had sort of really felt as though I
really belonged here. I would miss my brothers, sisters, and relatives,
but not anything that India really had to offer.

There was one thing, I mean, I should not hide it. When I was
growing up, one of my ambitions really was to be one of the top min-
isters in the central government. And because the kind of things, per-
quisites that you get with power is something not that you could get
just with a big job and a lot of money, as you can here. So that was,
for some years, that was one major thing I did miss, as though I'm sort
of giving up one of my life's goals.

After graduate work at various schools in California and a brief tenure
for Shenoy and Durga as instructors at a midwestern university, the family
settled in the Chicago area. Psalm, the elder daughter, remembers the early
days of family life.

I really think I was blessed with just a glowing, happy childhood. I was
born when my dad was still in graduate school. And I think those were
really, really happy days for my parents.

My dad was actually really, really idealistic back then in terms of
being real politically interested. Originally, he believed in socialism, and
then he also wanted to be kind of another Gandhi or something like
that. So he had really high political ideals. In the end, though, he really
started to believe in capitalism, because of the economics he studied.
Then he also lost all interest in any political interaction. But in school,
he was president of the international student body, and things like that.

I was five when we moved to Chicago, where I grew up. And I
think my parents were really good parents back then. I was very disci-
plined. I always had a certain really good self-discipline (which,
unfortunately, I feel I don't have as much now). I mean, I was just very
happy somehow. I loved my parents. I used to think I was going to
marry my dad.*

When they settled in Chicago, Durga devoted herself to raising her
children. Although she wanted to work, she felt that the child-care options
that were available provided neither the privacy nor the spontaneity that
young children need to mature and develop. A major concern in raising
her children has been to give them the support and encouragement to dis-

---

* Psalm begins to reveal the influence of parental examples in the Shenoy family. She
spontaneously recounts with a good deal of accuracy her father's early desire to participate
in public life. A commitment to public life is appreciated by all the Shenoy children, but
most strikingly, as we will see, by Psalm's brother Sanjay. Also evident here is the "disci-
plined" atmosphere of the Shenoy household. In Durga's childhood, discipline meant her
father's ordered and thorough approach to raising his kids. A similar sense of order and
intensity is characteristic of the Shenoy children's upbringing.

cover and develop their own unique talents and interests. This attitude follows from both her own early educational experiences and the strong-willed sense of purpose and individuality she inherited from her mother.

I found myself completely busy with the children's activities. My kids were very active in having all these lessons. Skating lessons, ballet lessons, music lessons, and various other activities. They had to be driven all around. I had become a typical mainstream mother, very, very busy with that.

There was a Montessori school here where my last two kids went to school. The idea was that in a wealthy society like the U.S., where you have safety programs in place, it's important for people to find happiness by finding a productive activity that they love. Whatever that might be. But the problem was how do you go about having the children become aware of what that is? What sort of education system should you have? And I felt that, in the early years, if they could somehow have a method where they're learning by discovery, and that allows them to think, and they have joy of learning, I just felt that that would be a good starting point.

So there was all this combination of Montessori school, all the private lessons, and all this. So that kept me very, very busy.

Did the kids seem really involved in private lessons and all that? Because there's some kids, you drag 'em by the hair . . .

No, my kids asked for lessons. And I think it has something to do with this method of discovering your interests. Your reading to them, for instance. Like my oldest one, she must have been, I don't know, two years old. Every morning, she would get up at six and sit down in the books and have me read to her. So this initiating of the lessons, wanting to learn, that came from the kids.

Music lessons came because my younger one was about six years old, she got a friend of hers to teach her how to play the piano, in school. At a friend's house I was visiting, the neighbor's house, she kept on begging for piano lessons, and played on the piano to show me, yes she can do it, see.

All three of them really loved that. My son was two and a half when he started sort of insisting that he wanted music lessons. So we said, "Well, what do you want to learn? What instrument do you want?" And he said violin. So we got him this little violin. It's still there in the basement.

So that's how that was done. The kids would ask for lessons. And we would follow through.

The two daughters especially remember the energetic pursuit of interests being encouraged. They also mention, however, that their parents expected extracurricular interests to be balanced with strictly academic pursuits. Padma, the second daughter, recalls:

It was always installed in us, every turn, my parents were always encouraging us to take classes. I was actually telling this story to someone. In second grade, I was in summer school taking Spanish, something like that. They were all laughing, like, "Second grade! What were we doing in second grade? My God, we were in our baseball caps!" But, you know, every step of the way, like every summer school, my mom was always encouraging us to take engineering and accounting and statistics. My God, I mean . . . and now I regret not having taken accounting and statistics. But I don't think we were ever pressured the same way a lot of other Indian kids are pressured to go into medicine and to maintain like a straight-A average and study.*

I think that I'm different. Because I think it was always recognized that I was not always a straight-A student. I think that my sister, they had higher expectations for her, because she was really, really smart, and she had always done really well in school. I know they just didn't expect the same sort of things from me.**

I had my own insecurities, too, about not being smart. I had always excelled in extracurricular activities and piano and violin, and in ice skating, and in whatever other activities I did. And a lot of this for me was happening when I was in debate. Debate was a way for me to show all these really intelligent honors students that I was smart, too, because I was doing really well. So I worked really hard at that. But then it was really hard to study, to be a really serious student and to be a debater at the same time.

Psalm, too, remembers the pressure to do well academically. Although she easily excelled at her purely academic pursuits, it is interesting that for her, like her sister, the achievements were tempered by a fear of failure, a need to prove that she really was at the top.

I think I was always expected to go to a top school, and the funny thing was I . . . in the end of high school, I was best friends with this one

---

* This is one of the clearest examples of the use of prototypes in the construction of identity. The "pressure to get straight A's" and "go into medicine" which were paramount in the public rhetoric of educational issues (see chapter 5) are characterized by Padma as typical of "other Indian kids." Her situation, however, deviates from this perceived norm. Padma could just as well have left this statement out of her description of her parents' encouragement of learning. It really adds no new information about her own experiences. However, we see over and over again that individuals use this type of comparative device and, in so doing, forge a link to the Indian community (simply by using it as a relevant point of comparison) at the same time as they distance themselves from it. The process of assimilation, then, is not a movement from "ethnic" to "mainstream American" but a progressive shift in the kind of "ethnic" one is.

** Padma shifts from a contrast with Indians to a contrast with her sister to further carve out her own unique identity.

girl who had a lot of problems with her parents and academically somewhat, and that somehow affected me. I got a D in French or something 'cause I was skipping it a lot. It was really bad. I felt so bad. I felt like no college would ever want me. And yet, in truth, I graduated, like, number nineteen out of, like, five hundred fifty kids. So looking back, I should have, like, applied to Harvard and stuff like that. And I think I probably could have gotten in if I'd just written some good essays. But I was really scared that there was no way. Tufts was the big safety school for me, for the honors track. I just applied to Tufts, and I applied to Yale and Stanford also. Typed the essays on my typewriter the day they were due. It was really terrible. I was pretty irresponsible about certain things. Not irresponsible, just not really knowing what I wanted to do, or what was going on overall as far as applying to college. I just didn't really know.

Did your parents help you at all with the college . . . ?

No, see, we didn't discuss any of that. Looking back, my mom's like, "Oh, we should have done this, we should have done that." I'm like, "Mom, don't worry about it. I'm happy now and everything. And it was good and everything." But on the one hand, they just expected, okay, I'm going to go to an Ivy League school; and on the other hand, it's like they didn't really get involved with trying to help me.

I don't even remember what happened with that whole thing, but in any case, I had this stigma of my own that I was ashamed to even share with my parents. Like, I couldn't talk to them about my D. It was like, "My gosh, I'm a failure."

Many of the educational goals and decisions made by the girls' younger brother, Sanjay, have also been driven by a desire to be at the top, to be not just excellent but perfect. After his first year of high school, despite his parents' objections, Sanjay persuaded them to let him attend a boarding school.

So then, the next year, I went to boarding school. They finally let me go to boarding school. I always knew that I wanted to get out. I knew I couldn't stay in the school system here. I needed a good boarding school to get me into a really good college. Because otherwise I wouldn't have been able to get in. And also I wanted to meet the right people, because I was very materialistic then.

What's the "right people?"

Well, all the wealthiest families send their kids to boarding schools like Andover and Exeter. The schools in the area aren't good enough for them. I wanted to be involved with that.

So, anyhow, I didn't get in. I didn't know there were other places like Cranbrook or Taft. In other words, I could still get something with a really good name but not perfect. So, instead, I heard about this school called the Cambridge School. A friend said that this school was a place where people who got into Andover and Exeter, didn't want to go there, went. Kind of like Reed, Bennington on a secondary-school level. That stuck in my mind. That notion that, "Okay, I couldn't get in there, so I go to a place where people who did get in, didn't go . . ."

I really liked it because there weren't any things to interfere with the learning process. The academics were in fact probably better in many ways than Andover and Exeter, because you had a system where you took only three classes a term. So you really dig into the learning. There are a lot of things I liked about it.

Sanjay, however, did not settle for his second choice. Throughout high school, he repeatedly tried to get himself to the top boarding school.

My parents never liked the Cambridge School because it was very liberal. So my parents then put me at a very conservative school. It's here in Chicago. I let them do that. I thought I could go to this school and bring up all the new philosophies I'd learned. Just like the idea of calling people by their first names and more democracy in education.

My parents had this philosophy, they thought they indulged me my first year. So they wanted to take back from that.

So at that point, I had achieved something at boarding school. I had done average work in math and sciences, which is my weak point, and above-average work in other things, humanities. And so I had the elements to get me into a good boarding school. And I remember when I applied to the school in Chicago, it was really terrible, because they wanted me very badly, and it was really easy to get in. I thought I'd be on a higher level than everybody else. It was kind of complicated. It's hard to explain. But then, when I realized that it was just a bad situation, I wanted to go back to my boarding school in Massachusetts. Or even go to Andover or Exeter. And my parents wouldn't let me at that point.

That was where a change took place in our family where my parents weren't going to support me in what I wanted. And they were going to do what they wanted in regard to my life. Which is something that should be done along with what I want, because it's my life. Of course, they didn't think that.

So, at that point, I applied to several boarding schools and got in. Several of the schools that rejected me in the past, because I had straight A's and everything. And still my parents wouldn't let me go.

Looking back on it now, I had to keep banging my head on the wall, kind of tripping and falling. Finally, I developed enough things to get me in. There were points when I was able to get into the right boarding schools and my parents didn't let me go. I look back on that very negatively. When I came back to school in Chicago, that was partly my fault. It was kind of by choice. A stupid one. But my senior year, at that point, I had wised up and realized that this is the right thing for me.

See, the thing is, I feel that getting the best education, whether you're a liberal or a conservative, or materialistic or not materialistic, is the best thing. Because one of the things is at Andover, you learn skills more than you learn anywhere else. You learn academic and social skills, far more than you learn anywhere else. And so, on any level, it's the best thing. Education-wise. Academic-wise. Social-wise. Any-wise. Future-wise. College-admissions-wise. Anything you want. It's the best place for a student.

There's a lot more to it than I'm describing. I still look back on that, and a lot of the things in my life, a lot of the problems I have now are the result of that period.

This sense that "the best" is really the only acceptable alternative echoes the Shenoy daughters' feelings of anxiety that they are not or may cease to be at the top. Anxiety about the possibility of failure is a theme that runs throughout members of the second generation's descriptions of their lives. In this family, as in the Kumars', though, there is a great deal of consistency in this feeling among the siblings. I will return to the role the Shenoys' "third identity" plays in this later.

In Sanjay's story, there is a strong element of independent thought. "What are *my* interests?" irrespective of, if not in opposition to, his parents' interests, is clearly articulated. The Shenoy daughters, too, have this sense of their own personal interests and styles. These individual interests, which have the potential to bring them into conflict with their parents, nonetheless are pursued vigorously. In Psalm's case, it is her interest in religion.

In the following excerpt, in addition to discussing the development of her interest in religion, Psalm lets us see something of her perception of Durga's parenting. Just as Durga's parents actively exposed their children to learning experiences (Durga's watching her father sort organ meats or accompanying him on medical rounds), Psalm describes Durga as a very "hands in the mud" type of parent.

> College was interesting in a lot of ways. I mean, I had actually a variety of different threads of experience while I was there. I was an economics major, but I didn't really love economics. I really loved the humanities. For a while, I was really taken with psychology and Carl Jung. Carl Jung is real into psychology of mysticism and religion.
>
> It was all very interesting, and where that all led to was me being really interested in mysticism and what mysticism was. Not interested in religion, the institution of religion, but more interested in, like, a personal individual spiritual search and connection. I just became more interested in that itself and really tired of, like, psychological terminology of religious experiences, which I felt reduced it. It was one step away from the heart of the matter.
>
> So I began to read a lot of different Hindu mysticism, Turkish mysticism. And I took a class with Elie Wiesel on Jewish mysticism. I

also got involved sort of with the New Age in Boston, which is a big thing there.

And when I graduated from college (this was like another thing to my parents' chagrin), I didn't know what I wanted to do. I interviewed with one company that was insurance or something. It turned me off so much, I felt like I really wanted to do some other stuff, and I didn't know what. So I did a variety of little things. I worked at a spiritual, like a metaphysical, holistic health bookstore which my parents couldn't stand because I was working for minimum wage after this expensive college education. I did that for, like, eight months, and they were really mad.

But while I did that, I also took some other classes, in all kinds of things, from Buddhist meditation to Tarot cards to astrology to psychology. And then I moved back home.

I was working for my dad for a while. While I was doing that, I audited three classes at Northwestern, two graduate philosophy classes and one at the divinity school which looked at right brain, left brain, at the two different sides of man's faith, an analytical and an intuitive. So I was trying to really figure out what I wanted to do.

My dad was really mad that I was spending time with that. He thought that that should be a hobby, that I should really be working first and foremost. We had some, like, interesting things, like he fired me because I was, like, not doing enough work for him. I didn't really care about the work. I was glad he fired me, I said.[2]

Luckily, out of the blue, I got a job offer in New Jersey, where a good friend of my mom's had seen my résumé that my mom had sent her. My mom had always taken a real active interest in what I've done. She's a person to put her hands in the mud and try to work with things. My dad, on the other hand, is not. He's much more hands-off. My dad's very there, but it's more verbal and intellectual. He tells you what should be done, and you're just supposed to understand that. He was not real interested in coming to all our school open houses and things like that. I mean, my mom would drag him along, and he would come, but if he could, he sort of stopped.

I also really kind of wanted to go back east. I just sort of felt, I mean, and not necessarily for the greatest reasons, I guess. Basically, the reasons, I think, were that I'd gone to school there, and I felt like that's where my growing still was. I somehow felt here [in Chicago], I couldn't connect with the things that would make me grow. I think that was sort of silly, but anyway, I did get this job offer, and I hadn't begun to look for a job here. Things were uncomfortable working for my dad. So I just said, "Fine, I'm going."

I went through this kind of interesting phase where I was really interested in this one spiritual writer who mixes a whole bunch of different spiritual traditions together. Kind of read that stuff on the side. Went to different lectures around the area, little workshops and things like that. But I'd go to my "Wall Street work" every day and do that whole routine.

In the meantime, I got real interested, through a funny turn of events, in Christianity. I started reading the gospels on somebody's recommendation. And I loved them. I had been reading through this other strange guy, a very convoluted picture of Christ and what the whole story was about. I was always intrigued, but I sort of wanted to know more. And when I read the gospels, I really felt like that was the truth about the whole story. They just had a lot of really beautiful human messages and that I felt were just full of heart and stuff like that. Plus, the guy that I was dating at the time was Catholic. I'd never known in my life anybody Catholic. And he was also practicing, which somehow was very unusual.

So I really began to get exposed through him and just really kind of, I mean, I don't know, I almost had like a real conversion experience. I haven't at this point been baptized, but I'm pretty sure that I'm going to do that at some point in the next couple years. I will probably, I'm pretty sure I will do that.

How do your parents feel about your plans to be baptized?

I think they understand and accept me, I mean, for "me" to some extent. And they've kind of always known I'm the kid who's kind of got, like, this sort of strange spiritual thing.

In some ways, it's a little bit of a crisis that it's not something I even share with my parents anymore, you know. Up until now, I've shared sort of everything with them. Everything in my life kind of fit with them, and stuff that I did wrong was rebellion against them. That was bad, but at least it all had to do with them. Now I feel like I have something that's my own. I sort of came of age. I got something that was really my own identity.

Padma's independent interests revolve around her desire to travel, to experience life away from her parents.

I had gotten into a law school in L.A., and I really, really wanted to go there. I had gotten a scholarship in Chicago, but I really wanted to go to Los Angeles. And my parents were paying, and they wouldn't pay for that. And that was a really major thing.

They felt if I went to L.A., I would never come back. And that was totally wrong, because I really like Chicago, and it's a great place to raise a family. I like it here, and I know that I would have come back after law school. And that really bothered me, because they've always encouraged us to be independent.

How come you finally made that decision, rather they saying, "I'll take out loans and go to L.A."?

Well, I could have done that, you know, but I don't think I have the guts to do that. I guess I really didn't have the guts to do it, or I really didn't want to go that much. It was something I didn't really think of.

While all three children have energetically pursued their desires, and to a large extent have succeeded in enlisting their parents' eventual support, as Padma points out, there is a point when the bonds to their parents, to their parents' wishes, have overwhelmed their individual desires.

For Padma, the issue of whose interests will prevail was put to the test in her choice of law schools. For Sanjay, it came when his parents refused to let him go to the boarding school of his choice. Padma describes her capitulation to her parents' desires as a result of the fact that alternatives didn't occur to her, but she does not, in retrospect, seem very bitter. Sanjay provides a similar interpretation, but, in contrast to his sister, one senses that had he thought of alternatives, he would have pursued them.

> So all the current dilemmas are a result of that period. All the things I'm dealing with are the result of mistaken decisions they made. And part of it is, what I was saying, is they don't know how to raise an adolescent male, because my dad didn't have a father when he was that age. So he doesn't know what it's like to be under somebody's authority. My mom doesn't, either, because she went away to boarding schools. So they don't really know what it's like to be bossed around.

Do you think it was different with your sisters?

> Yeah, well, my sisters did more of what they were told, and my sisters are much more positive people. They're much more conforming. They follow orders well.

But you, ultimately, followed. No matter how much grief was involved, you generally followed orders.

> Unfortunately, that was the result of my training, my upbringing. I was always taught that you do things within the system. In other words, if they can't be convinced . . . also, I didn't have grandparents, so I didn't have any authority they had to answer to. So they were the final arbiters, and I didn't realize I could do . . .
>
> You say I was obedient. Well, that's true, but I didn't know there were other channels I could go through. For instance, my dad's clients who provide his livelihood, I'm sure they would agree that if I had what it took to get into boarding school, I should go there. They sent their own kids there. I could have gone to his clients and said, "Look, you're the only person he'll listen to." In other words, there were other channels I could have gone through, but I didn't.

Psalm casts her capitulations to parents in a different light. Her younger brother and sister talk in terms of just giving up the fight at a certain point— for lack of energy, for lack of knowledge. Psalm, in contrast, sees giving up the fight in terms of a need to please her parents.

I think that I've had a big need to please my parents. I think that has to do a lot just with the Indian culture. That's the way things are. You respect your elders. You do what your elders want.

In fact, when I was in college and I was studying economics, a friend of mine said, "Well, why do you want to study it?" Whatever I said had something to do with my dad, and he thinks it's a good thing to study, or he thinks I should do that, and his business involves it, and he wants me to work in his business. And she's like, "That's awful, you should really be doing what you want to do," and stuff like that.

I asked Psalm how she had decided to go to business school, her current pursuit.

Well, that is one mystery to me. I think what happened was, I had taken a really wonderful class called "The Resurrection." It was looking at the resurrection in the four different gospels. It was almost like, okay, I have finally found something that I really, truly believe in, that I love, that I could really see dedicating the rest of my life to. Now, I can do what maybe my parents have wanted me to do. I can sort of get this over with. I can get this thing [i.e., the M.B.A.] that will help me in life in some way. I felt I had found something that would give me the strength to do that.

A similar decision was made when Psalm had the choice of going to business school on the East Coast near her boyfriend or in Chicago near her parents.

Bob was like, "Go to Yale," and my parents were like, "Go to Chicago." I think kind of deep down, I always sort of knew I was going to come to Chicago. I don't know exactly why. I really felt the need to return to my parents. I felt like I needed some distance from Bob. I felt like if I stayed there, I would just probably get married to him soon. Still probably will, but I'm not sure how soon. So I came here.

What struck me about the Shenoys was their strong emphasis on independent activity and development. Durga, in particular, was forced to develop a sense of independence quite early in life. While her early experiences with independence—separation from her mother in grammar school and separation from both parents when she was sent to school in India—left her with "hurts" that she remembered for a long time, one senses that by the time she was on a ship to America, she was quite proud of her ability to make her way on her own. Shenoy, too, talks about his desire to succeed economically and politically as very much a personal venture. There is no mention of being motivated by familial considerations, no mention of pleasing his parents.

The independence of the parents translated into individualism in their children. It is clear both that the parents encouraged and that the children did develop their individual, particular natures and interests.[3] At the same time, however, there seems to be a curious bond between parents and children that at times works against the fruition of the children's "self-enlightened, self-interested" desires.[4] Despite his strong feelings to the contrary, Sanjay did go along with his parents' preferences regarding school choice. Psalm did put her interests in religion on hold (at least as far as a career was concerned) and did go to business school. Padma went to law school in Chicago rather than Los Angeles.

It is only in Psalm's description of her bond to her parents that any family member spontaneously and specifically related some aspect of his or her experience to the family's Indian heritage. Based on my interviews with other families, Psalm's interpretation is quite plausible. There does seem to be a sense in the Indian community that the vestiges of Indian culture that persist in immigrant families do create a certain kind of parent-child bond that is different from the one Indians see in their non-Indian social and economic peers.

Most of the Shenoy family members did not interpret their family dynamics in light of their Indian heritage. One may think this is not surprising given that, in general, the Shenoys' concerns and values seem to be very American—almost to the point of caricature. There is a very strong emphasis on the individual. Each person should discover and develop his or her own talents and also nurture the other individuals in the family. The details of their day-to-day lives are not very different from the relatively Americanized Iyengar family. But, unlike the Iyengars, the Shenoys did not even speculate about their Indian heritage, debating what, if anything, was Indian about their values and lives. For the Shenoys, their Indian identity is not an issue. For them, identities are not created from elements that have national or cultural boundaries. They stress the universality of human experience and the connections among people as "citizens of the universe." While both parents clearly discussed their Indian upbringings in terms of culturally salient values and expectations, neither discussed current careers and activities or family life in relation to cultural heritage.

To try to understand the family's general inattention to its Indian heritage, I explicitly brought up the subject in some interviews. At one point in our conversations, I asked each parent about the role Indian heritage played in the way they have raised their children. Although my questions may have led to post hoc constructions of their concern with being Indian, the tone of their answers is significant. I broached the issue with Durga as follows:

> *When they were little like that, when they were in their preteen years, was there any way that you tried to share the Indian cultural heritage with them?*

I tried, but it was a very difficult attempt. I wanted them to learn, for instance, the Hindi language. And, in fact, a friend of mine sent me these stacks of books on the alphabet. So I made the attempt, but it was very difficult, because my husband is from South India, and I'm from North India. He learned the Hindi language as a foreign language. Both of us spoke English better than we spoke the Hindi language. So he could not speak my native language, I could not speak his native language. So the result was that the attempt I made to teach my kids the language came to nothing.

So then I thought, well, once they know what their interests are, and that they love to learn, that even when they're adults, it would be very easy to pick up the languages.

I did make an attempt to form a group which was centered around music. But that was very difficult, too, because families were very spread-out. I think the group met for probably almost a year. And somehow it was just not . . . just not satisfactory. I was finding myself so busy running around with the carpools Saturdays for all these private lessons, then also having that as an activity, and driving the distance was very difficult.

In terms of just your home life, how you set up your home, and the kinds of things you ate, was that at all Indian?

No, it was mixed. I think maybe one of the reasons could be that when I was growing up in India and Africa, I observed two groups of people who didn't want to change at all. In India, there are some communities that refuse to use English. The result was that by the time India became independent, all of the best jobs had gone to the people who were willing to learn the English language. And here, all people who learned this new language, new technologies, were able to become leaders. And this group that was left back started to demand all kinds of things, just because out of their own volition, they had not wanted to change. And many of us—when I say "us," I mean the people who did well—were stuck to foot the bill, for all the dissatisfactions.

The other people I observed in the same thing, and I think they're going to die off, are the Masai tribe in Kenya. The Masai also didn't want to change at all. The tribes that were willing to change moved into the industrialized level, the Kikuyu tribes and the Wakamba tribes. The Masai didn't want to change at all. They just wanted to keep their own old ways of tending the animals. They didn't want any schooling. So by the time independence came to Kenya, the Masai tribe was on the way to dying off.

That's what the whole thing about change is that you either change or you die. You perish slowly and steadily. And I think the same thing has happened to Indians in the United States. Out of their own volition, they have decided not to change. So I didn't want my kids to be that way. I just felt that I wanted them to learn the [English] language at a very early stage and move on from there.

I wasn't afraid of the change, either. That is, I didn't feel that just because they have learned English language, that they would not be aware of their roots. If it was necessary, they had this burning desire to go back and rediscover their roots, they had the initiative in them to do it, that would be their own decision, to do that.

At another point, Durga gave an example of an incident with her daughter that pointed up the need for her aggressive mainstreaming policy in regard to her children.

When my daughter, my second one, went to college, a white American professor of English asked her, "Did you speak English at home?" The reason he was asking was that she was doing freshman English writing, and her writing was not up to snuff. She was B level, but she could be getting better and so on. So he asked her that, and I told my daughter right away, I said, "That statement supposes that either you are Hispanic or that you never spoke English at home. And therefore, it's possible that your level of English is not as advanced. Even though your level of English may be just as advanced as any mainstream person's is." Right?

So I told my daughter, "Go back to that professor, and tell him that you were born in this country, one. Two, you spoke the English from the day one you were born. You've always spoken English at home. And then, three, that you still want to improve your English. What extra work should you do?" I told her that whenever people ask you these kinds of questions, they're trying to ask you, "Have you been raised in the mainstream way, or have you been raised in a . . . ?" So I said, just be aware of it. You have to immediately interact and verbalize and set the record straight. That's the only thing you can do.*

Aside from her attempt to organize a group devoted to Indian music, Durga also got the family involved with a group of other Indian families. This group, call the Country Club Group, was first brought to my attention by the daughters, who remember a lot of interfamily rivalry. The Shenoy family apparently used to win most of the little intellectual competitions of the group (e.g., story writing and poetry contests), which produced a certain amount of grumbling among some of the other families. I asked Shenoy about the Country Club Group.

Well, I don't like it, but . . . I guess as the years passed by, the Indian community did become large. Our kids were growing older, and we did feel that we should expose them to other Indians. And so we made

---

* Durga's concern over the way her daughter is categorized as a "mainstream person" or an "ethnic" reminds us that part of the assimilative process at work in these families is a dynamic that they share with other people who perceive themselves as potentially different from the mainstream. The affect of this dynamic on the developing identities of the second generation is in part a consequence of the parents' own feelings regarding their "minority" status. Durga and Shenoy, in choosing their occupations, their friends, and their lifestyles, have insisted that they themselves are fundamentally mainstream (though they may retain some interest in things Indian, as Durga seems to). As Durga asserts of the years when her children were young, "I had become a typical mainstream mother."

some conscious efforts to find other families who had similar interests. For instance, we never exposed them to our religion. So we made some attempts to get to know some couples who would Xerox stories from the scriptures. Kids would meet and discuss it. We were some fifteen, sixteen families. There are many doctors in the group, some accountants, one or two engineers.

This is all my wife's doing, and you want to keep the family tight. You've got to make compromises, so . . . I have never really enjoyed this group, but I still continue to go there. We have, I think, something like six meetings altogether. And, as I recall, four or so meetings we didn't go, all through the year. So that is tolerable for me. You know, because in my overall scheme of things in life, that has absolutely no significance, this group.

You say one issue was that you wanted to expose them to other Indians. Why did you think that was important?

First of all, we do stand out because of our color. And so it is better to know what your roots are and where you came from. If you have that awareness, it won't be as difficult to be different. Another reason, which was something that I went along with my wife, which is that if we found eligible sort of mates for them in our own community, with the same kind of a background as ours, maybe it will last longer.

I don't think we are trying to impart any Indian culture per se. But I do want them to be aware of what Indians were all about. So that whatever idiosyncrasies I have, or their mother has, they would appreciate it. But I'm not really trying to impart any Indian culture per se.

Shenoy states explicitly that he is not trying to pass on something called "Indian culture" to his children. Durga, in contrast, has made explicit efforts, however minimal, to expose her children to some aspects of Indian culture—language, music, and so on. But she, too, does not seem to be interested in passing on an essentialized Indianness that is bound up with personality and identity. When she talks about the dangers of resistance to change, she is talking about "ethnicity" standing in the way of a group's efforts to join in the "mainstream." Ethnicity, or in this case an essential Indianness, should not form the core of one's identity. One must be able to develop a personal identity that enables one to functional well in one's present circumstance. The Shenoy children must develop a personality that is in tune with the mainstream if they are to succeed and flourish.

In general, the kids' recollections of what was Indian about their upbringing reflect the sort of haphazard, half-hearted attempts of the Shenoys to impart Indian culture to their children and a general absence of concern with creating an Indian identity. In our first meeting, Padma said that her family led a very "non-Indian" home life, pointing out that the family had gone on European vacations and listened to Western classical music. I asked her more about this on a later occasion, asking what *was* Indian about her childhood home life. Did they eat Indian food? Did her parents tell her traditional Indian stories? Yes, her mother did tell her traditional stories, they did eat a lot of Indian food, but, she added:

> I guess what I meant when I said that it wasn't very Indian, it was like when we'd go over to other people's homes, and they'd have a lot of Indian things in the house, or they'd have a little praying area, and the house would always smell of Indian food. We did have a lot of Indian artifacts and things like that. But it wasn't overpowering in our house. That you'd come in there and know, you know.

When I asked about religious observances, Padma reported her one memory of visiting a Hare Krishna temple with her uncle. She didn't remember "going to any Hindu temples that were straight, or whatever." Christmas and Easter were celebrated with their Jewish neighbors. Other Indian families would invite the Shenoys to festive Divali parties, but Padma couldn't recall any religious ceremonies or activities during this Hindu holiday.

Despite this tangential attachment to Indian food, decor, or religion, both daughters do have vivid memories of their parents pointing out other Indians as the family passed them on the street. Psalm's words are illustrative.

> But one thing that my parents would always do, when we'd be driving around Chicago or something, was point out Indian people. But not necessarily saying, "We like them" or "That's good." There's different classes of people. I think my parents, my father sort of felt like, maybe this is a caste thing, but they both came for graduate school, for education. And a lot of the merchant class who have come here subsequently were not of the same class. There's certain lines between them and those people. Some ways me and them, too. But that's just sort of general. There's hundreds of thousands of people, you can't just come in contact with everybody.

When Durga argued Indian culture was something that her kids could pick up should they ever develop the interest, she was referring to concrete aspects of culture—language, religion—that one could read about in books.

As her daughters have moved into their twenties, both have developed interest in their Indian heritage, but it is the inarticulable, essentialized aspects of Indian culture that have drawn their attention, rather than the more accessible components. While both daughters had a vague sense of their connection with other Indians growing up (both say that their childhood friends were mostly Jewish), in their adulthood both have developed a new interest in other Indians of their generation. Padma reports:

> Some friends of the family had a wedding, and I met a bunch of other Indians. For the first time, I met a whole bunch of Indians who were very American, just like me. And that was a first.

Whenever my parents have seen someone who's Indian walking in Chicago, or we pass by another Indian family, they'd always make eye contact. "Oh, I think they're Indian." We were just sort of like, "Who cares?" But now, I'm the same way. I'll pass by somebody I see who's Indian, and I'll always smile at other Indians and other Indian families.

There's this girl in law school who's Indian. It was really funny the way we met, because we had seen each other. When we'd see each other, we'd smile and say hello, but I never really introduced myself. Then, one day, we just saw each other in this hallway at school and started talking. It was really odd, because we were both talking with each other on a very, very personal level. There was just this unbelievable trust which, I guess, you know, because maybe there aren't so many Indians, or so many Indians who are American, there's just sort of more of a feeling of closeness. Something like we were Indian and that we both grew up in the U.S. Let's see if I can expand upon that.

Well, because we came from the same heritage, the same family. I'm really a bad person to talk to. Because I know I can't really articulate my Indian heritage. And I told you about my boyfriend, and how he's Jewish. I'd want my kids to know about the Indian culture, too, in addition to the Jewish culture. He's like, "Well, what is the Indian culture?" I'm like, "Well, I don't know. When I have kids, I'll find out." But right now, you know, I don't know.

Psalm, too, reports a sudden discovery of her rapport with other second-generation Indians.

There's, like, all these Indians here [at business school], and they're really nice. There's this extra unspoken bond that's just there. A little bit of extra respect or something, in the relationship. I just find it, actually, an incredible support to have those relationships here. And it's not something I ever had before. I never had an opportunity where I was with all these Indian people.

Is there any way that you share anything with them that you don't share with your non-Indian friends? Is it that you look like them? Or something cultural?

I think there is to some extent looks. I think also, though, there's an understanding. A shared culture. Similar motivations.

There's this similar feeling about relationships. Relationships with your parents, with your family, with your friends, even with the system, with authority. I think you just understand that those are important, that you kind of try to cherish and nurture them, that they nourish you back. That's what I think is the understanding that's similar between us. I don't really know. All I know is we call each other and say hi. We see each other at social events, and there's something fun.

I went to this Indian dinner. They ordered out from Devon Street. And they had a movie, a video. There's this romance between an Indian man and woman in this movie, and it's so melodramatic. It's practically sickening. But I definitely felt a relationship to that.

I feel like Indians have also this romantic male-female thing, which is such a huge part of the culture. Not that, probably other ones have it also, but theirs is always sickeningly sweet. Just like the way their desserts are sweet. Maybe that's the other thing that we share. We all kind of, like, have a feeling for that. And I like that. I definitely like that.

Yet, despite this feeling of rapport with other Indians, neither daughter sees herself devoting much energy to including Indian culture in her life. I asked Psalm:

In terms of your longer life, what role do you see the fact that your family is originally from India, or of Indian heritage, playing?

I didn't see it as being a real big deal until, again, recently, that I've met all these Indians. It would be really nice to go to India again. It would be nice to learn the language, if possible. I feel it would really help me to relate more to all these Indians, that I already feel I have a special kind of kinship with.

But I think, in reality, I don't know how much of a role it's going to play. If I were to, say, have a relationship with Ravi [a second-generation Indian at business school she had dated] or something like that, then I'm sure it would start to play a big role. We'd start to do all this stuff. But, you know, I will probably marry Bob, and then I don't think it will play a big role at all.

I feel like my values, on the bottom, are Indian. There's sort of a work ethic, emphasis on education, big emphasis on family. Loyalty, a certain kind of ethic in the way you do things, caring for each other, stuff like that. But also I feel like I've sort of adopted, or been adopted by, Christianity at this point. That's kind of got all the ethics and all the values that I need. To some extent, that can be scary. Sometimes, I wonder, "Am I letting myself be completely subsumed by this whole engrossing thing that seems to have the answers to everything?" To me, it's also a very living thing that I grow with. It fits into everything I do, in some way.

So I don't know what will be left of the Indian except for looks and maybe certain feelings. Like I said, the way I feel about romance. I think I've got this notion that's very Indian about that.

Padma described her search for a religious identity through a comparative religion course at college. Like her sister, she is interested in learning more but doubts her commitment to follow through.

I think I was at the soul-searching part of my life, when I wanted to know what religion I was and why. So many of my best friends are

Jewish, and I always felt a certain kinship with a lot of Jewish people. And I was wondering if I was Jewish and should I convert.

   I told my parents that if I felt that any of the three religions we were going to study was what I sort of identified with, I was going to convert, because, you know, they never really taught me about Hinduism. And we've never really had a religious household. They were like, "Fine, do whatever you want." They didn't care. Like, my sister will probably talk your ear off about Catholicism, and about how she is going to convert one of these days. I'll get a call. "Padma, you know, I really want to convert." I'm like, "Okay," you know.

   And so I studied Christianity and Islam and Judaism. I read and I studied these religions, and I didn't really feel like any one of them really spoke to me. They were all foreign in a way. They were always outside of me. But I could understand them, and they were all beautiful in their own way. And then I just picked up some paperback book on Hinduism. I started reading it, and I just felt like, "This is just common sense," you know, and I didn't really read it that much, but what I did read I just felt very comfortable with. And I was like, "Okay, I'm a Hindu." My junior year, I started reading about Hinduism again. A lot of the times, because people who were friends of mine, they'd say things about Hindu mythology, the *Mahabharata*, or other things, and I didn't know what they're talking about. I'd just feel dumb. But I've never really followed through on learning about my heritage. I say that I would like to be more Indian, and yet I guess I must not totally care. I guess that maybe if I had kids, I'd probably start to be more serious about it. I don't know.

For the girls, the discovery of their Indianness in adulthood has much more to do with feelings than with gaining book knowledge about the culture. Unlike his sisters, Sanjay has not made a discovery of his heritage in terms of a rapport with other Indians. He sees his minimal connection with India as more political and philosophical than personal.

One thing that hasn't come up in the conversation is the fact that your family's originally from India. Has that been at all important in your life?

At times. I always admired that my dad started out with nothing and made it here. When I was in grade school, I wanted him to teach me the language, but he never did that. He said, "Well, do well in school first." Which meant, like, get straight A's.

   Unfortunately, the thing that was really depressing was that they didn't transmit the Hindu religion. Some of the philosophical elements like sacrifice and altruism. But, of course, you can't transmit that if that's not evident in your life. I'm really concerned with the internal attributes of being Indian, which to me means the Hindu religion, Buddhist religion.

Also, India was under colonial rule for many years, which was the result of Western imperialism. India hasn't really been given enough compensation for that period of exploitation by the West. And I'm very angry about that. I studied that at school. The West got the money for their wars through starving out India. Completely exploiting the country. That really touched me when I read Nehru's work on India.

And so I think part of being Indian is to realize that we were screwed over. We should take some of it back.

In general, the Shenoy children's attitude toward their Indian heritage is very similar to that of the Iyengar boys. In neither family do the children consider their houses or habits particularly Indian. Except for the Iyengars' younger son, Bob, all the children express an interest in learning more about India or Indian languages or religions. Yet all also recognize that their desire is not strong enough to bring about action. This similarity is partly a consequence of the similarities in their parents' attitudes toward their own Indianness. Neither set of parents sees themselves as *essentially* Indian. Unlike Vaidehi Nagar or the Kumars, they have no core Indianness that fundamentally distinguishes them from non-Indians. Instead, Indianness is found in the histories of the parents and in the few Indian practices that remain part of their lives. Indianness is incidental for both generations.

The one obvious difference between the families, however, is the Shenoy girls' sense of connection to other Indians. Many in the second generation speak about a mutual bond rooted in their similar experiences negotiating the two worlds of Indian and American. The Shenoy girls' sense of connection is different. It is a romantic notion of an inexplicable bond that seems rooted not in shared experience but in an essential Indianness.[5] This difference from the Iyengar boys' sense of Indianness is related to subtle differences in the way the two sets of parents conceive of their incidental Indianness.

In the Iyengar family, Lakshmi and Shivan have ambiguous feelings about Indianness as an essentialized concept.[6] Their critique of essential Indianness, however, has developed alongside a strong connection to their "historical" Indianness. They remain very connected to the country and the family they have there.[7] Relatives here are very active in political and human rights organizations that focus on India.

The process at work in the Shenoy family is very different.[8] Moreover, a real identity shift has taken place. The Shenoys have developed and articulated a philosophy of life, a family idiom, that has very little connection to any of the traditional elements of Indian philosophy or social practice. In addition to lacking any positive connection to traditional Indian society or culture, their philosophy does not even seem to be a reaction to their Indian upbringing, based on a critique of traditional Indian culture. Unlike the Iyengars, they do not express a particular dissatisfaction with Indian culture.[9] Rather, their philosophy of life has grown out of their experiences in the United States. Their outlook has not grown from where they have been but is preparing them for where they are going. I asked Shenoy:

In raising your children here, what do you think were the major issues, or what are the most important things that you were trying to teach them?

I wanted them to really get good education. I didn't want them to have any bad habits. Drugs. Learn to get along with people. Be active physically and otherwise. Get to see the world, which of course we tried to do. So those were the kinds of things that as far as I know, I did emphasize, I still do. That is to me the way to participate with the rest of the elite.

How did you try to impart those values to your kids? Verbally, or example, or . . . ?

I felt that I tried to do both equally. I'm quite proud of who I am and where I stand and how far I've come. So I feel that through examples also I have done.

In my conversations with Shenoy and Durga, I came to view the core of their outlook as an individualistic ethic geared toward economic success and driven by rational decision making. Durga repeatedly used the phrase "self-enlightened self-interest" to describe the counsel she has given to her children. (She is quick to point out, however, that realizing one's "self-enlightened self-interest" does not make one selfish and isolated. Rather, this realization takes place in the context of a family and global community in which respect for other individuals and mutual support for and nurturance of their personal development are highly valued.) For Shenoy, a driving force clearly has been economic success.

To the extent that this individual rational approach is joined by a concern with financial success, the overarching concern becomes one of class. In many ways, Shenoy was explicit about this connection when he discussed wanting his children to marry people "with the same kind of background, sociologically, economically, and other ways."

In trying to understand the Shenoy family's central identity as grounded in class rather than ethnicity, I once described their motivation as "economic" when I commented on a story Durga had told about their decision to remain permanently in America. Durga promptly corrected me.

So in the final analysis it was for mainly economic reasons?

No, because, you see, I beg to differ with that question, because to me, economics, your condition in the physical world, reflects your philosophy and religion. They are all interactive, you see. That's the way we look at life. We felt more in tune with wanting to be free, wanting to discuss openly whatever we felt, wanting to work on that basis.

We just felt that this country offered the best possible kind of freedom, both spiritual freedom, religious freedom, freedom to work, freedom to travel. And so we just felt that that's what we wanted to do.

So we decided to get the green card. That was in 1965. We both became citizens in 1974. We decided we will make our philosophical and spiritual commitment to this country, and that's another reason why I wanted my kids to be raised as Americans.

Durga's comments here may or may not be read as "class" concerns. She disagreed with my interpretation of the family's primary identity as class-based in a strict sense. She sees her family as more broadly concerned with freedom and self-discovery than with something commonly called class.[10]

However, Shenoy and the children seem more sensitive to the class elements in their lives. It is interesting that Psalm explicitly used the term *class* when accounting for the family's peculiar connection to other Indians. That is, they would seek out and acknowledge other Indians on the street but would feel a certain distance between themselves and Indians from the "merchant class." Sanjay interprets his parents' failure to pass on the Hindu religion, which he views as the essence of Indianness, with the absence of "sacrifice and altruism" in his family's lifestyle. He repeatedly criticized the family's and his own "materialistic" desires.

The class-based, individualistic outlook that has shaped the family's core identity has affected the way the children have dealt with their Indian heritage. Since the parents have not tried to raise their children as Indians, have not been overly concerned with exposing the kids to Indian material culture, and have raised them in an environment in relative isolation from other Indians, it is not surprising that the children do not talk about themselves in terms of their Indian or dual heritage, or express much commitment to learning about Indian culture.

Moreover, the girls' recent discovery of the kind of romantic appeal and fascination they feel is rooted in the way Indian identity has been overshadowed by a class-based identity throughout their upbringing. It seems they are discovering India and Indians almost as a tourist would discover them. They are able to sustain these romantic notions because India is being discovered for the first time. Had some connection to a real India or real Indians been a part of their early experience (like, for example, the Iyengar boys' visits to India and with Indian relatives over the years), this kind of romance with India—perhaps an idealized notion of their heritage—would not be possible.

One point of contact, then, is between the Shenoys and the Iyengars. Both families have led much less Indian daily lives than the other families profiled here, and neither set of parents seems to view themselves as definitively and essentially Indian in quite the same way as the other sets of parents. However, the two families differ in that the Iyengars have cultivated a sense of themselves as Indian in a historical sense. They preserve that history through visits to India and frequent contact with family members from India and their extended family that has moved to America. The Shenoys, in contrast, have created a life for themselves that is very much grounded in their current situation. They have developed a rather distinct and coherent philosophy of life which supports their concerns (with education, economic success, the discovery and development of each individual's potential, community responsibility) and guides their family dynamic (open and frank discussion, strong guidance, and a supportive environment for their children). The Shenoys are geared toward the future and seem (in comparison to the Iyengars) to have at most a benign interest in their past.

The Shenoys also have something in common with the Kumars in the role a "third identity" plays in shaping the second generation's understanding of the process of adjustment. For the Kumar children, Christianity intervened between Indian and American, allowing them to see themselves as closer to Americans than some of their non-Christian Indian-origin peers, and to understand their overall process of adjustment not as a cultural transformation but rather as a cultural diffusion. For the Kumars, Christianity blurred the sharpness of the assimilation process.

Similarly, the existence of a strong class-based identity has made the Indian-American dichotomy less distinct for the Shenoy children. On the one hand, their class has enhanced the ability of the Shenoy children to move comfortably in the mainstream (or at least their class-specific part of it). In describing his efforts to get to boarding school, Sanjay did not mention Indians as a reference group. He compared his position to that of other wealthy people, other elites. The daughters talk about their mainly Jewish childhood friends, about activities centered on "lessons."

On the other hand, the Shenoy children, like the Kumars, talk about a fear of failure and feelings of inadequacy. Only in these two families was this anxiety so profound. Perhaps when a third identity obscures the clear contrast between Indian and American, the ability of the second generation to locate and articulate its path of change is impaired. Perhaps the inability to see a clear division between where the parents have been and where the children are going makes the adjustment process more problematic (or at least different). Instead of talking about themselves as "caught between two cultures" or "proud to be Indian" or "pretty much American," these children just fear that they will fail to live up to their parental models, to their own hopes and expectations.

11

The Shankars:
Searching for a
Close Family

When I talked with the Shankars, their daughter, Veena, age twenty-two, and their son, Ganesh, age twenty-six, about something called Indian culture, about the core values that the parents have tried to pass on to their children, about the way they see themselves in relation to American culture, every family member talked about the special Indian "sense of family" as a distinguishing characteristic of their own family and of the Indian community in general. When I asked the father about his aspirations for his children, his hopes for their lives ten years down the road, he worried that they would be "completely detached from the first-generation friends and relatives," although he is reassured that his children do "talk about being close to parents and all that kind of stuff. Taking care of [us] when [we're] old." When I asked about the most important values that she has tried to pass on to her children, the mother replied:

> First thing, to love your family members. To share, care for them. And charity begins at home. First, you have to do whatever you have to do at home to help family members. Then, if you have energy, then you go out and do it.

Ganesh and Veena both describe the "sense of family" as something they value and something that grounds their Indianness. But what is this Indian sense of family?

In the other families profiled here, the foundation of the undeniably "close" relationship between parents and children is usually left unspeci-

fied. Lakshmi Iyengar describes her relationship to her sons as "clingy."
Psalm Shenoy talks about a feeling of loss when parts of her life, specifically her interest in religion, "no longer had to do with [her] parents."
Minakshi Kumar talks about the sense of obligation she feels toward her
parents, given all the sacrifices they have made on her behalf. But what does
it mean to have close familial relationships? What is the basis of this feeling of closeness?

Before talking to the Shankars, it hadn't occurred to me that "closeness" and "a sense of family" were problematic concepts. These terms are
commonly used in American English. Everyone knows a close family. Siblings, parents, and their adult children talk a lot. They are concerned with
the ins and outs of one another's lives. They are concerned with creating
and maintaining an image of themselves as emotionally close. The closeness they experience within the family is very similar to the closeness they
try to find with friends.

But the Shankars' daughter, in discussing her life's history, articulated
something about closeness in the context of Indian culture that caused me
to think again about this Indian sense of family. What is called a sense of
family by the Indian immigrant community refers to a very different constellation of emotions and expectations from what is commonly understood
as a close family in the American context.

I came to know the Shankars through their daughter, Veena, whom I
had first seen at an area college as a member of a panel discussing intergenerational problems in the Indian community. I ran into her at another
community function, and we discussed our research projects. As an undergraduate, she was working on a paper about the mental health implications
of bicultural tensions experienced by second-generation Indian Americans.
I was in the process of trying to locate a fairly traditional family to include
in these profiles and asked her to send out some feelers. A couple of weeks
later, she informed me that she couldn't find any traditional families who
would be willing to participate but that her family, which she characterized as "very traditional," would agree.

Mr. and Mrs. Shankar and Veena live in a large house in a new development in a suburb of Chicago. Like many of the Indian homes I visited
in the new suburban developments, on entering the house, one feels a sense
of spaciousness. The contemporary furnishings complement the architecture in this regard. Also like many of the homes I visited, there is relatively
little that signals that the occupants are of Indian origin. There are some
family portraits and an Indian batik on the walls. A display case in the family
room contains a model of the Taj Mahal and some Indian figurines. The
family's shrine, as in many homes, is tucked away in the kitchen. There is
no dramatic differentiation of formal and informal space on the ground
floor. On different occasions, I was received in both the living room and
the family room.

The story of the Shankar family's immigration to America is quite typical. Both parents come from large farming families in the South Indian state of Karnataka. Shankar's father was the thirteenth child in his family. At age twelve, he left his natal village and went to live with an aunt in one of the large cities in the state and began working. As an adult, he owned a grocery wholesale business. Shankar's brother went into the grocery business with their father. Shankar, however, describes himself as "somehow not inclined" to go into the family business. Instead, he went to college and received an engineering degree.

At age twenty-six, he married Parvathi. With the encouragement of friends and his wife's brothers, who were settled in America, he decided to come to the United States to receive some more advanced training. However, it was not until after both his parents had passed away that he was able to come. Freed from family obligations at age thirty, he received an immigrant visa and, once in America, decided to take advantage of his immigrant status and work rather than pursue his studies. Six months after he immigrated, he was joined by Parvathi and the two children. They had planned to stay for a few years, see America, and then settle down in India. Like most families, however, they shortly found themselves with adolescent children rooted in America. This made it difficult to return. Parvathi also had become accustomed to the freedom she enjoyed. She was able to work and was not consumed by the responsibilities of living with a large extended family.

I began my work with this family by interviewing Parvathi. More so than any other life story I heard, Parvathi's stories about her family, her education, and her marriage illustrate in a lively and evocative way the dynamics of a "very traditional" home life for a woman of her generation. Parvathi was the eighth of twelve children in her family. When she was born, her father and mother maintained their own household, because her father was changing locations with his government service position every couple of years. However, the feeling and politics of a joint family household prevailed.

> When my father was in service, my grandmother was not living with him, but my mom used to take care of so many children, my dad's nephews. They were all from the village, so they would stay with our family. That way, my mom can help them to get an education. She helped them so much because in the villages there were no colleges, and their parents were not willing to spare time or money. We were actually farmers, and we had lots of grains but not enough money, not much circulation. But still, because my father was in service, he was able to own something. He would get the grains from my grandma's place.
>
> See, like in India, it's joint family. We all live together, brothers and their wives, their children. And husband's parents. It used to be

most of the time, the parents would always stay with their sons. The daughters would be married to some other family. When I was born, my grandfather was dead already. I had only a grandmother, and she was the boss. I had my uncle, his family, our family, and my grandmother had adopted a son for the purpose of getting some help for harvesting and everything. And then my uncle's son was already married, his wife, his children, we were all together. It was fun. We didn't have the luxury of going to the movies or living in the city, but we were happy. We were a happy family. There was a lot of affection.

And my father had a high school diploma. At that time, that was worth like a master's today, or Ph.D. And he knew English very well. And he was always pushing us to get education, so that, you know, we will have good life in future.

In our community, there were not too many lady graduates. When I was born, this is forty-seven years ago, especially in the villages, the elderly people, grandparents would say, "Oh, you don't need to get educated. One day, you are going to be married anyway. So what are you going to do with a degree? You will never be able to avoid cooking or cleaning, or bearing children, or raising them." But in our community, there was only one lady graduate, and my fantasy was to get a degree.*

On top of school, we had to help at home also. Every weekend, because it was a joint family, there would be bushels and bushels of clothes to be washed. And where we used to live, there was not taps or anything. So we used to go one and a half miles to a pond where there is soft water. But there you have to have rocks, right? To do like this [she demonstrates beating the clothes on a rock]. And always *dhobis*[1] would have rocks, they would reserve it. And before they come, we have to go. So we used to go early in the morning, like five o'clock, we used to walk there. So cold and sleepy. And we used to wash all those things. With a joint family, there are so many boys going to college. So their clothes, white clothes, we have to put tinge of blue. And for our saris, most of those were cotton. So we had to starch. There were no cans or anything, especially back in India. Lots of work in the weekends, but we enjoyed it. It was fun.

And I was valedictorian in high school, and my grandma would never send me to college. That was the case. I had paternal auntie, my dad's sister. When I was a very young child, I had some kind of infection on my ear. My dad had shown it to so many doctors. Back then, technology was not this advanced, either. So no doctor could do any-

* Note that Parvathi repeatedly refers to what takes place "back in India." This is her version of the Indian prototype. The joint family "back in India" should be understood in contrast to the nuclear family she lives with today. What "grandparents would say" should be understood in contrast to her own fantasy to get a degree. She constructs the kind of Indian she is today (for, as we will see, Parvathi is still "essentially" Indian) by contrast to the India and Indians she knew in her past.

thing. My paternal auntie, his sister, came to visit us. She used to come quite often. And my father was so fed up with my doctor bills. He was scared, especially a girl when she doesn't have an ear, then nobody would marry her, right? So he told his sister, "I don't know what to do with this girl. I tried so much. So why don't you take her to your village? Why don't you keep her? So she is yours whether she is dead or alive. You can have her." She took me to her house, and she used some kind of juice from the leaves. She was able to cure it.

So when my grandmother said that she is not going to send me to college, and they were already looking for a groom for me, and I was kind of very upset, I said, "No. In that case, I'll go to my auntie's house." And I took her permission, and I went there. But at that time, my maternal uncle, my mom's brother, who was helped by my mother to get education, he was in London doing his FRCS. He is a surgeon. He was so mad when he heard that even after me being a valedictorian, my family was not going to send me to college. At that time, my brothers were already working. They had double E, engineering. And my uncle wrote to them a nasty letter that being working, they couldn't even support me to send to college? He asked them to stand up and fight for it. So you see, back in India, whoever the boss is, their word always goes. So my grandmother was handling everything because she was the boss. So then my brothers came, and they convinced my grandma, and finally they decided to send me to college. On one condition, my grandma agreed to send me to college only if I travel every day, back and forth. She wouldn't let me stay in the dorm. They thought it's not a good idea to live a girl in the dorm. There is a myth that all the girls will be spoiled if they stay in the city. That was happening, but it depends upon the children and how they were raised. In my case, no matter where I would have been, I wouldn't have been spoiled. But again, the fear is going to be there for the parents and grandparents who care more for you.

But see, living with a joint family, there was always help needed. And in my family, all the other ladies, except my own sisters and my mom, were kind of jealous because I go to college. I go to the city, and, you know, I dress up, this and that. At the same time, they were also jealous I was not helping. So they would never cook meals on time before I leave. I would have never had any good meal before I leave. Then my grandma never used to give me any money for me to use at the lunch room to buy food.

In a joint family, nobody can save food for me. See, back in India, people would just drop in, and they expect you to feed them. By the time I get home, there is nothing. And then, it's not like here—there is always refrigerator, there is always food, you know. In India, there is only certain timing to cook. So I had to wait till dinner. Even after dinner is ready, see, the custom is, the men first sit down and eat. And then ladies. By the time we sit down, it's ten o'clock in the night. I would be so hungry. So my father used to bring some bread. He used to hide it for me, because, see, it's so expensive, he cannot buy it for everybody. I never liked bread, from my childhood, but I used to eat it.

So many times I used to think, "Is it worth going through all this?" So many times like that. I should quit and just enjoy my life with other people. And settle down. Then I would think, "Even though I have to work hard today, I'm sure it will pay me off one day." Which is paying me off today. I'm so glad I got education. Otherwise, if I had not had the degree, I don't think I would have married my husband. He has double degree. I would have been married to another family, a farmer family. It would be typical, girls of the village. So anyway, my fantasy was to finish my degree.

So how did you get married?

Well, I was in final year of degree. One of his friends brought my husband to our house. One day, since he [her husband] was talking to a friend, he was saying, "If you know somebody, why don't you let me know?" So he [her husband's friend] said that he knew our family, and he would introduce us to him.

One day, he came. You know, back in India, the custom is always the groom has to come to see the bride. Actually, first the elderly people, like groom's sisters, married sisters, and mother, they come and they have a look at the girl. And if they approve it, then only the boy will come. See, in olden days, it's like arranged marriage. But in my case, things have changed a little bit. So I had the chance of giving my opinion. They would say, "We have a boy here. If you want to, you can meet. We would have him come over, you can see if you like." So there were a few offers. Some of them I didn't like. And when he came, I wasn't actually thinking of marriage, because my fantasy was to get the degree. I knew if I get married before the degree, I'll never finish my education. And then there goes my dream. So I had told them only if the groom's side is going to agree that he will wait till I have my finals, then only I will be willing to marry.

He came, but see, we didn't know that he was coming. His sisters or mother didn't come first. He, my husband, went to his friend's house, and then his friend sent somebody for my mom to go to his place to see the groom. So my mom went there, and then she just have a glance at him, and then she went inside and she talked to the lady of the house. And she comes and tells me that I have to get ready. I had to get to school, and I said no, because it's not been prearranged and I don't have time. I don't want to miss classes. It's like a show, you know. See, back in India, the custom is that the boy would come, and the girl would be dressed, and she will offer him some sweets or some snacks and some coffee or whatever he wants.

So I didn't see him, but he saw my picture. After seeing my picture, it seems he went home and said to his family, "The girl is okay.

The family is very nice. The girl is very smart, educated." Especially I was very dear to him. Nobody had studied in his house, and he was the only graduate in his whole house. I mean, he had seven sisters and a brother, and nobody went to high school, either. So, you know, he was impressed. But his family had an impression, like, if my husband marries me, an educated girl, I'll be splitting the family because I don't want to live with illiterate people.

But I was never raised like that. I was raised in such a way we should not get down to the level of illiterate people. Even if they make mistake, you're supposed to understand it because you have education. You can understand them, and you can train them, or you can do something to help them out. But see, back in India, that's how it is. They were thinking in a different way.

I wanted to wait until my exams are over. But in the meantime, my father-in-law was very, very sick. So he didn't want to wait anymore. He thought he will die, and he wanted to have the wedding done right away.

But because of this reason, I had to take exam early. I had to produce my wedding invitation and everything, for this wedding reason.

I couldn't even dream of my marriage because I was so much concentrating on exams. Because his family was bigger than mine, I knew if I don't pass, then I'll never continue. I knew they would never encourage me to continue studying. So I couldn't even dream of my wedding. I don't even know how it was done [laughing].

And back in India, usually, three months, they don't send the girl to the husband's place, because they want to train the girl right and, you know, teach them whatever they can. But in my case, I didn't even have that opportunity because of my father-in-law. He was very sick, and he wanted to see me in their house. So I had to go there in the next few weeks. I didn't even know how to cook. My parents were going to train me after I got married.

But in the meantime, when I got engaged to my husband, my cousin-brothers, for some reason, they didn't want my parents to have me married to my husband because he owned a car. They were well-to-do, and the boy was a double graduate. So they were opposing to that. But my parents were determined. And they said, "No matter what, we want to have this marriage performed." And then they wanted to split the family. So the day before my engagement, they sent us out. We didn't even have a kitchen for my mom to cook for the people who were coming for the engagement.

So I got married, and within a couple of weeks, I had to go to my husband's house. They were nice people, but it was hard on me. These people were not educated. My husband wanted me to go for a walk every day, but I would be scared.[2] I would be thinking about what other people would think. Because they don't know about walking and all those things. It's beyond their imagination because they were never raised like that. Especially, you know, leaving the family to go for a walk. I was feeling very uncomfortable. But my husband used to tell me that I had to please him. Forget what other people think. Somehow I managed, and then everybody was very happy. Even today they admire me, they adore me, for staying in their house and liking them, loving them.

Parvathi's experiences of her own and her husband's families, her portrayal of the intricate extended-family interactions, were for me particularly evocative. The life she described was very similar to the all-encompassing family life I witnessed when I lived with a similarly situated family in India. I understood this Indian experience of family in terms of its differences from my own experience of family. The stereotypically close Indian family was, from my perspective, too close, too encompassing. But I saw the differences between my images of a close American family and a close Indian family as differences of degree. In the Indian family, there were more people involved, and their involvement was more intrusive. I did not, however, pick up on differences in the nature of closeness. I thought that whether Indian or American, closeness meant that people cared for one another, wanted the best for their children, and so on.

But through my conversations with the Shankars, I have come to feel that the interactive dynamics that build and maintain this feeling of closeness are very different in the Shankars' experience from my own. One day, the Shankars' daughter, Veena, and I were discussing her marriage prospects. (I worked with the Shankars through the months surrounding their son's marriage, so marriage was a topic on everyone's mind.) In the excerpts below, Veena describes differences in the interpersonal styles of Indians raised in India and those raised in America. These differences set the stage for the way her parents, on the one hand, and she and her brother, on the other, define familial closeness.

Veena had been saying that when they were younger, she and her brother were very open to marrying someone outside their culture. But as time has gone on, and since her brother has found a second-generation Indian woman to marry, her views have changed.

> I really want to marry an Indian guy for a couple reasons. One is, I don't want to cause the devastation that I know it will. My parents will never disown me or anything like that, but I know that they will be devastated that I didn't marry an Indian person. And also, growing up, it was always Kannada,[3] you know, our own type. But then I started dating a North Indian. So they're like, "Okay, any Indian," you know. And then I started dating an American, and it was more, "Okay, any Indian."
>
> But I see my brother and his fiancée and the families interacting, and it's so wonderful. They get along so well. The plain fact is, if I were to marry someone who wasn't Indian, I could probably get along great with the in-laws and have a great relationship, but I know my parents

can't. 'Cause they can't even with my [American] friends. And for me, a family, a good, tight-knit family is very important.*

I guess it's selfish in that sense. I don't ever want to deal with that, you know. I mean, in the future, if anything were to happen, any type of family conflict, any type of marital quarrel, it won't be just that—a marital quarrel. It would be, well, I married an American, and that's why he's doing this. And holidays and stuff. I want us all to be together. So . . . it's hard, though, I mean . . . it's so hard meeting these men, you know.

Have you had some introduction?

No, not yet, because, well, like I said, I'm going to graduate school. I think I'm ready to get married, but as far as where I am in life right now, I have a couple of things I want to take care of. I don't think I'll necessarily wait till I'm done with graduate school, but I want to get into a routine and know what I'm in for before I make some sort of commitment. The way these arranged things work, there's always the underlying theme of marriage. Where here, when it's a blind date, it's just a date. Go out, see if you like each other, and marriage isn't really the end result. But if I were to start meeting people through my parents, I would have to decide somewhere along the line, and I'm not ready to do that.

Is marrying someone from India an option?

No, absolutely not. I know I'm generalizing, but the risks are too high that my assertiveness and independent attitudes will really clash with the male-dominant attitude of India. It's happened in my family, and I don't want a similar situation.

And the other thing that I've found, people in India are not trained with social skills too much. Interpersonal skills. They're not taught how to communicate with parents. How to resolve conflict. Anything like that. And, in fact, one of my brother's best friends is marrying a girl from India. He says it's very difficult to get to know her because they've never had this relationship. They've never dated. They've never even with the opposite sex had close relationships. And how am I supposed to get to know a guy under those circumstances? I don't want that, you know.

Do you think the young men of Indian heritage who are raised here are different?

* This comment harkens back to Anar Nagar's description of the way her friend Dave and her mother could never get to know each other. There is something radically different in the social worlds in which Indians and Americans move. The second generation, for the most part, views the social world around them as do other Americans. At times, however, they are pulled into social worlds governed by their parents' rules. For individuals like Anar and Veena, crossing back and forth between these different plains entails significant challenges as they struggle to construct unified identities and lives.

They're more skilled socially and interpersonally. They know how to flirt. I mean, just open up and discuss things. Whereas in India, especially, a woman going to India asking a lot of personal questions about a guy, being assertive in that sense, is threatening to them. And that's not expected, and that's not acceptable. And, you know, especially me, I'm the type of person that really needs these connections with a person before I make any kinds of commitments. And I don't see that happening, back there.

Veena drew a distinction between the interpersonal skills available to second-generation Indians in America and their counterparts in India. I was struck, however, by the similarity between Veena's conception of interpersonal distance in India and the Shankar family members' descriptions of the dinner parties that constituted most of the family's contact with other Indians in America. Veena's brother Ganesh recalls:

My parents' life revolved around us and their community. Like all of my parents' friends for the most part are from the same region we are. So their social life was having dinner parties. Every weekend, either go to someone's house or have someone come over. And that to them was socialization. We would go with them, and we would come home. Us going out separately from them was sort of a different concept. Everywhere they go, they would really make us go. It wasn't until really I started college I stopped going to these dinner parties. And they would always get upset that we wouldn't go because they felt like we didn't want to socialize with their friends. I don't think they ever understood. Maybe they did and they didn't want to admit it. But I don't think they ever understood the difference in age and the generation gap. 'Cause we'd be bored when we'd go there. And it wasn't like there were a whole lot of kids our age.

Veena adds:

Well, it's funny, because, yes, and we were forced to [go to dinner parties and big association events]. Especially, the one thing I remember clearly is that, you know, they'd give us this line about how we're going as a family, and we'd get there, and I'd never see my parents. They'd be off. So the women were off doing their thing, and the men were off doing their thing, and the kids were, you know, whatever . . . and yes, we went there in one car and we came back in one car, but where was the family interaction? I don't know.

Later, Veena suggested:

One of the things I was telling my parents the other day is that I don't remember us doing things as a family unit. It was always when we went someplace, or we had company over. I can't ever remember just us going to the park, or us sitting down and playing cards together. That's one of the things I really want to have—a good-quality family life. That's one of the things I'm going to make time for.

See, in India, you have the extended family. Okay. And also, if you're not wealthy, your whole life is spent working, you know. The mothers are with the kids all day, the fathers are out earning, and communication between parents and children just doesn't exist, only because there's that hierarchy.* It's almost like, okay, males, elders, and then kids. They come here, and that's just how it is, in the family, and especially here, you have the nuclear family, right? So what do they do? Their form of an extended family is social functions with other Indians. So that's how it is. And also, the other thing is that a lot of Indian couples don't know how to relate to each other because their whole lives are their kids. And then their kids grow up, and it's like, "Oh, no. Who is this person that I'm married to?" Because generally speaking, in India, when you get married, you have kids right away. There's none of this, "Oh, well, I just got married, I'm going to wait a couple years and spend it with my husband." No, it doesn't happen that way. And so communication, I think, is very rare thing in Indian families. Very, very rare.

When taken together, these comments illustrate an important feature of familial closeness in the Indian immigrant context. Both children—Veena in the above excerpt and Ganesh elsewhere in our conversations—identify a close family life as something that they value and something that they want to have in their adult relationships with both their parents, spouses, and children. Ganesh talks of eventually having his parents come live with him and his wife—something that he and his fiancée have thought about even before their marriage. Veena talks about needing to spend holidays comfortably with her parents. However, both siblings also recall their own childhood experiences of "doing things as a family" as not particularly fulfilling emotionally. The family would go out together, but there was little time spent conversing. Veena talks about Indians raised in India as being socially inept, not able to open up to one another.

What is closeness if it's not "getting to know people"? In Parvathi Shankar's description of her childhood, for her, the stories that she tells about herself, that connect her to her family, center around the actions of daily life (washing clothes, cooking) and the decision-making process in the family (will she or won't she go to college?). It is these routine interactions, which are the consequences of people living together, that made

---

* Veena's description of a lack of communication between parents and children in Indian families in India is reminiscent of Durga Shenoy's description of her natal family, where communicative norms were not developed enough for her to just say to her parents that she missed them and wanted to come home. Instead, she silently suffered the "hurts" that resulted from her parents flying her brothers from school in India back to Africa for visits, but not her.

her family life "happy" and "fun" and made her in-laws "adore" her. The pleasure and satisfaction Parvathi feels in her family relationships are rooted in family members' common participation in daily life.

In Shankar's reflections on his life in America, there is a similar sense that it is physical, practical interactions that make for a fulfilling close family life. He was the thirteenth of fourteen children and was very involved with his siblings before he moved to America at age thirty. After coming to America, he tried on two occasions to persuade his wife to return to India: "The main reason why I wanted to go was I had a big family back home." In a very moving exchange, Shankar expressed regret that he was unable to return to his family.

> I think in 1982, when my son was graduating from high school, that time I raised that same question, "Let's go back." Because I was missing my family. My brother was getting weak because his heart became, I don't know how to put it, missed me, I think. So every time when I go, I used to fear that we got separated for no reason or something. Because we lived together. I missed him, and he also missed me. So that was main reason, and also I though it was my duty being a first educated person to guide other people, but I think I failed.

> *In what way did you hope to guide them?*

> We really, somebody, a knowledgeable person, at least you could direct them to go to some good jobs, or concentrate on studies, or try to make a better living or something. For example, my brother's two sons, they were in college, and I tried to help them from here. But if I had stayed there, probably it would have been different. 'Cause from here, you can only send some money. That's all. Monetarily, you can help them, but morally it's difficult to communicate and try to educate them in certain ways. So anyway, I think that's over.

Later, I asked Shankar if he ever regretted coming to the United States.

> Yes. Sometimes I do. Because, I don't know what to say, like for everything and anything, we missed a lot of things being away from our big family. Sometimes I feel lonely. That's not the type of a life I lived before I came to this country. It was full of people in the home, activities. So here it is just, we are okay ourselves, but other things, we are not active in other things. So that aspect I do regret. Financially, we are okay. Socially, we miss some things. When I say socially, within our own [extended] family.

> *Do you think you would come again if you had the choice to make again?*

> Come back here?

> *If it was thirty years ago in India again, knowing what you know now about how your life has been here, do you think you would come again?*

> No. I would stay.

When the Indian community in general, and the Shankars in particular, talk about a sense of family, it is based in this kind of practical interaction. Although Veena desires a more psychological connectedness in her eventual relationship with her husband, she suggests that this kind of psychological closeness, open communication about feelings and desires, is not the characteristic tone of traditional Indian family life.

Ganesh and Veena, however, supplement their desire for a close family in the traditional, practical sense with a more psychologically oriented desire for closeness. Their parents, in contrast, do not talk about this kind of psychological closeness when they discuss their lives and their vision of family.[4] Their notion of a close family rests, as Shankar will tell us, on children "sticking close to home."

Disagreements between parents and children about the nature of familial closeness and cohesion is at the root of many incidents identified by both generations of Shankars as serious parent-child problems. The Shankars, like many other families, disagreed about dress, friends, dating, and the limits of teenagers' activities. Among the Shankars, as in most families, these disagreements are glossed as differences in cultural practices—"You were raised in India, and things here are different" from the child, or "I wasn't raised that way, and these changes are difficult to get used to" from the parent. These explanations mirror the folkways of American families—"You grew up in the '50s. Times are different," or "That's not the way we behaved when I was growing up." Whether practices are varying across space or time, the logic of the explanation is the same.

For the Shankars, what is really (or at least additionally) at stake is something much more fundamental: the definition of the family unit itself. This differs from what was at stake in parent-child disagreements in the Nagar and Iyengar families. Those families struggled over the roles that family members were to play. Vaidehi Nagar's exasperation when Anar wanted an explanation for why she was prohibited from putting pennies in the loafers was a struggle over the proper roles of parent and child. Lakshmi Iyengar's worry that Bob's extreme individualism will leave him isolated was a struggle over the individuation of children. In the Shankar family, in addition to negotiating members' roles within the family, the very meaning of family is being challenged. What is a satisfying, close family life for parents is not the same for children. The Shankar children, in the particular way each dealt with adolescence, were looking for a psychologically based sense of interpersonal closeness with their parents. Parent-child disagreements were as much a search for open communication and psychological closeness as they were instrumental tactics to get one's way.

The following excerpts present parent-child disagreements from the perspectives of both parents and children. The parents see children trying to do what they want and themselves as gatekeepers. They argue with their children but at a certain point conclude, "What can we do?" and let the children have their way. The children, in contrast, desperately want their parents to understand them and come to share their feelings that their intended actions are desirable. The Shankar parents would be happy if the children gave in. The children are not satisfied when their parents give in—they really want them to understand.

In the Shankar family story, Veena was the "rebellious child." Ganesh's adolescence is understood as much less problematic. Shankar recalls:

> In the beginning, we had some problem. Especially with my daughter. She was very outgoing. Going and staying late. Spending time with friends. Not that we had suspicion about her, but we were afraid that she may be hurt or something. We used to tell her, "Come home early," you know. As all parents say. But she wouldn't even care. She used to be always opposing to whatever we say.
>
> Dress, for example, or hairstyle, for example. Things like that. I was encouraging her to be modest. Stick to home. Spend time with parents. And, you know, get up early in the morning, and don't go late to the bed. She used to go out and come home late in the night. And morning, we would get up, she was not around. She will be in bed. So it's a kind of a 180 degrees type of a life. When you are up, she is asleep. When she is asleep, you are up. I didn't like that kind of life.
>
> The one thing we observe, even though she was spending too much time with her friends, academically she was okay. She was doing pretty good at school, very intelligent and all that. So then we realized, "Well, probably, she wants to be friendly. That type of person, why should we discourage it?" I think now we realize that maybe that's the way she wants to be. Her lifestyle.

Did you have similar kinds of issues with your son?

> No. He was a different person altogether. [He was] very easy. Very easy, and he was very considerate. He never opposed for things we used to tell him. We don't know his daily routine when he was in college, away from home. But as long as he was in the house, very, very methodic and studious, and limited in his activities. He had friends but never used to go and stay late. On occasions, birthdays, once in a while, but not on a regular basis. And if we tell him, "Okay, we have something to do," or "Don't go," he would say, "Yes, okay, I'm not going." But not the same situation with my daughter. If she says she is going, she is going.

Parvathi, with a little more attention to her own role in the process of her kids' maturation, notes the same issues, the same differences between her two kids.

> See, when my kids were young, it didn't bother me, because young children, it's just like, we raise our children. Only disturbing part will be when they become teenagers and they start going out with other kids. Try to do whatever the other kids do. That was hard on us. Like, we would never talk back to our parents. No matter what. Parents are like next to gods. They knew everything. And we were not rebellious.

We were trying to pull our children back from bad things because we knew their mind is very tender. Anything they see will look good for them. They will follow that. So we were trying to pull them back from exposure to drinks, drugs, sex.

Stay out late. We were never going out once it's dark. Especially girls. Even boys. Once it gets dark, the way we were raised, you go and wash up and pray to God for a few minutes, and then sit down and study. Evening is for you to study.

And we were never fed till we finished our homework. We were very systematically brought up. My father was in service. He was like an army leader. Today, my house is so clean because of him. He didn't want to see a piece of hair on the floor. He was very clean. And, you know, although he was very strict, he loved us. He would bring some snacks. He would have all of us sitting in a circle. He would peel the peanuts, and he would feed us. Something that had to be peeled, he would peel and cut into pieces, to feed. He would bathe us. He would help my mom. Lot of affection. Lot of things he was sharing, which my husband doesn't do today. There was teamwork between husband and wife. Caring and sharing and bringing the children up together. So he taught us, and they taught us, they raised us very well. Very systematically. So which I would expect my children to be.

I had taught both, same things to both of them. But he [her son] is different. He has to take bath in the morning. He makes the bed. His room has to be spick-and-span. Veena is quite opposite. Sometimes I wonder, I raised both of them in the same way, why are they different?

Veena had a lot of influence from the kids from here. She was only two and a half. She was raised along with other kids. Maybe she learned those things from them. Maybe she's different.

So, you know, I would not support her going out later in the evening. Some curfew . . .

But we have changed a lot, compared to what we were. For the sake of the children. Because we had to. We didn't want them to feel bad. But there's only so much you can change, right? You can't give up everything that you have learned in your custom, your culture, your heritage. So that was hard.

It was really hard when Veena started going out with boys. She used to go in groups, but still it was hard. We were never like that. I was so innocent, I didn't even know how the babies were born. Even when I got ready to get married. See, back in India, even when the girls get their periods, they won't even train them beforehand. They don't talk all these things publicly. And making love, kissing the husband, it's only inside four walls. We never kiss each other, we never hug together in front of the kids. We are, you know, brought up in such a way, it's something you should share only with your husband. It's not a public affair. Kissing or hugging or necking . . .

These were very hard for us. I never had any problem with my son, because we usually normally give lenience to the boys. We're always concerned about the girls. The reason being, the girl has to be a virgin. Ninety-nine point nine percent back in India, the girls are virgins. And there is only one husband in their life. You share your body only with that person. And all other men are like your brothers or fathers, okay? See, that's how I was raised. So I didn't want Veena to get all these ideas from these people. One boyfriend today, another boyfriend tomorrow.

I used to try to control them, I guess. So they would be upset. It used to be a lot of heartache when they were teenagers. I was walking on the eggshells. But the children really worked hard. They prospered well. And they know what's right and what's wrong.

I used to worry too much about Veena. Till she was nineteen, twenty years old. But now . . .

You don't worry.

No, because I know what she is. Even though I had to keep an eye on her because I was worried about her, I always wanted the best for her.

But even today, I worry about her much, because, see, back in India, they usually have the girls married off when they are nineteen, twenty, twenty-one. Veena is going to be twenty-three in November. I always think it's our responsibility to protect her till she gets married to somebody. Then our responsibility is over. If her husband lets her do whatever she wants to do, we will never butt into that. But till then, when she is under our roof, there are certain things we don't want her to do. Even though she doesn't want to follow.

From the perspective of both parents, then, disagreements with their kids about the limits of behavior were resolved by sometimes saying no, sometimes giving in, and always keeping a watchful eye on their activities. Neither parent, however, discusses trying to convince the kids that parental points of view are the preferable ones. Parvathi simply contrasts what her kids want to do with the practices back in India and argues that the kids might be spoiled if they are given too free a rein. The exact mechanism through which this spoilage would occur (after all, Parvathi recognizes that hers are good kids with sound judgment) is not articulated.

The children also note the temperamental differences between them observed by their parents. Ganesh was the less outgoing and had as his best friends other second-generation Indian Americans. This made his parents feel safe in the knowledge that he was not getting spoiled. However, even for Ganesh, a major disagreement did arise when in his senior year in high school, he wanted to start going to dances sponsored by one of the area Indian associations.

My parents wouldn't let us go to the dances, because they didn't think it was right. My other friends were going, like Prakash and these other guys. I felt really bad about it, so we'd argue a lot. And they finally let me go to one once I was able to drive, at sixteen. And that's when I got more interested in what the Association of Indians in America was trying to do.

When you would argue with your parents about these dances, how did it go? Did you say, "Can I go?" and they would say no, and there's no more discussion, or were there reasons going back and forth?

There were reasons, because by then, I was old enough to be able to rationalize things and to try to explain my point of view. When I argued with them, it was never a yelling-type thing. Whereas my sister did a lot of things that would get somewhat emotional. But I guess I just sort of accepted the fact that they didn't like it and that I wasn't going to be able to go. Their biggest thing was just that, you know, you're not supposed to date. Why? Well, from their perspective, you're just not supposed to. And there really isn't a need to. And you really don't need to be dancing with girls and things like that. And also staying out late.

So somehow or the other, they eventually agreed. It was a really long process. I'd say it took over a year to get them to the point where they'd even allow us to go out with our friends. And they were a lot more reluctant with Veena than with me. Just because they're very protective of her being a girl.

So I got really active in that [AIA]. I just remember being in a lot of panel discussions. Giving speeches and stuff.

The biggest debate on everyone's mind was love versus arranged marriages and dating. Also, parents letting their kids get in the mainstream America and socializing with other people. Doing things versus being cooped up in the house like you're supposed to be. Good little Indian boy or girl. Go to school and study hard, and everything will work out. But they didn't understand that we needed to be more active if we were going to be able to relate more to Americans. To be honest with you, I was pretty geeky in high school. I don't know that I'm still not, but . . . I was. And if you stayed home all the time, you just tend to be sheltered, and you never really break out of your shell.

Overall, I know that Veena argued a lot with my parents. She was more one to keep asking "Why?" Never really backing down. She's very strong-willed. So she wanted to go out for pom-poms. And I think my parents kind of thought it was slutty, or you shouldn't be showing your legs like that, and doing things. So that was a huge argument. I'd have to say that Veena really went through a rough time, because they were trying to hold on to her more than anything. And also her personality made it difficult. She wasn't able to stay calm about things. For the most part, I always agreed with her and tried to side with her. I just didn't agree with how she went about arguing.

I do know that my junior and senior year in high school were a lot of fun for me. Just because I was seeing a change in myself. I was gaining so much more self-confidence, and getting involved in the community was really nice. But it was getting involved more, not on a social level but actually trying to make a statement. I always felt frustrated because I guess I always knew in the back of my mind that each family would deal with the generation gap and the cultural differences in their own way. I think when I first got into it, I was really optimistic about trying to get—especially my parents, at that point—to see my point of view and to see the kids' point of view. But as more and more activities happened, I just realized that there's not much you can do. Because once you get back into the family unit, your own house, it's a whole different ball game. No matter what you've heard that day or the week before, it doesn't really make a difference. It was up to the kids to be able to sit down and talk to their parents or communicate what they're feeling and why they need to do certain things. So even though I stayed active in it, I don't think I ever really believed that a whole lot could change.

Even though Ganesh's disagreements with his parents came rather late in his adolescence and were generally low-key, he was nonetheless interested in bridging the psychological space between himself and his parents. In describing his activities on AIA panels, he explicitly talks about the desire to make his parents' generation understand the kids' point of view. In the above excerpt, too (as well as elsewhere in our conversations), he expressed a sense of loss and disappointment that this psychological bridge building was impossible to achieve in the public realm of the Indian community. The community, in his opinion, could not be made to understand or value parent-child give-and-take. In his opinion, it was up to the kids in each individual family to build communication with their parents. But the fact that Ganesh even thinks of this problem as one that deserves discussion and solution at the community level is evidence that what is at stake is something more than individual roles and rights within the family.

Like her brother's, Veena's reflections on her adolescence also reveal a search for psychological closeness to her parents. On the surface, she tells a story of well-organized acts of rebellion, but underneath, there is a recurrent plea for emotional union.

Joining the pom-pom squad was one of the major acts of rebellion for Veena. In her description, it is important to note that the story does not end when she wins the pom-pom battle and is allowed to join the squad.

So what happened when you went to join the pom-pom squad?

We argued for two months. The answer was no, and I said, "Why?" And they said, "Because if you want to do sports, that's fine, but pom-poms is not respectable." And I said that it is a sport, we compete. "Well, we don't like you wearing those little short skirts and performing for people." And I said, you know, everything I do in school is academic. I was on the math team, I was on the newspaper. I said that

I want something fun, and social, and something where I can use my body. Not my brain. So, finally, my dad, I argued so much that they get to a point with me where it's like, "Well, there's no changing your mind. So, fine, go ahead." And the first night I tried out, I hurt my knee. So I didn't make it that year, and I blamed my dad. 'Cause I said, "You cursed me!" But the next year, I tried out, and I made it. And they got used to the idea, but not once did they ever come see me perform.

Did you ask them to?

Yeah, a couple times I did, but they never . . . and again, I understand it a lot more now. It's not that they were trying to hurt me. They just had never been used to that sort of thing in India.

Like, in college, I remember, all my friends would get care packages, you know, and I never got one. Even when I asked for one, they'd be like, "Oh, that's just a waste." It's not that they were trying to hurt me, it's just they never knew how to do it. So that hurt me at the time, and I was just like, darn, everyone else . . . you know. "My parents don't love me" sort of thing.

Veena's pom-pom story is about more than the usual battle between parents and children about the limits of behavior. Veena did not finish her story when she got to join the squad, when she had won that battle. Instead, for her, the ending is bittersweet. Her parents never came to see her perform. She was not able to establish, through this issue, the general openness and understanding she hoped for. This search for an emotional connection is also revealed in an addendum to Veena's discussion of her need to fit in at high school and college.

But even in college, I had to be in a sorority. Because all my life, I had been validated by what I was. Even by my parents. They never told me I was worthy as a person. I was worthy as a student, or I was worthy as a daughter. As long as I was the valedictorian, or as long as I was the newspaper editor, they were proud of me, but nothing else about me they were proud of. So I felt I had to be involved with everything, because my whole life, everyone was like, "Veena this and Veena that, Veena this and Veena that." And I felt like, in order to get any type of validation, I needed to do that.

And then, junior year, I slipped into almost clinical depression, because I was doing all this, and yet I knew I wasn't content and satisfied. It took me a couple years, just to kind of snap out of it and really figure out what I'm all about. I think that's where I made my change. I always wanted to do psychology, as a major. And my parents never encouraged it, because it was that whole . . . first of all, it's not respectable, you know, in the Indian community. Secondly, you have to go to graduate school, and they wanted me to be on my own and secure after four years. And so I said, "Well, I have to do what's right for me."

I was always looking for external cues for validation, and I needed to start doing it with myself.

Later, Veena was commenting on the way Indian families will support their kids financially until they can support themselves. Indian parents would never charge their children rent, for example, if they moved back home after college.

And in that sense, they are very, very supportive. It's almost a quanti- fying experience rather than a qualitative experience. Their idea of a close-knit family is parents shell out the orders and the kids do it, you know. That's family cohesiveness and family unity.

It's not like that here. And that's one of the things I always missed growing up. I felt a big void, because I could never talk to my mom about sex. I could never talk to her about my boyfriends. I could never feel respected for not agreeing with something that they said, feel respected for having my own opinions.

Currently, Veena feels that in her relationship with her mother, she is now developing the kind of psychological closeness that she missed as a teenager.

We really have a very close relationship now. See, it's really hard be- cause, in India, and I think here, too, in America, women, mothers especially, are taught to be all sacrificing. Don't let your problems interfere with your family's life. A lot of times, I have to drive it out of my mom if she's hurting. Especially with school, she doesn't want to disturb my mind, she doesn't want to tell my brother things a lot of times, because he's out of town, and he'll worry. I think, though, she's realizing that it worries me more when she doesn't tell me. She's been very open with me about a lot of things, and I feel very close to her. I feel like I can talk to her a lot. I think we've just come to more of a friendship, rather than a . . . because, that's another thing, you know, in American and Western families, I see a lot of friendships evolving between parents early. Starting in high school, when their kids are talk- ing about a lot of things. You don't have that in Indian families. Still that hierarchical mother, father, parent. Until you're out. I still see my parents trying to tell my brother, and he's getting married. I really like that. I really like being my mom's friend, and I think it's something that I've missed.

In the Shankar family, then, this search for a "close-knit family life" has been the dominant issue. The parents have missed the sense of familial closeness they felt in India. They have tried to recreate it here by urging their children to spend time at home and going to visit other Indian fami- lies. The children have tried to expand the interactions they have with their parents to include an emotional sharing. For them, it is not enough to lead parallel lives, simply to be with their parents. They are searching for a psychological closeness. While both Ganesh and Veena claim this type of psychological closeness with each other, they see only slight progress in this area in their relationships with their parents.

The interplay between a physical, practical sense of closeness and a more psychological sense of closeness based on sharing one's thoughts and emotions is, in retrospect, a concern for the Nagar family as well. Anar Nagar was trying to develop a "more open" relationship with her mother, in which she could share her true self with her mom, not just her "dutiful daughter" self. Vaidehi, however, still reports the sense of mutual satisfaction she thinks she and her daughter share when Anar occasionally asks to sleep with her mom. Mausami and Vaidehi are "close" because they cook and watch TV together.

This relationship between physical and psychological varieties of closeness, however, is less directly evident in the other families. The Iyengars, Kumars, and Shenoys all have what appears to be the kind of open communication leading to genuine understanding and empathy between parents and children that the Nagar and Shankar children long for. Yet these families also value the basic physical entanglements essential for familial closeness in the Indian context. Lakshmi Iyengar is happy that her elder son might return to live at home. The Kumar children, despite their busy college schedules, continue to live at home and participate faithfully with their parents in church activities on the weekends. Both Shenoy daughters have forgone opportunities outside the Midwest so that they could return to their familial home base in Chicago.

While it is unfair to say that physical and psychological varieties of closeness are aligned exclusively with Indian and American cultures, we can understand some of what occurs in these families surrounding the issue of closeness in those terms. In the families without a strong sense of psychological closeness, the push for its development is clearly coming from the generation raised in America. Anar Nagar and Veena Shankar explicitly point to this sharing as something they see among their non-Indian friends but they feel is atypical in Indian families. We should not conclude, however, that the families that do have this psychological sense of closeness are more Americanized than those that do not. While the Iyengars and the Shenoys clearly have lifestyles that are most similar to their non-Indian counterparts, the Kumars' lifestyle is as wrapped up in Indian cultural practices and an Indian social circle as are the lives of the Nagars or Shankars. Exposure to the American model clearly brings about some of the psychological closeness, but the communicative norms that characterized each family even before their immigration to the United States are equally significant. For the Iyengars and the Kumars, the parents' own experiences while growing up set a precedent for the open give-and-take style of communication they have established with their children. In the case of the Shenoys, it is the individual personalities of the parents that prepared them, when the opportunity arose, to adapt a different set of communicative norms from those that characterized their natal families.

Overall, then, one cannot make clear or straightforward inferences about the effects of immigration on the communicative norms and sense of closeness characteristic of particular families. Closeness, like assimilation in general, is a multilayered, complex phenomenon.

The next part of this book will bring together the variety of experiences and interactive dynamics that have characterized these five families and suggest that while we cannot make generalizations about what the trajectory of assimilation looks like (any more than we can predict the mix of the different senses of closeness in individual families), we can tease apart the strands, the different dynamics, that carry the process of assimilation along.

III

FAMILY AND COMMUNITY

12

Families:
A Model of
Intergenerational Change

It is clear from the preceding portraits that these five families share some common preoccupations; education, dating and marriage, and the quality of intergenerational communication are ubiquitous concerns. It is tempting to point to these commonalities and assert a common process of assimilation.[1] However, it is also clear that the formulation and the *meaning* of these issues in different families are far from uniform. So, rather than focusing on the most common issues and interpreting them in terms of broad differences between "Indian" and "American," we must understand the process through which issues take shape in individual families. Similarity in this *process* of articulating issues and the personal and familial identities that result from this process provide a general model of *how* assimilation takes place—a model that covers not only the Indian case but all situations of intergenerational change.

To begin, the particular issues that come up in any family, and the way parents respond to these issues, are rooted in the personal histories of the parents. The formative experiences of parents act as models for the way they deal with their children. There are two levels at which parental history affects family life. First, there is a straightforward connection between the issues in parents' own lives and the issues they have with their children. Second, there is a much more subtle connection between the way parents *conceptualize* certain issues and the way their children conceptualize these same issues. Parental history affects not only which issues will arise but also how they will be thought about by the second generation.

The particular issues that arise in different families are clearly rooted in parental experience. For example, although none of the parents in these five families had the experience of dating in the American sense, there is a relationship between the way parents met and married and the degree to which "dating" became an issue for their children. For the Shenoys and the Iyengars, two sets of parents whose unions were by choice, dating was not particularly problematic when it came to raising their children. Children dated freely, and there was no discussion of dating as an issue. In contrast, in the Shankar, Kumar, and Nagar families, dating was problematic. All the parents in these families had arranged marriages.

Similarly, Ravi Kumar and Durga Shenoy both discussed communication between themselves and their parents as salient issues in their early lives. Ravi describes his natal family as one in which there was constant serious dialogue about life decisions. The same concerns are carried over to his interactions with his own children. Durga talks about relatively poor communication between herself and her parents. This deficit in her background translates into a very active promotion of "good communication" with her own children. Indeed, her children recognize that she likes to get her "hands in the mud" when it comes to their lives.

It is not only particular issues that find their roots in parental experience. Subtle differences in the centrality of issues and the way particular issues are framed show a great deal of continuity from generation to generation. In the Nagar family, for example, the central issue was interpersonal dynamics—how one should treat others. The elder daughter, Anar, had to struggle with what she knew was her "duty" (to serve her elders) and what she felt was morally right, what her heart told her was right. In one example, she discussed asking her mother, Vaidehi, to bring her a glass of water. On the one hand, she felt that her mother "shouldn't do that. She should say no, get it yourself." It is improper for parents to wait on children; it should be the other way around. On the other hand, Anar rationalized her request for a glass of water, suggesting that it was somehow okay because her mother was just a considerate person. Anar clearly perceived and discussed the tension she felt between her two different interpretations of the event.

The way this dilemma was framed, as a dilemma between duty and heart, is clearly a formulation that finds a parallel in Vaidehi's life experiences. In discussing the difficulties with her in-laws after her husband's death, Vaidehi speaks of a tension between the traditional duties of a period of mourning—not to go out for a year—and her desire to see her daughters' lives get back to normal, to go to McDonald's once a week. Even in terms of her marriage, Vaidehi talks about the "arrangement" as a formal structure (the duty of a daughter) and as an emotional experience (the "romantic time" she had during her engagement). I suggest that the salience of interpersonal dynamics and the relationship between the formal and emotional aspects of interpersonal relationships were articulated in this way by Anar Nagar because these were issues and ideas with which her mother, Vaidehi, herself had struggled.

On the flip side, the issue of education was not particularly salient for the Nagars. Aside from the daughters speaking about being expected to do extremely well in school, the girls never discussed educational issues unprompted. Similarly, Vaidehi never brought up the subject; it was left to me to ask. Vaidehi talked about her daughters' educations in the context of their planned roles as wives and mothers. The girls, too, recognized the connection between education and family life (at least from their mother's perspective).

Again, the way her family talks (or doesn't talk) about education is rooted in Vaidehi's own experience. When Vaidehi and her girlfriends were musing about the qualities they hoped for in a husband, her girlfriends wanted rich husbands, but Vaidehi wanted an educated husband. However, her own higher education was something that she did between the time of her engagement and her marriage. After marriage and starting a family, she discussed going back to work as a search for the opportunity to use her knowledge to earn some money, to be helpful to her family. Education for Vaidehi had been structured around the family.

The girls employed this same formulation when they discussed educational issues. When the younger daughter, Mausami, discussed her mother's expectation that she study hard, she added, "But I don't mind that, because all my friends are really smart. My sister was smart. My dad was smart." It's not that Mausami doesn't mind studying because she personally finds it fulfilling (even though I would say this is undoubtedly true, based on my interactions with her). Rather, she frames her own education in relation to her family: she doesn't mind studying because her sister is smart. Similarly, when Anar talked about her career plans, she was quick to point out that this whole notion of education as a family affair was something she needed to address when discussing career plans with her mother. Even though Anar does not share her mother's outlook, she recognizes this as a central issue: Should one put career first, or must it be integrated into a family life?

To understand the process of intergenerational change, then, the first step is to recognize the importance of parental history. Parental experiences are important both in determining which potential issues will and will not be seen as problematic in raising children and, perhaps more importantly, in determining how particular issues will be framed. Common sense and personal experience should tell us that this particular aspect of the intergenerational change process, what I will call the *intergenerational dynamic*, is common to all families, immigrant and nonimmigrant alike.

The second element of a model of intergenerational change has to do with "Indianness." In all the families studied here, Indianness was in some way important both in the kinds of interactions that took place between parents and children and in the extent to which Indianness was of concern to the second generation. However, this aspect of the change process is also generalizable to other immigrant and nonimmigrant groups. The key is whether or not a particular family views itself as part of the "mainstream." Families that think of themselves as in any way different from something they identify as the mainstream must in some way deal with their "x-ness," or that feature of themselves that separates them from the mainstream. Until people no longer are conscious of their x-ness—of their ethnic origin, race, religion, and so on—the *x-ness dynamic* will shape the process of intergenerational change.

In the case of immigrants, coming into a new social environment and changes in that environment over time can affect the way x-ness plays out in individual minds and in social relationships. Although we cannot definitively disaggregate the components of the x-ness dynamic that originate in some interior concept of identity (a sense of difference from the mainstream) and the elements that originate in the social environment, we can see that these two forces are both operative.

In these families, the effect of the x-ness dynamic, of Indianness, is channeled through four variables, two "internal" or psychological, and two "external" or contextual. The first internal variable is parents' sense of their own Indianness. The particular way in which parents conceive of their own Indianness and the role Indianness plays in their lives cannot but help affect the way Indianness works intergenerationally. I am not claiming that parental Indianness is a stable concept. Clearly, it changes over time. But at a specific moment in time, these five families illustrate that there is some relationship between the parents' thinking about their own Indianness and the interactions that are taking place within the family. The second internal variable is the particular personality of each child. Different children within the same family may respond very differently to their parents' and their own Indianness depending on their own peculiar personality traits.

One external variable is parents' early experiences as new immigrants to the United States. This experience contributes greatly to their overall comfort level and consequently to the way they view the connection between Indian and American. While their ongoing experiences are no doubt continuing to shape the way they deal with their Indianness, their initial experiences seem particularly important. First impressions set the stage for future contacts with "American culture."

Finally, the context in which children find themselves at school, in their life outside the home, affects the opportunities they have to deal with their differences from the mainstream. Particularly important is the recent incorporation of ethnic difference into the school experiences of the younger members of the second generation. Unlike their older siblings, younger members of the second generation are educated in increasingly diverse student bodies and through curricula that celebrate ethnic diversity. In addition, individuals raised in communities where their x-ness is not salient to those around them will have a different set of constraints placed on their developing sense of their own x-ness from individuals who are reminded of their x-ness on a daily basis.

To see how these four variables shape the transfer of Indianness, a couple of families can serve as illustrations. I am not claiming any statistical significance for the way these four variables shape a family's experience of Indianness. Neither am I claiming that these are the only elements that contribute to this particular aspect of the process of intergenerational change. However, by examining the concrete cases of the families profiled here, we can see how these variables come together in unique ways in different families and thus account for the variety of attitudes toward Indianness in the second generation.

In the Iyengar family, the parents have a very historical sense of their own Indianness. They are Indians because they were born and raised in India. In contrast to some other families, they do not seem to view Indianness as an essential characteristic, one that somehow defines and constitutes their inner, true self. Rather, coming from India is simply a fact of their existence. The extent to which this fact has shaped their values and outlook is clearly questionable for them. Again and again, they link their remarks about their values and practices with comments like "whether they're Indian or whatever" or "it's not exactly like we were orthodox Hindus or Indians, anyway."

Coupled with their own ambivalence about their Indianness (which I believe has roots in their preimmigration experiences),[2] the Iyengars' early experiences in the United States shaped their general comfort level with Americans and American culture. Although newly married, both came as graduate students and had host families that served as a significant early positive contact with Americans. Although they maintained an affinity with other Indians (because "you have an affinity with people you grew up with"), they both claim close personal relationships with non-Indians early in their graduate careers.

These two features of the Iyengar parents' experience have influenced the general approach to Indianness that has been part of the Iyengar home. Unlike some of the other families profiled here, the Iyengars never discuss the Indianness of their children in terms of demeanor and expectations regarding social interactions. In the Iyengar household, all talk of Indianness is limited to more concrete aspects of Indian culture—language, music, religious practice. Both parents wonder whether more "Indian culture" would have prevented some of the difficulties they are having raising their boys—disagreements about clothes and hair and educational choices. For them, Indian culture is a card that may or may not be played, not a constituent element of their efforts to raise their children.

The boys' take on Indianness reflects the general atmosphere created by their parents. In talking about his Indianness, Michael reiterates the historical view of Indian heritage characteristic of his parents' talk about their own Indianness: "I'm probably more American than I am Indian. It's just I have a pretty good knowledge of India as a country, its culture and stuff." Elsewhere, he talks about visits to India as similar in nature to visits to Japan, or any other country where he is a tourist. Bob has a similar historical sense: "Since I was born, I've felt like an American. Most of my friends have thought of me as American, and nobody really cares, actually . . . my parents were born in India, but that's it."

An additional important factor in allowing the Iyengar boys to maintain this relationship to their Indian heritage has been the community in which they live. The family has been settled for most of the boys' lives in a liberal, racially integrated area of Chicago. The boys attend a progressive private school that is also well integrated. As Michael points out, he has never been teased about being Indian. One can imagine that the boys' relative inattention to their Indian heritage would have been impossible if they had found themselves in a community where their Indian background was salient to others around them.

Finally, the personalities of the boys have not had much to do with their reactions to their Indianness. Despite the fact that Bob is "extremist in the way he's not willing to compromise" and Michael is much more easygoing and adaptable, the two do not seem to have very different attitudes toward their heritage or the role that Indianness plays in their lives. This lack of an effect of personality is a consequence of the other factors at work. Had their parents' Indianness or their experiences as new immigrants been different, or had the community context of the boys been otherwise, one can imagine that the personality differences between the two boys would be more important in differentiating their attitudes toward Indianness.

The stage for the second generation is set by their parents' views of Indianness and their experiences in the United States. Then, depending on the community context in which children are raised, children may be forced to acknowledge their Indian background and find a place for their personal sense of Indianness. At the same time, the particular personalities of individual children may shape their responses to their Indianness. If the parental view of Indianness and their own life experiences do not make Indianness a salient or important concept in their own lives, and the family lives in a community where external forces do not highlight the ethnic background of the children, then the personalities of children need not come into play.[3] This has been the case with the Iyengars.

The Shankar family illustrates a very different constellation of these four variables and a very different sense of Indianness. In the Shankar family, there was very little explicit discussion of Indianness. The central issue for this family revolved around a sense of closeness. Although each member of the family identified a "sense of family" as something he or she felt was "Indian," there was little self-conscious discussion of Indianness.[4] However, witnessing this lack of explicit discussion of Indianness, we can speculate about what this implies about the parents' sense of their own Indianness and the way Indianness has been dealt with by their children.

In our interviews, Shankar never brings up the fact that he is Indian and does not discuss Indians in the abstract (i.e., he does not discuss the qualities of Indians in general). Parvathi uses the customs of India as a way of explaining particular situations. She often uses the phrase "back in India" but always in the context of explaining some particular event. For example, in her natal family's discussions about whether or not she should attend college, there was a disagreement between her grandmother and her uncle. She pointed out, "Like back in India . . . the elderly people, grandparents would say, 'Oh, you don't need to be educated. One day, you are going to be married anyway. So what are you going to do with a degree'?" And later, "So you see, back in India, whoever is the boss, their word always goes. So my grandmother was handling everything, because she was the boss."

Although she used general references to the way things work "back in India" to explain some of the events of her life, Parvathi, like her husband, never discussed things Indian or Indianness as abstract concepts or as definable "essences." The customs of Indians are always introduced in concrete situations. They are introduced as explanations of behavior for my benefit. She does not bring them up as motivations on her part, but as a way to help me understand why events were as they were.

The only time Parvathi does mention something close to her sense of her own Indianness is in a part of our conversations where she had been telling me how she and her husband have changed a lot over the years in their attitudes and practices in child-rearing:

> But we have changed a lot compared to what we were. Like for the sake of the children. We didn't want them to feel bad. But there's only so much you can change, right? You can't give up everything that you've learned in your custom, your culture, your heritage.

Notice that Parvathi does not use the word *Indian* in this passage. For her, *Indian* is not something exterior to her inner self. It is not something she could choose to shed or something she can discuss as separate and identifiable. It is simply "everything that you've learned." If one were to give that up, what would be left? I think Shankar's nondiscussion of Indianness may be similarly motivated. For the Shankar parents, in contrast to the Iyengars, Indianness is essential to who they are. It is not something they discuss self-consciously.

In addition to their own sense of Indianness, the Shankars' early experiences in America have also set the stage for the way Indianness has worked out in this family. Unlike the Iyengars, who came as students and were exposed to host American families, the Shankars came as immigrants. They lived initially with Parvathi's brother and then in a small apartment of their own. Throughout their stay in the United States, their social interactions have been exclusively with other Indians. Shankar did not describe any particularly memorable aspects of his early experience. The only thing he did mention was some difficulty he had finding his first job because he had no work experience in the country.[5] Parvathi, however, did discuss one early, specific memory of a July Fourth spent at the beach a few days after she arrived in the States. "I saw all these people half naked, lying on these beaches. And their boyfriends sitting next to them, necking. Oh, God, I used to close my eyes. I used to scream." Her first contacts with Americans, at least those she described in our conversations, were shocking. Although elsewhere in our conversations she does talk about Americans having some good qualities, being "big at heart," there seems to be a persistent distance. She described no specific positive contacts with Americans. Both children confirm that their parents' current social life excludes non-Indians.

In the Shankar family, the parents' sense of themselves as Indian and their lack of intimate contact with Americans has contributed to making Indianness problematic for their children. Since Indianness was assumed by the parents, the children were not exposed to a language for discussing or thinking about their Indianness. It was left to Ganesh and Veena to develop this language for themselves.

The context in which the Shankar children were raised made dealing with their Indianness a necessity. Although there were others of Indian origin in their schools, both children suffered teasing because of their difference. In addition to attacks on their home with eggs and toilet paper and the like, which they attributed to the fact that they are Indians, name-calling seems to be the facet of their experience that both children recall most vividly. Common names included "monkey," "coal miner," "sand nigger," and "camel jockey."[6] So, unlike the Iyengar children, the Shankar children were reminded of their difference in the community in which they lived.

Partly because their parents did not provide a language for dealing with Indianness, the Shankar children's sense of their own Indianness is heavily influenced by their own particular personalities and experiences. In Veena's case, her sense of herself as a person of Indian origin is a practical matter connected with her overarching desire to maintain close family relationships. Veena has always had close friendships with both Indians and non-Indians. She seems to feel equal comfort with both. In discussing prospects for her marriage, however, she says that she will probably marry an Indian: "The plain fact is, if I were to marry someone who wasn't Indian, I could probably get along great with the in-laws and have a great relationship, but I know my parents can't. 'Cause they can't even with my American friends." Veena does not spend much time theorizing about what makes her Indian. For her, being Indian is more significant socially than psychologically. Even when she discusses Indians from India, she sees them as being different from herself because they haven't had the same social training; they don't know how to open up and talk.

For Veena, Indianness exists in the realm of the social. I think this is connected to a more general social orientation in Veena's personality. Both her parents comment that Veena was always very active socially from a young age. She herself describes how she has always been concerned about "fitting in" with her peers and how she has been "validated" by *what* she was rather than *who* she was. It seems natural, then, that Veena should view Indianness as a similarly social issue.

Ganesh's sense of his own Indianness is quite different. In the excerpts about the Shankars, Ganesh does not talk explicitly about his own Indianness. He does, however, mention that his closest friends were Indian. Further, he describes his participation in panel discussions of the problems of second-generation Indian Americans. In this context, he reflects that ultimately he sees the issues of parent-child relations being resolved within each family. "But I always felt frustrated, because I guess I always knew in the back of my mind that each family would deal with the generation gap and the cultural differences in their own way."

Even in these limited facts and comments, we can begin to see that Ganesh's view of Indianness is somewhat different from his sister's. While Veena's view is outward-looking and social, for Ganesh the Indianness problem is more inwardly directed. This is confirmed by a longer discussion I had with Ganesh specifically about his sense of his own Indianness. Although he says he is not conscious of his Indianness, it still exists as something that draws him to other Indians and distances him from non-Indians in some situations. Commenting on his group of Indian friends, Ganesh said:

> It's not so much the fact that we only want to be friends with Indians, it's just we tend to have, it seems like, an instant commonality. We've all grown up here. Have to deal with a lot of the same things. It's kind of strange, because everyone at work says they can't tell I'm Indian. Or they just think of me as the same as everyone else. Yet all of my friends are Indian.

On the subject of dating, he added:

> Even though in college I had a lot of opportunities to date Americans in the sense that I knew that they were interested in me, I just never did. I really didn't give them a chance. Meaning that I never was all that interested. And I knew that I would always prefer marrying an Indian because of my parents. And the other big thing that I always sort of had to come to grips with was I think I would have felt very self-conscious if I were dating an American and walking down the street holding hands. I guess I would have felt people were looking at us strange or something.

I asked Ganesh if he would feel similarly uncomfortable holding hands in public if his date were Indian. He replied, "Not at all."

On the surface, Ganesh's description of his not being conscious of Indianness seems similar to the way the Iyengar boys described their Indianness. For Ganesh, however, there remains a deeply inarticulable sense of himself as Indian or, perhaps more accurately, Indian-American.

This more contemplative view of Indianness fits with Ganesh's personality in general. While Veena was the rebellious, active child, Ganesh was softer in his approach. He approached disagreements with his parents through controlled reason. He did not become socially active until late in high school, and then never to the same extent as his sister.

In the Shankar family, then, each child has developed a very different way of articulating and thinking about Indianness. The combined forces of their parents' own essentialized Indianness and isolation from social interaction with Americans and the relatively hostile community environment put pressure on the children to find a place for their Indianness in their lives. If the children had been raised in a community where Indian-origin families predominated, the children might have shared their parents' tendency to treat Indianness as simply constitutive and not a topic for discussion. However, their Indian origin was highlighted in their community of peers. The way each has come to terms with his or her Indianness reflects larger patterns in their individual personalities.

The intergenerational and x-ness dynamics represent behavioral and ideological dimensions of adjustment or change, respectively. Ideological aspects of assimilation are related to abstract ideas, such as Indianness or x-ness. Behavioral components include dating, intermarriage, and choice of a college major. We must consider both to understand the social process guiding intergenerational change. At this level, the processes at work are more broadly applicable to all families with a consciousness of their own x-ness. What is special, if anything, about the experience of immigrants or about the experience of Indians is identified at a second level of analysis.

At this second level is a group of filters that influence the discussion and action taking place around behavioral and ideological issues. The filters that comprise this *cultural dynamic* are linked to particular features of Indian culture and social life. First, prototypes or images of what Indians do and what Indians are like enable immigrants to explain themselves with reference to these ideals. Second, anxiety about social worth and standing, an anxiety deeply rooted in an Indian worldview, informs parent-child interactions and children's sense of their Indianness. Finally, a specifically Indian view of parent-child bonds influences intergenerational and x-ness dynamics. Although I do not provide a complete catalogue of all possible filters, the three I discuss illustrate a second and necessary level of analysis required to understand the process of intergenerational change. It is important to recognize that a common base of *intergenerational* and *x-ness* dynamics constitutes a starting point for any analysis of intergenerational change. The peculiarities of experience that are characteristic of different groups in different circumstances should be dealt with only after one has taken a good look at what is common in intergenerational family process.

Prototypes

Prototypes, the comparisons people make of themselves to the "standard" Indian experience, influence both behavioral and ideological issues within the family. Eleanor Rosch has argued that prototypes or model members of categories are constructed and used to assist people in classifying perceptual information.[7] Rather than (or at least in addition to) using discrete attributes to determine whether a particular instance belongs in a particular category (which she terms a definitional approach to category membership), people also judge category membership based on the distance of a particular example from a conceptual prototype. For example, a Volkswagen Beetle is perceived as a "car" because it resembles the sedan-type "car" that most people picture when asked simply to imagine "a car." It is less likely that an individual will categorize a Beetle as a "car" because he or she makes an instantaneous inventory of specific features proving that the Beetle possesses the discrete characteristics of "a car." Rosch attests, "It is by now a well documented finding that subjects overwhelmingly agree in their judgments of how good an exemplar or clear a case members are of a category, even for categories about whose boundaries they disagree."[8] As a consequence of the existence of these prototypes, "categories can be made to appear simpler, more clear-cut and more different from each other than they actually are."[9]

Although Rosch's research focuses on the use of prototypes to categorize in attribute domains (color and form) and object categories ("chair," "car"), her concept of prototypes is useful in understanding intergenerational change as well. The Indian families studied here, and the Indian community in general, use prototypes of Indian and American in their adjustment process. Following Rosch, we can suggest that this use of prototypes accentuates the differences between Indians and Americans to a degree that exceeds any actual differences. One would imagine that by using prototypes of Indian and American to think about the adjustment process, the perceived difficulty of the adjustment process is accentuated. This appears to be true in the case of press rhetoric (see chapter 5), where the "two worlds" are thought to leave the second generation "stuck" between them.[10] However, for individuals in these five families, the function of prototypes is just the opposite. Most of the people I interviewed used prototypes to *soften* the perceived difficulties of cross-cultural and intergenerational adjustment.

The first common use of prototypes to make the adjustment process seem less dramatic is the use of phrases like "back in India" to explain certain events and behaviors. Parvathi Shankar repeatedly makes generalizations about the way things are "back in India" to make particular events she is discussing clearer or more understandable for me. Ratna Kumar exhibits a similar pattern. When she was describing how her father persuaded her to marry, for example, she said, "You know how in India, they usually say, this was my dad's logic" and then goes on to discuss the benefits of marrying an eldest son.

One might think that this use of models or prototypes of how things work "back in India" was only for my benefit. However, evidence from the second generation indicates that this "back in India" talk is something that goes on between parents and children as well. Lakshmi Iyengar points out that her Indian upbringing is something that her kids bring up to try to explain why they differ with her on certain issues. In discussing her parents, Minakshi Kumar reasons, "It's hard for them to let go of their authority on us because, you know, in India, the parents can even tell them what to do when they're forty."

All this "back in India" talk gives particular behavioral events a historical basis. Even though the Indian way of doing things might be very different from the American way, by explaining particular behaviors with reference to general patterns of behavior "back in India," behavior seems more grounded, understandable, or perhaps rational than it would had the "back in India" explanation been absent. References to the way things are done "back in India" also depersonalize the difference between Indian and American. Rather than differences being linked to intrinsic differences between Indians and Americans, differences are a consequence of place—where someone was raised, where someone was living. Finally, in addition to rationalizing and depersonalizing differences between Indian and American, the phrase "back in India" conjures up images of a distant time and place, pushing potential differences between Indian and American away from the immediate concerns of the here and now, at least at a metaphorical level.

A second common prototype centers on generalizations about the character of Indians or their beliefs and values. The Indians may be either here in America or back in India. The key, however, is that their characters, beliefs, or values form the core of the prototype, not, as in the case of the "back in India" prototype, the concrete events that take place in a certain locality. The "back in India" prototype is about what people in India do; the character prototype is about who they are and what they believe.

It might seem that references to essential differences between Indians and Americans would work in the opposite direction of the "back in India" prototype, making difference between Indian and American more personalized and immediate, thus accentuating the drama of adjustment. What is interesting about the use of the character prototypes, however, is that they usually are not mobilized as explanations for why the individuals in these families are the way they are. Rather, they are used so that individuals can communicate what they themselves are *not* like: "I am not like other Indians."[11] Of the thirty instances I identified of Indian prototypes, only one made a positive connection between the way Indians are and the way the speaker is. (This one positive instance occurred when Psalm Shenoy used the romantic sensibility of Indians in general to make sense of her own romantic feelings.)

The distancing of oneself from other Indians covered a very wide range of different Indian characteristics and particular contexts. Sometimes, what Indians were like was not specified. Shivan Iyengar, for example, commented, "It's not like we're orthodox Hindus or Indians anyway." Anu Kumar phrased the sentiment, "I can't be a true Indian or a total American." Specific traits that were identified ranged from Indians' reliance on social roles as determinants of behavior (e.g., what daughters should do), to their views of male-female relations, to their assertions of their own cultural superiority, to their "narrow" outlook on life.

The contexts in which these prototypes were used were similarly varied. The second generation used the character prototype to differentiate themselves from other second-generation Indians: "I didn't want to be like other Indian kids where they lie" (Anu Kumar). "I don't think we were pressured the way a lot of other Indian kids are pressured to go into medicine and to maintain a straight A average and study" (Padma Shenoy). Both generations used prototypes of Indians to differentiate themselves from their parents. Discussing the ambition she sees in her parents but not in herself, Minakshi Kumar reasons:

> Most Indians will adjust very easily. I think the entire Indian culture in a sense is very materialistic in the sense of wanting good jobs . . . they want to go up there so their ambition is fueled. And they're willing to let go of their culture . . . I see that in my parents.

In describing her family's reaction to her wish to marry her husband, Durga Shenoy explains:

> But they did put up a big fuss about the one fact that my husband . . . had lost his eye. How could he take a wife? And things like that. The other thing was that, like typical Indian families, they also thought it would be good to marry someone who had a profession. And I just didn't go along with that.

Parvathi Shankar uses a similar logic to explain how she was able to secure a college education:

> Elderly people would say, "Oh, you don't need to get educated. One day, you are going to get married anyway. So what are you going to do with a degree? You will never be able to avoid cooking or cleaning, or bearing children, or raising them." But my fantasy was to get a degree.

Thus, both the "back in India" and the Indian character prototypes have the effect of lessening the perceived drama of the adjustment process implied by a confrontation between Indian and American. "Back in India" talk rationalizes certain past behaviors by setting them in a context that is removed in time and space from the present. The character prototype facilitates a sense of integration into American society since people commonly distance themselves from what other Indians think and do.

In family dialogues, the content of these prototypes is quite varied, situating family life amidst a whole range of aspects of an Indian character or the memories of conditions "back in India." In the family context, prototypes are held up as exemplars from which family members see themselves drifting away. Therefore, there is no need to have a consensus of exactly what Indians are like or exactly what took place "back in India." When you

are concerned about situating yourself in the gray areas of category boundaries, the boundaries between Indian and American (or between India and
America), it is not necessary to have a well-defined categorical center, a very
precise and complete list of exactly what constitutes Indian and American,
to be able to draw contrasts. It is enough to have a specific instance of something Indian or American in mind. One can take what one's grandmother
once said to generalize a view characteristic of Indians as a group and tell
how one's own view differs from that.

This stands in contrast to the nature of prototypes in the public sphere,
where the key to creating a public conversation about adjustment is the
creation and solidification of precisely that categorical center that individual
families have the luxury of avoiding. Yet in the process of simplification and
standardization, that categorical center becomes increasingly unfamiliar to
individual families. This encourages the perception evident among the families profiled here that each family is more well adjusted, better able to cope,
and feeling more comfortable with the path it has chosen than its members imagine other families to be.

It is the interplay between public rhetoric and family idioms that allows people to come to grips with the variety of individual experiences that
collectively make up "the Indian immigrant experience." The *content* of
these prototypes surely reflects the particular character of Indian experience, but the *use* of prototypes and contrasts is one of the essential features
of the adjustment process in general—whether it occurs among Indian
Americans or in any other community.

Status Anxiety

A second filter that overlies the primary behavioral and ideological aspects
of intergenerational change is a persistent status anxiety, particularly on the
part of the second generation. In each of these five families, children express
fears and concerns about their social and occupational status.[12] The genesis of this status anxiety is unclear. However, it clearly influences the way
behavioral and ideological issues are constructed.

In the most straightforward examples, those in the second generation
talk about whether certain activities are respectable or adequately prestigious. As she tells it, Veena Shankar's desire to join the pom-pom squad
was complicated by her father's view that "wearing those little short skirts
and performing for people" was not respectable. Similarly, her desire to
major in psychology was complicated by a lack of support from her parents because psychology was "not respectable . . . in the Indian community." Anar Nagar worries that although she would like to go into psychology or sociology, "There's this other side of me that's like, 'Well, how
would that be seen? How prestigious is that?'" Sanjay Shenoy was concerned about attending *the* best boarding school.

A second manifestation of status anxiety is evident in a tendency for
members of the second generation to compare themselves unfavorably with

their parents. Mausami Nagar wonders whether she will be able to be the knowledgeable parent that her mother has been. Although her mother explains the meanings of rituals and stories to her, Mausami reflects, "I'm still concerned about when I'm a parent. What am I going to do? I won't know anything, you know. She knows stories, like little stories. I'll just know the basics . . . that's my only worry, that what kind of a parent am I going to be?" Minakshi Kumar expresses a similar concern about degradation in her generation. "They're very ambitious . . . at least that's with the first generation. And it's so sad because the second generation is not having the same feeling . . . they're so diffused. They have no ambition to take on their parents' dreams."

The final dimension of status anxiety is a fear of personal failure or a general sense of inferiority. Several in the second generation discussed their anxiety concerning low grades. Michael Iyengar describes trying to tell his parents that he had received a B: "When I was in high school, sometimes if I got a B, I'd feel really, really bad . . . I remember one time, I got my first B in high school, and I was coming home and trying to explain to my dad why I got a B. I was feeling so bad, like I disappointed him so much." Psalm Shenoy shared a similar experience:

> I got a D in French . . . It was really bad. I felt so bad. I felt like no college would ever want me. . . . It was like I had this stigma of my own that I was ashamed to even share with my parents. Like I couldn't talk to them about my D. It was like, 'My gosh, I'm a failure.'

Veena Shankar related this particular anxiety to the fact of her Indianness: "When I went out with my American friends, I was always feeling a little inferior because I was Indian." Padma Shenoy talks about her participation in the debate club as rooted in her "own insecurities about not being smart": "Debate was a way for me to show all these really intelligent honors students that I was smart, too."

Together, concerns with "respectability," intergenerational degradation of culture and ambition, and a sense of personal inferiority illustrate the phenomenon of status anxiety.[13] Where does this status anxiety come from? It may be that it is just a function of the age of the second generation and the times in which we live. Particularly when we consider the talk of members of the second generation concerning their general inability to live up to the cultural and career models of their parents, it seems that this may just be part of a general generational feeling of hopelessness. Much is made of the prospect in American society that the current generations of children and young adults will not be able to achieve the standard of living of their parents. The views of intergenerational economic decline expressed by these second-generation Indian Americans may just be reflecting this larger societal trend.

However, given the multifaced nature of status anxiety, this cannot be the whole answer. The talk about inferiority and personal failure (rather than failure relative to parents) suggests that part of status anxiety may come from experience as the second generation. The children of immigrants face a peculiar problem regarding the relation between the culture of their parents and the cultural environment in which they themselves have been raised. Members of the second generation have a tendency to reject the background of their parents yet may have difficulty being fully assimilated into the host culture.[14] Perhaps the fear of personal failure and inferiority reflects anxiety about the second generation's potential for acceptance by the mainstream. As noted in chapter 2, individual merit and success are the ideological building blocks of the American social order. Thus, a fear of *personal* failure may be a fear about their potential to fit in, as well as a fear of shaming themselves before their parents.

Finally, there is the talk about respectability and prestige. In most cases (with the exception of Sanjay Shenoy's talk about boarding schools), the "Indian community" is the judge of respectability and prestige. Status anxiety, then, may also grow out of a value system rooted in the second generation's Indian heritage, rather than the experiences its members share with all members of their generation or the experiences they share with other second-generation immigrants.

Regardless of the origin of this status anxiety, however, it affects the way behavioral and ideological issues are played out at the primary level of the adjustment process. On the behavioral side, for example, educational issues are clearly closely connected to this general status anxiety. On the one hand, anxieties about respectability and prestige and anxieties about the personal shame of bad grades connect educational issues to an Indian cultural context. The second generation is worried about choosing occupations that are not prestigious in the eyes of the Indian community; they are worried about not getting the grades their parents expect. On the other hand, however, anxieties over educational failures also have meaning in the American arena, where grades are a marker of individual achievement and being a doctor is still considered a high-prestige occupation. Status anxiety, like the use of prototypes, is a mechanism that integrates, or at least bridges, both Indian and American ideas and expectations.

To a lesser degree, status anxiety has a role in the way Indianness plays out in the second generation. At least for some in the second generation, defining their Indianness is complicated by a fear that Indian is inferior. (See, for example, the comment by Veena Shankar above or the equivocations about the relative status of Indian and American that appear in second-generation writings for the immigrant press.) Unlike the use of prototypes or the role that status anxiety plays in educational issues, status anxiety in relation to Indianness does not seem to soften the contrast between Indian and American. It does not, like prototypes, allow individuals to place themselves at the comfortable fuzzy margins between Indian and American. It does not, like status anxiety about educational achievements, have independent meaning in both Indian and American social contexts. Rather, status anxiety about one's own Indianness sets up a dilemma in which one is always testing one's feelings of Indianness to determine when it will be a source of pride and when it will be a source of shame. Sometimes it is okay to be Indian, and sometimes one wishes one's Indianness would disappear.

For most of the second-generation individuals profiled here, their sense of Indianness is unsettled. With the exception of the Iyengar boys and Mausami Nagar, all talked about how their Indianness had changed over time. (Mausami Nagar and Bob Iyengar, it should be remembered, are the youngest of the second-generation participants, ages twelve and fifteen, respectively.) While the x-ness of any maturing generation may be unsettled and perhaps clouded with a deep anxiety about the potential inferiority that may be implied by that x-ness, in the Indian context, this uncertainty about relative status has a resonance with the general problem of uncertainty that is part and parcel of an Indian worldview. The general difficulty in determining relative status, and the notion that it is on some level indeterminable because one can never know another's status for sure, accentuates the second-generation tendency to see Indianness as forever problematic. With other x-nesses, although there might be fears about x-ness being inferior, we can imagine that people can potentially exorcise these fears, becoming convinced that their x-ness is not a liability and may perhaps be an unmitigated source of pride. But given the particular role that uncertain status has in an Indian worldview, I would argue that for the Indian community, at least for generations of the community that retain some knowledge of what it means to look at the world through Indian eyes, working out the status of Indianness will be an ongoing task.

Parent-Child Bond

The third filter is the parent-child bond. The first aspect of this bond is a sense of obligation as a binding force. Minakshi Kumar talks about obligations to parents as a driving force in life decisions. Despite her attraction to theater and writing, she is pursuing a career in medicine according to her parents' advice. Speaking of her interest in drama, she says, "I feel that's where my talent lies. And I want to pursue that talent because I know I can excel in that. That's what I would take pride in, so . . . I mean, I want to make my parents happy, too. 'Cause they've done a lot for me, sacrificed a lot for me." Obligation works in the opposite direction as well. Parvathi Shankar says that she will worry about her daughter being "spoiled" until she gets married, because it is her "responsibility to protect her until she gets married to somebody. Then our responsibility is over."

A second element of the parent-child bond has to do with the maintenance of physical proximity. Padma Shenoy talks about her decision to go to law school in Chicago rather than Los Angeles as a capitulation to her parents' fear that if she went to L.A., she might never return. Her sister, Psalm, describes her choice of graduate schools similarly: "Deep down, I always sort of knew I was going to Chicago. I don't know exactly why. I really felt the need to return to my parents." Veena Shankar also does not want to move away from her family. Lakshmi Iyengar talks about her delight that her son might transfer to a college in Chicago. Vaidehi Nagar talks about the good feeling her college-age daughter still gets from crawling into bed with her.[15]

Finally, the parent-child bond is expressed in terms of the practical entanglements of everyday life. Shankar encourages his children to "stick close to home. Spend time with parents." Mausami Nagar describes her Friday nights spent with her mother watching TV or going shopping as the time when she most feels that they have a "mother-daughter thing going." Psalm Shenoy describes her mother as someone who gets her "hands in the mud" when it comes to helping the children manage their lives. It is spending time and doing practical, concrete things that bind parents and children, more so than sharing feelings and thoughts.

As is the case with prototypes and status anxiety, parent-child bonds contribute to the way the basic behavioral and ideological issues are constructed. The notion of obligation perhaps encourages members of the second generation to follow the wishes of their parents regarding issues such as educational choices or choices of marriage partners more often than would be the case if this sense of obligation were not present. It was very surprising to me that none of the children in these families ever defied his or her parents' desires. No one ever decided to move away and become financially independent in order to pursue his or her own, as opposed to his or her parents', desires. No one took out educational loans to secure the education of his or her choice.

The transfer of Indianness, too, has been shaped by these overarching parent-child bonds. In most families, what the children have absorbed about Indianness has originated in the practical entanglements of parents and children. The Nagar girls have learned about Indian demeanor from watching their mother interact with relatives. The Iyengar boys have learned about a sense of family from being hosts to visiting relatives (and non-relatives). The Shankar children, in seeing the way their parents have excluded non-Indians from their social lives, have learned that in their own lives a good family life will require that they marry only ethnic Indians. What members of the second generation have learned about Indianness they have learned through these practical interactions rather than through intellectual appeals and indoctrination. Although what and how much second-generation individuals have learned about material and philosophical aspects of Indian culture varies, what is consistent across the board is that they have developed much of their sense of Indianness in response to the practical, everyday interactions they have with their parents.

Conclusions

In order to understand the process of intergenerational change in these five Indian immigrant families, and in immigrant families in general, I suggest a two-tiered model of analysis. First, all families are subject to an *intergenerational dynamic*. Whether changes occur across time or across both time and space, the events that become issues for any family are, I believe, a consequence of parental history and the memories and expectations formed in the past coming up against the demands of the current environment in which their children live. Moreover, as long as a family is conscious of its difference from something its members identify as the mainstream, be it on account of national origin, religion, race, and so on, they must grapple with the *x-ness dynamic*, which introduces ideological or identity issues, above and beyond the particular behavioral issues that arise out of the intergenerational dynamic. The way the x-ness issue is resolved by the younger generation is a function of the intersection of parental history, community context, and personality.

At one level, this model focuses on processes that are common to all families, and processes that are common to families conscious of their x-ness. At a second level, a series of filters shapes the way these primary processes play out. First, families use prototypes of what Indians do "back in India" and what Indians in general are like to de-dramatize the process of adjustment. Second, a widespread status anxiety on the part of the second generation seems to shape the way primary behavioral and identity issues are resolved (or not resolved). Similarly, features of the parent-child bonds in these families significantly shape the process of intergenerational change. These filters are applicable to the process of intergenerational change characteristic of these five families, and perhaps of the Indian immigrant community in general. No doubt, other filters may be operative in this context (or, for that matter, some of these filters may apply in other contexts). It is important to try to separate out the universal aspects of the assimilation process from those that are particular to the Indian case—prototypes of Indians, status anxiety, and a particular kind of parent-child bond.

This model of intergenerational change has three advantages over previous models for the analysis of assimilation. First, as opposed to theories that focus on signposts along the adjustment road,[16] this model takes an interactional view of the process of immigrant adjustment. Rather than measuring the state or degree of assimilation—the assimilation process seen from a distance—an interactional approach opens up the door for an analysis of the variety of paths toward adjustment that characterize the experiences of different groups, assimilation seen close up. Although an aggregate, comparative analysis of immigrant groups has its own merits, an interactional approach allows one to appreciate the unique intersection of history, personality, culture, and context that accounts for the particular experiences of different immigrants and immigrant groups. This approach allows comparability of the process of assimilation but at the same time explains the origin of vast individual variation.

Second, other studies of Indian immigrants in the United States give a large role to "cultural" concerns. They tend to examine the experience of immigrants and their children in terms of a bifurcation of cultures. Problems grow out of being Indian in America or trying to live in two worlds.[17] In this study, I try to tease out the place of cultural forces (i.e., unique aspects of Indian culture) in relation to other variables such as personal history, community context, and personality. The danger of letting Indian culture loom too large in the analysis of immigrant experience is that it separates the experience of Indian immigrants from that of other immigrants. Although it is important to recognize the influence of the unique cultures of different immigrant groups, it is equally important to recognize that certain common forces are at work.

Finally, this model accounts for the multiple layers of experience in the situations of the five families studied. One part of their current experience grows out of their being simply families with teenage and young adult children. Another comes from their status as minorities in the United States. A third results from the fact that they are immigrants. Still another is shaped by their varying connections to Indian culture. The virtue of an interactional approach is that it avoids the pitfalls of much past research, which glossed over differences among immigrant groups in favor of theories about immigrant experience in general, or analyzed immigrants groups as isolated bundles that seem to have little in common with others.

13

Families and Organizations: A Division of Labor in Support of Community

This study consists of two distinct analyses of the Indian-American community. Part I examines the organizational life and public debates of the community, while part II examines issues of adjustment as played out within families. The two analyses also rely upon different methodologies. The organization analysis employs traditional methods of participant observation and interviewing and content analysis of newspaper articles. The family analysis uses somewhat unorthodox techniques in a series of family portraits. However, the central concerns of both parts are the changes that have taken place between the immigrant generation and their young adult children. The purpose of this final chapter is to integrate the two analyses in order to present an accurate view of the process of assimilation taking place among Indian Americans. A key element of this process is the division of labor between organizational and family life.

Organizational life is the arena in which most of the symbolic work of immigrant adjustment occurs. At the organizational level, ideas about being Indian and American, the prototypes for identity and behavior in the Indian-American community, are publicly examined. While organizational life adheres closely to the prototypes, family life does not. Although family members clearly understand and use prototypes of "Indian" and "American," their use of these prototypes is fluid and creative; they are not overly concerned with living out the symbolic prototypes that form the community's shared understanding of what it means to be an Indian immigrant in America.

Intergenerational Change in Organizational Life

At the organizational level, an understanding of intergenerational change begins with an appreciation of the way in which worldview shapes the organizational life of first-generation immigrants. In first-generation organizations, the community's preoccupation with disunity and its attribution of disunity to "ego problems" is in part a consequence of a worldview that considers groups, rather than individuals, to be the building blocks of social life. As long as groups are the social actors, all is well. When individual egos make claims to power, social life goes awry.

Yet a collectivist view of the social world alone does not account for the dynamics of group life in the first generation. A more subtle understanding of "ego problems" leads us to see the central role that ambiguity plays in structuring organizational life. A core feature of an Indian worldview is the potential fluidity of social relations and social status. The "person" is always being created and recreated through exchanges and in different social contexts. This potential for change introduces an uncertainty into social life. One is never quite sure of the status of the person with whom one is dealing. Along with this uncertainty comes ambiguity. Since one cannot know for sure whether another's motivation is selfless or selfish, and one cannot know the sum total of all the transactions that have created the person who stands before one today, there is a never-ending need to sort out the worthy from the unworthy, those who are working for the good of the community from those who are interested in lining their pockets. Ironically, in this effort to make distinctions in organizational life, the public recognition of individual achievement is central. Public recognition of someone's accomplishments becomes the proof of his or her moral fitness, and moral fitness is an important basis for legitimacy within the community.

In addition to elements of an Indian worldview and other ideas about morality, the particular history of this generation of immigrants has also shaped what its members have done with their organizational lives. This generation's heartfelt concern with "unity" has its roots in its members' experiences as the children of partition and their familiarity with the Gandhian idealism of the independence movement. Similarly, the setup of their organizations along religious, ethnic, and caste lines draws on their historical experiences of the "natural" social grouping in Indian society.

The organizations of the second generation face many of the same issues as first-generation organizations. There are ego problems that disrupt organizational elections and the fair allocation of work. Moreover, ambiguity plays a central role in the discussions of second-generation religious organizations. How is it that Indians who profess Hindu values, including the lack of attachments to the fruits of one's labors, can be so concerned with the cars they drive and the neighborhoods they live in?

Although the issues facing the organizations of the two generations have some surface similarities, the ways the two generations work toward resolution of these issues are very different. The first generation seeks social solutions; issues should be settled in the public, shared arena; there should be interpersonal and intergroup consensus. The second generation, in contrast, takes a much more individualistic approach. Its members tend to see ego problems and organizational infighting as "personal" matters and to seek resolutions of conflicts and contradictions by declaring that each person should make decisions for himself or herself. The first generation understands its organizational life as directed toward the benefit of the community. The second generation is much more concerned that its organizations meet the needs of individual members.

At a general level, the differences between the organizational behavior of the two generations may be understood in terms of differing worldviews. It is my belief that the first generation is engaged in an essentially Indian organizational game. The sentiments that are mobilized (unity, division, selfishness, selflessness) all have substantive meaning in the context of that generation's shared experiences of Indian history and Indian values. Problems are solved by establishing and maintaining a proper order in social relationships.

Members of the second generation distance themselves from this Indian view of organizational life. Their feelings about the relation between individuals and voluntary organizations is much more along American lines. While community is important, it is important as a collection of individuals each of whom is responsible for his or her own well-being and peace of mind. Organizations enhance the lives of individuals but do not have a great symbolic life of their own. In the first generation, there is a lot of handwringing about the disunity of the organizational network and the consequences of that for the community. The second generation takes a much more instrumental view of its organizations. Organizational problems are seen more as practical matters than as matters with symbolic import.

The distance between first- and second-generation organizations is dramatized by the relationship between the Hindu Temple youth organization In the Wings and its first-generation parent. In the relation between these two linked organizations, the youth branch is clearly trying to assert an independent identity. Instead of moving gracefully into the extant structure of temple participation and leadership, the young people are claiming that their Hinduism is not the Hinduism of their parents. The second generation, having grown up in an American rather than Indian context, must define its own connection to an Indian heritage, a connection that is uniquely Indian-American.

At the organizational level, then, at least from the perspective of the second generation, there is serious work going on to define its members as distinctly different from their parents. In discussing the first generation, they often reminded me that all the language and caste divisions of their parents' organizational network "are not manifested in us." Moreover, the way they resolve the problems endemic to organizational life by claiming that everything boils down to the actions and decisions individuals make has a distinctly American tone.

Intergenerational Issues in Families

In analyzing the intergenerational change that takes place in the context of family life, greater sensitivity must be paid to interactional dynamics than has been characteristic of previous studies of Indian immigrants. In order to understand the dynamics of intergenerational change in the family setting, we should not put too much stock in the rhetoric of "two worlds." To talk about the second generation as stuck between two cultures and, if they are lucky, as being able to select the best of both is to greatly oversimplify what actually takes place between children and parents.

What is needed is a multilevel analysis that first tries to isolate what is common to all families and what is common to families that see themselves as different from the mainstream. Only then can we appreciate the specific aspects of Indian culture and Indian ethnicity that shape the interactions between parents and children.

In contrast to the media rhetoric (see chapter 5) that revolves around a standardized plot for the "adjustment" process (whether individual authors argue for or against this standardized version), each of the five families studied creates its own particular idiom for understanding what is happening within it. These family idioms rely heavily on parental history but also leave room for the contributions of individual personalities and the residential and social situations of the family. The practical problems of everyday life that provide the content for families' stories about life in America do not rest upon idealized notions about what it means to be Indian or American.

Moreover, the very filters that overlie these basic family dynamics obscure the definitions of "Indian" and "American." For example, prototypes about India and Indians are most frequently used as a point of contrast between what is happening now or the ways people see themselves now and the way things were before or the way "other people" behave, thereby blunting an otherwise sharp distinction between Indian and American. Status anxiety obscures the contrast between Indian and American through its operation in both the Indian and American contexts. Anxiety about worth does not just have meaning vis-à-vis other Indians. Rather, the status anxiety expressed by the second generation seems to concern its members' worth and abilities to succeed in *both* Indian and American contexts. Finally, the parent-child bond obscures a boundary between Indian and American by the way it shapes children's behavior and ideas through example rather than indoctrination. These bonds expose children to Indianness through everyday interactions. Only rarely are parent-child bonds used to force explicit contrasts between Indian and American (e.g., by parents claiming, "You are ours. You are one of us. And we are different from them").

Within families, the process of intergenerational change is highly idiosyncratic. It is rooted in practice rather than ideology. Whatever a family has to say about being Indian grows out of the way its members lead their lives. Families do not seem very concerned with living up to ideas about Indianness. In the absence of this ideational aspect of adjustment, family life exists on the boundaries between Indian and American and consequently is free to exhibit wide variations and highly idiosyncratic patterns of interaction and adjustment.

Organizations and Families: A Division of Labor

Taken together, these analyses of organizations and families illustrate a division of labor in the realm of assimilation. At the organizational level, there is serious symbolic and definitional work going on. The first generation's organizational network, through the problems its members perceive and the resolutions they propose, creates a social life grounded in a worldview that has been part of their Indian upbringing. Although the second-generation organizational network in and of itself does not seem to have a rich symbolic life, it is nonetheless used to declare and define the second generation's difference from the first. It is important to second-generation organizations that their members find resolutions to their problems and answers to their questions that are uniquely their own. They do not want to be restricted to the ideas and values that shape their parents' organizational life.

While organizations are concerned about defining themselves as "a community" (as for the first generation) or as "a collection of similarly situated individuals" (as for the second generation), families are concerned about everyday life. "Who we are as a family" is something that is worked out in the mundane activities, in the agreements and disagreements, in the sacrifices and the celebrations that take place over time. In families, "who we are" remains largely unarticulated. It is precisely the fact that a family idiom is constructed through behavior rather than through self-conscious discussion that allows families to exist on the boundaries between Indian and American. Families can be spontaneous and creative in ways that organizations cannot.

Comparing organizations and families as distinct units that make up the Indian immigrant community, we see that organizations have taken on the task of creating, maintaining, and perfecting the prototypes that exemplify what it means to be an Indian immigrant or the child of one. Leaders and members of organizations stage the rituals and, along with the media, speak the words that shore up the community prototypes. Families, on the other hand, drift away from the prototypes and seem to exist in the fuzzy areas of categorical boundaries. In these boundary areas, little definitional work takes place (at least not in the sense that collective or uniform prototypes emerge).

There are several possible reasons for this decoupling between organizations and families in the Indian immigrant community. First, it may be that the methods I have used have influenced this picture of what organizations and families are up to. In the organizational study, I relied heavily on organizational leaders for information. It may be that in their roles as spokespersons, they have developed standardized stories that make organizational life seem more coherent and symbolically loaded than it actually is. In contrast, in the life-history interviews with individual family members, I was getting a much more well-rounded picture of events, seen from several different perspectives. Undoubtedly, this difference in methods has affected the kinds of information I have gathered. However, I would argue that these methodological differences capitalize upon rather than create the differences that exist between organizations and families. It is simply a fact that organizations nurture and support spokespersons in ways that families do not. Moreover, when I did have the opportunity to examine organizational life as an observer, there was still serious attention to definitional and symbolic issues. I found no evidence for this kind of definitional work in family interactions.

A second possible explanation for the differences between organizations and families is rooted in the very different natures of families and voluntary associations as organizational forms. Although the core memberships of many of the voluntary associations I studied were, in fact, no bigger than medium-sized families, the interactions that are possible in associational versus family contexts are quite different. Unlike members of families, members of voluntary associations do not interact on a daily basis. When they do interact, the larger audience to whom they are responsible is an ever-present concern. The knowledge that their own positions as core members are not permanent (or at least that the overall composition of the core membership may change) weighs on the interactions. Families exist as bounded, stable organizations with little concern for an external audience. Voluntary organizations have fluid boundaries, circulating personnel, and a permanent audience.[1]

These differences push voluntary organizations to do definitional work and allow families the luxury of not doing it. In order to continue to exist, to deal with potentially changing personnel, and to legitimize their existence to an audience, associations must make abstract statements of purpose and codify their rules for action. Families, on the other hand, have no need for manifestos; they can engage in continual face-to-face negotiations as a means to create and recreate their collective identity. The differing features of voluntary associations and families as organizations provide the opportunity for the division of labor I outline above.

A third possible reason for the differences between organizations and families is the particular characters of the individuals I happened to observe. I should note that none of the five families profiled here is heavily involved in the organizational network of the first generation. Had I studied instead the families of the immigrants most active in the organizational network, I might have observed more continuity between what went on at the organizational level and the kinds of concerns and discussions that took place in their families. Based on some of the interactions I have had with the families of organizational leaders, I think that this would probably be the case. However, *most* families in the Indian immigrant community are *not* heavily involved in the organizational life. There exists quite a bit of cynicism toward and criticism of the community organizations from non- and marginal participants. Particular families may engage in more or less definitional work, yet overall the assertion that families and organizations perform quite different functions in the life of the community is valid.

Finally, the Indian worldview may facilitate the division of labor between organizational and familial life. Again, the fluidity inherent in the Indian worldview plays a central role. The context-dependent nature of social interactions entailed by an Indian worldview makes it easy to understand why families in the Indian community should not, by and large, feel pressured to conform to the standardized prototypes of Indians in America and the rhetoric of adjustment that is offered up by the first- and second-generation organizational networks and the ethnic press. As Ganesh Shankar observed, no matter how many public forums were held:

> Each family would deal with the generation gap in their own way. . . . Once you get back into the family unit, your own house, it's a whole different ball game. No matter what you've heard that day or the week before, it doesn't really make a difference.

One can imagine that if the cultural background of the Indian immigrant community had been less accepting of contextual variations, then the ability of families to distance themselves from the prototypical patterns of immigrant adjustment and community identity, but still remain part of the community (both in their own and others' eyes), would have been diminished.

The notion that uncertainty and ambiguity are an inescapable part of social life has allowed a genuine division of labor between organizations and families. It is not that families have simply withdrawn from the definitional game, leaving the problems of community life to be ironed out by organizational officials and community leaders. Rather, organizations do the definitional work that surrounds the prototypes, and families do a different kind of work at the margins. Families push the boundaries of what it means to be Indian and to be Indian in America. But they do not push the boundaries by drawing ever more complicated and sensitive lines between Indian and American; they are not specifying the boundaries in a definitive sense. Rather, they are engaged in making the boundaries ever more uncertain and ambiguous. In a sense, they act as a counterpoint to all strivings for unity and uniformity that exist at the organizational center. While the organizational network is busy trying to abolish ambiguity, trying to sort out the worthy from the unworthy, staging contests for the role of *the* voice of the community, families are constantly reinfusing the community with new uncertainties and ambiguities. As their children mature and their relatives immigrate and their parents age, the first generation and its members' families inject ever greater complexity into the mix of community life.

Although each family develops its own unique identity, its own unique idiom, these tendencies toward particularity do not isolate families from one another and from the community at large. Rather, they provide the base upon which organizational life and the definitional prototypes for what it means to be Indian in America are built. Families provide the raw materials from which organizational life distills the "standard experience" of Indians in America.

The Consequences of the Division of Labor

This division of labor between families and organizations is what keeps, and will continue to keep, the Indian community viable. Families, in their diversity, generate a host of potential issues and problems for the community. The issues that arise in individual families are linked to the community by virtue of the fact that families, by and large, continue to identify themselves as in some way affected by their Indianness. An organizational network has arisen which addresses itself to the task of sorting out all the chaotic diversity that exists at the level of individual families. By virtue of their existence as voluntary associations (with their associated organizational characteristics), these associations are primed to sort things out, through the creation of standardized interpretations, or prototypes, that codify the life of the community.

When seen from a distance, this division of labor seems quite universal and rather unremarkable. Most immigrant communities (or, for that matter, any identifiable social subgroup) are, arguably, engaged in the same type of division of labor. Families are inherently messy. They are by nature very particularized social units that can rely on ongoing face-to-face interactions to work through their problems. In any community, one can find organizational entrepreneurs who create community organizations to codify and standardize the meaning of the community and give it a united voice.[2]

However, the *meaning* of this division of labor must be sought with reference to the particular cultural traditions that serve as a backdrop to both organizational and family life. It is only when we understand the dynamics of community life in this way that we can make reasonable arguments about the likely consequences of these dynamics for the life of the community over time.

In reference to the Indian immigrant community, it is not enough to see self-interested organizational entrepreneurs trying to divvy up social goods. We need to see the actions that take place in the organizational network in relation to the ongoing contests between the selfish and the selfless. We need to understand why it is that anyone should be concerned with sorting them out. We need to understand the tension between a well-ordered organizational life based on consensually defined social groups and the ultimate inscrutability of individual social status.

Similarly, it is not enough to look at the division of labor and see families, by and large, as unconnected to the actions of organizational entrepreneurs. We need to understand the different types of status anxiety that figure into family life as a base that both grounds and challenges organizational concerns with status. We need to see the connection between the central role of parent-child bonds in orchestrating family life and the central role that the second generation plays in providing a justification for first-generation organizations—"All this is for our children." We need to view the continuities (ego problems and election fraud) and discontinuities ("Everyone should decide for himself") between first- and second-generation organizational life through the prism of parent-child bonds as well.

If we understand the division of labor between organizations and families in terms of the beliefs and values and worldviews that inform the Indian community, we can see it as a source of continuity and cohesion rather than disruption and division. First, the notion that uncertainty and ambiguity are a fundamental part of social life, serving as an impetus for activity directed at clarification, renders the relationship between families and organizations a symbiotic one. Families, in their diversity, generate uncertainty and ambiguity about the identity of Indians in America. Organizations try to sort it all out. This whole process becomes part of a culturally grounded game. One can surely imagine a social group in which uncertainty and ambiguity are considered not natural and endemic but pathological, a sign of moral ill health. In such a social group, a division of labor between families and organizations (in the fashion of the Indian community) would not be keeping the social game afloat but would hasten its demise.[3]

Second, the division of labor promotes community integrity because the parent-child bond helps keep families and organizations linked in a community. First-generation organizations see themselves upholding and preserving Indian culture and gaining a voice for the community in the mainstream, all for the sake of their children. Second-generation organizations are still trying to define themselves in relation to their parents. This intergenerational sensibility, by fostering a kind of familial analogy, links organizations to families as part of an extended kinship network. Both organizations and families are caught up in the intergenerational enterprise.

In contrast, we can imagine a social group in which different ideas regarding the bond between parents and children would not support an intimate symbolic connection between organizational and family life. If families were viewed mainly as socializing units preparing their children for independent lives,[4] then any familial analogy at the organizational level would not have the same integrating effects as it does for the Indian community.

Finally, despite all the concern voiced within the Indian community about unity, the very disunity that is a source of organizational anguish is in fact a source of community strength. The first-generation organizational diversity, much like the messiness of family life, infuses the organizational network with ambiguities and uncertainties that allow the organizational network collectively to claim that its business is to sort things out and create an integrated unified Indian community; it provides its members with a mission. Much as the rhetoric of Indian independence idealized a united India that has yet to be realized, the first-generation Indian immigrants have idealized their own unity. Yet a large part of what keeps the community enterprise afloat is the struggle for unity. If one day the community became unified, with a single organizational spokesperson, the vitality of community life would likely diminish. The "struggle" would be over.

While the centrality of ambiguity in an Indian worldview, parent-child bonds, and the struggle for unity all support the integration of family and organizational life for the first generation, it is less certain whether a division of labor between family life and organizational life will remain functional for the second generation, or even if such a division will continue. The outlook of the second generation is very different from that of the first. We should not expect them, then, to filter unceremoniously into the first-generation organizational network as they mature. At the present stage of development, however, the second-generation organizations perform some of the same functions as the first-generation network in terms of sorting out and defining what it means to be a second-generation Indian American. Mirroring first-generation organizations, the present task depends on the raw materials of family life: problems with parents.

The prospects for the second generation as its members begin to form their own families, however, are difficult to predict. It may be that once the major identity questions of late adolescence are settled, the second-generation organizational network will lose its reason for existence. Looking at some of the older members of the second generation in the five families studied here, one senses that this may be the case. For example, Ganesh Shankar and the Shenoy girls seem relatively more comfortable and settled with their Indianness than younger members of their cohort. It has become part of them, but a part that does not inconvenience them or stand in the way of their full participation in the careers and lives they have chosen. However, it may be that when the second generation begins to raise a third, some of the messiness in its family lives will cry out for extrafamilial clarification. But based on the individualistic orientation of the present second-generation organizations, I would be surprised if the messiness of second-generation families would support the kinds of social, collective solutions that are offered by the first-generation organizational network. I would bet that second-generation families will more often find themselves in therapy than in community forums discussing what it means to be second-generation parents and third-generation children of Indian descent.

Appendix A
Organizations of
the Indian Community

The following is a list of all the first-generation organizations active in the Chicago area between July 1990 and December 1991. It was compiled from a list of area organizations held by the Indian Consulate in Chicago; the "Pink Pages," a list of area businesses that are owned by or cater to the Indian community; the organizations reported on in the ethnic media; and my own interviews with organizational officials and other community members.

Among the religious organizations, those in the "Other" category are so classified either because they are service-oriented (e.g., yoga centers) or, as in the case of the Vivekananda Society, because they have a significant proportion of non-Indian members. All of these organizations, however, have roots in the Hindu tradition.

General

Alliance of Midwest Indian Associations (1986)
Association of Indians in America (founded 1971)
Federation of Indian Associations (1980)

Religious

Muslim

Chicago Foundation for Religious and
   Cultural Reflection
Consultive Committee of Indian Muslims
Gujarati Muslim Association of America
Islamic Correctional Reunion Association
Islamic Foundation (Villa Park)
Islamic Society of America (Frankfurt)

Islamic Society of North America
   (Rolling Meadows)
Mahadavia Islamic Center of Chicago
Muslim Community Center
Muslim Community Center of Elgin
Muslim Education Center (Morton
   Grove)

Christian

Chicago Mar Thoma Church
Council of Kerala Churches of Chicago
   (includes six Syrian Orthodox and two
   Church of South India)
Federation of Indo-American Christians
   of Chicago

Gujarati Christian Fellowship and Hindi
   Fellowship
India Catholic Association
India Catholic Association of America
India Christian Fellowship Church
United India Christian Ministry

Hindu

Arya Samaj of Chicagoland
Balaji Temple
Bochasanwasi Swaminarayan Sanstha—
   Swaminarayan Hindu temple
Chinmaya Mission Chicago
Geeta Mandalam
Gita Mandal
Hare Krishna temple
Hindu Cultural Center
Hindu Foundation

Hindu Satsang
Hindu Society of Metropolitan
   Chicago—Om Hari Mandir
Hindu Temple of Greater Chicago
International Society for Krishna
   Consciousness
Manav Seva Mandir
Satkala Mandir
Vishwa Hindu Parishad of America

Sikh

Sawan Kirpal Rhumani Mission
Sikh Religious Society of Chicago

Jain

Jain Society of Metropolitan Chicago

Parsi

Zoroastrian Association of Metropolitan Chicago

Other

Chicago Raja Yoga Center
Himalayan International Institute of Yoga Science and Philosophy
Vivekananda Vedanta Society of Chicago

Cultural

American Telegu Association
Association of Rajastanis in America
Bengali Association of Greater Chicago
Bihari Association
Chicago Tamil Sangam
Gujarati Cultural Association
Gujarati Pragati Mandal
Gujarati Samaj
Hyderabad Foundation of Chicago
Kannada Kuta
Kashmir Overseas Association
Kerala Association

Maharashtra Mandal Committee
Maharashtra Mandal of Chicago
Malayali Association of Chicago
Malayali Cultural Association of Illinois
Orissa Society of the Americas
Posan Samaj
Punjabi Heritage Organization
Rajput Association
Sindhi Association
Telegu Association of Greater Chicago
Tri-state Telegu Association
Uttar Pradesh (U.P.) Association

Professional/Business

American Association of Physicians
    from India
American Association of Sikh Professionals
Asian Indian Business Association
Association of Indian Pharmacists in
    America
Association of Scientists of Indian Origin
    in America

Indian Dental Association
Indian Medical Association of Illinois
Indian Microbiologists Association of
    America
Indo-American Business Forum
Indo-American Manufacturers Association
International Council of Medical
    Associates

Alumni Associations

Aligarh Muslim University Alumni Association
Association of Kerala Medical Graduates
BVM Alumni Association of Engineering College Vallabh Vidyanagar
Maulana Azad Medical College Alumni Association
Rajastan Medical Schools Alumni Association

Women's

Club of Indian Women
South Asian Women's Society

Political—U.S. Focus

Indian-American Forum for Political Education
Indo-American Democratic Organization
Indian American Republican Association
Sikhs for Democracy

Political—India Focus

India Alert
India Development Service
TOUCH (The Organization for Universal Communal Harmony)

Arts/Leisure

Ameer Khusro Society of America
Golf Association
Hindi Literary Association
India Cultural Society
India Forum
Indian Classical Music Society
Singles Exclusive Club

Service

Apna Ghar
Indo-American Center
South Asian Family Services

Other

Indian Community of Skokie
India League of America
West Suburban India Society

Appendix B
Some Notes on Method

Sociological studies of immigrant populations very often rely on social survey or census data as the basis for their analyses. However, even carefully designed and thoroughly pretested sample surveys necessarily limit in an a priori manner the types of information that will be gathered by the researcher.[1] More open-ended research techniques enable one to uncover a wide range of information and gain access to the extensive, often very subtle variations in individual experience. In designing this study, then, the first methodological decision I made was to use open-ended interviews and participant observation techniques to garner a richer, more developed picture of patterns of adjustment in the Indian immigrant community.

After making a general commitment to this field study orientation, I began to consider the units of analysis that would enable me to examine how people of Indian origin were structuring and making sense of their lives, both as individuals and as a community. Developing a plan to study the community was the easy part. There is a long tradition of studies geared to the public aspects of immigrant communities that rely on analyses of ethnic organizations, ethnic media, and ethnic leaders.

I began the community study with a series of semistructured interviews with organizational officials, concentrating on the structure and activities of organizations. Initially, much of what I needed to learn about the community was concrete information about the size, scope, and composition of the organizational network. I was also a newcomer to the community and needed to establish myself as a familiar face. Soon, I was invited to participate in and observe organizational events, functions, and meetings. The initial meetings provided valuable information on the public face of the organizational network. As I immersed myself in the affairs of some organizations, I also came to understand the way individual participants used and shaped organizations to create an identity both for themselves as individuals of Indian descent and for the Indian community as a whole.

But there are many more people of Indian origin who make up Chicago's Indian community than those I met through the network of ethnic organizations. How I should study these people was not so self-evident. Since I was particularly interested in the question of intergenerational change and the manner in which an Indian worldview may be socialized into the children of the immigrant generation, I decided that it was important to talk to people not as isolated random individuals but as individuals linked in networks that facilitate socialization. I decided to concentrate on nuclear families. Despite a tradition of extended family households in India, the pattern among Chicago's Indian immigrants is predominantly one of nuclear family residences.

Since it is not as easy to engage in participant observation in people's homes as it is in the comparatively public settings of voluntary organizations, I chose to rely mostly on life-history interviews with individual family members, supplemented by some group interviews. I told each participant that the general purpose of the interview was to get to know the person and his or her life experiences, to get a sense of that person's life history. In the first interview, I simply asked people to tell me about their lives and suggested that they begin with where and when they were born and what they remember about growing up. From there, my questions sought clarifications of events or ideas that the interviewee introduced. This technique allowed me not only to let the participant's understanding of his or her experiences guide my research but also, since I was interviewing members of the same family, to reconstruct more accurately the everyday process of interaction. By hearing about the same event from different family members, I was able to reconstruct what happened, who said what, and to appreciate what different participants felt and understood about the event. These interactions proved to be the essential mechanisms of the process of assimilation.

The presentation of this interview material as a series of family portraits was inspired by what I learned as I conducted them. I found that the really interesting stories were family stories. Each family had its own unique climate, its own unique pattern of interaction. I came to feel that introducing my readers to this aspect of immigrant Indian life was of paramount importance, since it was not a feature of the immigrant experience that had found its way into any of the scholarly literature I had read.

I also began to see that the process of assimilation within families did not work as I had expected. I had thought that the extent to which parents succeeded in socializing their children into an Indian worldview would be a function of parents' own acceptance of that worldview, and particularly of the family's contact with the Indian community at large. Are they attending enough functions? Are they getting support from the community in what they're trying to pass on to their kids?

Instead, I began to see that the whole problem revolves around subtleties of interaction, around ideas that are *perceived* to be shared with different communities (Indian, American, Tamil, Gujarati), whether or not they are. The process is not decomposable into broad variables, such as level of contact with the Indian community. Therefore, these family portraits, in presenting overlapping, conjoined individual voices, became a necessary first step in analyzing of the mechanisms of assimilation.

The creation of the family portraits as they appear here was guided by a careful editing process. After I completed the interviews with each individual, I edited the transcripts of our dialogues, eliminating most of the hesitations and repetitions of spoken language. I also changed some but not all of the grammatical deviations from standard American English. All interviews were mainly in English. English was not everyone's first language, but all those interviewed were very comfortable conversing in English. In all households, English was spoken frequently, if not exclusively. I decided to leave much of the speech of the first-generation immigrants in the grammar of "Indian English." Although at times this makes reading their speech more difficult, it reveals the subtly different thought patterns that stem from the two versions of English.

I also consolidated the dialogue into more extended passages of prose in the interviewee's voice. I deleted questions and responses I interjected with the intention of encouraging the interviewee to continue or to provide more detail. However, any of my speech that redirected the conversation or revealed a significant event in our effort to communicate (such as a misunderstanding or a question that caused discomfort) was left intact. Finally, I brought together discussions of a particular event that took place at different times to create more complete stories. This edited version of the conversation was returned to each interviewee. I wanted to both preserve confidentiality (was there anything they would not like other family member to know they said?) and to check that I had not distorted or misinterpreted anything in my editing.

After negotiating an individual portrait with each family member, I combined the portraits into family composites. At this stage, there were few rules that directed the analytic process. I began by reading through the series of interviews for the family several times and picking out the stories and incidents that revealed something about family dynamics, the backgrounds and memories of family members (particularly their childhoods), or the problems and concerns people identified in their lives. What was omitted at this stage were discussions of memories that seemed random and those that people did not connect to any other incidents in their lives. I also omitted or edited down many of the first-generation stories about work lives and health problems. Although these were clearly important to the informants, they were not in general relevant to my interests in the intergenerational aspects of immigrant adjustment and family dynamics. (Where the work stories did seem relevant to adjustment issues, I have included them.) In assembling the discrete passages from different interviews into the family portrait, I followed commonsense rules of storytelling. There is generally a temporal flow. I have also juxtaposed different family members' interpretations of the same incident or used themes introduced by one family member as a prelude to other members' speech regarding similar themes or concerns.

Although this editing process has reduced the volume of the interviews tremendously, I have tried to preserve the self-portrait that each family member presented during our interviews. I have interjected my thoughts about particular passages throughout each portrait, but the large passages of speech are first and foremost the family members' presentation of self. They are not discrete passages that I have somehow chosen to illustrate a point I wish to make. What drives the narrative of these portraits are the interviews themselves, rather than any analytic plan I had beforehand.

Each member of the family had the opportunity to read, correct, and comment on the family portrait in its entirety. At this stage, family members were considering not only my portrayal of their speech but also the story I had constructed about their family. All the commentary contained in the portraits has been approved as "accurate" or at least "plausible" by the family. The major exception is the portrait of the Shenoy family. Family members objected to my original description of their third identity as a "class" identity. I have modified my portrait according to their suggestions but have also self-consciously incorporated the story of our negotiations into the portrait.

The order of the family portraits is random—purely a reflection of the order in which I completed the interviews with the families. However, I found that as I wrote successive portraits, what I had come to think about previous families affected the way I wrote about subsequent ones. For example, as I wrote about the Nagar family (chapter 7), I was taken by the differences between the way the two daughters responded to their Indianness. The Nagar household was very close to what I had imagined as a "typical" Indian immigrant family from what I had read about the adjustment process in the immigrant press. Coming to terms with Indianness was serious business. There were many parent-child disagreements about the appropriateness of certain behaviors, such as wearing makeup or dating, for Indians. After finishing a draft of the Nagar family portrait, I began reading over my interviews with the Iyengars (chapter 8). What struck me was the very different way that they dealt with their Indianness. For the Iyengars, Indianness was not about culture or behavior but about history, about having been born in India. Had I not been thinking about Indianness based on my writing of the Nagar family portrait, I might very well have picked up on a different aspect of the Iyengar interviews to focus on. Similar carryovers in attention and consciousness have affected all the family portraits. By dealing with the raw interviews in a linear fashion and retaining a great deal of that linearity in the family portraits that emerged, I have tried to bring the reader into the process of analysis, or at least to make clear the roots and evolution of my analysis of the raw interview data.

Notes

Preface

1. Social scientists frequently talk about primary and secondary labor markets. The primary labor market offers a living wage and relative job security. The secondary labor market is comprised of low-wage, insecure employment and poor working conditions—a traditional immigrant port of entry into the economy. In addition to being part of the primary labor force, many in this new class of immigrants work in settings populated not by fellow ethnics but by a cross section of the American populace.

2. Anthony P. Cohen, *The Symbolic Construction of Community* (Chichester, England: Ellis Horwood, 1985). Cohen makes the point that communities always have been both concepts and more tangible entities. He suggests, however, that we move "away from the earlier emphasis our discipline placed on structure [and] approach community as a phenomenon of culture: as one . . . which is meaningfully constructed by people through their symbolic prowess and resources" (p. 38). The social interactions that are responsible for the construction of a consciousness of community must be approached as repositories of meaning rather than as "a set of mechanical linkages" that somehow outline community boundaries (p. 98).

Although even the nongeographic, institutionally weak new immigrant communities do have some places they can call their own, the symbolic character of these communities has had to develop *without* the numerous opportunities for social interaction that shaped the daily lives of earlier immigrant cohorts.

3. Ethnicity is a rather special basis for an identity-based community, particularly when it overlaps with race. Communities based on less observable characteristics are in a sense more voluntary than those constructed by people of color.

The experience of immigration also places a distinctive twist on the problem of fitting into "American society." However, the class position and occupational and residential integration of Asian Indians afford them a flexibility in the development of identity and the process of assimilation that compares to a wider range of contemporary identity communities than was true even of their European immigrant predecessors.

Chapter 1

1. In the 1990 census, those identifying their race as Asian Indian comprised about nine-tenths of one percent of the Chicago area's total population (Cook and Dupage counties). In the census tracts surrounding the Devon Avenue shopping district, the Indian population was 5.8 percent, with the highest individual tract concentration reaching 13.7 percent. Only 33 of the 1,468 census tracts in Cook and Dupage counties had concentrations of 5 percent or better.

2. I use the term *assimilation* to refer to the process through which people carve out a place for themselves in American society. To assimilate does not necessarily entail abandoning any sense of ethnic identity and blending seamlessly into the mainstream. Rather, assimilation is about becoming an integral part of the American patchwork.

3. For example, Thomas and Znaniecki's famous study of Polish immigrants, although it recognized the primary role played by the family in the daily lives of immigrants, stressed the integral part that boardinghouses, mutual aid societies, churches, and the ethnic media played in the "reorganization" of Polish society in America. W. I. Thomas and Florian Znaniecki, *The Polish Peasant in Europe and America*, 2nd ed. (New York: Knopf, 1927), pp. 1511–44.

4. "Mainstream" is used throughout this manuscript in the way Asian Indians themselves use it—to refer to white, middle class, native-born Americans.

5. Madison Grant, *The Passing of the Great Race; or, The Racial Basis of European History* (New York: C. Scribner, 1916). This, though, was not the first nativist movement in the United States. An earlier wave of nativist sentiment peaked in the mid-nineteenth century, when the Know-Nothings, alarmed by the influx of Irish Catholics and the supposed challenge these newcomers posed to an America heavily identified with Protestantism, agitated for immigration reform and the exclusion of foreigners from public office. See Philip Gleason, "American Identity and Americanization," *Harvard Encyclopedia of Ethnic Groups*, ed. Stephen Thernstrom (Cambridge: Harvard University Press, 1980), pp. 35–38. However, this earlier nativist movement waned with the onset of the Civil War and never became the inspiration for scholarly attention to immigration.

6. Horace Kallen, *Culture and Democracy in the United States* (New York: Arno, 1924), 67–125.

7. Henry Pratt Fairchild, *Immigration* (New York: Macmillan, 1913).

8. Louis Wirth, *The Ghetto* (Chicago: University of Chicago Press, 1928); William Carson Smith, *Americans in the Making: The Natural History of the Assimilation of Immigrants* (New York: Appleton-Century, 1939); Everett V. Stonequist, *The Marginal Man: A Study in Personality and Culture Conflict* (New York: Charles Scribner's Sons, 1973).

9. Robert E. Park and Ernest W. Burgess, *Introduction to the Science of Sociology*, 2nd ed. (Chicago: University of Chicago Press, 1924), pp. 161–164, 280–87, 506.

10. Nathan Glazer and Daniel Patrick Moynihan, *Beyond the Melting Pot* (Cambridge: MIT Press and Harvard University Press, 1963); Michael Novak, *The Rise of the Unmeltable Ethnics* (New York: Macmillan, 1972).

11. Anny Bakalian, *Armenian-Americans: From Being to Feeling Armenian* (New Brunswick, N.J.: Transaction, 1993); Herbert Gans, "Symbolic Ethnicity: The Future of Ethnic Groups and Cultures in America," *Ethnic and Racial Studies* 2 (1979): 1–20.

12. Mary Waters, *Ethnic Options: Choosing Ethnic Identities in America* (Berkeley: University of California Press, 1990).

13. Milton M. Gordon, *Assimilation in American Life: The Role of Race, Religion, and National Origin* (New York: Oxford University Press, 1964).

14. Nancy W. Jabbra, "Household and Family among Lebanese Immigrants in Nova Scotia: Continuity, Change, and Adaptation," *Journal of Comparative Family Studies* 22 (1991): 39–56; Darrel Montero and Ronald Tsukashima, "Assimilation and Educational Achievement: The Case of Second Generation Japanese-Americans," *Sociological Quarterly* 18 (1977): 490–503; Mary Stopes-Roe and Raymond Cochrane, "The Process of Assimilation in Asians in Britain: A Study of Hindu, Muslim, and Sikh Immigrants and Their Young Adult Children," *International Journal of Contemporary Sociology* 28 (1987): 43–52.

15. Yen Lee Espiritu, *Asian American Panethnicity: Bridging Institutions and Identities* (Philadelphia: Temple University Press, 1992); Joane Nagel, "The Political Mobilization of Native Americans," *Social Science Journal* 19 (1982): 37–45; Felix M. Padilla, *Latino Ethnic Consciousness: The Case of Mexican Americans and Puerto Ricans in Chicago* (Notre Dame: University of Notre Dame Press, 1985).

16. Padilla, *Latino Ethnic* Consciousness, pp. 3–12.

17. Mary C. Waters, "Ethnic and Racial Identities of Second Generation Black Immigrants in New York City," *International Migration Review* 28 (1994): 795–820.

18. Alejandro Portes and Min Zhou, "The New Second Generation: Segmented Assimilation and Its Variants," *Annals of the American Academy of Political and Social Science* 530 (1993): 82–83.

19. Nazli Kibria, *Family Tightrope: The Changing Lives of Vietnamese Americans* (Princeton: Princeton University Press, 1993), p. 168.

20. Karen Leonard, *Making Ethnic Choices: California's Punjabi Mexican Americans* (Philadelphia: Temple University Press, 1992), p. 13.

21. Fran Markowitz's study of Soviet Jewish immigrants also focuses on the mechanisms of community formation. She, too, notes the important role of talk and informal everyday social interactions with close friends in the creation of community among the geographically dispersed population. However, her study does not address intergenerational issues. Nor does she construct a theory to bridge the specific experience of New York's Soviet Jews and those of other communities. The current study does both. Fran Markowitz, *A Community in Spite of Itself: Soviet Jewish Emigres in New York* (Washington, D.C.: Smithsonian Institution Press, 1993).

22. Ronald Takaki, *Strangers from a Different Shore: A History of Asian Americans* (Boston: Little, Brown, 1989), p. 445.

23. *1990 Census of the Population, General Population Characteristics, United States,* Table 3. Indian ancestry is recorded by the "race" question on the U.S. Census, for which "Asian Indian" is one of the choices provided. The 815,447

persons claiming Asian Indian ancestry also include people who wrote in the racial identifications Bengalese, Bharat, Dravidian, East Indian, and Goanese. The racial identification "Asian Indian" presumably includes almost all of the 450,406 people actually born in India.

24. This figure for the population of Asian Indians in the Chicago area is the combined count of Asian Indians in Cook and Dupage counties reported in the 1990 census. Both New York and Los Angeles contain larger concentrations.

25. However, immigrants from the state of Gujarat predominate. Although Gujarat is not India's most populous state, it is one in which the people enjoy reputations for an affinity for long-distance travel and an adventurous, entrepreneurial spirit.

In addition to immigrants coming directly from India, there are also "twice-migrants"—immigrants whose ancestors emigrated from India to other areas of the British Empire. Although dispersed all over the globe, the "twice-migrants" who end up in the United States tend to come from East Africa or Guyana, sometimes by way of Britain. Based on my own experience and the opinions of community members, the proportion of "twice-migrants" is small, certainly less than 10 percent.

26. Caste is much too complicated to explain here in detail. In Sanskritic Hindu religious texts, there are four major caste groups. A fifth group, once called untouchables and now called scheduled castes, includes, in traditional thinking, people without caste. In everyday life, however, caste is more frequently though of in terms of *jati*, the multitude of endogamous communities that live side by side in geographically particular status hierarchies. My sense of the caste backgrounds of Chicago's immigrants is based on my conversations with community members about their own caste backgrounds and their perceptions of the community as a whole, rather than on a systematic survey.

27. There has been some remark in the community about the less advantaged class backgrounds of the most recent immigrants. As the highly educated professionals who immigrated in the 1960s and '70s sponsor relatives under the family reunification provisions of American immigration laws, the class composition of the foreign-born Indian population does indeed become more diverse. In 1980, for example, 51 percent of foreign-born Asian Indians were employed in managerial or professional occupations, as compared to today's 48 percent. Obviously, the shift is not too dramatic. *1980 Census of the Population, Asian and Pacific Islander Population in the United States: 1980*, Table 39.

28. In the case of communities based in identities other than ethnicity, particularly communities without an intergenerational component, the role of the family may be taken over by some other personal social network. Indeed, even in the case of intergenerational communities, other social networks, such as friends or other relatives, also exert an influence on the socialization process. I have chosen to focus on families as an example of one of these small-scale intimate social networks.

Chapter 2

1. In defining *worldview* in terms of ideas about the organization of the social world, I am following Clifford Geertz, "Ethos, World View, and the Analysis of Sacred Symbols," *The Interpretation of Cultures* (New York: Basic Books, 1973).

2. This is not to say that worldviews exist as complete and coherent sets of articulated ideas passed down from generation to generation. Rather, each in-

dividual, in the process of growing up or living in a particular cultural milieu, gradually constructs a set of ideas about the social world based on his or her experience of everyday life. Worldview is a set of assumptions, ideas, and beliefs that are in some sense constructed on the fly by each individual over the course of time as a way of making sense of the social world he or she lives in. Some of these notions, however, will become articulated as people discuss their ideas about the nature of social life, particularly when they perceive a difference in the way "we" behave versus the way "they" behave. The fact that people do communicate about their ideas of social order ensures a certain uniformity in and publicity about worldviews. Therefore, worldview is at once both private and public.

The existence of a common culture that serves as the basis for a shared worldview has been widely debated. Both cultural boundaries (who is to be included within the culture?) and cultural consensus (is there really a single culture that is shared by all?) are problems that challenge the notion of a common culture. As an alternative to this problematized version of a common culture, I take an emic approach to the definition of cultural boundaries and cultural consensus. Such an approach accepts as a cultural unit any group that talks about itself as belonging to a particular cultural tradition, such as being Indian or being American. The fact that "Indian culture" may mean different things to different people does not undermine the importance of the concept to those who use it.

3. Robert N. Bellah, Richard Madsen, William M. Sullivan, Ann Swidler, and Steven M. Tipton, *Habits of the Heart: Individualism and Commitment in American Life* (New York: Harper and Row, 1985), p. 20.

4. This is true of Dumont's treatment of the ideologies of hierarchy and equality, Marriott's contrast of "dividual" and "individual" persons, Shweder and Bourne's "egocentric" and "sociocentric" solutions to the problems of social order, Roland's "familial" and "individualized" selves, and Ramanujan's "context-dependent" and "context-free" social worlds. Louis Dumont, *Homo Hierarchicus: The Caste System and Its Implications*, trans. Mark Sainsburt, Louis Dumont, and Basia Gulati (Chicago: University of Chicago Press, 1980); McKim Marriott, "Hindu Transactions: Diversity without Dualism," in *Transactions and Meaning: Directions in the Anthropology of Exchange and Symbolic Behavior*, ed. Bruce Kapferer (Philadelphia: Institute for the Study of Human Issues, 1976); Richard Shweder and Edmund J. Bourne, "Does the Concept of the Person Vary?," in *Culture Theory: Essays on Mind, Self, and Emotion*, ed. Richard Shweder and Robert A. Levine (Cambridge: University of Cambridge Press, 1984); Alan Roland, *In Search of Self in India and Japan: Toward a Cross-cultural Psychology* (Princeton: Princeton University Press, 1988); A. K. Ramanujan, "Is There an Indian Way of Thinking?" in *India through Hindu Categories*, ed. McKim Marriott (Delhi: Sage, 1990).

5. Dumont, *Homo Hierarchicus*, p. 4.

6. Alexis de Tocqueville, *Democracy in America*, trans. George Lawrence, ed. J. P. Meyer (New York: Harper and Row, 1969), p. 508.

7. Marriott, "Hindu Transactions," p. 111.

8. Roland, *In Search of Self*, p. 205.

9. Shweder and Bourne, "Does the Concept of the Person Vary?" pp. 175–178.

10. Ibid., p. 188.

11. Ibid., p. 190.

12. Dumont, *Homo Hierarchicus*, pp. 9–10, 41.

13. Ibid., p. 4.

14. Ibid.

15. Alan Roland suggests that in addition to a structural hierarchy based on one's position in the social order, there is also a "hierarchy by quality of persons." The particular qualities of individuals may generate respect, idealization, and veneration. Roland, *In Search of Self*, pp. 218–20.

16. Dumont, *Homo Hierarchicus*, p. 66.

17. Marriott, "Hindu Transactions," pp. 109–10. Steve Barnett articulates substance code somewhat differently; substance is hereditary but can be altered by behavior (code). Steve Barnett, "Coconuts and Gold: Relational Identity in a South Indian Caste," *Contributions to Indian Sociology* 10 (1976): 133–56.

18. Marriott, "Hindu Transactions," p. 110.

19. Bellah et al., *Habits of the Heart*, p. 167.

20. Allan Silver, "The Curious Importance of Small Groups in American Sociology," in *Sociology in America*, ed. Herbert Gans (Newbury Park, Calif.: Sage, 1990), p. 63.

Chapter 3

1. Fashion shows feature community members (often young people) wearing the latest in Indian fashions. Cultural shows include an assortment of skits, songs, and dances presented by amateurs from the community. A favorite activity at cultural shows is lip-syncing to Indian movie music. While several of the major cultural shows are more polished and elaborately designed, part of the fun clearly is seeing one's friends and colleagues in the limelight.

2. Although there has been a sizable immigration of Indian nationals throughout the 1980s and '90s, these later immigrants do not figure prominently as officers or active members of Indian community organizations.

3. What I recount below is the *story* of organizational development that community members tell. There is a very rough correspondence to the actual patterns of growth, but the founding dates of any one type of organization vary widely. The pattern is not as neat as community members suggest.

4. Phrases in this chapter and the following one that appear in quotes were used by members of the Indian community during interviews or during community events at which I was an observer.

5. Most immigrants of the '60s and '70s came to the United States with the intention of returning to India within a few years. However, as time passed, immigrants began to realize that their children would face great difficulty readjusting to India and that their own careers would suffer if they went "back home." This pattern holds both for the immigrants I interviewed and for Indian immigrants throughout the United States. See Sathi S. DasGupta, *On the Trail of an Uncertain Dream* (New York: AMS Press, 1989).

6. While the stages in the expansion of the organizational network are explicit in the story community members tell about how the organizational network got to be what it is today, these dual motives are not. I have extracted them from the variety of stories people have told me about how they became involved in various organizations.

7. *Mainstream* is the way members of the Indian community refer to non-immigrant Americans. I have often heard *mainstream* and *white* used inter-

changeably, and I think in general that when Indian immigrants and their children refer to the "mainstream," they mean nonimmigrant Americans of European stock.

8. Although people would often call this other story the "true" one, I would resist that label. What they meant, I think, was not that the first story was untrue in comparison but simply that the second side of organizational life was what really deserved attention. It was here where the community was in distress and where the energy of the community should be focused.

9. In addition to being the dominant rhetoric used to describe the current state of affairs in the Indian community, "splits" are also seen as a dynamic of growth. When I asked some interviewees why there were so many organizations in a particular category, they cited splits as an important source of new organizations.

10. The choice of language here is revealing. In more informal settings, first-generation Indians usually refer to themselves as "the Indian community." This meeting, however, sponsored as it was by the governor's office and open to a few non-Indian observers (both whites and other Asians), promoted this explicit recognition of the community of Indians as "Asian Indian Americans." In this context, I think, the Indian leaders were more aware of their relation to the mainstream than they routinely are and, further, were more concerned than usual with stressing the fact that they belong here.

11. Division does not seem to be a feature only of the local community in Chicago. A recent guest column in the Indian immigrant press by a Maryland Indian laments: "The Indian community in the U.S. . . . is divided vertically along religious lines. There is no communication between subcommunities and each is espousing its own party line. Whatever happened to bringing these people together and espousing an Indian party line, associating with each other socially and eliminating division?" Kaleem Kawaja, "Kissa Kursi Ka: A Story of the Throne," *Spotlight*, Nov. 24, 1990, p. 14.

12. Informants have recounted in detail seven different organizational splits in the course of our interviews. In many interviews, these splits were brought up spontaneously. In some later interviews, we would discuss them as I was checking the completeness of my organizational lists. For example, I would show an interviewee my list of other organizations in his category and ask if I had missed any. I would also ask what the differences were between them. This generally led to their bringing up the history of organizational division.

13. It may seem that in lumping these kinds of intragroup divisions together, I am missing some subtle differences in the dynamics of organizational splits. It may seem that divisions that arise on the basis of caste or class are creating rankings or hierarchies of organizations and that language-based splits are somehow more egalitarian. However, in the Indian understanding of what is at issue when differences of language, caste, or class are found, there are consistent references to lifestyles (cooking in the same fashion) and compatibility (feeling "more comfortable" with those who are members of the same group). Although differing social and economic status also may be evident, my informants tended to frame these differences in terms of "different cultures."

14. To say there is a "ranking" of community organizations does not mean that there is a clear vertical pecking order. There is, however, among organizations of the same type—organizations that could, conceivably, draw on the same

constituency—a kind of contest to be recognized as *the* representative of a particular constituency. Whichever organization is more frequently recognized as *the* representative—by the city government, by the Indian consulate—is generally seen as more legitimate by the community at large.

15. Salman Rushdie, *Midnight's Children* (New York: Avon Books, 1980).

16. "Communal" conflict in the Indian context refers primarily to tensions between different religious communities (Hindus and Muslims in particular), but has also come to refer to tensions among all sorts of religious, regional, and caste groups. Communal tensions, however, are not only a post-independence phenomenon. They have been a constituent feature of discussions about Indian social and political life since the early days of British colonial rule. See Gyanendra Pandey, *The Construction of Communalism in Colonial North India* (Delhi: Oxford University Press, 1990). But since independence, and particularly in the last fifteen years, the validity of a single unified "India" has been challenged with increasing vigor and frequency by various religious, regional, and caste interests. Secessionist movements of Punjabi Sikhs, Kashmiris, Tamils, and tribals in eastern India; conservative Hindu voices which demand a Hindu Rastra; reactionary movements among middle and upper castes against government suggestions of increased job and academic reservations for the "backward" sectors of Indian society are all recent examples.

17. The Ram Janmabhoomi/Babri Masjid controversy, involving the dispute over a plot of land in the city of Ayodhya that was once the site of a Hindu temple, now the site of a mosque, is one of a number of issues that focused the immigrant community's attention on issues of national unity in India. Prime Minister V. P. Singh's call for the implementation of the Mandal Commission Report advocating increased reservations of governmental and educational positions for members of the "backward" sectors of Indian society, the elections that brought down the Singh government, and the assassination of Rajiv Gandhi have all prompted general discussions of the communal threats to national unity. I will focus on the *mandir/masjid* issue because it has held media and community attention for most of the period of this study and for a much longer period of time than these other issues.

18. Since this study was completed, the Babri Masjid/Ram Janmabhoomi crisis has continued to flare. On December 6, 1992, a huge mob tore down the mosque, brick by brick. In the wake of the demolition of the mosque, there were severe riots in several Indian cities, most notably Bombay. As with the earlier developments, the Chicago community strongly denounced the demolition of the mosque and the violent riots that followed.

19. "Is Myth of India's Composite Culture Disappearing?" *Spotlight*, Nov. 17, 1990, p. 4.

20. Atul M. Setalwad, "Why We Must Remain Secular," *Spotlight*, Jan. 25, 1991, p. 8.

21. "India's Unity at Stake: Palkhivala," *Spotlight*, Nov. 17, 1990, p. 4.

22. Setalwad, "Why We Must Remain Secular," p. 8. Emphasis added.

23. Michael Neri, "In India, United We Fall, Divided We Stand!" *India Tribune*, Feb. 16, 1991, p. 2. Emphasis added.

24. A. M. Khusro, "Understanding, Tolerance Keys to Nationhood," *India Tribune*, Feb. 16, 1991, p. 2.

25. Jose Kalleduckil, "My Heart Bleeds for India," *Spotlight*, Jan. 18, 1991, p. 8.

26. "Arif Begins Indefinite Fast for Communal Harmony," *Spotlight*, Dec. 22, 1990, p. 1.

27. Prem Prakash, "Indian Democracy at the Crossroads," *Spotlight*, Nov. 17, 1990, p. 9.

28. Kawaja, "Kissa Kursi Ka," p. 14.

29. "Economic Disparity Causes Communal Violence," *Spotlight*, Feb. 8, 1991, p. 10. V. P. Singh is cited as one who opposed the Hindu fundamentalists on the *mandir/masjid* issue, and the BJP is the party that supported the fundamentalists.

30. At present, Muslim personal law supersedes the national civil code in adjudicating certain disputes. One recent famous case concerned the denial of alimony to a Muslim woman based on Muslim personal law. The "special treatment" of minorities that the Hindu fundamentalists object to encompasses both the Muslim laws and the reservation of educational and job slots for India's former untouchables, the scheduled castes.

31. Tarun Basu, "BJP, Condemned by Some, Hit by Ideological Ferment," *India Abroad*, Nov. 9, 1990, p. 17.

32. "Is Myth of India's Composite Culture Disappearing?" p. 9.

33. "Silent Walk Most Impressive," *India Tribune*, June 1, 1991, p. 23.

34. Kalleduckil, "My Heart Bleeds," p. 8.

35. Kawaja, "Kissa Kursi Ka," p. 14.

36. *The Bhagavad Gita*, Barbara Stoler Miller, trans. (Toronto: Bantam, 1986).

37. The condemnation of greed in the epics is not the whole story of the place of money in Hinduism. Hindu practice encompasses the worship of Lord Ganesh and Goddess Lakshmi, whose blessings are sought to ensure financial and material success. Lord Ganesh is often worshiped at the beginning of new endeavors to ask that the undertaking be successful. Although not limited to requests for financial success, material rewards are a strong incentive for Ganesh worship. Lakshmi is worshiped for fertility of body and field, luck, and general well-being as well as material wealth. Throughout much of North India, Ganesh and Lakshmi are paired (although they are unrelated in mythological genealogy), reinforcing their common role in granting material prosperity. See Paul B. Courtright, *Ganesa: Lord of Obstacles, Lord of Beginnings* (New York: Oxford University Press, 1985); David R. Kinsley, *Hindu Goddesses: Visions of the Divine Feminine in the Hindu Religious Tradition* (Berkeley: University of California Press, 1986).

Yet the notion that money and wealth are goods in their own right does not undermine the question of motivation raised in the *Mahabharata*, since the desire for prosperity is not the moral equivalent of an undue attachment to the fact of prosperity. See Balbir Singh, *Hindu Ethics: An Exposition of the Concept of Good* (Atlantic Highlands, N.J.: Humanities Press, 1984).

38. Singh, *Hindu Ethics*, p. 129.

Chapter 4

1. Several area high schools also have Indian student associations. However, I chose to forgo any investigation of these organizations because of the administrative complexities of gaining access to public schools.

2. When I began this phase of the study, there was only one Hindu religious group at an area university. During the course of the study, however, sev-

eral others were founded. Muslim student associations have been around for many years, but these organizations include students of Middle Eastern origin as well as those from the Indian subcontinent.

3. Instead, most first-generation organizations sponsor organizational activities specifically designed to attract and amuse the children of their members. In these cases, the youth are nominally "in charge" of the events, but impetus for activities still comes from the parental generation of organizational leadership.

4. I chose to work with the Indian student organizations at the two universities, one public and one private, to expose any differences in the organizational concerns and dynamics that might be related to the differences in the student populations at the two schools. The public university draws its student body mainly from the Chicago area. I thought that students whose parents were involved in local first-generation organizations might develop their own organization with strong similarities to their parental models. At the private institution, students are from all over the country and thus do not share a common organizational experience. I chose Om, since it was the only exclusively Indian campus religious organization when the study began. In the Wings was likewise the pioneer of autonomous youth branches.

5. Space constraints prevent the inclusion of all four case studies. I have chosen one example from each of the three types of second-generation organizations, including the postcollegiate organization, which was not a full case study but was the only organization of its type in existence. The omitted case studies also evidence the individualistic orientation to group life illustrated in the cases below.

6. The Awareness Week was organized at the request of the dean's office as part of a series of Awareness Weeks intended to reduce racial tensions on campus. The dean's office had suggested an Indian Awareness Week but was informed by the Association's leaders that given the history of Indo-Pak tensions, it would be best to include Pakistani students as an independently defined group rather than under the general rubric of "Indian."

7. There is, however, considerable feeling among the second generation that the ISA should not divide into ethnic subgroups and that the intra-Indian divisions in the first generation are wrong.

8. Although I did not participate in the youth activities of any other organization, I have interviewed both first- and second-generation leaders of other organizations with youth activities. In all those cases, the relationship between the first generation and the youth did not have the independence (in the perception of either generation) that was evident at HTGC.

9. Discussion topics provided by the counselors took the form of either questions about the participants' feelings (how do you feel about going to the temple?) or passages from religious texts which participants were asked to interpret.

10. This notion of religion as a "personal thing" also characterized group discussions that took place in Om, the campus religious organization.

11. It is interesting that this criticism was directed toward "our parents' generation" rather than toward anyone's parents in particular. It might be supposed that this only reveals a reluctance to criticize one's parents directly, but group members were generally not shy about making direct complaints about their own parents in regard to other issues. Rather, I think the group was criticizing a widely shared image of first-generation participation in the temple. Many in the first generation have also expressed their feeling that the temple is "too social." So I think this complaint by the second generation is more a response to a stereotyped

notion of first-generation behavior than it is a response to actual events they have witnessed.

12. Around the time of this formal transition in the HTGC youth group, notices of many other youth activities began appearing in the immigrant press. There were, for example, the Arya Samaj Youth Function, the FIA Youth Forum Gala, the Hari Om Mandir Youth Group, and the FOKANA Youth Leadership Conference.

13. This last comment is a clear dig at the first generation. As noted above, the second generation is very critical of all the division evident in the first-generation organizations and very proud that the divisions of language, caste, and so on are not manifest in its members' own behavior.

14. NETIP's press release argues that members of the second generation have been "raised in this country and thereby subjected to great social and cultural conflicts. They have, however, overcome the barriers they faced, and now stand tall and proud as unique members of the Indian community."

15. In addition to people allegedly using membership lists to further their careers, NETIP has been a cosponsor along with other Indian community organizations of a professional development seminar aimed at giving career advice to young adults.

16. This was true not only of ISA members but also of many other members of the second generation whom I interviewed. However, in the organizations I studied, only the ISA used these terms in an organizational context.

Chapter 5

1. The adjustment problems of immigrants are addressed sparingly in the ethnic media. The largest Indian American newspaper, *India Abroad*, features an occasional column entitled "Reflections on Life Abroad," covering everything from the problems of wearing turbans to laments about the replacement of moviegoing in India by home VCRs. Chicago's local weekly television show "Chitrahar" has sponsored special programs on a number of adjustment issues, such as dealing with elderly parents. However, the adjustment problems of the immigrant generation were not salient during the period of this study. If the immigrant generation did have one serious adjustment issue, it was dealing with its children.

2. The analysis that follows is based on the adjustment rhetoric that appears in the ethnic press. I have focused on print rhetoric, both because its printed form renders it amenable to content analysis and because it is representative of the rhetoric I heard in public discussions of the second generation. The analysis is based on 105 articles collected from immigrant newspapers. The majority of these articles came from a systematic monitoring of *India Tribune* and *Spotlight*, two Chicago-based weeklies, from June 1990 through September 1991, and February to November 1991, respectively. All articles that addressed any aspect of second-generation experience were included in the sample. In addition, a few articles were included that came from *India Abroad* and *News India*. These were articles I had clipped from these papers in the years prior to this study or articles that appeared during the period of study in issues I happened across. Neither of these latter papers is based in Chicago, and neither maintained a regular feature devoted to youth issues. Therefore, I chose not to monitor them systematically during the course of this study.

3. Priya Jenveja, "Growing Up in America," *Spotlight*, Nov. 17, 1990, p. 13.

4. Shelu Bhandari, "Dating Is Good But . . . ," *Spotlight*, Dec. 15, 1990, p. 13.

5. Lalita Gandbhir, "Response to 'Does Brain Drain Hurt India?'" *Spotlight*, June 16, 1990, p. 8.

6. Swamy Brahamchari Sudhanshu, "Why We Should Denounce Dating," *Spotlight*, June 9, 1990, p. 9.

7. Pran Vohra, "Young Indians, Wake Up and Be Proud to Be Hindu," *India Tribune*, June 1, 1991, p. 19.

I have chosen to use the term *superior/inferior* rather than *hierarchy* in the majority of instances in this chapter. As suggested in chapter 2, *hierarchy* implies a relation of the "higher" unit *encompassing* the "lower" unit, in addition to their simply being ranked as higher and lower in a linear sense. In the context of adjustment rhetoric, the distinctions one finds between "better" and "worse," "moral" and "immoral" seem to me to be closer to the straightforward scaled ranking than to the notion of hierarchy. The one exception to this is the relationship between parents and children. In discussing the intersection of the concept of ranking with that issue, I will use the term *hierarchy*.

8. Nausheen Moinuddin, "Student Get-together Fosters Unity, Pride," *India Tribune*, June 22, 1991, p. 17. I do not mean to suggest that this view of American society is universal or even dominant in the Indian community at large. While critics tend to be more vocal than supporters (and thus more frequently represented in the press), there are instances where the opposing view of American society makes an appearance. An article from the "Reflections on Life Abroad" series in *India Abroad* instructs parents: "We need to recognize that stereotypes about the immorality of Westerners . . . will not be helpful." Mathew Zachariah, "Solving Youth-Parent Conflicts," *India Abroad*, Nov. 9, 1990, p. 3.

9. Sailesh Harwani, "New Generation Reviews Itself," *Spotlight*, Dec. 8, 1990, p. 12.

10. Sailesh Harwani, "Children of Two Cultures," *Spotlight*, March 8, 1991, p. 12. The four articles by Harwani that are part of this analysis are collections by this young man of the thoughts of his peers. Therefore, there are many different voices quoted within each article.

11. Shobha Sairam, "Accept the Future Generation's Ideas," *Spotlight*, Sept. 27, 1990, p. 14.

12. Zainab Burney, "Teenager Speaks Out," *Spotlight*, Dec. 28, 1990, p. 10.

13. Clare Talwalker, "It's Time for Indian Americans to Prepare for Threat of Racial Attacks," *India Tribune*, Feb. 23, 1991, p. 12.

14. Darshan Thakkar, "Balvihar of Indiana Opens Up Children," *India Tribune*, March 16, 1991, p. 17.

15. Bangalore Sureshwara, "Early Experiences: Amusing and Confusing," *Spotlight*, Sept. 1, 1990, p. 8.

16. Harwani, "Children of Two Cultures," p. 12.

17. Ibid.

18. Ibid.

19. Ibid.

20. However, the academic/nonacademic distinction remains important, with greater emphasis on the former. Scores were determined by the following formula: 40 percent for academic achievement, 20 percent for academic extracur-

ricular activities, 25 percent for nonacademic extracurricular activities, 15 percent for activities related to Asian Indian affairs.

21. Zachariah, "Solving Youth-Parent Conflicts," p. 3.

22. Thakkar, "Balvihar of Indiana," p. 17.

23. "Ramesha Jagsi of Texas Leads Nehru Youth Excellence Awards Parade: 5 Winners," *India Tribune*, May 25, 1991, p. 25.

24. Moin Khan, "How to Combat Dating Virus," *Spotlight*, June 9, 1990, p. 9.

25. Meera Komarraju, "Being a Parent in Two Worlds," *India Abroad*, Aug. 17, 1990, p. 2.

26. This reason is confirmed by the father quoted above, who sees "sexual activity" as incompatible with "achievement," or at least something that must be postponed until education is complete.

27. Khan, "How to Combat," p. 9.

28. Bhandari, "Dating Is Good," p. 13.

29. Thakkar, "Balvihar of Indiana," p. 17.

30. Khan, "How to Combat," p. 9.

31. In the rhetoric of the second generation, I have never heard or read the common Indian rhetoric of "arranged" versus "love" marriages. In the U.S. context, the discussion always revolves around whether the second generation will have marriages arranged by their parents or marriages in which they will make the final decisions regarding the choice of partners. The position of love in this formulation is not clear. It may be that love is presumed, whether the marriage is arranged or choice, and therefore not deserving of comment. What is more likely, in my opinion, is that for the second generation in the United States, marriage is an issue of *choice*. Whose choice will it be? This is in contrast to the understanding of the marriage issue as it applied to the lives of immigrants before their arrival. There the concern was with the *reason* for marriage—for status and comfort and family connections, or for love.

32. Kavitha Ravella, "Arranged Marriage: 2 Outlooks," *India Abroad*, Dec. 1, 1989, p. 2.

33. Sailesh Harwani, "Disadvantages and Advantages," *Spotlight*, June 7, 1990, p. 12.

34. Khan, "How to Combat," p. 9.

35. Harwani, "Disadvantages," p. 12.

36. It is problematic to suggest an interpretation based on the negative case—in this instance, parental silence on the issue of marriage. However, given the additional evidence that follows, I am confident of this reading.

37. Lucyamma Menezes, "A Message to Indian Parents," *Spotlight*, Jan. 25, 1991, p. 16.

38. Sailesh Harwani, "Teens Need Such Conferences to Understand and Communicate Better," *Spotlight*, Aug. 9, 1991, p. 14.

39. Sairam, "Accept the Future Generation's Ideas," p. 14.

40. Menezes, "A Message," p. 16.

41. Harwani, "Teens Need Such Conferences," p. 14.

42. Ibid.

43. Jenveja, "Growing Up," p. 13.

44. Menezes, "A Message," p. 16.

45. Although print media's output in the commercial realm are clearly the crafted products of editors, my discussions with editors of the Indian immigrant

press indicate that at least as far as the youth pages are concerned, there is a relatively open microphone. Submissions are not so numerous as to require much picking and choosing.

Chapter 6

1. Herbert Gans, "Comment: Ethnic Invention and Acculturation, a Bumpy Line Approach," *Journal of American Ethnic History* 12 (1992) : 42–52.

2. I left the task of choosing pseudonyms to the participants themselves. I asked only that they choose a family name that was consistent with their regional, caste, and religious background. Given names were at their discretion. This has resulted in quite an assortment of names, most of which will be unfamiliar to non-Indian readers.

Chapter 7

1. Draping flowers on images is a common practice in many Indian households. The pictures may be of Hindu gods, saints and gurus, or departed loved ones.

2. Krishna is an incarnation of the Hindu god Vishnu. Playful and mischievous, he is often depicted playing the flute and cavorting with *gopis*, the female cow herders who are his companions and devotees.

3. A *bindi* is the small dot, sometimes painted, sometimes peel-and-stick, worn by many Indian women in the center of the forehead.

4. *Bharata natyam* is a style of classical dance originating in South India. It has become a national form of classical dance, studied by young girls throughout India.

5. A dhoti is one type of traditional dress for men. It is a cloth wrapped around the waist and styled into baggy calf-length pants.

Chapter 8

1. Their unwillingness to identify particular features of their family life as Indian stems from their general construction of themselves as "only" historically Indian. The Iyengars, unlike other families, resist seeing life in "essential" terms. They see life as very concrete. For them, there is no spiritual or essential force that gives shape to particular life circumstances, except perhaps for a universalistic spirit of human nature and goodness. They seem much more comfortable understanding life "as it is," with all its idiosyncrasies, than understanding their lives as part of some master scheme rooted in a particular cultural milieu.

2. A *pankha* is a type of fan operated by a pull string which makes the fan move back and forth.

3. When I asked this question, we had been talking about their sons' educations for some time. I had asked a general question about the importance of grades. This had been prompted by earlier discussions with the sons in which they had brought up grade issues. To my general question about the importance of grades, Lakshmi responded that she felt grades were very important. A short discussion ensued concerning why grades were important. Then I asked about straight A's.

4. See in particular the portraits of the Kumars (chapter 9), the Shenoys (chapter 10), and the Shankars (chapter 11). Each of these families has children

who are somewhat older than the Iyengar boys. Even in their middle and late twenties, children in these families are still deeply attached to their parents in a way that was quite surprising to me as an observer.

5. As Bellah et al. suggest in their study of American culture, "In a culture that emphasizes autonomy and self-reliance of the individual . . . childhood is chiefly preparation for the all important event of leaving home. . . . [While] separation and individuation are issues that must be faced by all human beings . . . leaving home in its American sense is not." Robert N. Bellah, Richard Madsen, William M. Sullivan, Ann Swidler, and Steven M. Tipton, *Habits of the Heart: Individualism and Commitment in American Life* (New York: Harper and Row, 1985), pp. 56–57.

Chapter 9

1. The Nagar family actually did return to India after a few years' stay in the United States. The lack of career prospects, however, led them back to the United States. The Iyengar family originally intended to return to India but got caught up in their lives in the United States. Lakshmi Iyengar once told me that she still has a plot of land in India. She continues to hold on to it; she's not sure why. In other families as well, this sentiment prevails. However, I have not routinely incorporated discussions of it into the family portraits.

2. In the older generation, this norm of intense discussion was illustrated when Ravi and Ratna needed to make changes in their careers.

3. I sensed a comparable solidity in the Iyengar family. In their case, however, that solidity was built around a camaraderie between parents and children rather than a commitment to contentious dialogue and compromise. To be sure, Lakshmi and Shivan Iyengar had frequent discussions with their children, hoping to influence their children's actions (Michael's choice of major or Bob's performance in school). In that family, though, the decisions were, in the end, left to the children. Lakshmi and Shivan expressed their views which the children then took into consideration. This is not the same dynamic I found with the Kumars and the Shenoys. For the Kumars and the Shenoys, the discussion process was supposed to lead to a mutual recognition by parents and children that a particular course of action was preferred and would be carried out. The similarities in a family idiom governing the process of decision making between the Kumars and the Shenoys are, like all family idioms, grounded in the particular historical experiences of parents. While those experiences have been different for the two sets of parents, we can see clearly in each case the genesis of this pattern.

Chapter 10

1. The five Pandavs are the brothers who are the heroes of the Indian epic *Mahabharata*.

2. Psalm's recounting of her father's attitude toward her interest in mysticism is reminiscent of similar attitudes expressed by Shivan Iyengar and Ravi Kumar. Shivan Iyengar stressed choosing an occupation with a guaranteed comfortable income. Music, for example, was not a good choice, no matter how strong one's inclinations to music over medicine. Similarly, the Kumar daughters talk about their own interests in theater or journalism, which they have subordinated to more practical career pursuits on the advice of their father.

3. I do not mean to suggest, however, that the Shenoy family philosophy renders family members isolated and self-centered. All the nurturing of individual characters and talents takes place in an overarching framework, as Durga puts it, "of responsibility to family, society, and fellow human beings of the universe." While nurturing one's own interests, one is also expected to treat others around one with care and respect.

4. "Self-enlightened, self-interested" was a phrase used repeatedly by Durga in discussing her realizations about herself and about the decisions she has made, and in discussing what she has tried to accomplish in raising her children.

5. Although Psalm does articulate some specific Indian values and the basis for this bond, her speech contains disclaimers that suggest these specifics are post hoc rationalizations of an almost primordial feeling.

6. They consistently equivocate about whether their values and sentiments are Indian and openly criticize members of the Indian community who see themselves as fundamentally different from (and perhaps superior to) non-Indians.

7. They travel back and forth, and relatives from India spend long periods residing with the Iyengars in Chicago.

8. They have lost contact with friends and relatives in India and express no interest in the political or social conditions there.

9. Durga, however, did speak about developing a critical attitude toward the tradition of male dominance in Indian culture and about her activities as a student to protest the caste system. However, these critiques were and are arenas of cultural debate within the Indian context. These are not ideas that placed her outside the cultural interests of her Indian contemporaries.

10. I am using *class* here in a vernacular rather than sociological sense. Class encompasses not only life chances but also general status attributes—clothing, language, style, demeanor.

Chapter 11

1. People who wash clothes for a living.

2. For a young woman, walking around alone is considered unseemly.

3. Kannada is the language spoken in the family's home state of Karnataka.

4. Although Shankar does say, referring to his nephews in India above, that from America "morally it's difficult to communicate and try to educate them in certain ways," this communication is not the kind of open sharing of thoughts and desires for which Veena and Ganesh long. I sense that had Shankar stayed in India, he thinks that through the sheer force of his presence and the process of day-to-day communal living, he would have been able to provide for his relatives moral guidance—perhaps through example more so than through language.

Chapter 12

1. In fact, this tendency is realized in most studies of Indian immigrants. Priya Agarwal, *Passage from India: Post-1965 Indian Immigrants and Their Children* (Palos Verdes, Calif.: Yuvati Publications, 1991); John Y. Fenton, *Transplanting Religious Traditions: Asian Indians in America* (New York: Praeger, 1988); Margaret A. Gibson, *Accommodation without Assimilation: Sikh Immigrants in an American High School* (Ithaca: Cornell University Press, 1988); Proshanta K. Nandi, *The Quality of Life of Asian Americans: An Exploratory Study*

of a Middle-sized Community (Chicago: Pacific/Asian American Mental Health Research Center, 1980); S. Parvez Wakil, C. M. Siddique, and F. A. Wakil, "Between Two Cultures: A Study in Socialization of Children of Immigrants," *Journal of Marriage and Family* 43 (1981): 929–40.

2. For example, both Iyengar parents grew up in rather nontraditional households in India. Both families were nationally mobile. Lakshmi's family, in particular, promoted a kind of secular, nonessentialized identity. As she points out, her parents didn't want her "going around with dots and saris."

3. I would allow, however, that the personalities of children may in some instances bring their x-ness into play even when their parental examples and immediate social environment do not make it a salient feature. One could imagine a child developing an interest in his or her x-ness to call attention to his or her individuality in an ethnically bland environment.

4. The exception here was the son, Ganesh. In a part of our interview not included in the family portrait presented in chapter 11, he did discuss his feelings about his Indianness. I will introduce some of his comments below.

5. This recollection is not included in the family portrait here. As noted in appendix B, I edited out much talk about the work experiences of the first generation.

6. I have not included the children's discussions of name-calling and teasing in the excerpts about the Shankars. For both children, the references to name-calling occurred in the context of discussions of other issues. For example, Veena comments about being called names in the context of her discussion of an overwhelming need to "fit in." A large part of the "fitting in" discussion is excerpted in the chapter. Ganesh introduces his experiences with name-calling in the context of a lengthy chronology of the events of junior high and high school. In composing the chapter about the Shankars, I decided to concentrate on the "sense of family" issue. The Indianness issue was much more tangential to the family dynamic as a whole, as I hope to be demonstrating here.

7. Eleanor Rosch, "Principles of Categorization," in *Cognition and Categorization*, ed. Eleanor Rosch and Barbara B. Lloyd (Hillsdale, N.J.: Laurence Erlbaum and Associates, 1978).

8. Ibid., p. 36.

9. Eleanor Rosch, "Human Categorization," in *Studies in Cross Cultural Psychology*, Vol. 1, ed. Neil Warner (London: Academic Press, 1977), p. 3.

10. In fact, much of the literature on Asian Indians in America also posits this bifurcated experience, for both the first and second generations. See DasGupta (*On the Trail*) and Fenton (*Transplanting Religious Traditions*) for the first generation and Arthur Helweg and Usha Helweg (*An Immigrant Success Story: East Indians in America*) (Philadelphia: University of Pennsylvania Press, 1990) and Gibson (*Accommodation without Assimilation*) for the second generation. However, similar to the families studied here, close attention to individual statements reported in the literature reveals a much less bifurcated reality, particularly for the second generation. The persistence of the "two worlds" image in scholarly literature perhaps results from the focus of these studies on the public "community" voice or on snapshots of the lives of first- or second-generation individuals rather than on the intergenerational interactions that actually constitute lived experience.

11. I have concentrated here on the use of Indian rather than American character prototypes because of the relative infrequency of the latter compared to the

former. It is interesting, however, that American character prototypes were most frequently used by second-generation individuals expressing the sentiment that they and their peers (and sometimes their parents) are "pretty American." Unlike the Indian character prototype, the content of the American prototype was very rarely specified. So, unlike the Indian prototype, where specifics were used to draw contrasts between self and prototype, the American prototype was nonspecific and overwhelmingly used to draw parallels between self and prototype. This difference can be accounted for by the particular position of these two prototypes in relation to the users. Indian immigrants are not particularly concerned with fleshing out what it means to be American. Rather, they are concerned with what it means to be Indian in the American context. Alternatively, it might be that individuals did not feel the need to flesh out the American prototype because they assumed that I, as an American, already knew what it entailed.

12. I argued in relation to the Kumar and Shenoy families that the children displayed a fear of inadequacy or failure that was related to the existence of a strong "third identity." This third identity dissipated the contrast between Indian and American. I think that the consistency with which each of the three children in each of these families expressed this fear is unusual and is at least in part linked to this notion of a third identity. However, the kind of status anxiety I am discussing in this section is more widespread, peppered throughout the five families. There are other conditions, beyond the existence of a third identity, that contribute to this less intense and uniform but still notable pattern.

13. In this case, "status" is not a technical status (i.e., not a status with an associated role) but rather a colloquial usage of the term. Status anxiety here, is concern over one's worth, one's adequacy, the opinions others have about one.

14. Herbert Gans, "Second Generation Decline: Scenarios for the Economic and Ethnic Future of Post-1965 American Immigrants," *Ethnic and Racial Studies* 15 (1992): 173–92. This is a very simplistic argument with which the thrust of my analysis here is at odds. However, I bring this idea up as one possible part of the complex process of intergenerational change. Moreover, I am taking some liberty with Gans's argument. His focus is on those immigrant groups that have relatively little access to the mainstream economy. While the children of these immigrants may adopt American expectations regarding the type of and compensation for employment, they are unable to compete in the mainstream economy. Gans does not fully expand this logic to the realm of acculturation (as distinct from economic integration). However, he does make some suggestions in that direction.

15. I should note that no males ever discussed any aspect of physical proximity in their conversations with me. However, the possibly gender-specific idea of the importance of physical proximity as an expression of the parent-child bond is not a topic I will address here.

16. Milton M. Gordon, *Assimilation in American Life* (New York: Oxford University Press, 1964).

17. Das Gupta (*On the Trail*); Fenton (*Transplanting Religious Traditions*); Gibson (Accommodation Without Assimilation); Helweg and Helweg (*An Immigrant Success Story*).

Chapter 13

1. One may argue that these differences are found more in theory than in practice. Indeed, concern for how things will play "in the community" sometimes

shapes what happens in families. Likewise, the core members of organizations sometimes behave as if they are the only ones concerned with their behavior. While there are clearly overlapping concerns and behavior patterns, I do not think it is unreasonable to suggest that on balance, organizations function very differently from families.

2. Indeed, other studies of immigrant groups have noted patterns of inter-organizational competition and attention to community identity that are very similar to what I observed in the Indian community. For the case of Korean immigrants, see Hyung-Chan Kim, "Korean Community Organizations in America: Their Characteristics and Problems," in *The Korean Diaspora: Historical and Sociological Studies of Korean Immigration and Assimilation in North America,* ed. Hyung-Chan Kim (Santa Barbara: ABC-Clio, 1977); or Ilsoo Kim, *New Urban Immigrants: The Korean Community in New York* (Princeton: Princeton University Press, 1981). For Caribbean immigrants, see Philip Kasinitz, *Caribbean New York: Black Immigrants and the Politics of Race* (Ithaca: Cornell University Press, 1992).

3. One problem here, which has not been directly addressed, is why this ambiguity and uncertainty should lead to a division of labor *between* families and organizations and not an overarching concern in *both* families and organizations with sorting things out. To address this issue, we can turn again to the particular qualities of voluntary associations and families as organizational types and the position each holds in proximity to the immediate crises that arise in people's lives. In crisis management, the family is the first line of defense. When a child says he or she doesn't want to go to temple, mosque, or church, the family is the arena in which an immediate decision is made. Although parents (and children) sometimes may look to community organizations for advice, support, and validation, they cannot do so on a daily, hourly basis. Because of the immediacy of family life, families are inhibited from devoting a lot of energy to categorical sorting. Families are, by and large, "on the fly" propositions, where parents make individual yes/no decisions. Any sorting at the level of family interaction is bottom-up; the sorting is the *result* of the decision making. Organizations, on the other hand, feel no such immediate pressure. They can accomplish their sorting in a top-down fashion, considering whether a particular action measures up to the prototype; in practice, ideology is more functional in the organizational than in the familial setting.

4. This kind of parent-child bond typifies white, middle-class America. Robert N. Bellah, Richard Madsen, William M. Sullivan, Ann Swidler, and Steven M. Tipton, *Habits of the Heart: Individualism and Commitment in American Life* (New York: Harper and Row, 1985), p. 56.

Appendix B

1. Annabel Farraday and Kenneth Plummer, "Doing Life Histories," *Sociological Review* 27 (1979): 773–98.

Index